# Early Families of Southern Maryland

## Volume 2

Elise Greenup Jourdan

HERITAGE BOOKS
2007

# HERITAGE BOOKS
*AN IMPRINT OF HERITAGE BOOKS, INC.*

**Books, CDs, and more—Worldwide**

For our listing of thousands of titles see our website at
www.HeritageBooks.com

Published 2007 by
HERITAGE BOOKS, INC.
Publishing Division
65 East Main Street
Westminster, Maryland 21157-5026

Copyright © (1993) 2001 Elise Greenup Jourdan

All rights reserved. No part of this book may be reproduced or transmitted in any form or by any means, electronic or mechanical, including photocopying, recording or by any information storage and retrieval system without written permission from the author, except for the inclusion of brief quotations in a review.

International Standard Book Number: 978-1-58549-269-5

# TABLE OF CONTENTS

| | |
|---|---|
| Numbering System and Abbreviations | iv |
| Introduction | v |
| The Plummer Family | 1 |
| The Lawrence Family | 41 |
| The Skinner Family | 63 |
| The Stephen West Family | 88 |
| The Letchworth Family | 92 |
| The Mariarte Family | 98 |
| The Child-Childs Family | 105 |
| The Boarman Family | 128 |
| The Nuthall Family | 163 |
| The Gover Family | 185 |
| The Cowman Family | 205 |
| Corrections and Additions to Volume I | 209 |
| Index | 225 |

## NUMBERING SYSTEM

The custom of using and reusing given names in these families is both a help and hindrance in identifying the various generations. The following system has been devised to show relationships.

Explanation of numbering system:

Example: 1133-1 Benjamin Plummer (p. 5)

1133-1   Benjamin Plummer is the first child listed in the family of 113-3 James Plummer. Since many of the families were reconstructed from legal documents with unknown birth dates, the children may not be numbered according to their order of birth.
113-3   James Plummer, son of 11-3 Samuel Plummer
11-3   Samuel Plummer, son of 1-1 Thomas Plummer (3)
1-1   Thomas Plummer (3), son of 1. Thomas Plummer (2)
1.   Thomas Plummer (2), son of Thomas Plummer (1)

In instances where there were more than 9 children, ( ) has been used to keep the numbering straight. The 10th child listed in a family would appear as -(10). The eleventh child of the tenth child would be numbered as (10)-(11), etc.

## ABBREVIATIONS

| | |
|---|---|
| ? | this event or person may not belong in this place |
| £ | pound sterling, British currency |
| bapt. | baptized |
| bur. | buried |
| ca | about the time of |
| ch./chr. | christened |
| d/o | daughter of |
| (f) | female |
| (m) | male |
| m/1 | first marriage |
| mb. | marriage bond |
| mi. | marriage intent |
| ml. | marriage license |
| s/o | son of |
| wit. | witness |

INTRODUCTION

This volume contains two expanded and corrected families from the first edition of volume I of this series, the Plummers and the Boarmans. They have been re-done because of material which became available to me from other researchers interested in getting more (and corrected) information about these families in publication.

Missing records, names misspelled in documents and using the same given names over and over makes it difficult to sort out some of the families. In all cases where it was possible, print-outs have been sent to others researching the line for review and correction, but all mistakes are mine.

No claim is made as to having the "correct" spelling for every family name. Clerks frequently spelled the same name as many as 3 ways in a single document and various branches of the families adopted different spellings of the family names.

Most of my sources came from published 17th and 18th century records of Maryland and family histories and are listed with the material presented.

I wish to thank all the people who have shared information with me including the following who were especially generous in pointing out errors in the first volume and/or donating material for this volume:

> Agnes Millikin Winkelman, Englewood, Ohio
> Ann Scrivener Agee, Crofton, Maryland
> Brice M. Clagett, Friendship, Maryland
> Ernest C. Allnutt, Jr., Baltimore, Maryland
> Gale Edwin Spitler Honeyman, San Francisco, California
> Judge James Trabue, Belleville, Illinois
> Michael L. Marshall, Mechanicsville, Virginia
> Nelson and Lindsay Nuttall, Bloomington, Indiana
> Robert Proctor Carter, Charlotte, North Carolina

Elise Greenup Jourdan<br>
Knoxville, Tennessee<br>
September 1993

*Any genealogical publication is merely a rough draft of the next edition.*

*There is always one more record waiting to be found.*

## PLUMMER

> In Volume I of this series the wives of the first and second Thomas Plummers were accidentally reversed. Because of the wealth of material obtained after publication of Volume I, the family is repeated in this volume with corrections and additions. Recognized authorities on the genealogy of this family are two descendants,
>
> Agnes Millikin Winkelman of Englewood, Ohio, and
> Gale Edwin Spitler Honeyman of San Francisco, California,
>
> who contributed their own research and copies of original documents, and reviewed the final draft in this volume, but any and all errors are mine.

According to Skordas, Richard Plumer was transported in 1653 (Liber 6, folio 95), John Plummer in 1673 (Liber 17, folio 456) and Thomas Plummer in 1667 (Liber 11, folio 171). Two men named Plomer also came to Maryland: Henry transported in 1675 (Liber 18, folio 306) and John, service in 1677 (Liber 15, folio 520).

A Thomas Plummer patented 207 acres 28 Oct 1642 in Virginia for transportation of 4 persons (Cavaliers and Pioneers).

### PLUMMERS in the QUAKER MOVEMENT

The Plummer name is prominent in the history of the Quaker movement in the early days of Maryland and Virginia. The first and second Thomas Plummers do not appear to have been Quakers. Of the 10 sons of the second Thomas Plummer, three sons, Samuel, Jerome and Yate were Quakers, and a 4th son, James, who once signed as a Quaker, appears to have been deleted from the records after his marriage to a non-Quaker.

An indenture in Frederick Co., dated 16 Mar 1768, shows that for 5s Thomas Plummer, son of Samuel, gave 4 acres of land called *Saplin Hall* to William Ballinger and Joseph Plummer as trustees "to build thereon one or more house or houses as they shall see convenient for the people called Quakers to meet and assemble together to worship Almighty God." (Fr. Co., Liber L, folio 266). This was the original home of the Bush Creek Meeting. Several more post-1800 documents exist in

Frederick Co. records regarding this land in the trusteeship of descendants of the founders of the Meeting.

### THOMAS PLUMMER

Thomas Plummer (1), d. ca 1694/5; m. Elizabeth Stockett (1662-1700); d/o Thomas Stockett and Mary Wells; children:

1. Thomas Plummer (2); m. Elizabeth Smith
2. Margaret Plummer; m. Hugh Riley
3. Mary Plummer; m. William Jackson
4. Susannah Plummer; m. Francis Swanston
5. Elizabeth Plummer; m. William Ijams

Thomas Plummer was brought from England in 1667 by William Stanley (Patent, Liber 11, folio 171). 100 acres of *Bridge Hills* in Anne Arundel Co., of the 663 acres granted Dr. Henry Stockett in 1669, was conveyed to Thomas Plummer in 1672. Elizabeth inherited 200 acres remaining unsold of 800 acres of *Rich Level* and 118 acres of *Level Addition* from the 1691 will of her step-father, George Yate, erroneously listed as "Joseph Yate" (Md. Cal. Wills, Vol. II, p. 48).

Thomas Plummer bought on 28 Jul 1686 for 3,000 lbs. tobacco from Francis Stockett, physician of Anne Arundel Co., 64 acres *Doden* in the woods northward of *Anne Arundel Manor* granted Stockett; containing 664 acres; bounded by *Bridgehill* (Abstracts of Land Records of Anne Arundel Co.).

On 20 May 1676 Thomas Plummer, Anne Arundel Co., planter, obtained "for valuable consideration" 100 of the 663 acres of *Bridge Hill* from Henry Stockett of *The Ridge*, Anne Arundel Co. (Abstracts of Land Records of Anne Arundel Co.).

> WILL of THOMAS PLOUMER of Anne Arundel Co.; written 12 Jul 1694; probate 26 Feb 1694
> To eld. (only) son Thomas, 100 acres *Seaman's Delight* in Calvert Co.
> To eld. dau. Margaret, wife of Hugh Reily, 5 shillings because of advances already made
> To sec. dau. Mary, wife of William Jackson, and hrs., rights in certain tract of land, and 300 acres *Scott's Lott* in Calvert Co.
> To 3rd dau. Susanna, wife of Francis Swanson, personalty

To wife Eliza. extx., home plantation, being 164 acre part of *Bridge Hill* and *Doden* during life
To young. dau. Eliza: and hrs., sd. plantation at death of wife afsd.
In event of death of sd. Eliza. without issue, sd. plantation to pass to 2 daus. afsd., Mary Jackson and Susanna Swanson, equally
Wit: Henry Hanslap, Edw. Brucebank, Jos. Hanslap
(Md. Cal. Wills, Vol. II, p. 86; Wills, Liber 7, folio 56)

Inventory of Thomas Plumar of Anne Arundel Co.; £110/15/0; 12 Mar 1694 (10.399); Account of Thomas Plumer; #4740; 15 Jul 1700; ex. Elisabeth Plumer (20.42). Testamentary papers; 25 Jul 1706 show Elizabeth was still alive (Box 11, folder 17).

1. Thomas Plummer (2), est. b. ca 1670s; d. ca 1728; s/o Thomas Plummer and Elizabeth Stockett; m. Elizabeth Smith (\_\_\_\_-1736) sister of John Smith; lived on *Seaman's Delight* Prince George's Co. [formerly Calvert Co.], 100 acres inherited from his father, 201 acres by patent 1716; *Dundee* of 50 acres patented in 1716; owned part of *Swanson's Lot*; Elizabeth patented *Lyford* in 1734; children:

    1-1  Thomas Plummer (3)
    1-2  Samuel Plummer - Quaker
    1-3  George Plummer
    1-4  James Plummer - Quaker
    1-5  John Plummer
    1-6  Jerome Plummer - Quaker
    1-7  Philemon Plummer
    1-8  Micajah Plummer
    1-9  Yate Plummer - Quaker
    1-10 Abezar Plummer
    1-11 Priscilla Plummer
    1-12 Phoebe Plummer

WILL of THOMAS PLUMMER, JR., Prince Geo.'s Co.; will written 29 Jun 1726; probate 26 Jun 1728
To eldest son Thomas 10s; son Samuel 20s; son James 5s; sons Philimon and Jerom, personalty
To 5 sons, viz., George, John, Micajah, Yate, Abezar and their heirs, 4 tracts, viz. *Seaman's Delight*, pt. of *Swanson's Lott*, *Dundee*, *Part of Dundee* and interest in all lands afsd. Co. Sons to dispose of afsd lands only to sd. 5 brothers or to their bro. Jerom; shd. any die without issue, survivors to divide portion of dec'd; shd. wife marry, 3 youngest sons to be of age at 16
To daus. Priscilla and Phebe, 10s each
To wife Elizabeth, extx. residue of personal estate, shd. she die during minority of 3 youngest children sons John and Jerom to take care of child. and their estates until of age

Wit: Thomas Stockett, Jr. and Thomas Still, Thomas Waitt
(Md. Cal. Wills, Vol. VI, p. 64; Wills, Liber 19, folio 409)

WILL of ELIZABETH PLUMMER, Prince George's Co.; written 27 Mar 1736; probate 8 Jul 1736
To eldest son Thomas, 2nd son Samuel, 3rd son George, 4th son James, 5th son John, 6th son Jerome, 7th son Phillimon; eldest dau. Priscilla Ouchtclony, youngest dau. Phoebe Williams, 8th son Micajah, 9th son Yate, and 10th son Abiezer, personalty. Legacy to Abiezer to be in poss. of son Yate until Abiezer arrives at age of 21
To 2 sons, viz: Micajah and Yate tract called *Liford*. Residue to personal estate to be divided bet. two youngest sons, Yate and Abiezer
Exs: Sons Micajah and Yate
Wit: John Evans, Sr., John Evans, Jr., Eliner Evans
(Md. Cal. Wills, Vol. VII, p. 181; Wills, Liber 21, folio 617)

Estate of Elisabeth Plummer of Prince George's Co.; £167/10/6; ____ 1736; 24 Nov 1736; next of kin: George Plummer, Jeremiah (?Jerome) Plummer; exs. Micajah Plummer, Yate Plummer (22.161).

1-1 Thomas Plummer (3); d. ca 1773/4 Frederick Co.; s/o Thomas Plummer (2). and Elizabeth Smith; m. 6 Feb 1715 Queen Anne Parish to Sarah Wilson; d/o Edward Wilson, Sr.; he inherited 10s from will of father; granted *Greenland* in 1744; their children from his will:

11-1 John Plummer
11-2 Thomas Plummer (4)
11-3 Samuel Plummer
11-4 Dorcas Plummer
11-5 Priscilla Plummer
11-6 Phebe Plummer
11-7 Mary Plummer
11-8 Susannah Plummer
11-9 Ruth Plummer
11-10 ? William Plummer

WILL of THOMAS PLUMMER, SR., Frederick Co.; written 27 Nov 1773; probate 20 Feb 1774
To son Thomas Plummer, Ex., all of my estate both real and personal except the following legacies
To son and 6 daus., Samuel, Dorcas, Priscilla, Phebe, Mary, Susannah and Ruth Plummer, 5s each
Test: Thomas Plummer, John Hilton, James Hilton, George Kirk
(Wills, Liber 39, folio 600)

11-1 John Plummer; d. ca 1758 Frederick Co.; m. 18 d. 3 mo. 1736 West River Friends Meeting to Rachel Miles; d/o Thomas

Miles and Elizabeth ?Griffith, widow of Guy White II; Rachel was half-sister to Sarah who m. Samuel Plummer; Test. Papers filed 25 Nov 1758; Edward Wilson, Sr. and Jerome Plummer sureties; inv. of estate shows admnx. Rachel Plummer; next of kin: Edward Willson, Jr. and Sr.; 2 Dec 1758; 26 Oct 1759; value £77.11.5 (68.100); account filed 27 Oct 1759 by Rachel Plummer who rec'd the estate (she did not sign as a Quaker); no mention of children in estate proceedings; John not named in father's will

11-2 Thomas Plummer (4); m. unknown; given *Greenland* for "love and affection" by Thomas (3); Frederick Co. deed 17 Oct 1806 names children (L. WR30, f. 12-14):

    112-1 James Plummer; went to Brook Co., WV
    112-2 Ann Plummer; m. 13 Sep 1796 Frederick Co. John Turner; went to Brook Co., WV
    112-3 Eleanor Plummer; m. 16 Apr 1785 Frederick Co. Leonard Wayman; went to Jefferson Co., OH
    112-4 Amelia Plummer; went to Brook Co., WV
    112-5 Jerome Plummer
    112-6 Joshua Plummer

11-3 Samuel Plummer; d. ca 1777 Frederick Co.; m. Sarah _____; will filed Frederick Co. (Liber GM1, f. 12); children:

    113-1 Joseph Plummer; m. 12 May 1789 Mary Cash; moved to North Carolina

        1131-1 William Plummer, b. ca 1794 MD; m. Rebecca Jones, b. ca 1804; went to Lee Co. VA ca 1830/2

    113-2 George Plummer; no wife or children known
    113-3 James Plummer; m. 10 Dec 1783 Dorcas Cash; in 1795 they moved to Mason Co., KY; 1805 to Fleming Co., KY; known child:

        1133-1 Benjamin Plummer, b. 15 Jun 1793 MD (Marylanders to KY); d. 6 Jan 1866 KY; farmer and miller; served War of 1812; m. 15 Aug 1816 Mary M. Seever; 9 children

113-4 Mary Plummer; m 29 Apr 1786 Frederick Co.; 2nd wife of John Bennett; went to KY
113-5 Martha Plummer
113-6 Jane Plummer
113-7 Ann Plummer
113-8 Rachel Plummer
113-9 Thomas Plummer

11-4 Dorcas Plummer; may have m. Daniel Veach; lived Woodford Co., KY
11-5 Priscilla Plummer
11-6 Phoebe Plummer
11-7 Mary Plummer; may have m. John Waters III; he d. ca 1771 Anne Arundel Co.
11-8 Susanna Plummer
11-9 Ruth Plummer

The following William Plummer may have been another son of Thomas Plummer not named in his will. He is placed here by circumstantial evidence only; there is no proof. Daniel Veach, who was involved with his estate, had a wife named Dorcas, who was possibly [11-4] Dorcas Plummer; his son Jeremiah named a child Dorcas. William Plummer and Daniel Veach both had leases on land belonging to the Hepburn family in Montgomery Co.

11-10 ?William Plummer; d. Oct 1763 Frederick Co.; m. Mary _____; d. after 1763; estate settlement, 11 Nov 1762; 22 Jan 1763; next of kin: Mary Plumer, Jeremiah Plumer; admn. Zephaniah Plummer (79.439, Skinner; Accts, Liber 50, folio 88); children:

        11(10)-1 Zephania Plummer
        11(10)-2 Jeremiah Plummer
        11(10)-3 Mary Plummer
        11(10)-4 Drusilla Plummer

Indenture; 3 Aug 1645; 6 Oct 1746; from John Greenup, Thomas and Mary Johnston to William Plummer; for 2,500# of tobacco; a tract of land of 64 acres now called *Plummer's Purchase*, part of a tract in Prince George's Co. called *Beal's Pleasure*; bounded by Thomas Gordon and a branch that falls into Beaverdam Branch; /s/ John Greenup, Thos. Johnston, Mary Johnston; wit. To. Belt, Jr., Jno. Riley, Nicholas Rhoades (Land Records, BB#1 p. 458).

Indenture; 12 May 1756; 2 Jun 1756; from William Plummer, turner, to Samuel Carmole; both of Prince George's Co.; for £20; part of *Plummer's Purchase* laid out for 64 acres; being part of *Beal's Pasture*; /s/ William Plummer (mark); wit. J. Hepburn, I. Rawlings; Mary, wife of William Plummer acknowledged deed

### 11(10)-1 Zephania Plummer; d. 1767; unmarried

Will of ZEPHNIA PLUMER, Frederick Co., planter; 5 Jan 1767; 16 Jan 1767
To bro. Jeremiah Plumer, clothing
To sister Donesphlar (Drusilla ?), £5, to be paid by Daniel Veach
To mother, cattle
To sister Mary
Ex. Daniel Veatch
Wit: Mathew Compton, Thomas Raye
(Md. Cal. Wills, Vol.. XIII, p. 147; Wills, Liber 35, folio 88)

Zephaniah Plummer, estate settlement, 4 Apr 1767; 22 Aug 1767; ex. Daniel Veach (95.192, Skinner).

### 11(10)-2 Jeremiah Plummer; d. ca 1809 Jefferson Co., KY; m. ca 1762 Nancy Banfield; children:

11(10)2-1 William Plummer; remained in Maryland
11(10)2-2 Zephaniah Plummer; d. ca Sep 1846; m. 15 Jan 1791 Frederick Co., MD Charity Hempston/e (Will, GM 3, folio 192)
11(10)2-3 Charles Plummer; to Clark Co., IN
11(10)2-4 John Plummer
11(10)2-5 Nelly Plummer
11(10)2-6 Anna Plummer
11(10)2-7 Dorcas Plummer
11(10)2-8 Patsy Plummer
11(10)2-9 Charity Plummer

Jeremiah leased 100 acres, part of *Hanover* for 18 years from John Hepburn in Frederick Co. 13 May 1769 (Liber M, folio 212). In 1790

Jeremiah with his wife and children, except William and Zephaniah, and Samuel Banfield, Sr., Jr. and some of Jr.'s children moved to KY

   11(10)-3  Mary Plummer
   11(10)-4  Drusilla Plummer; d. 1767; unmarried

Will of DRUSILLA PLUMER, Frederick Co.; 10 Mar 1767; 13 Apr 1767
To Mathew Compton, cattle and the legacy my bro. Zephariam Plumer left me in his will
Ex. Mathew Comptom
Wit: Samuel Henson, Mary Henstone
                    (Md. Cal. Wills, Vol. XIII, p. 162; Wills, Liber 35, folio 204)

1-2 Samuel Plummer, b. 9 Feb 1691/2; d. 12 Dec 1759 Prince George's Co.; s/o Thomas Plummer (2) and Elizabeth Smith; marriage dates found: 13 d. 1 mo. 1723 West River, 1 d. 4 mo. 1723/4 at Indian Springs, 2 d. 12 mo. 1724 West River, to Sarah Miles, b. ca 1705 Wales; d. 3 d. 10 mo. 1788 near New Market; d/o Thomas Miles, Sr. and his 1st wife, Ruth Jones; he inherited 20s from will of his father; all children wed in Quaker ceremonies except Joseph:

| | |
|---|---|
| 12-1  Ruth Plummer, b. 1725 | 12-7  Abraham Plummer, b. 1736 |
| 12-2  Thomas Plummer, b. 1726 | 12-8  Rachel Plummer, b. 1738 |
| 12-3  Joseph Plummer, b. 1728 | 12-9  Ursula Plummer, b. 1742 |
| 12-4  Samuel Plummer, b. 1730 | 12-10 Elizabeth Plummer, b. 1744 |
| 12-5  Cassandra Plummer, b. 1731/2 | 12-11 Anna Plummer, b. 1747 |
| 12-6  Sarah Plummer, b. 1734 | 12-12 Susannah Plummer, b. 1751 |

Samuel witnessed will of John Turner, Sr. in Prince George's Co. with his brother, James, written 2 Dec 1720; probate 9 Dec 1723 (Md. Cal. Wills, Vol. V, p. 152); will of Thomas Miles of Prince George's Co. written 2 Aug 1725 leaves daughter Sarah, wife of Samuel Plummer, personalty (Md. Cal. Wills, Vol. VI, p. 10); on 28 Jun 1743 four more surveys filed for *Hunting Lott*, *Pleasant Meddo*, *Rich Hills* and *Food Plenty*, located near New Market; listed in taxables of Patuxent Hundred in 1719 and 1733. This family left the West River-The Clifts area when certificates to Monocacy were given to Joseph and Thomas on 26 May 1749. After the death of Samuel, the entire family followed the lead of the 2 eldest sons and moved to Frederick Co.

18 d. 2 mo. 1775 Sarah Plummer presented a certificate from West River to Pipe Creek Monthly Meeting for herself, daus. Ursula and Susanna, and granddaughter Sarah Harris (Quaker Records of No. Md.)

The plantation called *Rose's Purchase* came into the family through the following will of Richard Rose:

WILL of RICHARD ROSE of Prince George's Co.; written 30 Apr 1716; probate 29 Jun 1717
To friend Sam. Plummer and hrs., plan. and tract, *Rose's Purchase* and personalty
Thos. Plummer, Sr., ex., and residuary legatee
Test: John Evans, John Turner, Sol. Turner
(Md. Cal. Wills, Vol. IV, p. 109; Wills, Liber 14, folio 385)

Will of SAMUEL PLUMMER, Prince George's Co.; written 13 Jan 1754; probate 2 Feb 1760
To wife Sarah, land where my dwelling house is, one tract whereof is called *Rose's Purchase* and one other tract adjoining, *Upper Getting*
To eldest son Thomas, land in Frederick Co., *Hunting Lot* of 226 acres
To sons Joseph, Samuel, Abraham, and daus. Cassandra Ballenger and Sarah Plummer, tracts of land in Frederick Co.
Wife Sarah to make over to son-in-law Richard Holland, a tract of land in Frederick Co. upon Linganore, called *Rich Hill*
Extx: Wife, Sarah
Wit: Richard, Thomas and Mary Moore (1.519, WM - Bowie)

WILL of THOMAS MILES, Prince George's Co.; 24 Apr 1760
To sister Sarah Plummer and hrs., all estate after decease
Ex. Sister Sarah Plummer
Wit: Joseph Richardson, Zach and Margery Lyles
(Md. Cal. Wills, vol. XII, p. 232; Wills, Liber 31, folio 1125)

12-1 Ruth Plummer, b. 10d. 3 mo. 1725; d/o Samuel and Sarah; m. 14 d. 12 mo. 1743 to Richard Holland; d. ca 1788; s/o Thomas Holland and Margaret Waters; Quaker marriage; resurveyed *Rich Hills* in 1761 inherited from her father; *Bush Creek Mountain* surveyed 20 Sep 1755 for Richard; no children; his will names wife Ruth (Liber GM 2, folio 290-292).

12-2 Thomas Plummer, b. 8 d. 7 mo. 1726; s/o Samuel and Sarah; m. 29 d. 4 mo. 1761 to Eleanor Walker; d/o William and Sarah

Walker; widow of John Poultney; inherited *Hunting Lott* from his father; children:

122-1 Isaac Plummer, b. 15 Feb 1762; m. 25 May 1785 Grace Taylor: children:

    1221-1 Israel E. Plummer; unmarried
    1221-2 Mary P. Plummer; m. 28 Apr 1825 Richard Plummer; s/o Yate Plummer (2)
    1221-3 William B. Plummer; m. Elizabeth _____
    1221-4 Abner M. Plummer; m. 21 Sep 1831 Ruth Haines
    1221-5 Ellen Plummer; ml. 19 Mar 1821 Jacob Thomas
    1221-6 Elizabeth Plummer; unmarried

122-2 Jesse Plummer, b. 28 Oct 1763; m. 18 Jul 1786 Ruth Griffith; children:

    1222-1 Greenbury Griffith Plummer; m. Jane Millhouse
    1222-2 Eleanor Walker Plummer; m. 15 Apr 1809 Caleb Flemming
    1222-3 Thomas Griffith Plummer; m. Mary Ralston
    1222-4 Ann Plummer; d. young
    1222-5 Ruth Plummer; m. 20 Nov 1817 Howard Griffith, Jr.
    1222-6 Lydia Griffith Plummer; m. 1816 William P. Burgess
    1222-7 Philip Plummer; m. 6 May 1823 Anna Marie Waters
    1222-8 Jesse Baker Plummer; m. Ellen Clark
    1222-9 Sallie Plummer; m. Stephen Hussey
    1222-10 Anna Plummer; m/1 John H. Holmes; m/2 Dr. J. T. Hobbs

122-3 Ruth Plummer, b. 24 Dec 1765; unmarried
122-4 William Plummer, b. 27 Nov 1770; m. 1 Nov 1792 Bush Creek Meeting to Rachel Morsell; d/o William and Mary Morsell; 1 Jun 1793 he laid out part of New Market, MD [co-founder]; Nicholas Hall was also selling land for this town, which was part of *Dorsey's Partnership*; children, probably not in order of birth:

    1224-1 Thomas Morsell Plummer; m. Mary West

1224-2 William W. Plummer
1224-3 Rachel Plummer
1224-4 Rebekah Plummer
1224-5 Mary Plummer; m. Abraham Johns
1224-6 Elizabeth Plummer; unmarried
1224-7 Ellen Plummer
1224-8 Jesse Plummer; m. Mary G. Russell

12-3 Joseph Plummer, b. 3 Jul 1728; d.18 d. 2 mo. 1806 Fayette Co., PA; s/o Samuel and Sarah; m. Sarah Sollers, b. 2 Feb 1729 Queen Anne Parish; d/o John Sollers and Mary Stockett; inherited *Pleasant Meddo* from his father; increased land holdings to 1,777 acres in 1764; lived on *Land of Promise*, the resurvey of *Pleasant Meadow*; member Bush Creek Meeting House; see wills following information on children:

123-1 Joseph West Plummer; m. 4 Apr 1775 Mary Taylor; moved to Jefferson Co., OH
123-2 Anna Plummer; d. by 1806; m. 17 Aug 1780 Israel Janney; 18 d. 10 mo. 1780 Anna Janney requested certificate to ____ Meeting
123-3 Ezra Plummer
123-4 Samuel Plummer
123-5 Moses Plummer; m. 11 Mar 1785 Elizabeth Webb; d/o George and Ann Webb of Lancaster Co., PA; moved to Muskingham Co., OH; children:

1235-1 Ann Plummer
1235-2 Sarah Plummer; may have m. 23 Apr 1811 James Woellas
1235-3 Ruth Plummer; may have m. 8 Mar 1815 Joseph Mills

123-6 Aaron Plummer
123-7 Marian/Miriam Plummer; m. _____ Ball; 16 d. 11 mo. 1782 Bush Creek Preparative Meeting reported that Miriam Plummer moved within the verge of Fairfax Monthly Meeting with consent of her father.

123-8 Asa Plummer; m. 12 Jan 1796 Grace Burgess; moved to Clinton, OH; children:

1238-1 Eli Plummer, b. 11 Nov 1797
1238-2 Deborah Plummer, b. 20 Oct 1798; d. 1802
1238-3 Anna Plummer, b. 10 Apr 1802; d. 1804
1238-4 Jesse Plummer, b. 12 Jul 1803
1238-5 Ezra Plummer, b. 21 Nov 1805
1238-6 Tacy Plummer; m. Thomas Gilpin
1238-7 Lot Plummer
1238-8 Emily N. Plummer; m. Thomas Sanders
1238-9 ? Mahala Plummer, b. 14 Jun 1814; m. John Harvey

123-9 Susannah Plummer; d. by 1806; m. 31 Dec 1772 Samuel Waters; children:

123(10)-1 Sarah Waters, b. 20 Dec 1773
123(10)-2 Margaret Waters, b. 3 Sep 1776; m. 22 Jan 1801 Nathan Woods

Joseph Plummer sold his Maryland land in bits in pieces after moving to Berkley Co., VA (now WV); he left VA and, traveling through Pennsylvania on his way to Ohio on 18 d. 2 mo. 1806, he wrote a will (copy on file) which mentions his son Moses and 4 daughters. This will was probated first before the earlier will written in VA.

Will of JOSEPH PLUMMER, Berkley Co., Virginia; 17 d. 10 mo. 1805; 23 Jun 1806
To son Joseph West Plummer, 5s Maryland currency and no more
To dau. Marian Bawl (Ball), £5 Maryland currency
To grand-dau. Margarete Wood 25 ? Maryland currency
1/5 of estate to be divided among the children of dau. Ann Janney
4/5 of estate to my sons, Samuel, Moses, Aaron and Asa
To Isaac, son of my brother Thomas Plummer, right and title to a lot for the Bush Creek Meeting House
Ex. James Mendinhall
Wit: John Chenowith, George Harris, Arthur Chenowith

12-4 Samuel Plummer, Jr., b. 30 Oct 1730; s/o Samuel and Sarah; m. 18 Dec 1764 Mary Tucker; d/o Robert and Lydia Tucker; in

1740 he patented 50 acres known as *Plummer's Delight* on the west side of Bennett's Creek and east side of Sugar Loaf Mtn. in what is now Montgomery Co.; on juries 1750 and 1754; on grand jury 1764; granted certificate to Monocacy, Frederick Co. 25 Jun 1756; overseer of Bennett Creek-Monocacy Ford road in 1760; patented *Resurvey to Plummer's Delight* in 1760; children:

124-1 Jonathan Plummer; m. 21 Dec 1789 Ann Ward; children:

    1241-1 Elisabeth Plummer
    1241-2 Deborah Plummer; m. Lilben Williams
    1241-3 Dorilla Plummer; m. George Gray
    1241-4 Samuel W. Plummer

124-2 Evan Plummer; will, 12 Aug 1817; unmarried
124-3 Israel Plummer; d. by 1817; m. 29 Oct 1795 Rebeckah Morsell; children:

    1243-1 Maria Plummer; m. Benjamin Benton, Jr.
    1243-2 Elisha Plummer; m. Ann Langton
    1243-3 James Plummer
    1243-4 William Plummer; unmarried

124-4 Sarah Plummer; d. 1833; unmarried
124-5 Elizabeth Plummer; m. 30 Dec 1790 Bush Creek Frederick Co. to John Talbott, b. 3 d. 1 mo. 1766; s/o John Talbott and Mary Johns; children:

    1245-1 Susannah Talbott, b. 12 Nov 1791; unmarried
    1245-2 Ruth Talbott, b. 25 Jun 1793; m. William Hughes
    1245-3 Samuel Talbott, b. 1 Apr 1797; m. 5 Feb 1822 Catharine Davis
    1245-4 John Talbott, Jr., b. 8 Jan 1802; m. 21 Feb 1833 Mary Coale; d/o William Coale and Anna Talbott; granddau. of Joseph Talbott and Ann Plummer

124-6 Sarah Plummer; unmarried
124-7 Rachel Plummer

124-8   Ann Plummer; m. 20 May 1813 Richard Roberts
124-9   Rebekah Plummer; unmarried in father's will

12-5   Cassandra Plummer, b. 3d. 5 mo. 1732; d. 12 Jul 1820; m. 3 d. 8 mo. 1751 William Ballinger; d. 1 Jan 1787; s/o Henry Ballinger & Hannah Wright of Frederick Co.; Quaker marriage; inherited part of *Hickory Plains* from her father; 17 d. 4 mo. 1773 Cassandra Ballinger appointed overseer of Bush Creek (Women's Minutes); children:

125-1   Sarah Ballinger, b. 8 Nov 1752; m. 18 d. 9 mo. 1777 2nd w/o Isaac Brown of Frederick Co., VA; s/o Daniel and Susanna Brown; Sarah Brown requested certificate to Hopewell Meeting
125-2   Mary Ballinger, b. 16 Jun 1754
125-3   Daniel Ballinger, b. 25 Jun 1756
125-4   William Ballinger, b. 22 Jul 1758; m. 20 Jul 1797 Lydia Smith, b. 3 Mar 1775; d/o John and Elizabeth Smith; Jefferson Co., OH
125-5   Hannah Ballinger, b. 10 Jul 1761; unmarried
125-6   Rachel Ballinger, b. 28 Sep 1763; unmarried
125-7   Henry Ballinger, b. 29 Sep 1765; unmarried
125-8   Ann Ballinger, b. 28 Sep 1767; d. 18 Mar 1805; unmarried
125-9   Samuel Ballinger; b. 10 Feb 1770; d. 15 Nov 1808; unmarried
125-10   Elizabeth Ballinger, b. 19 Oct 1772; unmarried

12-6   Sarah Plummer, b. 30 Aug 1734; s/o Samuel and Sarah; m. 29 Aug 1758 to Mahlon Janney; s/o Amos Janney and Mary Yardley; Amos Janney began settlement of present-day Waterford, VA; Sarah listed as d/o Samuel of Prince George's Co.; Quaker marriage
12-7   Abraham Plummer, b. 16 Jul 1736; d. by 7 Jul 1810 Belmont Co., OH (probate of will); s/o Samuel and Sarah; m. Sarah Ward; d/o Robert and Elizabeth Ward; intention to marry 29 Jan 1762; Quaker marriage; inherited part of *Hickory Plains*; Mahlon

Janney assigned right to *Supply* to him in 1667; children's name from Quaker records.

17 d. 6 mo. 1775 Abraham Plummer, Sarah his wife, three children named Samuel, John and Robert, presented certificate from West River to Pipe Creek Monthly Meeting (Quaker Records of No. Md.).

> 127-1 Samuel Plummer, b. ca 1763; d. before 1810; m. [194-2] Priscilla Plummer; d/o Yate Plummer and Artridge Waters; in will of father
> 127-2 John Plummer, b. ca 1765; m. Ann Sidwell
> 127-3 Robert Plummer, b. ca 1771; m. 3 Oct 1793 Rachel Talbott, b. ca 1774; d/o John Talbott and Mary E. Johns; Belmont Co., OH; children:
>
>> 1273-1 Elisabeth Plummer, b. ca 1794; m. Jeremiah Patterson
>> 1273-2 John Plummer, b. 1796; m. Rachel Patterson
>> 1273-3 Abram Plummer, b. ca 1799; m. Elizabeth Strahl
>> 1273-4 Mary Plummer, b.1809; m. Elisha Starbuck
>> 1273-5 Robert Plummer, b. 1813; m. Jane Bailey
>
> 12-8 Rachel Plummer, b. 16 Feb 1738; d/o Samuel and Sarah; m. 11 Mar 1760 to John Harris of VA; another record states marriage accomplished 23 d. 11 mo. 1759; inherited part of *Hickory Plains*; her certificate to Cedar Creek, VA 25 d. 3 mo. 1760
> 12-9 Ursula Plummer, b. 16 Mar 1742; d/o Samuel and Sarah; never married
> 12-10 Elizabeth Plummer, b. 29 May 1744; d/o Samuel and Sarah; int. to marry 27 d. 11 mo. 1761; m. 3 Dec 1761 West River to Moses Harris of VA; they lived Frederick Co., MD; known child:
>
>> 12(10)-1 Sarah Harris; m/1 14 Oct 1780 Jacob Janney II; s/o Jacob Janney and Hannah Ingledue of Loudon Co., VA; m/2 16 Dec 1784 Samuel Gover
>
> 12-11 Ann/Anna Plummer, b. 26 Oct 1747; d/o Samuel and Sarah of Prince George's Co.; m. 3 Mar 1772 to Joseph Talbott III of

Calvert Co.; s/o Joseph Talbott and Mary Burket; Quaker marriage at house of Sarah Plummer; he was Friends Elder of Fairfax Monthly Meeting Loudon Co., VA; children:

12(11)-1 Samuel Talbott, b. 18 Dec 1772; m. 6 Nov 1794 Rachel Littler; Cincinnati, OH
12(11)-2 Sarah Talbott, b. 8 Jan 1776; m. 30 Jan 1799 Stephen Scott
12(11)-3 Mary Talbott, b. 18 Mar 1778; m. 1 May 1799 John Pancoast
12(11)-4 Joseph Talbott, b. 12 May 1779; m. 4 May 1800 Jane Daniels
12(11)-5 Rachel Talbott, b. 3 Mar 1780; d. young
12(11)-6 Elisha Talbott, b. 1 Jan 1782; m. 2 Oct 1806 Sarah Saunders
12(11)-7 Jesse Talbott, b. 28 Aug 1783; m. 1 Jun 1808 Hannah Lytle
12(11)-8 Anna Talbott, b. 31 Jan 1786; m. 21 Jun 1804 William Coale
12(11)-9 Elizabeth Talbott, b. 29 Apr 1788; m. 26 Dec 1810 Richard Humphreys Lytle

12-12 Susannah Plummer, b. 16 Oct/Dec 1751; d. 9 May 181_; will probated 13 Jan 1814 Frederick Co. (RB1.291); m. 22 Jul 1777 to Anthony Poultney, b. 31 Mar 1752; d. 25 Jul 1805 ?; s/o John Poultney and Eleanor Walker; Quaker marriage; children:

12(12)-1 John Poultney, b. 15 Aug 1778
12(12)-2 Samuel Poultney, b. 18 Jan 1780; m. 1 Oct 1812 Elisabeth Wright
12(12)-3 Sarah Poultney, b. 1 Mar 1781; m/1 23 Apr 1807 Caleb Farquhar; m/2 18 Mar 1813 Jazar Garretson
12(12)-4 Elizabeth Poultney, b. 2 Dec 1782; m. 21 Jun 1804 Joel Wood
12(12)-5 Mary Poultney, b. 15 Jul 1784; m. 22 Sep 1803 Allen Farquhar, b. 15 d. 9 mo. 1773
12(12)-6 Thomas Poultney, b. 27 Apr 1786

12(12)-7 William Poultney, b. 12 Aug 1788; d. 5 Aug 1800 or 1806
12(12)-8 James Poultney, b. 26 Nov 1790; d. 15 May 1813
12(12)-9 Rachel Poultney, b. 24 Aug 1793; d. 24 Feb 1809
12(12)-10 Jesse Poultney, b. 16 Feb 1796; d. 187_

1-3 George Plummer; d. ca 1754 Prince George's Co.; s/o Thomas Plummer (2) and Elizabeth Smith; inherited land in father's will; never married

WILL of GEORGE PLUMMER, Prince George's Co.; written 8 Jul 1753; probate 14 Jan 1754
To Abyzer Plummer, stock
To George Plummer, son of the widow Plummer, and to Abyezer Plummer, stock
To George Plummer, son of the widow Plummer, cattle (son living at Linganore)
To Aby Ezar Plummer, furniture
Wit: John Evans, James Whiten
(Md. Cal. Wills, Vol. X, p. 16; Wills, Liber 29, folio 78)

1-4 James Plummer, b. ca 1696; age 50 in 1746 (Md. Deponents); d. ca 1772 Frederick Co. (Will); m/1 Mary Ouchtalong; d/o John Ouchtalong and his m/1 Frances Wells; John Ouchtalong m/2 Priscilla Plummer, sister of James; inherited 5s from will of father; wit. will of John Turner, Sr. of Prince George's Co., 2 Dec 1720; signed as a Quaker; purchased 103 acres of *Tewkesbury* in Prince George's Co. 27 Aug 1734 from Robert and Mary Tyler; Michael Buckley, age 10, bound to him for 11 years (DD 20); children:

14-1 Jeminia Plummer; m. Thomas Ramsey Hodge
14-2 Sarah Plummer; m. _____ Wells
14-3 Anne Plummer; m. Joseph Jones

In 1723 *Wickham's Good Will* of 270 acres on Muddy Branch in Montgomery Co. was surveyed for James Plummer; land patent 1726

1-5 John Plummer, est. b. late 1690s; d. ca 1740; s/o Thomas Plummer (2) and Elizabeth Smith; unmarried; inherited land in father's will; next of kin estate of John Crichtealony (?Ouchtalong) and Yate Plummer with Samuel Plummer as executor (25.30,).

WILL of JOHN PLUMMER, Prince Geo.'s Co.; written 17 Jan 1739; probate 2 Feb 1739/40
To bros. Samuel, ex., Thomas, George, James, Jerum, Philimon, Yate, Cager, Bezor and sis. Prisila and Phebee, entire estate
Test: George Wills, John Lamar, Abraham Lee (mark)
Note: Samuel Plummer in the presence of Joseph Williams, Sr., and Nathan Welles made over his interest in above will to Jerome Plummer
(Md. Cal. Wills, Vol. VIII, p. 74; Wills, Liber 22, folio 158)

1-6 Jerome Plummer, est. b. ca late 1690s; d. 12 day 3rd mo. 1751; bur. West River; s/o Thomas Plummer (2) and Elizabeth Smith; m/1 7 Jun 1737 Herring Creek to Margaret Child, widow of Henry Child, Jr.; both of Anne Arundel Co.; m/2 11 Feb 1741/2 West River to Mary Harris; d/o George and Anna Harris; he inherited personalty from will of his father; estate settlement shows James and Yate Plummer as next of kin; executors Mary Plummer, Quaker, and Samuel Galloway, Quaker; known child:

16-1 John Plummer, b. 5 d. 10 mo. 1750; m. 25 Dec 1772 at Indian Springs to Johanna Hopkins; d/o Garrard Hopkins II and Mary Hall; children from West River Meeting:

161-1 Jerome Plummer, b. 3 d. 1 mo. 1774; m/1 Anne Arundel Co. 19 Dec 1796 to Elizabeth Hopkins; m/2 24 Jun 1807 Henrietta Hopkins
161-2 Gerrard Plummer, b. 7 d. 9 mo. 1775; m. 18 Feb 1802 Mary Hopkins; sister to the 2 wives of his brother Jerome
161-3 Mary Plummer, b. 13 d. 3 mo. 1777; m. 16 Apr 1793 John Carmon
161-4 Ann Thomas Plummer, b 12 d. 1 mo. 1779
161-5 John Plummer, Jr., b. 20 d. 4 mo. 1781; m. Caroline Shoemaker; lived Washington, DC
161-6 Joseph Pemberton Plummer, b. 4 d. 10 mo. 1783; m/1 13 Mar 1806 Susanna Husband, 29 d. 9 mo. 1782; m/2 1819 Lydia Husband; sister of m/1; they were d/o Joseph Husband and Mary Pusey

WILL of JEROM PLUMMER of Anne Arundel Co.; written 29 Nov 1750; probate 14 Aug 1751
To wife Mary Plummer, plantation called *Plummer's Purchase* alias *Brousley Hall*; mentions unborn child
Wife and friend Samuel Galloway of West River, merchant, exs.
Request friend Kinsey Johns of West River, merchant, to be overseer and trustee of my will
Wit: Benj. Owens, Samuel Jones, Jacob Jones, Henry Jones
(Md. Cal. Wills, Vol. IX, p. 165; Wills, Liber 28, folio 111)

Jerrum Plummer of Anne Arundel Co.; £1232/7/4; 29 Dec ____; 3 Sep 1754; next of kin: James Plummer, Yate Plummer; exs. Mary Plummer (Quaker), Samuel Galloway (Quaker) (57.292).

1-7 Philemon Plummer, est. b. ca 1700; d. 1744; no will; s/o Thomas Plummer (2) and Elizabeth Smith; m. Elizabeth ?Turner; d/o John and Sarah Turner [James and Samuel Plummer were witnesses to the 1723 will of John Turner (Md. Cal. Wills, Vol. V, p. 152)]; Elizabeth m/2 1756 as 2nd wife of Abraham Crum, a non-Quaker, and was dismissed from Quaker congregation; he inherited personalty from will of father; Abraham Crum was living in All Saint's Parish, Frederick Co. in 1756 (Pioneers of Old Monocacy); children:

|  |  |
|---|---|
| 17-1 John Plummer | 17-6 Philemon Plummer |
| 17-2 Kezia Plummer | 17-7 Jerome Plummer |
| 17-3 Sarah Plummer | 17-8 George Plummer |
| 17-4 Ascah Plummer | 17-9 Dorcas Plummer |
| 17-5 Elizabeth Plummer | |

Philemon granted warrant for 40 acres called *Batchelor's Choice*, 5 Dec 1722; *Addition to Batchelor's Choice* of 97 acres granted 4 Dec 1733/4, both in *Calverton Manor*; patent for *Debutt's Delight* documented under grandson Philemon (171-1).

Guardian Bond; 24 Aug 1748; Elizabeth Plummer, widow; Micajah Plummer and Samuel Plummer, son of Thomas of the same Co., planters; bind themselves unto Ascah, Elizabeth, Philemon, Jerome, George and Dorcas Plummer in the amount of £88/2/9; /s/ Elizabeth Plummer (mark), Micajah Plummer, Samuel Plummer (mark) (Guardian Bonds, 1708-1777, p. 162)

17-1 John Plummer, b. ca 1726 Prince George's Co.; of age in 1748; d. ca 1768 Frederick Co.; m. Rachel _____; warrant dated 29 Nov 1754, survey dated 6 Mar 1752; for 54 acres *Helleber's Spring* in *Conigochigee Manor* in Frederick Co. on a small draft which runs into Linganore about 1/2 mile above the mouth (BC & GS 9, folio 162); in Debt Books until 1772; in Debt Books as possessing *Debutt's Delight* until 1767/8; Rachel listed in Debt Books 1768-1773; children:

   171-1 Philemon Plummer, b. ca 1749 MD; d. bond posted 25 Aug 1807 Montgomery Co., OH; m. Sophia _____; inherited his father and grand-father's lands, *Helleber Spring* and *Debuts' Delight*; on tax list Guilford Co., NC in 1785; later moved to Montgomery Co., OH; children:

     1711-1 Sarah Plummer, b. 25 Aug 1780; d. 13 Jul 1841; m. NC to George Sinks II; moved to OH

     1711-2 Rachel Plummer, b. ca 1781; d. 18 Mar 1867; m. NC to Frederick Summy, Sr. (ca 1777-1849); moved to OH then settled in IN

     1711-3 Sophia Plummer, b. 15 Jun 1783; d. 19 Jul 1859; m/1 1800 NC Daniel Waymire, Sr. (1776-1825); m/2 Henry Hoover, Jr.; moved to OH

     1711-4 Elizabeth Plummer, b. ca 1784; d. 12 Oct 1848; m. NC to Jacob Fouts (1781-1864); moved to OH

     1711-5 Philemon Plummer, b. ca 1786/7; d. 14 Nov 1823; m. NC to Mary Means; moved to Indiana Territory

     1711-6 John Plummer, b. 31 Dec 1789; d. 7 Sep 1846; m. 13 Aug 1811 Wayne Co., IN to Isabella Harvey (1786-1864)

     1711-7 Catharine Plummer, b. 26 Sep 1791; d. 2 Oct 1861; m. 21 Jun 1810 Montgomery Co., OH to John Cress, Sr. (1790-1866)

     1711-8 Susannah Plummer, b. 8 Oct 1793; d. 28 May 1862; m. 7 Mar 1811 Preble Co., OH to Elijah Fox (____-1837)

     1711-9 Caroline Plummer; m. 6 Jul 1814 Wayne Co., IN to John Biggs, Sr.

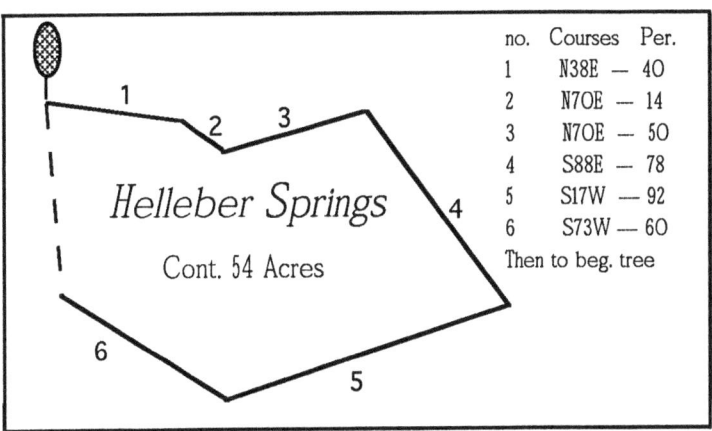

6 Jun 1739 patent to Richard Snowden of Anne Arundel Co. for 100 acres; 50 acres assigned 10 Sep 1739 to Philemon Plummer of Prince George's Co.; called *Debutt's Delight* lying in Prince George's Co. in *Calverton* or *Conegscheigue Manor*; surveyed 13 Sep 1739; on back of certificate: Philemon Plummer of Prince George's Co. petitions for patent on foregoing land; Philemon Plummer, Sr., dec'd, land descended to petitioner; 22 Jul 1768 (Land Records BC&BS37, p. 221)

6 Sep 1777; Philemon Plummer, son and heir of John Plummer, dec'd; sold to Nathan Hammond *Debutt's Delight* and of 50 acres by patent and a parcel called *Helleber Springs* containing by patent 54 acres; also a parcel called *Beatty's Range* conveyed him by Charles Beatty ca 25 Mar 1769 of 8 acres; all land in Frederick Co. (Land Records RP-1, p. 235)

 171-2 ? John Plummer; found in Davidson Co., NC; probably s/o John and Rachel
 171-3 ? Thomas Plummer; found in Rockingham Co., NC; probably s/o John and Rachel

 17-2 Kezia Plummer, b. 4 d. 1 mo. 1728/9 Queen Anne Parish; may have been 2nd wife of William Hendrickson, Sr. living in Allegany Co. in 1800; she was disowned by Quakers in 1757
 17-3 Sarah Plummer, b. 28 d. 9 mo. 1730 Queen Anne Parish
 17-4 Achsah Plummer; m. 28 d. 1 mo. 1755 George Hinkle; lived Allegany Co., MD; children:

  174-1 Elizabeth Hinkle; m. 1780 William Drake

174-2 Charlotte Hinkle; m. 6 Jan 1778 William Hendrickson, Richland Co., OH
174-3 Sarah Hinkle
174-4 George Hinkle; m. Hariet Beall
174-5 Margaret Hinkle; m. David Drake
174-6 John Jacob Hinkle
174-7 Barsheba Hinkle, m. 1 Aug 1796 Adam Gross

17-5 Elizabeth Plummer; she was disowned by Quakers in 1757 for supporting her mother's second marriage

17-6 Philemon Plummer; m. Sarah _____; d. by 1820; signed Oath of Fidelity 1778; will written 21 Sep 1818 Montgomery Co.; codicil 29 Aug 1820, proved 15 Sep 1820; children:

176-1 Philemon Plummer, b. 7 Aug 1764 Rock Creek Parish; will proved 24 Mar 1829 Montgomery Co.; no wife or children

176-2 Joseph Plummer; may have m. 21 Jan 1812 Montgomery Co. to Verlinda Veatch; known child:

1762-1 Philemon Plummer; named in will of (17-6) grandfather and (176-1) uncle Philemon

176-3 William Plummer, b. 17 Jan 1769; d. 17 Mar 1855; m. 19 Jan 1795 Frederick Co. to Rachel Hobbs; d. 1833; moved to Scott Co., KY ca 1790; children:

1763-1 Amey Plummer; named in uncle Philemon's will; remained in Montgomery Co.
1763-2 Philemon Plummer, b. 13 Sep 1807 Scott Co., KY; named in (17-6) grandfather Philemon's will; one descendant moved to Tipton Co., IN
1763-3 William Plummer; moved to KY

176-4 John Plummer; d. by 1818; m. ?Eleanor _____; children:

1764-1 Joseph Plummer
1764-2 William Plummer

176-5 Sarah Plummer; m. Stephen Anderson, Sr.; children:

  1765-1 Philemon Anderson
  1765-2 Joseph Anderson

176-6 Nancy Plummer; m. John Moon; children's names unknown

176-7 George Plummer; m. Delilah Riggs; moved to KY but no records found there; daughter's names unknown

17-7 Jerome Plummer; d. ca 1806; m. Elizabeth ____; moved to Brooks Co., WV after son's death in Allegany Co., MD; children:

  177-1 Jerome Plummer; d. will proved 26 Aug 1796 Allegany Co., MD (Liber A, folio 21-22)

    1771-1 George Plummer; lived with grandfather; d. 3 Oct 1865, bur. Wells Burying Ground., Avella, PA; m. Leah Wells
    1771-2 Rebecca Plummer; remained in Maryland
    1771-3 Christina Plummer; remained in Maryland
    1771-4 Elizabeth Plummer; m. Henry Perregory; Elizabeth Perregory named in will of [17-7] Jerome Plummer's will

  177-2 George Plummer
  177-3 Elizabeth Plummer; m. _____ Lazsher

    1773-1 Asa Lazsher
    1773-2 Jefferey Lazsher; of age in 1806; ex. of grandfather [17-7] Jerome Plummer's will
    1773-3 Elizabeth Lazsher
    1773-4 Sally Lazsher

17-8 George Plummer, b. ca 1737 (Fr. Co. Deed, Liber H, folio 386); m. Hannah _____; estate settlement 1777 Frederick Co., MD; he was disowned by Quakers in 1757; children:

  178-1 Abraham Plummer
  178-2 Joshua Plummer

178-3 Elizabeth Plummer
178-4 Alice Plummer

Will of GEORGE PLUMMER, Frederick Co., planter; 21 Jun 1774; 23 Jan 1777
Land where I now live to be sold and the profit used to purchase another tract of land to be equally divided between my 2 sons
To my son Abraham Plummer, a roan mare
To my son Joshua Plummer, a bay colt
To my beloved wife Hannah, my personal estate to be divided at her death between my two daughters Elizabeth and Alice Plummer
Ex. my brother Philemon Plummer of Frederick Co.
Wit: Aaron Gartrell (mark), John Penn, Ezekial Waters (Box P, folder 32)

17-9 Dorcas Plummer; may have m. James McClane; she was disowned by Quakers in 1757

1-8 Micajah Plummer, est. b. ca early 1700s; planter; s/o Thomas Plummer (2) and Elizabeth Smith; m. Margaret Childs; d/o Henry Childs and Margaret Preston; witnessed will of Charles Scraggs of Frederick Co. 28 Mar 1949 (Wills, Liber 26, folio 34); inherited land in father's will; 50 acres surveyed 7 Apr 1743 in what is now Frederick Co.; co-legatee with brother Yate in will of mother land called *Liford*, and to share residue of personal estate with brother Yate; in 1750 he was sent to the Grand Jury for stealing a colt belonging to Adam Buttner; owned *Plummer's Delight* which he sold 10 May 1753 to Joseph Bell (Land Records E, p. 169); 21 Jul 1753 he sold Samuel Plummer *Plummer's Hunting Lott* for £16 (Land Records E, p.234); Margaret gave up dower on both transactions; children, if any, unknown

1-9 Yate Plummer (1), est. b. ca 1716; d. 23 Jul 1764 age 48 (obit.); s/o Thomas Plummer (2) and Elizabeth Smith; (Wills, Liber 32, folio 341); m. Priscilla ?Yate; he inherited land in father's will; to share residue of personal estate of mother with his brother Micajah; possessed 434 acres *Howard's Range*, Town Neck Hundred (Rent Rolls, #6, folio 115).

19-1 John Plummer
19-2 William Plummer
19-3 Thomas Plummer
19-4 Yate Plummer (2)
19-5 Robert Plummer
19-6 Daniel Plummer
19-7 James Plummer
19-8 Susanna Plummer
19-9 Elisabeth Plummer

WILL of YATES PLUMMER, Anne Arundel Co.; written 1 Sep 1763; probate 31 Aug 1764
To wife: Priscilla Plummer, 200 acres *Howard's Petapsco Range*, including the now dwelling plantation and slaves
To sons: John, William, and Yate, tract called *Howard's Petapsco Range*
To sons: Robert, Daniel, Thomas and James, tract called *Plummer's Pasture* to be divided between them
Profits from iron ore to wife and children: John, William, Yates, Robert, Daniel, Thomas, James, Susannah, and Elizabeth Plummer
To daus. Susannah and Elizabeth, residue of personal estate
Wit: Gerrard Hopkins (Quaker), Nehemiah Miller, William Rowles
(Md. Cal. Wills, Vol. XIII, p. 54; Wills, Liber 32, folio 341)

19-1 John Plummer; m. Nancy _____; children

    191-1 Anne Plummer
    191-2 Harriet Plummer

19-2 William Plummer; m. unknown; d. will 16 Jan 1836 (Liber TTs-1, f. 241); children:

    192-1 Elizabeth Plummer; m. Stephen Lee
    192-2 _____ Plummer; m. Beale Gaither; children:

        1922-1 Susanna Gaither
        1922-2 Elenor Gaither
        1922-3 Massey Ann Gaither

19-3 Thomas Plummer; d. ca 1818; will probate 15 Dec 1818 (Box P, folio 35, Anne Arundel Co.); estate left to wife and children of his brother John; land left to Stephen Lee if he releases obligation to brother James Plummer

19-4 Yate Plummer (2); m. 23 d. 12 mo. 1768 Indian Springs, Anne Arundel Co. to Artridge Waters; d. 17 Oct 1823, in her 75th year; d/o Samuel Waters; 15 d. 4 mo. 1775 Yate Plummer presented a certificate from West River to Pipe Creek Monthly Meeting for himself, Artridge, and his dau. Sarah; children:

194-1 Sarah Plummer, b. 9 Apr 1773; m. 19 Sep 1799 William Ward; children:

1941-1 Yate Ward; named in Richard Plummer's will

194-2 Priscilla Plummer, b. 13 Jul 1775; m. [127-1] Samuel Plummer; s/o Abraham Plummer; moved to Ohio; Priscilla and son Samuel named in will of father-in-law Abraham and her brother Richard; in 1850 she was living with son in Buckeys Town district, Frederick Co., MD; known child:

1942-1 Samuel Plummer, b. ca 1802; unmarried

194-3 Samuel Plummer, b. 13 Aug 1777; d. Ohio
194-4 Richard Plummer, b. 12 Feb 1780; m. Mary Plummer; d/o Isaac Plummer and Grace Taylor; no children mentioned in his will
194-5 Rachel Plummer, b. 21 Jul 1782; m. 18 Jan 1816 Joseph Jackson
194-6 Yate Plummer, b. 22 Dec 1784; d. 2 Oct 1795
194-7 Gulielma Plummer, b. 18 Apr 1787
194-8 Rebecca Plummer, b. 9 Aug 1791

19-5 Robert Plummer; m. Elizabeth _____; sold land 5 Feb 1797 left him by his father; later had mortgage on James Watkins' household
19-6 Daniel Plummer; had no heirs; sold land to John and Andrew Ellicott
19-7 James Plummer; no heirs
19-8 Susannah Plummer; might have m. Samuel Waters, Jr.
19-9 Elizabeth Plummer; d. ca 1774; unmarried

1-10 Abiezer Plummer, b. after 1715; d. ca 1770; s/o Thomas Plummer (2) and Elizabeth Smith; acquired *Swanson's Lott*, his home plantation, and *Dundee* from his brothers; under age 21 when his mother died and Yate to care for his portion until he became of age; m. Ann _____; children from his will:

    1(10)-1 Thomas Plummer
    1(10)-2 John Plummer
    1(10)-3 Joseph Plummer

WILL of ABIEZER PLUMMER, Prince George's Co.; written 31 Sep 1770; probate 8 Oct 1770
To sons Thomas and John tract called *Dundee*
To son Joseph, *Swanson's Lott*, his dwelling plantation, after death of wife Ann Plummer
To sons Joseph and John, remainder of estate after death of mother
Ex: Son Joseph
Wit: Charles Ramsey Hodges, Jos. Jones, Peter MacLaughlin
                                                            (T. 1.105 - Bowie)
Codicil: Thomas not to receive any land, but it is to be given to his two sons, and for wife.

1(10)-1 Thomas Plummer, b. 3 Jan 1744; m. ca 1766 Mary Hodges; most of his family moved to Indiana; children:

    1(10)1-1 Abiezer Plummer, b. 22 Jan 1767
    1(10)1-2 Mary Ann Plummer, b. 30 May 1768
    1(10)1-3 Elisabeth Plummer, b. 28 Aug 1769
    1(10)1-4 Charles Plummer, b. 30 Jan 1771
    1(10)1-5 John Plummer, b. 6 Sep 1772; m. Nancy Ladd; lived Cass Co., IN
    1(10)1-6 Thomas Plummer, b. 27 Mar 1774; m. Barbara _____
    1(10)1-7 Joseph Plummer, b. 27 Jul 1775
    1(10)1-8 Levi Plummer, b. 14 Mar 1777; d. 1870; m/1 Martha Brock; m/2 Sarah Richards; lived Hendricks Co., IN
    1(10)1-9 William Plummer, b. 19 Nov 1778
    1(10)1-10 Barrach Plummer, b. 23 Jul 1780; m. Nancy Piper; lived Marshall Co., IN
    1(10)1-11 Sarah Plummer, b. 28 Aug 1782
    1(10)1-12 Charity Plummer, b. 17 Jan 1784
    1(10)1-13 Elijah Plummer, b. 3 Mar 1787
    1(10)1-14 Elisha Plummer, b. 17 Mar 1790; m/1 Sarah _____; m/2 Nancy _____; m/3 _____; lived Marshall Co., IN

1(10)-2 John Plummer; d. ca 1813;? m. 1 Aug 1782 Sarah Hodges; children:

1(10)2-1 Charles H. Plummer
1(10)2-2 Ann Plummer; ml. 14 Dec 1808 Grafton Tyler (1788-1886); s/o Samuel Tyler (1737-1805) and Susannah Duvall; member Holy Trinity Church; Ann inherited a number of slaves from the 1789 will of her father
1(10)2-3 John Plummer
1(10)2-4 Benjamin Plummer
1(10)2-5 Sarah Plummer

Will of JOHN PLUMMER; Prince George's Co.; 13 Mar 1813; 10 Jul 1813
To son Charles H. Plummer, all my lands in Anne Arundel Co., *Browzley Hall, Hopkins' Search* and *White Plain*; except 100 acres adjacent Patuxent River and the land of John Weems devised to dau. Sarah Plummer
To son John Plummer, 1 Negro
To son Benjamin Plummer, dwelling plantation in Prince George's Co. part of *Swanson's Lot* and part of *Strife*
To dau. Ann, wife of Grafton Taylor, Negroes, etc.
To dau. Sarah, 100 acres above, furniture, etc.
Exs. sons Charles H. and Benjamin Plummer
Wit. Benjamin H. Clark, James Lamar, John McGill
(Prince George's Co. Wills, TT#1.71)

1(10)-3 Joseph Plummer; d. ca 1789; m. Esther/ Hester Smith; d. by 1819 Prince George's Co.; d/o Nathan Smith and Cassandra Childs; lived *Swanson's Lott* Prince George's Co.; children :

1(10)3-1 Mordecai Plummer, b. ca 1775; d. 28 Mar 1839; m. 15 Nov 1803 Margery Lyles (1794-1855); inherited part of *Dundee* from will of his father
1(10)3-2 Joseph Plummer
1(10)3-3 Abiezar Plummer; m. 3 Nov 1793/5 Susanna Wells; went to Washington Co., KY
1(10)3-4 Ann Plummer

1(10)3-5 Sarah Plummer; m. 23 Jun 1802 Fielder Bowie Smith, b. 14 Nov 1775; d. 20 Jun 1844; s/o Mordecai Smith and Phoebe Finch; Fielder m/2 Lucy Middleton Smith

1(10)3-6 Esther Plummer

WILL of JOSEPH PLUMMER; Prince George's Co.; written 9 Jan 1789; probate 18 Apr 1789

Estate to wife Esther for schooling and maintenance of children during widowhood, and after her death or marriage to son Mordecai "all the land he then possessed in Prince George's Co."

In event of death of Mordecai without heirs, to son Joseph; should he die without issue to son Abiezer

Mentions daughters Ann, Sarah, Ester

Wit: Daniel Clark, Walter Wills, Clement Smith, Richard J. Duckett

(T. 1, 277 W.M., Bowie)

1-11 Priscilla Plummer; d/o Thomas Plummer (2) and Elizabeth Smith; m. 2nd wife of John Ouchterlong, b. Scotland; she inherited 10s from will of father and personalty from will of mother; John Ouchterlong m/1 Frances Wells according to 2 depositions made in 1770 (Maureen Duvall of Middle Plantation); known children:

1(11)-1 Margaret Ouchterlong, b. 30 Jan 1731/2 Queen Anne Parish, Prince George's Co.

1(11)-2 Agnes Ouchterlong, b. ca 1733 (deposition of Elizabeth Tyler)

1-12 Phoebe Plummer; d/o Thomas Plummer (2) and Elizabeth Stockett; m. Joseph Williams, Sr.; she inherited 10s from will of her father and personalty from will of mother

2. Margaret Plummer, est. b. ca 1670s; alive 1694 (father's will); d. by 1696; d/o Thomas Plummer and Elizabeth Stockett; m. Hugh Riley, b. ca 1653; age 61 in 1714, 63 in 1716, 66 in 1719 (Md. Deponents); he m/2 by 1698 Mary _____; d. by 1712; Margaret inherited 5s from will of father, plus "advances already made"; children from land records:

2-1 Lydia "Leady" Riley; d/o Hugh Riley and Margaret; m. Thomas Swearingen; d. ca 1726; Thomas was illiterate; children from Queen Anne Parish:

21-1 Thomas Swearingen, b. 8 Apr 1708
21-2 Mary Swearingen, b. 11 Aug 1710
21-3 Laurana Swearingen, b. 15 Oct 1713
21-4 Margaret Swearingen, b. 17 Feb 1716
21-5 Van Swearingen, b. 22 May 1719

Deed of Gift, 17 Nov 1716; from Hugh Riley to Leady Riley, his daughter, wife of Thomas Swearingen; 120 acre portion of *Riley's Gift* (Pr. Geo.'s Co. Land Records, Liber F, folio 571).

Deed of Gift, Dec 1722, 24 May 1723; from Hugh Ryley of Prince George's Co. to Thomas Swearingen, son-in-law, planter of Prince George's Co.; 120 acre part of *The Forrest* called *Ryley's Gift*
(Pr. Geo.'s Co. Land Records, Liber I, folio 440)

WILL of THOMAS SWEARINGEN; [Prince George's Co.]; written 12 Apr 1726; probate 12 May 1726
To eldest son Thomas and hrs., 70 ac. *The Forest* had of father-in-law Hugh Riley
To youngest son Van and hrs., 70 a. of afsd. tract and 20 a. of *Hill's Choys* had of father _____
To daus. Margarit and Lurana and their hrs., each 40 a. of *Hills Choys*
To eldest dau. Mary and hrs., 96 a. *Swerengen's Pasture*, Prince George's Co.; shd. either sons Thomas or Van die before of age, the survivor to inherit portion of dec'd; shd. either of girls die before of age, survivor of them to inherit portion of dec'd
Test: John Sherwood, Joseph Chaplin, Ann Clarke
(Md. Cal. Wills, Vol. V, p. 225; Wills, Liber 18, folio 501)

2-2 Hugh Riley, Jr.; s/o Hugh Riley; m. by 1712 to Rebecca _____; d. ca 1748 (Index to Wills, Admn. & Inv., Prince George's Co.); land records refer to him as a planter; he sold 100 acres of *Ryley's Range*; 444 acres of *Weston*; 40 acres of *Cope's Hill* taken from *Hugh's Labour* and *Riley's Folly*; 100 acres of *Poplar Thicket* on the Eastern Branch of the Potomac(Land Records of Prince George's Co.); son:

22-1 Hugh Riley; admn. estate of mother 1748

2-3  Elizabeth Riley; d/o Hugh Riley and Mary; m. ca 1706 William Chapline; children from Queen Anne Parish:

23-1  Joseph Chapline, b. 5 Sep 1707
23-2  William Chapline, b. 25 Oct 1709; ?d. young
23-3  Mary Chapline, b. 17 Sep 1712
23-4  Anne Chapline, b. 2 Dec 1714
23-5  Moses Chapline, b. 11 Jun 1717
23-6  Elizabeth Chapline, b. 14 Nov 1722
23-7  William Chapline, b. 17 Apr 1726

Deed of Gift, undated (ca 1715/6); from Hugh Ryley to Elizabeth Ryley, wife of William Chapplin of Prince George's Co.; 139 of the 259 acres of *Ryley's Gift*; bounded by land of Thomas Swerington
(Prince George's Co. Land Records, Liber F, folio 579)

Indenture, 19 Nov 1718; William Chaplain, planter of Prince George's Co., sold John Oliver a tract of 37 acres called *Hope* on the "lowermost draught of the long branch of the northeast branch of the Eastern Branch" of the Potomac; acknowledged by wife Elizabeth
(Prince George's Co. Land Records, Liber I, folio 123)

Indenture, 19 Aug 1721; William Chaplin, ship carpenter of Prince George's Co., sold Dr. Richard Pile, 100 acres of *Expedition* on Piney Hedge Branch; acknowledged by his wife Elizabeth
(Prince George's Co. Land Records, Liber I, folio 215)

Deed of Gift, Dec 1722, 24 May 1723; from Hugh Ryley to William Chapline, son-in-law, planter of Prince George's Co.; 135 acre portion of *The Forrest* of 259 acres; acknowledged by wife Rachel.
(Prince George's Co. Land Records, Liber I, folio 438)

PART of HUGH RYLEY'S LAND RECORDS in
CALVERT & PRINCE GEORGE'S COUNTIES:

5 May 1688, Calvert Co., *Riley's Horse Pasture*, 330 acres, granted Hugh Ryley
16 May 1689, Calvert Co., *The Beginning* and *Hugh's Labour*, granted Hugh Ryley
19 Feb 1694, Calvert Co., *Ryley's Range*, 800 acres, granted Hugh Ryley
3 Sep 1694, Calvert Co., *Rylys Lott*, granted Hugh Ryley
25 Aug 1696 Hugh Riley, carpenter of Prince George's Co., sold 50 acres part of *Riley's Folly* and *Hugh's Labor* on east side of Collington Branch to George Coope of Anne Arundel Co.; no wife's acknowledgment

23 Jun 1696 Hugh Riley, carpenter of Prince George's Co., sold Nathaniel Brothers part of a tract called *The Beginning*; no acknowledgment

28 Jun 1698, Hugh Riley, sold 130 acres deducted from *The Beginning* and *Riley's Folly* called *Second Lott* to Solomon Rothery of Anne Arundel Co.; acknowledged by Mary Riley, his wife

28 Jun 1698 Hugh Riley sold 107 acres called *The First Late* deducted from a tract called *The Beginning*; acknowledged by Mary Riley, wife of Hugh

9 Sep 1699, Hugh Riley, gentleman of Prince George's Co.; sold to John Baptistyler 100 acres called *Duchman's Imployment*, part of *Riley's Range* in the woods above the head of Collington; and 200 acres called *Widdow's Purchase* to Sarah Rodery from same tract; acknowledged by Mary Riley, wife of Hugh

13 Apr 1698, for Hugh Riley, Thomas Addison filed a resurvey of an 800 acre tract called *Major's Lott* on Collington Branch

3 Jun 1702, Hugh Riley sold Samuel Brashear a 60 acre tract in Prince George's Co.; acknowledged by Mary Riley, wife of Hugh

15 Feb 1703, Hugh Ryley sold 510 acres of 1000 acres of *Ryley's Discovery*, called *Ware Park*, to Edward Dawson and 380 acres of same to Thomas Ricketts; acknowledged by Mary Riley, wife of Hugh

13 Feb 1703, Hugh Ryley, gentleman, sold 150 acres called *Stoney Plaines*, part of *Ryley's Discovery*, to Richard Isaac; acknowledged by Mary Riley

10 Jan 1704, Hugh Ryley, carpenter, bought 50 acres called *The Beginning* from Charles Hyatt

8 May 1712, Hugh Ryley, gentleman of Prince George's Co., sold 103 acres of land called *Rose Purchase* taken from *Scott's Lott*; no acknowledgment by wife

3. Mary Plummer, est. b. ca 1670s; d/o Thomas Plummer and Elizabeth Stockett; m. William Jackson; she inherited rights in "certain tracts of land and 300 a. *Scott's Lott* in Calvert Co." from will of her father

4. Susannah Plummer, est. b. ca 1670s; d/o Thomas Plummer and Elizabeth Stockett; m/1 Francis Swanson; d. by 1714; she inherited personalty from will of father; m/2 James Ward; Francis and Susannah Swanstone of Calvert Co. sold a tract of land called *Swanston's Lott* 12 Mar 1693 (P. G. Co. Land Records, Liber F, folio 254); 10 Dec 1714, James Ward and Susannah his wife, formerly Susannah Swanson, acknowledged the right of George Wells to ownership of a portion of *Swanston's Lott*; [Francis may have been the only son of Dr. Francis Swanston of Calvert Co. who d. ca 1675 (Md. Cal. Wills, Vol..

I, p. 119); Dr. Swanston patented *Swanson's Lot* 17 Jul 1670 in that part of Calvert which became Prince George's Co.]

5. Elizabeth Plummer, est. b. ca 1670s Quaker; bapt. 19 Jun 1698 All Hallows Episcopal Church (as wife of Wm. Ijams, Jr.); d. ca 1762 (Wills, Liber 31, folio 741); d/o Thomas Plummer and Elizabeth Stockett; m. 27 Aug 1696 All Hallow's Parish to William Ijams, Jr. (1671-1738); s/o William Ijams, Sr. [bur. 29 Jul 1703] and Elizabeth Cheney; Elizabeth inherited 164 acres of *Bridge Hill* and *Doden* at mother's decease; William Ijams "requested the re-recording [of *Doden* and 100 acres of *Bridge Hill*] in the right of his wife [Eliza.] the legatee, daughter of Thomas Plumer" (Abstracts of Land Records of Anne Arundel Co., MD, 1662-1703). They lived at *Bridge Hill* where the children were all born. Children from will and All Hallow's Parish records:

   5-1 Elizabeth Ijams, b. 1697   5-6 John Ijams, bapt. 1718
   5-2 William Ijams, b. 1699    5-7 Plummer Ijams, bapt. 1718
   5-3 Richard Ijams, b. 1702    5-8 Charity Ijams
   5-4 Mary Ijams, bapt. 1705    5-9 Ann Ijams
   5-5 Thomas Ijams, b. 1708

WILL of WILLIAM IJAMS, planter, Anne Arundel Co.; written 28 Jun 1734; probate 17 May 1738

To wife Elizabeth, entire personal estate, except following legacies. Shd. sd. wife marry personal estate to be divided bet. sons John and Plummer and dau. Ann.

To son William and hrs., 100 acres *Cheney's Resolution*; and 5s

To sons Richard and Thomas and daus. Elizabeth, Mary and Charity, 5s each

To son John and hrs., after his mother's decease, 100 acres *Bridge Hill*; sd. son dying without issue to pass to son Plummer and hrs., he dying with issue to son Thomas and hrs.

To son Plummer and hrs., 64 acres *Doden* adj. to dwelling plantation *Bridge Hill*

To dau. Ann, personalty

Exs.: Sons Thomas and John

Test: Richard Williams, Richard Welsh, John Nicholson, Jr., Richard Williams, Jr.   (Md. Cal. Wills, Vol. VII, p. 246; Wills, Liber 21, folio 878)

WILL of ELIZABETH IJAMES, Anne Arundel Co.; written 5 May 1762; probate 22 Sep 1762
My deceased husband William Ijams' will that all effect that I should die possessed with should be equally divided between sons John and Plumer Ijams and dau. Anne Williams
It is my will that they should settle it and dispose of it in the following manner: that the slaves should not be divided between my 3 children until the 1st day Dec next but kept on plantation of John Ijams and my provisions to be for the use of the family, some furniture, etc.
To son John Ijams, looking glass; to dau. Anne William, Clothing
To daughter-in-law Ruth Ijams, my side saddle and other
Sons John and Plumer Ijams and daughter Anne William to give son Thomas Ijams £10 currency
If any one of the rest of my children should have a right to any part of the estate I give each of them 1 shilling, but I think they have no right by my deceased husband's will
Wit: Richard Harwood, Jr., John J. Phelps, Ariana Ijams, Mary Tull
(Md. Cal. Wills, Vol. XII, p. 150; Wills, Liber 31, folio 741)

The family name Ijams is found with a variety of spellings in the early records. Court and church records show spellings as Eyoms, Eyams, Iiams, Iams, Ijames, Jiams, etc. The origin of the name is unclear according to Harry Wright Newman in *Anne Arundel Gentry*, Vol. I, which contains more detailed information on this family.

William Ijams (____-1703) m. Elizabeth Cheney; their children were William Ijams (1671-1738); Richard Ijams (1676-____); George Ijams (1690/1-1763); George had children named George, William and Jacob, Mary and Susanna Ijams (Md. Deponents and Md. Cal. Wills).

5-1 Elizabeth Ijams, b. 15 Jun 1697; bapt. 19 Jun 1697; m. Gassaway Watkins, b. 31 Mar 1695 All Hallow's Parish; d. ca 1746; s/o John and Anne Watkins; children from will and All Hallow's Parish:

51-1 John Gassaway Watkins, bapt. 6 Aug 1718
51-2 Anne Watkins, bapt. 27 Mar 1719; m. 9 Feb 1737/8 Richard Harwood; bapt. 19 Oct 1707 St. James Parish; s/o Richard and Mary; children listed under Richard Harwood.
51-3 Elisabeth Watkins, b. 16 Sep 1720; m. _____ Rawlings

51-4 Margarett Watkins, b. 11 Feb 1722; this might be the same person as "dau. Mary" in father's will
51-5 Gassaway Watkins, b. 3 Jul 1723
51-6 Nicholas Watkins; bapt. 9 May 1731; d. ca 1770; m. Margaret _____; wit. will of William Coller 20 Feb 1742 (Md. Cal. Wills, Vol. X, p. 34).
51-7 Jane Watkins; bapt. 9 May 1731
51-8 Thomas Gassaway Watkins; bapt. 9 May 1731

WILL of GASSAWAY WATKINS, Anne Arundel Co., written 23 May 1746; probate 9 Jul 1746
To son John Watkins and hrs., land on the side of branch called *Jacob's Branch*, where his dwelling house now stands, bounded with the water of the river
Remainder of my plantation called *Townhill* to be divided between my son Gassaway Watkins, Jr. and son Nicholas Watkins
To dau. Elizabeth Rawling, 1 slave
To dau. Mary
To son John Gassaway and Nicholas, my son-in-law Richard Harwood, and son Gassaway Watkins, exs.
Wit: Jno. Jiams, Wm. Jiams, Will Chettin
(Md. Cal. Wills, Vol. IX, p. 71; Wills, Liber 24, folio 400)

5-2 William Ijams, b. 22 Dec 1699; bapt 26 Jul 1700; age 57 in 1757 and 66 in 1765 (More Md. Deponents); m. 9 Oct 1720 Elizabeth Jones; d. after 1774; inherited *Cheny's Resolution*; children:

52-1 William Ijams, b. 22 Nov 1721; d. ca 1774; carpenter
52-2 Cassandra Ijams, b. 20 Sep 1722; m. 16 Dec 1736 Henry Leeke
52-3 Margaret Ijams, b. 13 Aug 1724
52-4 Sarah Ijams; unmarried 1774

5-3 Richard Ijams, b. 9ber 1702; bapt. 4 Mar 1702/3; m. 19 Jan 1737 Mary Nicols
5-4 Mary Ijams, bapt. 26 Aug 1705; m. 14 Feb 1720 to John Waters
5-5 Thomas Ijams, b. 7 Aug 1708; bapt. 24 Feb 1708; m. ca 1730 Artridge _____; he bought *Duvall's Delight* on 17 Apr 1730 from Charles Carroll; children from will and family Bible:

55-1 Elizabeth Ijams, b. 19 Aug 1732
55-2 Sarah Ijams, b. 8 Dec 1734
55-3 Artridge Ijams, b. 6 Feb 1736
55-4 Charity Ijams, b. 15 Jan 1739
55-5 Susanna Ijams, b. 15 Dec 1742; m. _____ Pumphries
55-6 Thomas Ijams, b. 20 Apr 1745; d. ca 1805; m/1 Sarah Ijams; d/o John and Rebecca; m/2 Sarah Marriott; d/o Joseph Marriott; children:

    556-1 John Ijams, b. Jun 1775; ml. 15 Feb 1794 Anne Arundel Co. to Rachel Marriott; d/o Joshua Marriott and Anne Homewood; confirmed by 1805 will of Joshua
    556-2 Rebecca Ijams, b. 5 Sep 1777; ml. 25 Mar 1796 to Joseph Marriott

55-7 John Ijams, b. 20 Oct 1747; d. 2 Jun 1785; ml. 5 Jun 1778 to Susannah Watkins; believed to be Susannah Taylor, widow of Joseph Taylor; she next m. Marsh Mareen Duvall
55-8 Richard Ijams, b. 15 Feb 1749; m. Eleanor Musgrove; he was a millwright; settled in Frederick Co.; children:

    558-1 Thomas Musgrove Ijams, b. ca 1774 Frederick Co.; m. Nancy Carvel, b. ca 1778; d. ca 1850; settled in that portion of Rowan Co. which became Davidson Co., NC; children:

        5581-1 Henrietta Ijams, b. 7 Jul 1796; d. 1 May 1846 NC; m. 13 Aug 1817 Samuel Cecil; s/o Philip and Julia Cecil, formerly of Frederick Co., MD
        5581-2 Sarah Ijams, b. ca 1798; d. Johnson Co., MO; m. 23 Apr 1821 Rowan Co., NC to Daniel Livingood
        5581-3 Richard Ijams, b. ca 1800; d. 12 Mar 1857; m. Ellen Colt; d. Davidson Co., NC
        5581-4 William Ijams; m. Mary Leonard
        5581-5 Mary Ijams; m. Philip Clinard
        5581-6 Rachel Ijams; d. ca age 17 unmarried
        5581-7 Thomas Ijams, b. 8 Jul 1812; d. 11 Sep 1874 Johnson Co., MO; m. 3 times

5581-8 Nancy Ijams; b. 29 May y 1815; d. 8 Feb 1901 Johnson Co., MO; m. Salathial Stone

5581-9 George Washington Ijams; b. 4 Aug 1817; d. Johnson Co., MO; m. Elizabeth Cecil

5581-10 Ellen Ijams; d. young

5581-11 John Ijams; d. young

558-2 Nancy Ijams, b. 10 Mar 1792; d. 2 Feb 1858 Johnson Co., MO; m. 18 Dec 1812 Rowan Co., NC to John B. Cecil, b. 29 Oct 1785 Frederick Co.; d. 21 Jan 1861 Johnson Co., MO

55-9 Mary Ijams, b. 10 Jun 1752

55-10 William Ijams, b. 26 Nov 1755; ml. 5 Jan 1782 to Charity Ryan; he was a blacksmith

5-6 John Ijams, bapt. 6 Aug 1718; d. ca 1783; m. Rebecca Jones; d/o Isaac Jones; inherited *Bridge Hill*; children:

56-1 Elizabeth Ijams; m. Robert Fenley

56-2 Anne Ijams; m. Lewis Stockett

56-3 Mary Ijams; ? m. Thomas Ijams

56-4 William Ijams; m. Elizabeth Howard

56-5 Isaac Plummer Ijams; ml. 4 Aug 1795 Prince George's Co. to Elizabeth Beck; d/o James Beck and Rebecca Walker; widow of Richard Williams

56-6 Thomas Plummer Ijams, b. 4 Apr 1773; m. 10 Feb 1794 to Sarah Duvall; m/2 20 Dec 1814 Elizabeth Manly; child of m/1:

566-1 Lewis Ijams, b. ca 1798; m. Elizabeth \_\_\_\_\_, b. ca 1808 PA

Child of m/2:

566-2 William Fletcher Ijams, b. 7 Jul 1816 OH; m. Elsie Robinson, b. ca 1819 OH

56-7 John Ijams; ml. 21 Mar 1782 Frederick Co. to Mary Waters; d/o John and Rachel Waters

56-8 Rebecca Ijams; m. Thomas Sunderland

WILL of JOHN IJAMS, Anne Arundel Co.; written 9 Oct 1782; probate 21 Apr 1783
To dau. Elizabeth Ijams £5
To grandchildren, John and Rebecca, of my dau. Mary Jiams, 20s
To eldest son William, son-in-law Thomas Ijams, son John, son Isaac Plummer Ijams, negroes
To wife Rebecca Ijams the dwelling plantation and at her decease to be divided between his minor sons Isaac and Thomas, if they died without issue then to son William
Extx: wife Rebecca
Wit: Plummer Iams, John Iams of Plummer, Joseph Williams and Christian Parrott (Anne Arundel Gentry, Vol. I)

5-7 Plummer Ijams, b. ca 1716; bapt. 6 Aug 1718; d. 26 Nov 1792; m. Ruth Childs (1700-1794); he inherited *Doden*; children:

57-1 Plummer Ijams, b. 29 Oct 1748; d. ca 1793; m. Jemina Welsh, b. 27 Oct 1760; d. 16 Apr 1789 Frederick Co.; d/o Benjamin Welsh and Rebecca Hoen; children from will:

571-1 Anne Ijams, b. 17 Sep 1778; ml. 29 Jan 1799 Anne Arundel Co. to George Sanks
571-2 Plummer Ijams, b. 8 Mar 1781; ml/1 15 Mar 1804 Frederick Co. to Rebecca Ijams; d. 10 Nov 1809; d/o of John Ijams and Mary Waters; ml/2 27 Feb 1815 to Mary Montgomery
571-3 Ruth Ijams, b. 13 Nov 1783; ml. 19 Dec 1799 Frederick Co. to Christopher Mussetter
571-4 Rebecca Ijams, b. 18/28 Oct 1785 Frederick Co.; d. adm. acct. 18 Dec 1829; ml. 12 Jan 1805 Benjamin Duvall (1778-1827)
571-5 John Ijams, b. 3 Apr 1789 Frederick Co.; m. 22 Apr 1813 to Catherine Barnes; raised by his aunt, Elizabeth Drury of Anne Arundel Co.; settled in Baltimore

57-2 Elizabeth Ijams, b. 3 Dec 1750; m. William Drury
57-3 Margaret Ijams, b. 1 Oct 1753
57-4 John Ijams, b. 5 Jun 1756; d. 1791; unmarried
57-5 Ann Ijams, b. 2 Jul 1759; m. Samuel Drury

WILL of PLUMMER IJAMS, Anne Arundel Co.; written 18 Feb 1792/3; probated 4 Jan 1793
To wife Ruth the dwelling plantation (parts of *Bridge Hill* and *Dodon*); if she remarried, then only her 1/3 and at her decease to son Plummer
To daus. Elizabeth Drury and Ann Drury, slaves and other personalty
Wit: John Jacob, Isaac Ijams          (Anne Arundel Gentry, Vol. I)

5-8  Charity Ijams; m. 28 Jan 1724 to John Waters, b. 10 Oct 1698 at *Jerico*, Prince George's Co.; d. ca 1774; a John Waters m. Ann Purnell 9 Jan 1717/8 in All Hallow's Parish; Charity may have been his second wife; their children:

58-1  Samuel Waters, b. 28 Jan 1726; m. Elizabeth _____
58-2  Elizabeth Waters, b. 25 Jan 17__; never married
58-3  John Waters, b. 11 Dec 1735
58-4  Thomas Waters
58-5  Arnold Waters; m. Rachel Franklin
58-6  Mary Waters; m. Stockett Williams
58-7  Sarah Waters; m. _____ Norris
58-8  Ann Waters; m. Nathaniel Pigman
58-9  Susannah Waters; m. ca 1773 George Robertson
58-10 Charity Waters
58-11 William Waters

WILL of JOHN WATERS, JR., Prince George's Co.; written 17 Nov 1768; probate 27 Oct 1774
To son Samuel Waters, Ex., part of tract *Maden's Fancy*, 280 acres, personalty
To son William Waters, part of tract *Maden's Fancy*, 280 acres
To son Thomas Waters, part of tract *Indian Town Land*, part of Resurvey at upper part of *Indian Town Land*, 200 acres
To dau. Eliza. Waters, tract *Water's Purchis*, 150 acres, 1 negress during life, son Samuel Waters to take care of dau. Elizabeth Waters and at her death to have her lands
To son Arnold Water, Ex., my now dwelling house and plantation, 280 acres, called *Jericho* and *Cherry Walk*, 1 negro, personalty
Two parcel of land one *Water's Purchis* and the other *Maden's Fancy* to be sold and money equally divided between son Arnold Waters, Mary Williams, Sarah Norris, Ann Waters, Susannah Water, and Charity Waters

To 3 unmarried daus. Ann, Susannah and Charity Waters, 1 negress, personalty, each
To grandson Jno. Williams, son of Stockitt Williams, 1 negress
To sons Wm. and Thos. Waters, £5
To children Arnold, Ann, Susannah, Charity Waters, Mary Williams and Sarah Norris, residue of personal estate equally
Wit: Jno. Jiams, Mordecai Waters, Jacob Holland Waters, Richard West
(Wills, Liber 40, folio 101)

5-9 Anne Ijams; m/1 Richard Williams; m/2 William Ijams; s/o George Ijams

### THOMAS PLUMMER

The following family of Thomas Plummer moved to Belmont Co., OH and lived near the Quaker descendants of [171-1] Philemon Plummer (1749-1807). The names and dates do not fit the family of Philemon and the relationship, if any, is unknown at this time.

Thomas Plummer of Lancaster Co., PA, m. 15 d. 11 mo. 1758 to Phebe Cook; d/o John Cook; their children from *Nottingham Quakers*:

1. John Plummer, b. 22 d. 8 mo. 1759
2. Hannah Plummer, b. 13 d. 4 mo. 1761; m. 27 d. 6th mo. 1778 to John Webster; both of New Britain
3. Dinah Plummer, b. 23 d. 8 mo. 1763
4. Phebe Plummer, b. 15 d. 10 mo. 1765
5. Eli Plummer, b. 14 d. 1 mo. 1768
6. Cineh Plummer, b. 14 d. 5 mo. 1770; m. 3 d. 2 mo. 1791 at Little Britain to Henry Sidwell; s/o Henry and Margaret Sidwell of West Nottingham Hundred, Cecil Co.
7. Elinor Plummer, b. 15 d. 5th mo. 1772

The above family moved to Belmont Co., OH and seemed to live with the Quaker descendants of [171-1] Philemon Plummer [1749-1807]. The names and dates do not fit the family of Philemon and the relationship, if any, is unknown at this time.

### Benjamin Lawrence

Benjamin Lawrence (1); m. Ann Ascomb; he came from Accomack, Virginia, where he owned land north of the 150 acres Richard Robinson patented 5 Apr 1666, originally surveyed for John Custis, on the bay side of the north side of Muddy Creek branch (Cavaliers and Pioneers). 16 Mar 1670 Benjamin Lawrence of Somerset Co., MD, planter, proved rights to 200 acres of land for transporting himself, his wife, Ann Lawrence, and his sons Benjamin Lawrence Jr., and Nehemiah Lawrence out of Accomack, VA into Maryland to settle (Book 16, p. 319); on 26 Sep 1674 Benjamin Lawrence of *The Deserts*, Calvert Co., proved his rights for 500 a. of land (Book 18, p. 39). *Deserts* was taken up by Benjamin Lawrence, Nathaniel and Samuel Ashcom (Md. Cal. Wills, Vol. II, p. 15).

Ann Ascomb may have been a sister of Nathaniel and Samuel, children of John and Winifred Ashcom, born after the family settled in Virginia in 1638 and prior to their settling in Calvert Co. ca 1650, although she is not mentioned in any family wills. She might also have been the Ann Ashcomb, transported by John Senier, who was given land in 1650 on Cortoman Bay in Virginia for transportation of several people including Ann (Cavaliers and Pioneers).

1. Benjamin Lawrence (2)
2. Nehemiah Lawrence
3. Thomas Lawrence
4. Lucy Lawrence
5. ?Mary Lawrence

1. Benjamin Lawrence (2); d. ca 1685; m. ca 1676 2nd husband of Elizabeth Talbott, b. ca 1656; bur. 15 Jan 1702 All Hallow's Parish; d/o Richard Talbott and Elizabeth Ewen; Elizabeth Talbott m/1 ca 1672 James Preston of Calvert Co. who d. ca Dec/Jan 1673/4, leaving a daughter named Rebecca Preston b. by 1673; fate unknown (Chancery Records, L1R5, f. 574; Md. Cal. Wills, Vol. I, p. 77); Elizabeth m/3 10 Dec 1686 West River to Richard Galloway; their son, Richard Galloway, b. ca 1691; [see end of this section for a review of the marriages relating to these families]; children:

Children of Benjamin & Elizabeth:   Children from her other marriages:
1-1 Benjamin Lawrence (3), b. 1677   [Rebecca Preston, b. by 1673]
1-2 Elizabeth Lawrence; b. 1678/9    [Elizabeth Galloway, b. by Sep 1689]
1-3 Lucy Lawrence; b. 1685           [Richard Galloway, b. ca 1691]

Benjamin wit. will Sophia Beedle 1674 Anne Arundel Co.; 30 Oct 1681 Benjamin assists in building Patuxent Meeting House; 1 Oct 1682 Benjamin removes and takes Patuxent records with him overseer John Hillen's 1682 will and Richard Arnell's in 1683; wit. will Thomas Hooker of West River 1683; (Md. Cal. Wills, Vol. I, p. 86, 121, 128, 150; Quaker Records of So. Md.).

*Descendants of Richard and Elizabeth (Ewen) Talbott of Poplar Knowle, West River, Anne Arundel Co.* by Ida Morrison (Murphy) Shirk is an excellent source of information on this family (published 1927).

WILL of BENJAMIN LAWRENCE, West River, Anne Arundel Co.; written 6 Jan 1684; probate 3 Jul 1685

To wife Eliz:, execx., and dau. Eliza: and hrs., land in Calvert County on the n. side Patuxent [formerly taken up by Samuell & Nathaniell Ascomb and myself]

To sd. wife and unborn child, land in Somerset Co. obtained from brother-in-law Edward Gibbs [formerly mortgaged and delivered to me by my bro.-in-law Edward Gibbs]

To son Benjamin [at age 21] and hrs., 150 [115] a. *Benjamin's Fortune*, Anne Arundel Co., and tract bought of John Wattkins [at West River]

[To sister-in-law Jane Simmonds one cow and calfe]

To brother Thomas, sister Lucy Smith and Quaker ministry, personalty

[Personal estate: son Benj. 1/4, dau. Elizabeth 1/8, unborn child 1/8]

Overseer: Wm. Richardson, Richd. Johns, Edward Talbot, Saml. Galloway

Test: Jno. Griffin, Henry Hewit, Wm. Wheeler, Nich. Rollson
(Md. Cal. Wills, Vol. I, p. 154; Wills, Liber 4, folio 142)
(Brackets [ ] show additions from original will not in abstract)

1-1 Benjamin Lawrence (3), b. 13 May 1677; d. by 27 Mar 1721 Baltimore Co.; Quaker; s/o Benjamin and Elizabeth; m. 6 day 11 mo. 1701/2 Rachel Mariarte, at the house of Col. Thomas Tailor; d/o of Edward and Honor Mariarte; Rachel m/2 by 13 Sep 1726 to John Norwood (Quaker) (Baltimore Co. Families) or Thomas Norwood (Shirk); Benj. & Rachel wit. will of Solomon Sparrow 1718 Anne

Arundel Co. (Md. Cal. Wills, Vol. IV, p. 183); Benjamin inherited the family plantation, *Benjamin's Fortune*, from his father and sold it to his step-father, Richard Galloway; ca 1753 Rachel Norwood held 87 acres of *Talbott's Resolution* (Rent Rolls); children from West River Monthly Meeting:

11-1 Elizabeth Lawrence, b. 1702   11-4 John Lawrence, b. 1709
11-2 Benjamin Lawrence (4), b. 1705   11-5 Levin Lawrence, b. 1711/2
11-3 Sophia Lawrence, b. 1707   11-6 Margaret Lawrence, b. 1716/7

6 Feb 1690 deed for parcel called *Barren Neck* includes the following: 30 Dec 24th year of the reign of Charles II, indenture between John Keyes of Marlbourough, ex. of Joseph Burgess, dec'd, and Benj. Laurence; Indenture 17/18 Aug 1st year of reign of James II between Benja. Laurence of Marlborough afsd., grocer, and Thomas Curtis, John Smith and Thomas Smith of Marlborough, grocer (Land Records of Anne Arundel County)

8 Nov 1700 Benjamin Lawrence, planter of Anne Arundel County exchanged land called *The Favour* lying on the north side of West River in the woods, containing 115 acres; *Benjamin's Fortune* of 115 acres adjacent to land of Richard Talbott (Land Records of Anne Arundel County).

8 Nov 1700; from Benjamin Lawrence, Anne Arundel Co., planter to Richard Galloway, Anne Arundel Co., Gent.; exchange of land called *The Favour* [or *Benjamin's Favour*] on the north side of West River in the woods, containing 115 acres; /s/ Benja. Lawrence; lying between *Ewan upon Ewanton* and *Ewings Addition*, by land of Ferdinando Battee, by land of Richard Talbott; rerecorded by Richard Galloway (IH2.218; 11T.27).

Depositions of Thomas Bordley, Anne Arundel Co.; Benjamin Lawrence, Sr., s/o Benjamin and Elizabeth, m. sister of Capt. Daniel Mariarte; 1717 (More Md. Deponents).

    11-1 Elizabeth Lawrence, b. 8 d. 10 mo. 1702; d/o Benjamin and Rachel
    11-2 Benjamin Lawrence (4), b. 27 d. 11 mo. 1704; d. 4 Jan 1755; s/o Benjamin and Rachel; m. Ruth Dorsey, b. 15 Oct 1710; d/o John Dorsey and Honor Elder; Benjamin granted 1/4 *Dorsey's Grove* near Glenelg, Howard Co.; attended Christ Church, Queen Caroline Parish; the 4 daus. of John each inherited 1/4 of 783 acres of *Dorsey's Grove*; Ruth m/2 (?as 2nd wife of)

Nathaniel Rumney of Anne Arundel Co.; from his will written 25 Oct 1772, probate 4 May 1773, Ruth inherited *Holland's Choice, Leaf's Forrest* during widowhood (Wills, Liber 39, folio 260); wit will of Peter Barnes 1747 Anne Arundel Co. (Md. Cal. Wills, Vol. XI, p. 228); wit. will of Edward Dorsey, Jr. 1753 (Md. Cal. Wills, Vol. X, p. 247); Ruth wit. will of Peter Shipley 1736/7 (Md. Cal. Wills, Vol. VII, p. 213).

Benjamin Lawrence, planter of Elk Ridge, died last Saturday (Jan 4), when walking across a field with a pipe in his mouth; he fell forward, ran the pipe stem into the roof of his mouth (Maryland Gazette, 9 Jun 1755).

Benjamin Lawrence, Anne Arundel Co.; £578.12.1; 20 Jul 1755; 8 Sep 1755; next of kin: Leven Lawrence, John Dorsey, Jr.; admn. Ruth Lawrence (61.236)

11-3 Sophia Lawrence, b. 2 d. 4 mo. 1707; d/o Benjamin and Rachel

11-4 John Lawrence, b. 11 d. 9 mo. 1709; s/o Benjamin and Rachel; this may be the same person as:

John Lawrence, Anne Arundel Co.; £22.7.1; 27 Aug 1737; 4 Jan 1737; next of kin: N. Gassaway, Leavin Lawrence; admn. Benjamin Lawrence (22.533).

11-5 Levin Lawrence, b. 6 d. 1 mo. 1711/12; d. 1756 Anne Arundel Co. after he fell from his horse in the hunting field; built a brick house on a portion of *Dorsey's Grove* on Poplar Spring Branch called *Poplar Spring Garden* in 1741; s/o Benjamin and Rachel; m. Susannah Dorsey, b. 12 Dec 1717; d/o John Dorsey (1688-1764) and Honor Elder; Susanna rec'd 1/4 *Dorsey's Grove* of ca 1,100 acres for her dowry; she inherited £20 from 1764 will of her father (Will, Liber 33, folio 44); their 4 sons served in the Revolution; they owned *Benjamin's Addition, Cumberland,* and *The Invasion*; children from his will:

115-1 Rachel Lawrence, b. 1739
115-2 Benjamin Lawrence (5), b. 1741
115-3 John Dorsey Lawrence, b. 1743
115-4 Ruth Lawrence, b. 1745
115-5 Levin Lawrence
115-6 Betsy Lawrence
115-7 Peggy Lawrence, b. 1751
115-8 Richard Lawrence, b. 1756

Christ Church, Queen Caroline Parish: In 1750 Levin Lawrence sold 1 acre for 50s to build a Chapel of Ease in the western portion of the parish. William Fee was hired to build the chapel, but something changed as Levin Lawrence finished it (Founders of Anne Arundel and Howard Counties).

WILL of LEVIN LAWRENCE, Anne Arundel Co.; written 7 Feb 1756; probate 9 Nov 1756
To son Benjamin Lawrence, 156 acres called *Benjamin Addition* and one Negro boy
To son John Lawrence, land called *Poplar Spring Garden* and one Negro boy
To son Leaven Lawrence, remainder of *Poplar Spring Garden* and one Negro boy
To daus. Rachel, Ruth, Betsey, and Peggey Lawrence, one Negro girl each
To child my wife now goes with, one Negro boy
Test: Henry Howard, Michl. Dorsey, Vachel Dorsey, Jno. Dorsey, son of John                    (Will Book #30, BT#2, pp. 287/8)

115-1 Rachel Lawrence, b. 3 May 1739; d. 12 Aug 1808; d/o Levin and Susannah; m. 13 Dec 1759 to her mother's 1st cousin, Capt. Philemon Dorsey, b. 20 Jan 1714/5; d. ca 1772; s/o Joshua Dorsey and Ann Ridgely; he m/1 19 Feb 1738/9 Katherine Ridgely; Rachel m/2 19 Jan 1775 Nathan Harris, b. 19 Oct 1747; d. 23 Apr 1820 on his farm ca 3 mi. n. of Mt. Airy, Carroll Co.; s/o Thomas Harris and Sarah Offutt of Calvert Co.; children from his m/1 from Christ Church records; from his and her m/2 from family Bible possessed by Albert Jones:

Philemon & m/1 Katherine:
Ann Dorsey, b. 2 Oct 1740
Elizabeth Dorsey, b. 13 May 1742
Philemon Dorsey, b. 7 Feb 1742/3
Katherine Dorsey, b. 30 Nov 1745
Sarah Dorsey, b. 9 Sep 1747
Unknown mother:
Amelia Dorsey

Philemon & m/2 Rachel:
1151-1 Joshua Dorsey, b. 30 Jan 1762
1151-2 Henrietta Dorsey, b. 20 Feb 1766
1151-3 Ariana Dorsey, b. 24 Mar 1769
Rachel & m/2 Thomas:
1151-4 Harriet Harris, b. 6 Nov 1775
1151-5 Cordelia Harris, b. 10 Apr 1778
1151-6 Orrellana Harris, b. 27 Aug 1781

WILL of PHILEMON DORSEY, Anne Arundel County; written 1 Dec 1771; probate 7 Apr 1772
To wife Rachel the dwelling-plantation *Brother's Partnership* and *Pillage Resurveyed* during life then to his nine children, that is, Philemon, Ann, Catherine, Elizabeth, Sarah, Amelia, Joshua, Henrietta and Maria [Ariana]
To son Philemon *Friendship* whereon he dwelt and portion of *Sapling Range* near Frederick Town
To son Joshua *Beyond Far Enough*, also 60 acres of *Barnes' Purchase*
To sons-in-law viz., John Dorsey of Michael and Ann his wife, William Ridgely of William and Elizabeth his wife, Benjamin Warfield and Catherine his wife, Vachel Warfield and Sarah his wife, Samuel Riggs and Amelia his wife the following plantations, *Silence* of 434 acres, *Peace* of 65 acres, *Second Thought* of 60 acres, *Disappointment* of 100 acres and *Defiance Resurveyed* of 497 acres        (Anne Arundel Gentry)

1151-1 Joshua Dorsey, b. 30 Jan 1762 Queen Caroline Parish, Anne Arundel Co.; d. 1818 Frederick Co.; s/o Philemon and Rachel; ml. 15 Apr 1795 to Janet Kennedy; d/o Philip Kennedy; Joshua was an attorney and member of Maryland House of Delegates (Scharf); known child:

11511-1 Elizabeth Dorsey, b. ca 1797; ml. 25 Jan 1814 Dr. Thomas W. Johnson

1151-2 Henrietta Dorsey, b. 20 Feb 1766; m. 13 Dec 1786 William Hobbs; s/o Samuel Hobbs; children (Shirk):

11512-1 Warner Hobbs, b. 22 Nov 1787
11512-2 Philemon Dorsey Hobbs; m. Anne Dorsey; d/o Edward Dorsey and Deborah Maccubin of *Clover Hills*; lived near Poplar Spring, Howard Co.
11512-3 Rachel Hobbs, b. ca 1791
11512-4 William Hobbs, Jr. b. 6 Dec 1793; m. cous. [11533-3] Susanna Dorsey
11512-5 Kitty Hobbs, b. ca 1795; unmarried
11512-6 Janet Hobbs, b. ca 1796

1151-3 Ariana "Maria" Dorsey, b. 24 Mar 1769; d/o Philemon and Rachel; m. 15 May 1788 [1154-2] Samuel Owings

Children of Rachel Lawrence and Thomas Harris:

1151-4 Harriet Harris, b. 6 Nov 1775; d. 27 Jun 1829; m/1 12 Aug 1792 cous. Basil Dorsey, Jr., b. 14 Feb 1768; d. 4 Apr 1823; s/o Judge Basil Dorsey and Mary Crockett; lived Frederick Co.; she m/2 Rev. James Higgins of Prince George's Co.; d. after 1829; children:

11514-1 Maria Dorsey, b. 6 Aug 1793
11514-2 Cordelia Harris Dorsey, b. 19 Feb 1798

1151-5 Cordelia Harris, b. 10 Apr 1778; d/o Thomas and Rachel; m/1 1795 2nd w/o Beale Owings; s/o Richard Owings of Baltimore Co.; m/2 her 1st cousin Dr. Thomas Beale Owings, b. 26 May 1767; children:

11515-1 Nathan Harris Owings
11515-2 Harriet Harris Owings, b. ca 1798; m. John Ijams
11515-3 Mary Owings, b. ca 1802

1151-6 Orrellana Harris, b. 27 Aug 1781; d/o Thomas and Rachel

115-2 Benjamin Lawrence, b. 17 May 1741 at *Dorsey's Grove* now in Howard Co.; d. 5 Mar 1814; d/o Levin and Susannah; m. 28 Jan 1762 Urith Owings, b. 26 Jun 1738; d. 17 Sep 1807; d/o Samuel Owings and Urith Randall of Owings Mills; Benjamin built a mill on *Delaware Bottom* (Warfield); he was commissioned 2nd Lt. 6 Jan 1776 in Soldier's Delight Bat. of Baltimore Co. Militia (XI.467); moved to Jefferson Co., KY in 1799; both bur. *Eden* plantation in Jefferson Co.; children:

1152-1 Samuel Lawrence, b. 1762
1152-2 Samuel Lawrence, b. 1764
1152-3 Polly Lawrence, b. 1767
1152-4 Susannah Lawrence, b. 1769
1152-5 Rebecca Lawrence, b. 1771
1152-6 Levin Lawrence, b. 1774
1152-7 Elizabeth Lawrence, b. 1778

Two of Benjamin Lawrence's first cousins became his sons-in-law; his cousin's daughter became his daughter-in-law and aunt to her own first cousin; his cousin's granddaughter married his grandson (Founders of Anne Arundel and Howard Counties).

6 Aug 1773 Samuel Owings of Baltimore Co. gave his dau. Urith Lawrence 4 tracts in Baltimore Co.: *The Mill Place*, part of *Rich Meadows*, *Strawberry Patch* and another (Book AL#H, p. 251).

    1152-1 Samuel Lawrence, b. 30 Oct 1762; d. 16 Nov 1763

    1152-2 Samuel Lawrence, b. 29 Oct 1764; d. 17 Sep 1822 KY; s/o Benjamin and Urith; m. 22 Jun 1790 Frederick Co. Sarah Hobbs, b. 3 Jul 1769; d. 19 Sep 1828; d/o Nicholas Hobbs and Elizabeth Cumming of Linganore Hundred; moved to Louisville, KY 12 May 1799 from Baltimore Co.; children:

        11522-1 Urith O. Lawrence, b. 27 Jun 1791 MD; d. 3 Jan 1854; m. James Brown, b. 10 Oct 1780 MD; d. 9 Apr 1853 Jefferson Co., KY

        11522-2 Benjamin Lawrence, b. 7 Sep 1793; d. 24 Aug 1794

        11522-3 Benjamin Lawrence, b. 7 Aug 1795

        11522-4 Elhannan Lawrence, b. 23 Nov 1797; d. 12 Sep 1798

        11522-5 Elias Dorsey Lawrence, b. 1799; d. 1828; buried with his parents in the Brown and Lawrence Cemetery, Jefferson Co., KY (Md. Dep.)

        11522-6 Washington Lawrence, b. 3 Dec 1800; d. 31 Jul 1801

    1152-3 Mary Lawrence, b. 28 Feb 1767; d. 20 Aug 1810; bur. *Merryvale* plantation; (? same person as Polly); d/o Benjamin and Urith; m/1 17 Feb 1786 Elias Dorsey; d. ca 1794; s/o Vachel (d. 1762) and Ruth Dorsey; he was partners with Thomas Dorsey and Benjamin Lawrence in milling; Mary m/2 William Chambers, b. 1 May 1764/70 NY; d.

Jefferson Co., KY; s/o Rowland Chambers and Phoebe Mullican; known children:

11523-1 Mary Dorsey
11523-2 Ruth Dorsey
11523-3 Mary Lawrence Chambers, b. Aug 1810

1152-4 Susannah Lawrence, b. 4 May 1769; d/o Benjamin and Urith; m. 4 Feb 1786 Baltimore to bro. of her sister Mary's husband, Edward Dorsey, b. ca 1762 Queen Caroline Parish, Anne Arundel Co.; d. ca 1804 Jefferson Co., KY; will probate 5 Nov 1804 Jefferson Co. and 26 Aug 1808 Baltimore Co.; s/o Vachel and Ruth Dorsey; children:

11524-1 Urith Dorsey, b. Dec 1788; d. young
11524-2 Patience Dorsey, b. 23 Apr 1789
11524-3 Mary Ann Dorsey, b. 13 Sep 1791; m/1 19 Apr 1808 Basil N. Hobbs; m/2 James Hobbs
11524-4 Matilda Dorsey, b. 1794; m. Nimrod Dorsey (1789-1845); s/o Joshua Dorsey and his m/2 Sarah Hammond; Nimrod went to KY as a child
11524-5 Elias Dorsey, b. 7 Jun 1796; m/1 1815 Martha Booker; m/2 the Widow Williamson
11524-6 Susannah Dorsey, b. 22 Aug 1798; d. young
11524-7 Levin Lawrence Dorsey, b. 19 Dec 1799; m. 25 Jan 1820 Susan O'Bannon
11524-8 Benjamin Lawrence Dorsey, b. 13 Feb 1802; m. Nancy Booker
11524-9 Urith Owings Dorsey, b. 5 Oct 1804; d. 27 Mar 1867; m. John D. Hundley

1152-5 Rebecca Lawrence, b. 4 Jul 1771; d. KY; d/o Benjamin and Urith; m. 1789 Richard Winchester; b. 17 Apr 1759 Frederick, MD; children:

11525-1 Benjamin Winchester, b. 17 Aug 1790
11525-2 Lavina L. Winchester
11525-3 Mary Winchester

11525-4 Amanda Winchester, b. 14 Nov 1798
11525-5 Olivia Winchester
11525-6 Louisa Winchester
11525-7 William Chambers Winchester, b. 21 Feb 1809

1152-6 Levin Lawrence, b. 8 Apr 1774; d. 1852; s/o Benjamin and Urith; m. Mary Snowden Dorsey; d/o Elias Dorsey and Susan Snowden; they were in Nelson Co., KY in 1802 (Marylanders to KY).

1152-7 Elizabeth Lawrence, b. 2 May 1778; d. 15 Jan 1814; m. 16 Nov 1800 Baltimore Co. to William Rose Hynes, b. 27 Jan 1771; d. 10 Apr 1837; lived Bardstown, KY (St. James Marriages states his name was William Bois Hines of KY)

115-3 John Dorsey Lawrence, b. ca 1743; d. 18 Dec 1798; lived *Linganore Hills* Frederick Co.; m. Martha West, b. 13 Dec 1738; d/o Stephen West and Martha Hall; he inherited slaves from the 1764 will of his grandfather, John Dorsey (Md. Cal. Wills, Vol. XIII, p. 59); children from Warfield and Shirk:

1153-1 John Stephen Lawrence
1153-2 Ann West Lawrence
1153-3 Susannah Lawrence
1153-4 Upton Sheredine Lawrence
1153-5 Mary Elizabeth Lawrence
1153-6 Rachel Lawrence
1153-7 Margaretta Lawrence

1153-1 John Stephen Lawrence, Jr.; s/o John and Martha; m. Sarah Maria Shriner; only d/o Peter Shriner of Frederick Co., a wealthy farmer; children from family history:

11531-1 Josephine Elizabeth Lawrence
11531-2 Julianna Mahala Lawrence; m. Evan Dorsey, s/o Evan (1767-1823); moved to Tiffin Co., OH
11531-3 Martha E. Lawrence
11531-4 John Peter Lawrence
11531-5 Sarah Margaret Lawrence
11531-6 Charles Augustus Lawrence
11531-7 Stephen Decatur Lawrence

11531-8 Emma West Lawrence; Sister Juliana of the Convent of the Visitation, Frederick, MD
11531-9 Anna Lavinia Lawrence; m. Peter War; moved to St. Paul, KS

1153-2 Ann West Lawrence; eldest d/o John and Martha; m. Thomas Mansell; mentioned in 1767 will of William Hall (Md. Cal. Wills, Vol. XIV, p. 156); children's order of birth unknown:

11532-1 Mary Lawrence Mansell
11532-2 Martha West Mansell
11532-3 Louisa Mansell
11532-4 Susan D. Mansell (twin)
11532-5 Cordelia Mansell (twin); killed by tree in storm
11532-6 Estella Mansell; m. Philip Price; descendants once lived around Bardstown, KY
11532-7 Elizabeth Lawrence Mansell, b. 21 May 1800
11532-8 Ann West Mansell
11532-9 John L. Mansell; d. unmarried
11532-10 Thomas Mansell; died young

1153-3 Susannah Lawrence; d/o John and Martha; m. 6 Jan 1789 Evan Dorsey (1767-1823); eldest s/o Judge Basil Dorsey of Frederick Co. and Hannah Crockett of Baltimore; Susannah mentioned in 1767 will of William Hall (Md. Cal. Wills, Vol. XIV, p. 156); children:

11533-1 Evan Dorsey, Jr.
11533-2 Upton Lawrence Dorsey
11533-3 Susanna Dorsey; m. 2nd cousin [11512-4] William Hobbs, Jr.

1153-4 Upton Sheredine Lawrence, b. ca 1780; d. 31 Mar 1824; s/o John and Martha; m. 31 Jan 1803 Elizabeth Hager, b. 1 Aug 1785; d. 15 Aug 1867; only d/o Jonathan Hager, Jr. and Mary Magdalena Ohrendorff; and only grandchild of Capt. Jonathan Hager, founder of Hagerstown, MD, and Elizabeth Kirschner (monument)

1153-5 Mary Elizabeth Lawrence; d. Jessamine Co., KY; s/o John and Martha; m. Judge William Shreve, b. 16 Aug 1761 MD; d. Jan 1837 at *Anchor-in-Hope*, near Nicholsville, Jessamine Co., KY; s/o _____ and Catherine Shreve; he m/2 1808 Mrs. Ann Barnett Wake, b. 20 Sep 1775 Rappahannock River, VA; d. 13 Apr 1849; children:

11535-1 Levin Lawrence Shreve, b. 27 Aug 1793 Hagerstown, MD; d. 3 Apr 1864 Louisville; m/1 Flemingsburg, KY to Hannah Andrews; m/2 Mary Esther Sheppard of Matthews Co., VA; he was a wealthy businessman; no children

11535-2 Thomas Talliaferro Shreve, b. 4 Feb 1796 Hagerstown

11535-3 Catherine Lawrence Shreve, b. ca 1799 Jessamine Co.

11535-4 Eliza Ann Shreve, b. 6 Jan 1801 Jessamine Co., KY

11535-5 William Martin Shreve, b. ca 1803; m. Caroline Boyce of Fayette Co., KY

11535-6 Upton Lawrence Shreve, b. ca 1806; d. Oct 1826 Jessamine Co., KY

1153-6 Rachel Lawrence; d/o John and Martha; m. _____ Thompson

1153-7 Margaretta Lawrence; d/o John and Martha; m. Richard Talbott; moved to VA; children:

11537-1 Antionette Talbott
11537-2 Upton L. Talbott

115-4 Ruth Lawrence, b. 22 Dec 1745; d. 27 Jul 1827; d/o Levin and Susannah; m. 27 Nov 1760 Thomas Owings, b. 18 Oct 1740; d. 23 Aug 1822; s/o Samuel Owings and Urith Randall; their children from Shirk:

1154-1 Levin Lawrence Owings, b. 4 Oct 1761; d. 1812; m. Achsah Dorsey, b. 5 Aug 1766; d/o Caleb and Rebecca Dorsey

1154-2 Samuel Owings, b. 12 Jun 1763; m/1 15 May 1788 [Methodist] to 1st cous. [1151-3] Arianna Dorsey; children:

11542-1 Maria Owings, b. 1789
11542-2 Joshua Owings, b. 1794
11542-3 Ariana Owings, b. 1796
11542-4 Rachel Owings, b. 1799
11542-5 Samuel Owings, b. 1802
11542-6 William Owings, b. 1803

1154-3 Thomas Owings, b. 7 Jul 1765; d. 1786
1154-4 Thomas Beale Owings, b. 26 May 1767; he was physician; m/1 1803 Ann Johnson; m/2 1806 1st cous. [1151-5] Cordelia Harris, widow of Beale Owings
1154-5 Elizabeth Owings, b. 30 Apr 1769; m. 11 Nov 1800 3rd w/o Capt. John Downey
1154-6 Isaac Owings, b. 9 Apr 1771; m/1 Baltimore Co. to Achsah Dorsey; d/o Nicholas Dorsey and Elizabeth Worthington; moved west; m/2 Rebecca Williamson; d/o Capt. John Williamson; his son Dr. Thomas Owings m. Sarah Lawrence d/o [1155-2] John Lawrence
1154-7 David Owings, b. 8 Apr 1773; d. 12 Jul 1778
1154-8 Susanna Owings, b. 27 Jun 1775; d. 227 Aug 1861; m. 25 Aug 1800 Basil Sollers; d. 20 Aug 1839; s/o Thomas Sollers and Arianna Dorsey; made and sold hats in Baltimore
1154-9 Ruth Owings, b. 31 Jul 1777; m. 26 Nov 1801 to Joseph Sheetz
1154-10 Jesse Owings, b. 14 Sep 1779; d. 19 Sep 1812; m. 10 Dec 1801 Hannah Hood, b. 6 Mar 1786; d. 28 Jan 1838; d/o John Hood, Jr. and his 3rd wife Elizabeth Gaither; she m/2 Samuel Kennedy Jennings, M. D.
1154-11 Anne Owings, b. 4 Nov 1781; m. Benjamin Arthur
1154-12 Levin Owings, b. 10 Jun 1784; d. 1816; m. ____ Harnet
1154-13 Harwood Owings, b. 2 Oct 1786; d. 6 Sep 1793
1154-14 Matilda Owings, b. 7 Oct 1789; m. Edwin Downey; d/o John Downey; they had 2 children; one of whom was

the 2nd wife of Benjamin Arthur who m/1 [1154-11] Anne Owings

115-5 Levin Lawrence, Jr.; of *Dorsey's Grove*; s/o Levin and Susannah; m/1 29 Aug 1786 Sarah Dorsey, b. 31 Oct 1763; d. after 1790; d/o Caleb Dorsey (1740-1795) and his m/2 Rebecca Hammond (1741-1797); m/2 Rebecca Dorsey of Howard Co.; Levin inherited part of *Poplar Spring Garden* and all of William Dorsey's lands in Illinois; Sarah mentioned as already having received her portion in her father's will probated Anne Arundel Co. 10 Aug 1795; their children:

1155-1 Caleb Dorsey Lawrence, b. 1 Jan 1787; d. 31 Aug 1787 (Dorsey Bible); there may have been a second child with the same name who lived to be an adult as a Caleb Lawrence inherited the law library of his uncle, William Dorsey, from his 1802 will - or this Caleb may be from another line of the family not identified

1155-2 John Lawrence; eldest s/o m/2; m. M. J. or Nancy Wilson; lived near Frankfort, KY; [although no dates have been found for the m/2 or his birth, all family histories located place him as the 2nd child of his father]; two known children; his dau. Sarah m. Dr. Thomas Owings, s/o [1154-6]

1155-3 Larkin Lawrence, b. ca 1792; went to MO with Col. Edward Dorsey

1155-4 Rebecca Lawrence, b. 6 Dec 1796; d. 5 Feb 1853; ml. 20 Sep 1820; m. 3 Oct 1820 Baltimore Co. to David Waters, b. 12 Oct 1796; d. 20 Jun 1838; s/o Nathan Waters; she inherited portions of *Cumberland* and *Popular Spring Meadows Garden* from her father's estate in Anne Arundel Co.

1155-5 Hammond Dorsey Lawrence, b. ca 1797; d. 1844; moved to Baltimore; m. Louise Shipley (1802-1858)

1155-6 Sarah Dorsey Lawrence, b. 25 Dec 1805; m. 26 Sep 1831 Baltimore to John Henry Keene, b. 12 Dec 1806 Talbot Co.

1155-7 Caroline Dorsey Lawrence

115-6 Elizabeth "Betsy" Lawrence; d/o Levin and Susannah; m. Christopher Owings, b. 16 Jan 1744; s/o Samuel Owings and Urith Randall

115-7 Margaret "Peggy" Lawrence, b. ca 1751; d. 1835 Leonardstown, MD; d/o Levin and Susannah; unmarried

115-8 Richard Lawrence, b. ca 1756 after death of his father; of *White Hall* at Guilford; s/o Levin and Susannah; m/1 6/22 Mar 1780 Frederick Co. to Anne Warfield; d/o Rezin Warfield (1740-1767) and Honour Howard (b. ca 1740); m/2 7 Sep 1824 Charlotte Warfield, b. 25 Oct 1793; d/o Joseph Warfield (1758-1837) and Elizabeth Dorsey; they lived at *White Hall* on the Patuxent near Guilford, Howard Co., which Anne Warfield inherited from her father; said to have m/3 _____; children of m/1:

    1158-1 Otho William Lawrence, b. ca 1790; d. ca 1840; m. 1815 Katherine Murdoch Nelson, d/o Gen. Robert Nelson of Frederick, MD, and Mary Brooke Sims

    1158-2 Benjamin Lawrence

    1158-3 Richard Lawrence

11-6 Margaret Lawrence, b. 17 d. 11 mo. 1716; d/o Benjamin and Rachel

1-2 Elizabeth Lawrence, b. 25 Feb 1678/9; bur. 7 9ber 1700 West River Meeting House (All Hallow's Parish); d/o Benjamin Lawrence and Elizabeth Talbott; m/1 Capt. John Gassaway, bur. 2 Sep 1697; s/o Capt. Nicholas Gassaway and Hester Besson; he inherited 300 acres on the Gunpowder River, and, after the death of his sister, Hester Groce, he inherited the land she lived on and other property; Elizabeth m/2 John Rigbie of Anne Arundel Co.; d. 1700; children:

    12-1 Nicholas Gassaway, b. 1696/7
    12-2 Elizabeth Rigbie

7 Aug 1703 *The Addition* and *Hall's Inheritance* were resurveyed for the orphans of Col. Nicholas and John Gassaway, dec'd (WT2.64). 7 Sep

1706 a writ was granted for a water mill on 20 acres, part of land called *West Puddington* held by Moridcay Moore, Thos. Stimpson, and Nicholas Gassaway, son and heir of John Gassaway (WT2.557).

WILL of JOHN RIGBIE, Anne Arundel Co.; written 26 Oct 1700; probate 23 Nov 1700

To mother-in-law Eliza. Galloway, father-in-law Richard Gallaway, brother-in-law Benjamin Lawrence, Leucey Lawrence, Eliza. Galloway, son-in-law (unnamed), brother James and Eliza. his wife and their 4 children (unnamed) and to Balderfort Lambrest, personalty

To wife Eliza., extx., and dau. Eliza., residue of estate real and personal; dau. to be of age at 18 yrs. In event of death of either wife or dau. survivor to inherit deceased's portion

Test: Chas. Greenbury, Henry Pennington, Francis Todd

(Md. Cal. Wills, Vol. II, p. 209; Will, Liber 11, folio 28)

12-1 Nicholas Gassaway, b. 6 Feb 1696; d. ca 1757; s/o Elizabeth Lawrence and John Gassaway; m/1 2 Jun 1719 All Hallow's Parish to Elizabeth Hawkins; m/2 Sarah Shipley; d/o Robert Shipley; m/3 Rachel Howard; d/o Joseph Howard and Rachel Ridgely; moved to Queen Caroline Parish; ca 1753 Nicholas held 300 acres *Talbott's Resolution* (Rent Rolls); children from will and *Anne Arundel Gentry, Vol. I*:

| | |
|---|---|
| 121-1 Anne Gassaway | 121-8 Thomas Gassaway |
| 121-2 Elizabeth Gassaway | 121-9 James Gassaway |
| 121-3 Susanna Gassaway | 121-10 Hannah Gassaway |
| 121-4 Nicholas Gassaway | 121-11 Mary Gassaway |
| 121-5 Benjamin Gassaway | 121-12 Sarah Gassaway |
| 121-6 Richard Gassaway | 121-13 Lucy Gassaway |
| 121-7 Robert Gassaway | 121-14 Rachel Gassaway |

WILL of NICHOLAS GASSAWAY, Queen Caroline Parish, Anne Arundel Co.; written 18 Feb 1757; probate 21 Apr 1757

To heirs of dau. Ann Peirpont, 1s

To daus. Elizabeth Selman and Susanna Mansill and son Nicholas Gassaway, 1s

To sons Benjamin, Richard and Robert *Talbot's Resolution Manor*; Benjamin to have 1st choice; if either die before age 21, survivor or survivors to share

Personal estate to children Thomas, James, Hannah Porter, Mary
Gassaway, Lucy Nicholson, Benjamin, Sarah Gassaway, Richard,
Robert, and Rachel Gassaway
Nephew: Samuel Pierpont
Ex: Wife Rachel
Wit: John Dorsey (of John), Wm. Jean, Wm. Aldridge, Caleb Dorsey (of
John) (Anne Arundel Gentry; Md. Cal. Wills, Vol. XI, p. 167; Wills, Liber 30, folio 297)

   121-1 Anne Gassaway; d. by 1757; m. 10 d. 6 mo. called August
1737 at Meeting near Elk Ridge to John Pierpoint; d. ca 1753;
s/o Charles Pierpoint and Sydney Chew; brother of Margaret
who m. [121-4] Nicholas Gassaway, Jr.; children from his will:

      1211-1 Samuel Pierpoint, b. ca 1738-1753
      1211-2 John Pierpoint, b. ca 1738-1753
      1211-3 Henry Pierpoint, b. ca 1738-1753
      1211-4 Ann Pierpoint, b. ca 1738-1753
      1211-5 Rachel Pierpoint, b. ca 1738-1753

WILL of JOHN PIERPONT, Frederick Co.; written 21 Jun 1753; probate 9
   Aug 1753
To sons Samuel, John and Henry Pierpont, 252 acres
To daus. Ann and Rachel Pierpont, each 1 Negro
Ex. brothers Henry and Joseph Pierpont
Wit: Richard Richardson, Francis Pierpont, James Mankin (all Quakers)
                                                    (Wills, Book BT, #1, p.9)

Estate of John Pierpoint, Frederick Co.; £171/12/10; 30 Aug 1754; 21 Nov
1754; ex. Joseph Pierpoint (58.267).

   121-2 Elizabeth Gassaway; m. _____ Sellman; a probable
descendant: on 16 Sep 1779 Gassaway Selman rec'd license
to marry Catherine Davis in Frederick Co.; in 1790 a
Gassaway Selman was in Delaware Hundred, Baltimore Co.
with 12 family member and in Frederick Co. with 9 family
members; unable to locate in 1776 census
   121-3 Susannah Gassaway; m. _____ Mansill
   121-4 Nicholas Gassaway, Jr.; m. 4 d. 9 mo. 1747 Elk Ridge
Meeting to Margaret Pierpoint; moved to Baltimore Co.;

children [this does not agree with *Anne Arundel Gentry, Vol. I*, but does agree with *Baltimore County Families*]:

1214-1 John Gassaway; d. ca 1768

WILL of JOHN GASSAWAY, s/o Nicholas of Elk Ridge, Anne Arundel Co.; written 20 Dec 1767; probate 30 Aug 1768
Ex: father Nicholas Gassaway
Wit: Jacob Myer, Wm. Lux, Alex. Mcmachan   (Wills, Liber 36, folio 556)

1214-2 Rachel Gassaway, b. 15 d. 12 mo. 1750

121-5 Benjamin Gassaway
121-6 Richard Gassaway; m. 1 Oct 1778 Ann Arnold
121-7 Robert Gassaway; m. Sarah _____; 13 Apr 1772 Robert, planter of Elk Ridge sold Stephen West of Prince George's Co. 100 acres of *Talbott's Resolution* which was his share of 300 acres bequeathed his father by his grandfather John Gassaway (Anne Arundel Land Records, IB, N3, p. 257)
121-8 Thomas Gassaway; m. Jane Kelly
121-9 James Gassaway; m. Rachel _____
121-10 Hannah Gassaway; m. Philip Porter
121-11 Mary Gassaway
121-12 Sarah Gassaway
121-13 Lucy Gassaway; m. _____ Nicholson; [? did she marry twice; *Anne Arundel Gentry* says she m. William Richardson; father's will gives her name as Nicholson]
121-14 Rachel Gassaway

12-2 Elizabeth Rigbie, b. ca 1699; d/o Elizabeth Lawrence and John Rigbie; m. 19 Jan 1715/6 West River to Peter Bines Galloway, b. 2 d. 2 mo. 1696; 5th son of Samuel Galloway and Ann Webb; grandson of Richard Galloway, the immigrant; in 1740 they moved to Kent upon the Delaware, near Philadelphia; children:

122-1 _____ Galloway (f); living Oct 1778
122-2 Joseph Galloway, b. ca 1731 MD; d. 29 Aug 1803 Watford, England; m. 18 Oct 1753 Christ Church,

Philadelphia, to Grace Growden; d. 6 Feb 1782; d/o Lawrence Growden and Elizabeth Nicholas; both he and his father-in-law were in the Assembly in Pennsylvania; he earned a LLB in 1769 from Princeton; he was convicted of treason 6 Mar 1778 for his proposal that the US preserve the Federal system with England and his large estate confiscated; more about his career in *Pennsylvania Magazine of History and Biography*, XXVI, p.161-3; children:

1222-1 Joseph L. Growden Galloway
1222-2 Lawrence Growden Galloway
1222-3 Elizabeth Galloway; d. 7 Apr 1815; went to England with her father; m. William Roberts, Esq. of Portman Square, London; one child:

12223-1 Ann Grace Roberts; d. 12 Dec 1837; m. 30 May 1819 Lt. Benjamin Burton

{Note: Another Joseph Galloway was commissioned 2nd Maj. of South River Bat. of Militia 1776 (Warfield); the 1776 census of Anne Arundel County shows Joseph Galloway: 2 white women, 1 white boy, 1 white girl; several slaves.]

1-3 Lucy Lawrence, b. ca 1685; posthumous d/o Benjamin Lawrence and Elizabeth Talbott; m. 10 Feb 1701/2 All Hallow's Parish to John Belt; s/o John Belt and Elizabeth Tydings; "Lucy is also betrothed wife of Joseph Tilly, which action is contrary to the law of God and man;" moved to Baltimore Co. 1726; [*Shirk* says the children of Lucy and John Belt were John, Leonard, Higginson, Joseph, Sarah, Lucy, and Elizabeth - p. 30]; believe their children were:

13-1 John Belt, b. ca 1703; d. 1 d. 10 mo. 1788 aged 85 years; m. Lucy ____; children listed in Volume I of this series

WILL of JOHN BELT, Baltimore Co.; written 24 Sep 1788; probate 18 Feb 1789
To eldest son, John Belt, Jr., a tract of 222 acres

To sons Nathan and Joseph Belt, all of *Aquilla's Reserve*; 64 acres on a fork of Piney Run, descending to the west run of the Gunpowder, with reversion to his daughters, Sarah Randall, Lucy Malone and Mary Belt
(B'more Co. Wills, Vol. 4, p. 350)

13-2 Mary Belt; m. 18 Jun 1726 Greenberry Dorsey, b. 1710/1; s/o John Dorsey and Comfort Simpson; children listed in Volume I
13-3 Margaret Belt, b.10 Jun 1719; m. 1 Dec 1743 Basil Lucas

2. Nehemiah Lawrence; the "sister-in-law" Jane Simmonds mentioned in the 1685 will of Benjamin Lawrence could have been the wife of Nehemiah or Thomas. Nothing further could be found for her.

3. Thomas Lawrence; mentioned in the 1685 will of his brother Benjamin; unknown if any of the Anne Arundel Co. land records or any of the following has any connection to this Thomas:

A Thomas Laurence came into Maryland as a servant in 1668 (12,285) and a Thomas Lawrence was transported in 1674 (18.77).

Thomas Lawrence, Secretary of Maryland, d. in St. Mary's Co. ca 1700. His wife was Ann English (Marr. & Deaths in St. Mary's Co.). His will probated 19 Apr 1701 makes no mention of a wife, children or siblings (Md. Cal. Wills, Vol. II, p. 203).

4. Lucy Lawrence; m. _____ Smith

The following is the guesswork of myself and Agnes Winkelman:
5. ?Mary Lawrence; m. Edward Gibbs; the will of Benjamin Lawrence (2) calls Edward Gibbs "brother-in-law"; no connection can be made between the family of Elizabeth Talbott and the Gibbs family; therefore it is *possible* that Mary, wife of Edward Gibbs, was a d/o Benjamin Lawrence (1) of whom no mention has been found in the records to date.

Briefly: Nathaniel Gibbs, his wife Mary, and their 2 sons, Edward and William, were transported into Maryland in 1663 (5.467 & 6.19). After the death of Nathaniel, his widow Mary m/2 Alexander Gardner who with his wife Frances, sold Edward Gibbs part of a tract called *Leonard's Neck* in 1692. Several records can be found for this family in *Abstracts of Anne Arundel Land Records*.

Edward Gibbs and his wife Mary had 4 known children whose births are registered at St.Margaret's, Westminster Parish, Anne Arundel Co.:

5-1 William Gibbs, b. 4 Oct 1689; eldest son; was he named for William, brother of Edward?
5-2 Edward Gibbs, b. 31 Jul 1693
5-3 Ann Gibbs, b. 4 Sep 1697; eldest dau.; was she named for Ann Ashcomb, wife of Benjamin Lawrence, and possible mother of Mary?
5-4 Mary Gibbs, b. 11 Sep 1700; 2nd dau.

## A TANGLE OF MARRIAGES

Richard Ewen; m. Sophia ___; Ewen children: Elizabeth; Richard, Jr. (unmarried); John (m. Sarah), Susanna (m. James Billingsley), Ann, Sophia (m/1 Richard Wells; m/2 Henry Beedle)
Sophia (___) Ewen; m/2 as 2nd w/o William Burgess

Elizabeth Ewen; d/o Maj. Richard Ewen and Sophia _____;
  m/1 Richard Talbott (____-____); Talbott children: Elizabeth, Richard, Jr., Edward, John
  m/2 William Richardson (____-1691); Richardson children: William, Daniel, Sophia Elizabeth, Joseph, Sapphira and Elizabeth

Elizabeth Talbott, (____-1702); d/o Richard Talbott & Elizabeth Ewen
  m/1 ca 1672 James Preston of *Preston's Neck* in Calvert County (____-1673); s/o Richard Preston and Margaret _____; child Rebecca Preston
  m/2 after 1673 Benjamin Lawrence (____-1685); s/o Benjamin and Ann Lawrence; children: Lucy, Benjamin, Elizabeth Lawrence
  m/3 10 d. 10 mo. 1686 West River at home of William Richardson to Richard Galloway, b. 28 d. 11 mo. 1663; d. 17 d. 8 mo. 1736; bur. West River Meeting grave yard; s/o Richard and Hannah Galloway of London; children: Elizabeth, Richard Galloway

Richard Galloway (1663-1736)
  m/1 1686 Elizabeth Talbott
  m/2 30 d. 5 mo. called July 1719 Sarah Smith (____-1755); no known children

Sarah Smith (____-1755); d/o Thomas Smith, dec'd, and Alice
    m/1 30 d. 6 mo. 1690 Solomon Sparrow (____-1718); s/o Thomas Sparrow, dec'd, and his wife Elizabeth of Anne Arundel Co.; no known children
    m/2 1719 Richard Galloway (1663-1736); no known children
    m/3 14 Nov 1738 as 2nd wife [at least] of Henry Hill (____-1739) at the home of Henry Hill; he had children from previous marriage or marriages; no known children with Sarah

Note: Other Lawrence families lived in Maryland in this period. There were Lawrences of the Eastern Shore, at least part of whom were Quakers, and Laurence/Lawrence families of St. Mary's Cos., at least part of whom were Catholics.

## Skinner

Several Skinner families came to Maryland in the 1600s. Some apparently came directly from England, others by way of Virginia. They settled in various parts of Maryland including Calvert and Anne Arundel Counties, and the Eastern Shore. According to *A History of Calvert County, Maryland*, there is a connection between Robert Skinner who settled in Calvert County ca 1658 and the Skinners who lived on the Eastern Shore.

V. I. Skinner, Jr., author of the series of records of the Prerogative Courts of Maryland, states that although there may be a connection none has been proven between the lines of Robert of Calvert Co., Andrew of Talbot Co., and Thomas and William of Dorchester and Talbot Co.

The Skinner family of Calvert County is believed to have originated in Herefordshire, England, as the arms used by them are those of the Skinner family of that county.

### Robert Skinner

Robert Skinner; d. by Nov 1686; said to have immigrated from Bristol; merchant of Calvert County; m/1 Alice _____, probably in England; m/2 after 1672 Ann Storer, b. ca 1639/40; d. ca 1714; d/o Arthur and Katharine Storer; and widow of Dr. James Truman, b. ca 1622. Robert made his home on 256 acres *Truman's Reserve*, renaming it *Skinner's Reserve* or *The Reserve*, plus adjacent tracts called *Scrap* of 100 acres granted in 1679, *The Border* granted in 1680 and *Chance*; located near Prince Frederick. Children from wills:

| Children of m/1: | Children of m/2: |
|---|---|
| 1. Robert Skinner | 3. Clarke Skinner |
| 2. Mary Skinner | 4. William Skinner |
| | 5. Adderton Skinner |

In 1677 Robert Skinner, Sr. was one of the overseers of the will of Robert Rider of Calvert Co. (Md. Cal. Wills, Vol. I, p. 208).

WILL of ROBERT SKINNER, Calvert Co.; written 8 Mar 1685; probate 13 Dec 1686

To eldest son Robert and hrs., plantation and *Island Neck*; (1 chair, half my carpenter's and turners tools; 1 pewter dish; large concordance of ye Bible, 1 joynd table ...at *Island Neck*)

To dau. Mary Letchworth and to her first born child; (1 suite of children bed lining, 1 cradle, 1 child's chair, 1 religious book; to dau's first child...when 1 year old..a cow calfe)

To 2nd son Clarke and hrs., *The Border* (near his plantation), *The Reserve* and (part of) *The Scraps*; (one-half joyners and carpenter and Turner's tools with my large Bible)

To 3rd son William and hrs., *The Hatchet* on (the west side of the) Patuxent River (one of Mr. Cann's Bibles with Bishops Ushers Summary of Substance of Christian Religion)

To youngest son Adderton and hrs., *The Reserve*: (One of Mr. Cann's Bibles and 1 other religious book)

To wife Ann, personalty (with these conditions) to each son 3 able men servants when reach 20 & 1)

(Children's education and bringing up; each son benefit of own labor and crops at age 15; if Clarke or Adderton die remainder to William; if all 3 die to be divided amongst surviving children)

Son Robert appointed guardian of 3 youngest sons. Should he die, 2 sons-in-law Thos. Greenfield and Joseph Letchworth to act in his stead

Test: Robert Houldsworth, Arthur Storer, Elizabeth Cornall, William Moore     (Md. Cal. Wills, Vol. II, p. 9; Calvert County Wills; Wills, Liber 4, folio 430)

Estate of Robert Skinner, Calvert Co.; value £224/11/6; 26 May 1687; appraised by Joseph Letchworth and Thomas Hollyday; mentions servants and list of debts (Inv. Prerog. Ct., 9.410).

Estate of Robert Skinner in Baltimore County appraised 13 May 1693; value £10/10/0 (Inv. Prerog. Ct., 10.269).

WILL of ANN SKINNER, widow, Calvert Co.; written 4 May 1713; probate 19 Jun 1714

To dau. Greenfield, dau. Elizabeth Green and each grandchild, personalty

To eld. son Clarke (Skinner), 1/2 residue of estate, balance to be divided between 2 youngest sons William and Adderton

Exs. 3 sons afsd.

Test: Jno. Mackall, Mary Monk, Gabriel Parker

By codicil, 30 Jul 1713 - To youngest son Adderton Skinner, testator's portion of *The Reserve* as devised her by last husband Robert Skinner

(Md. Cal. Wills, Vol. IV, p. 14: Wills, Liber 13, folio 703)

Ann Storer was the sister of Arthur Storer, merchant, who died in Calvert County ca 1686/7. Arthur's will calls her "sister Ann Skinner, widow," and mentions brother Edward Storer, sister Katherine Storer and mother Katharine Clarke (Md. Cal. Wills, Vol. II, p. 50). His will, written 25 Nov 1686, probate Feb 1686, calls Martha Greenfield cousin. She was actually his niece, d/o his sister Ann and her m/1 to Dr. James Truman. (Md. Cal. Wills, Vol. II, p. 50 and Calvert Co. Wills, Clark, p. 67). The will of Nathaniel Trueman, Calvert Co., written 10 Jul 1676 calls her "sister-in-law Anne Skinner" (Md. Cal. Wills, Vol. I, p. 187).

Ann Storer m. England to Dr. James Truman, b. ca 1622; d. 1672 (tombstone). He was granted land in Maryland in 1666, probably not long after his arrival with his wife, 3 daughters and his brother-in-law Arthur Storer. The date of death of Ann Skinner is in question. Her will was probated in 1714. Although the tombstone reads 1717, the 1714 date is most likely correct.

> Here lyeth Mrs. Ann Skinner first Relict of James Truman Gent, afterwards of Robert Skinner, who died 3 of August 1717 aged about 75 years having lived near half the time a Widow (Tombstone, Basil Duke Farm, ca 2 mi. from Prince Frederick).

> Here lyeth the body of James Truman Gent who died the 7th of August 1672 being aged 50 (Tombstone at Trent Neck, near Mechanicsville).

By her first husband, Dr. James Truman, Ann is said to have had 4 daughters; 3 of whom are mentioned in his will. The 4th daughter, Ann, is mentioned in the will of Nathaniel Truman and land records of Prince George's County.

> Will of James Trueman, Calvert Co.; written 29 Jul 1672; probate 1 Nov 1672
> To wife Anne, execx., 1/3 of estate, real and personal
> To daus. Martha, Mary and Eliza:, residue of estate equally. In event of marriage of sd. wife Anne, brothers Thomas and Nathaniel to have charge of sd. children's estate
> Test: Nath. Trueman, Arthur Storer, Chris. Pinckney
> (Md. Cal. Wills, Vol. I, p. 70; Wills, Liber 1, folio 509)

(1) Martha Truman, b. ca 1658 England; d. 1739; m. ca 1674/5 Calvert Co. to Thomas Greenfield, b. Gedling, Nottingham,

England, b. ca 1648; d. 8 Sep 1715 Calvert Co. (tombstone); his will written 17 Aug 1715; probate 7 Nov 1715; leaves Martha the dwelling plantation and other lands; Martha, Thomas, Elizabeth bur. in what is now Prince George's Co. (Historic Graves of Maryland); their children from his will (Md. Cal Wills, Vol. IV, p. 39):

(1)-1 Ann Greenfield, b. ca 1675; m. John Wight
(1)-2 Thomas Truman Greenfield, b. ca 1682; m. Ann Smith
(1)-3 James Greenfield
(1)-4 Micjah Greenfield
(1)-5 Joan Greenfield; m. Henry Holland Hawkins
(1)-6 Martha Greenfield; m. 31 Jan 1709 Basil Waring
(1)-7 Elizabeth Greenfield, b. ca 1696; d. 2 Aug 1715 (tombstone); m. Gabriel Parker by 1714 (Pr. Geo.'s Co. Land Records, Liber F, folio 411)
(1)-8 Truman Greenfield

(2) Mary Truman, b. England; m. Thomas Hollyday

(3) Elizabeth Truman, b. England; m. Charles Greene, an apothecary of Kings Lynn, England

(4) Ann Truman; m/1 _____ Head; m/2 John Bigger, b. ca 1654; d. ca 1714; m/3 Patrick Andrew (Land Records of Prince George's Co., Liber I, folio 274); Ann may have been the eldest daughter and received her share of the estate at the time of her marriage or the youngest who was born after her father's will was written; the will of John Bigger of Calvert County written 26 Dec 1713; probate 18 Nov 1714 showed that he had large land holdings at the time of his death which he left to Kendall Head, s/o William and Ann Head, after the death of his wife. Ann was named extx. and received a life interest in all his lands; Adderton Skinner and William Head were overseers. William Head was the s/o Ann Truman and her 1st husband confirmed by this will and an indenture dated 23 Jun 1715 Prince George's Co. (Md. Cal. Wills, Vol. IV, p. 24; Land Records, Liber F, folio 453).

Ann Truman inherited 1/3 of a tract of 750 acres called *Indian Creeke with Addition* from her husband James Truman who d. ca 1672.

His daughters, named in his will as Martha, Mary and Elizabeth Truman, inherited 2/3. An indenture dated 17 Sep 1697 from Charles Greene of Kings Lynn and Elizabeth his wife, d/o James Truman, identifies ca 1,169 acres, being 1/3 of the land left the 3 daughters of James Truman, Martha, Mary and Elizabeth, and land inherited from Nathaniel and Thomas Truman by nieces Ann, Elizabeth, and Mary Truman. Ann and her second husband Robert Skinner conveyed their 1/3 portion to the 3 daughters mentioned in their father's will. No mention of 4th daughter named Ann who must have been born after James Truman's will was written (Land Records of Pr. Geo's Co., Liber A, folio 97).

The will of Thomas Hollyday, probated 20 Feb 1703, which leaves his mother (mother-in-law), Ann Skinner, personalty, was witnessed by William Greenup who sold him 100 acres *Cumberland* plantation, part of Cobreth's Lott in 1702 in that portion of Calvert Co. which became Prince George's Co. (Md. Cal. Wills, Vol. III, p. 1).

Nathaniel Truman left his sister-in-law Ann Skinner 1 hogshead of tobacco in his will written 10 Jul 1676, probate 4 Apr 1677 (Md. Cal. Wills, Vol. I, p. 187). These families lived in the area of Charles Town which no longer exists, being replaced upriver by Upper Marlborough.

1. Robert Skinner (2), b. of age 1686; d. by 1713; may have m/1 Ann Letchworth (Hist. of Calvert Co.); m/2 as 3rd husband of Ann Mackall, b. ca 1661, age 55 in 1716 (Md. Deponents); d/o James Mackall (1630-1693) and Mary ____ (b. by 1649-1718). Ann Mackall (ca1661-____); m/1 Andrew Tannehill (____-1694); m/2 John Taney; m/4 ____ Bussee/Busse/Bruse. Robert wit. will of Thomas Stirling of Calvert Co. 14 Jan 1684 (Md. Cal. Wills, Vol. I, p. 156); wit will of George Busse, planter of Calvert Co. who d. ca 1693 and will of Thomas Huchyson of Charles Co. in 1697 (Md. Cal. Wills, Vol. II, p. 64, 162); wit. will of Arthur Young of Calvert Co. 1711 (Md. Cal. Wills, Vol. III, p. 201). Robert was a justice of Calvert County and appointed Commissioner in 1707; children of Robert and Ann identified by wills of Mary Taney and Robert Skinner, Jr. and land records:

   [Mary Taney - step-dau.]    1-3 Mackall Skinner
   1-1 Robert Skinner          1-4 Nathaniel Skinner, Jr.
   1-2 Benjamin Skinner        1-5 Ann Skinner

Ann Mackall was married to Andrew Tannehill by 1687 when she witnessed the will of Richard Hall as Ann Tannehill (Md. Cal. Wills, Vol. II, p. 32). Andrew d. ca 1694 leaving the following will which mentions 3 minor children. Ann was not the mother of these children according to *A Biographical Dictionary of Maryland Legislature 1635-1789*.

> WILL of ANDREW TENNEHILL(sic), Calvert County; written 9 Jul 1693; probate 14 Jul 1694
> To eld. son John and hrs., 200 a. *Calendar* and part of 150 a. *Friendship*
> To young. son Andrew and hrs., 150 a. *Cooper* and residue of *Friendship*
> Sons to be of age at 18 yrs.
> To dau. Eliza., personalty at 16 yrs. of age
> In event of death of all child. without issue, real estate to pass to brother, John Tennehill, of Charles Co., and his hrs. (The abstract published by Raymond Clark states William Tennehill is the residual heir.)
> To wife Ann, extx., 1/3 of personalty; residue of personalty equally among 3 child. afsd.
> Overseers: Brother Wm. Tennehill, Walter Smith
> Test: Robt. Gillian, Geo. Cole, Dan'l Robertson
> (Md. Cal. Wills, Vol. II, p. 78; Calvert Co. Wills; Wills, Liber 7, folio 4)

Ann Mackall Tannehill married next to John Taney, s/o John Taney the immigrant who was transported into Maryland with his brother Michael by the Puritan leader, Thomas Letchworth. Proof of this second marriage lies in the will of Mary Taney, d/o of John, who was apparently raised by Ann and Robert Skinner. Robert's sons, Robert and Benjamin, might possibly have been from an earlier marriage to Ann Letchworth.

> WILL of MARY TANEY, Calvert Co.; written 10 Aug 1711; probated 29 Aug 1712
> To brothers Benjamin, Mackall, Nathaniel and Robert Skinner, Jr. and sister Ann Skinner, entire personal estate
> Ex: Father-in-law [step-father] Robert Skinner, who is to pay to sister Ann and brother Mackall [Skinner] afsd., money due testator from estate of father, John Taney
> Test: John Bigger, Richard Hildson, John Godsgrace
> (Md. Cal. Wills, Vol. III, p. 230)

1-1 Robert Skinner, Jr. (3); d. ca 1736 unmarried; served in Lower House of Maryland Legislature from Calvert Co. 1704-1707; justice of Calvert Co. 1700 to ca 1712/3

WILL of ROBERT SKINNER, gentleman, Prince George's Co.; written 25 Aug 1736; probate 1 Oct 1736
To bro. Nathaniel and hrs., marsh land
To bros. Nathaniel and Mackall and their hrs., residue of real estate. Shd. mother, Mrs. Ann Bruse, take her whole thirds out of land given to bro. Nathaniel then 1/3 of land herein given to bro. Mackall is bequeathed to bro. Nathaniel and hrs.
Bro. Nathaniel, ex. and residuary legatee
Test: Thomas Gantt, Alexander Magruder, William Read
(Md. Cal. Wills, Vol. VII, p. 194; wills, Liber 21, folio 677)

Robert Skinner, Prince George's Co.; £328.18.1; 27 Jun 1738; mentions: John Skinner, Mackall Skinner, Robert Whitaker, J. Lawson; ex. Nathaniel Skinner (23.365).

1-2 Benjamin Skinner; d. ca 1775 Calvert Co.; m. Henrietta Maria Smith; d/o John Smith and Mary Hall; Henrietta Skinner held 362 acres called *Smith's Farm, Good Prospect,* and *Land's Land* plus 17 slaves in Lyons Creek Hundred in 1782.

Benjamin Skinner, Calvert Co.; £761.7.11; 2 Aug 1775; 4 Jan 1776; next of kin: Truman Skinner, Frederick R. Skinner; admn. Hienriettamarea Skinner (124.149).

The Skinner notes state that John Smith and the Widow Erickson were the parents of Henrietta Maria Smith.
Another daughter of John Smith and Mary Hall m. _____ Brooks and another m. Mr. Cox. Mary Hall Smith m. Gunder Erickson after the death of John Smith. Her daughter Martha Erickson m. Samuel Roundall of England (Skinner notes). A Martha Erickson Skinner d. in Prince George's Co., ca 1819 (Probate Records).
Gunder Erickson, Gent., probably the father of the above Gunder, purchased land in 1721 and 1723 from Isaac Cecil, son of Judge Joshua Cecil of Prince George's Co., called *Stoke, The Farme* and *Twiver* as well as household goods, horses and livestock (Land Records).

12-1 Alexander Skinner; d. by 1829; sold part of *Purchase* and *Bussey's Garden* to Ann, Arthur, John H., Samuel, Rebecca and Mariah Allton on 6 Apr 1814 (Calvert Co. Land Records). In the Court of Prince George's Co. on 15 Jul 1829, Sarah Skinner petitioned the court for the appointment of a trustee to complete the sale of Alexander Skinner, trustee of Levin Skinner. Benjamin Skinner was appointed to handle the "said trust."

12-2 Elizabeth Skinner

12 Mar 1810 - Alexander Skinner sold to Elizabeth Skinner for $1,100, interest in law and equity to the undivided moiety or half part of two tract, *Reserve* and *Border's Enlarged*, which descended to Alexander and Elizabeth Skinner from their father, Benjamin Skinner (Calvert County Land Records).

1-3 Mackall Skinner, b. ca 1708; d. by 1754; he was a sergeant in Capt. James Wilson's Co. 20 Feb 1748/9 (Prince George's Heritage); ? did he m. Anne ____ who m/2 ____ Cox

Aug 1728; Mackall Skinner: (aged as tis said in court) twenty yers last January in his proper person here prays the Justices that he may be admitted to choose his guardian which is granted him whereupon he makes choice of his brother Robert Skinner who upon his declaring in Court here his willingness to accept the same is admitted accordingly (Orphans and Infants of Pr. Geo.'s Co. 1696-1750).

Estate of Mackall Skinner, Prince George's Co.; value £175/11/5; 3 Jun 1754; 26 Jun 1754; next of kin: Maryland Skinner, John Cox; admn. Mrs. Anne Cox (Prerog. Ct., 57.287).

1-4 Nathaniel Skinner, Jr. b. ca Apr 1711; d. ca 1743; Thomas Letchworth, admn. (Pr. Geo.'s Probate Records).

Aug 1728; Nathaniel Skinner: (aged as tis said in court) seventeen years last April in his proper person here prays the Justices that he may be admitted to choose his guardian which is granted him whereupon he makes choice of his brother Robert Skinner who upon his declaring in court here his willingness to accept the same is admitted accordingly (Orphans and Infants of Pr. Geo.'s Co. 1696-1750).

Nathaniel Skinner, Prince George's Co.; £687.17.4; 16 Jun 1743; 29 Mar 1744; next of kin: Mackall Skinner, Thomas Hollyday; admn. Elizabeth Letchworth, wife of Thomas Letchworth (28.499).

1-5 Ann Skinner; named in 1718 will of grandmother Mary Mackall

WILL of MARY MACKALL of Calvert Co.; written 25 Jan 1715; probate 15 May 1718
To son John and his wife, Susannah; son James and his wife, Ann; daus. Ann and Elizabeth Skinner, personalty
To Mary (d/o James Mackall) and Mary (d/o Wm. Skinner), £3 and personalty each at 21 yrs. or marriage
To Ann (d/o Robert Skinner), personalty
Son Benjamin ex., and residuary legatee
Test: Jonathan Cay, Tho. Howe        (Md. Cal. Wills, Vol. IV, p. 174)

2. Mary Skinner, b. est ca 1664-1670; m. by 1685 to Joseph Letchworth; d. ca 1713; s/o Thomas Letchworth; children listed under Letchworth family

3. Clarke Skinner, b. by 1677; d. ca 1714; m/1 Ruth _____; m/2 Ann _____; he might have been given the name Clarke in honor of Joseph Clarke who married his grandmother Storer; Clarke was an office holder in Calvert County and signed the memorial sent to King William in 1695 upon his narrow escape from an assassin; Clarke purchased *Hatchett* in Prince George's Co. from his brother William in 1702 (Land Records, Liber C, folio 14a). Clarke Skinner and his wife Ann owned an ordinary or inn in Charles Towne ca 1703 (Prince George's Heritage); child from will:

3-1 Ann Skinner, b. by 1710; d. by 1741; m. after 1714 as 2nd wife of Samuel Griffith

Clarke Skinner admn. estate of James Muffett 1700 (24,208); wit. deed between William Skinner and Ignatius Craycroft 12 Aug 1702; sold 110 acres of *Ladsford's Guift* in Prince George's Co. on 11 Aug 1707 to Phillip Tottershell; wife Ruth ack'd deed (Land Records, Liber C, folios, 1, 8, 189). Clarke was overseer of will of John Elsey probate 1700; wit will of Hugh Jones of Calvert Co. 1701; wit. will of John Fisher Calvert Co. 1702 (Md. Cal. Wills, Vol. II, p. 204, 228, 243); mentioned in estate of Joseph

Ireland and Thomas Blake 1703 (23.28; 24.256); wit. will of Robert Lyles of Calvert Co. in 1705, will of George Lingan 1705 & will of Richard Marsham 1713 (Md. Cal. Wills, Vol. III, p. 61, 107, 240).

WILL of CLARKE SKINNER, Calvert County; written Feb 1710; probate 18 Feb 1714

I, Clark Skinner of the County & province afsd. being very sick & weake in Body but of perfect mind & understanding & knowing that is appointed once for all me to die do make and appoint this my Last Will & Testament:

First & principally I recomend my Soul into the hands of Almighty God who gave it me hopin through the meritts, death & passion of my Saviour Jesus Christ to receive full pardon & remission of all my sins & to inheritt eternall life & my Body to the Earth from whence it came to be decently buried att the discretion of my Executors hereafter named & appointed.

Item    I give & bequeath to my daughter Ann Skinner & her heirs forever all that part or Tract of Land being my now dwelling plantation provided she deceases not before she attains to the yeares of twenty one

Item    I give & bequeath unto my sd. Daughter Ann to her & her heirs forever all that Tract of parcell of Land called *Skinner's Chance*, being the Land adjoyning to my sd. Plantation

Item    But in case my sd. Daughter Ann should decease before she attains to the age of one & twentie years & without lawfull Issue of her Boy that in such cases I give and bequeath my sd. Dwelling Plantation & the other Tract of Land called *Skinner's Chance* unto my loving Bro. Mr. Adderton Skinner to him and his heirs forever

Item    Whereas my father Mr. Robert Skinner late of the sd. County deceased did by his last Will & Testament appearing now upon record in the office of the Prerogative Court of this Province of Maryland afsd. did there give & bequeath to my young Bro. Mr. Adderton Skinner & his heairs for Ever all that Tract or parcell of Land called the *Reserve* Lying on the East side of a Branch commonly called or known by the name of the *Calf Pasture Branch* not withstanding the Right of property of the said Land properly belonging to me these presents therefore Testify unto all her Majesty's Liege people & others whome it may or shall concern hereafter That I the sd. Clarke Skinner in Humble Obediance to my deceased Father's last will & Testam't doe make over conferme & convey the sd. Land & Houses & orchards & all other appurtinances thereunto belonging unto the sd. Adderton Skinner to him & his heirs for Ever

Item   I give & bequeath to my sd. Bro'r Adderton Skinner all my apporhicaries scales & weights together with one Box of Chirugeons pocket (?) instrum'ts, my London Dispensitory, Dorum Medicum together with severall other Books of the Practice of Art of Physick comonly abiding in my Closett together with two plain scales and one pr. of dividers.

Item   I authorise & appoint my Loving wife Ann Skinner my sole & whole Executrix of this my last Will & Testam't whome I request to take care that just debts & funerall Charges be justly & honestly staisfyed. To whome I give & bequeath all the remainder part of my Estate not already bequeathed.

In Wittness whereof I have herewith set my hand & Seale this (date not shown) day of Feb'y Anno Domi 1710 (may have been miscopied into record...see below)   /s/ Clarke Skinner (seal)

Sealed & Acknowledged as my
Last Will & Testam't in the Presence of
Sam'll Griffith jun.
Rich'd Mills               And at the foot of w'ch Will was thus
Darby (x) Sullivan             written (viz)
Leonard Hollyday       Feb'y the 18th 1714 Ten came Rich'd Mills &
             Darby Sulivan & made oath on the holy Evangelist
             that they saw Clark Skinner signe & acknowledge
             this to be his last Will & Testam't
Sworne before me, James Mackall, Dep'ty Com., Calvert County

(Wills, Vol. 14, p. 21 - Courtesy Judge James Trabue)

4. William Skinner; d. ca 1738; physician; m. Elizabeth Mackall, b. ca 1665; d/o James Mackall (ca 1630-1693) and Mary ____ (b. before 1649-1718); lived at *The Reserve* which he and Adderton owned in 1714; sold 189 acres of *Hatchett* in Prince George's Co. in 1702 (Land Records, Liber C, folio 1); wit. will of Mary Parker of Calvert Co. 1714; wit. will of James Mackall Calvert Co. 1716 (Md. Cal. Wills, Vol. IV, p. 24, 96); wit. will of Peter Sewell Calvert Co. 1725 (Md. Cal. Wills, Vol. V, p. 207); sold 111 acres of the *Hatchett* to his brother Clarke 12 Aug 1702; owned 10 slaves in Hunting Creek tax list of 1733; children from will and *A History of Calvert County*.

| | |
|---|---|
| 4-1 Martha Skinner | 4-5 John Skinner |
| 4-2 William Skinner | 4-6 Joseph Skinner |
| 4-3 James Skinner, physician | 4-7 Mary Skinner |
| 4-4 Leonard Skinner | 4-8 Elizabeth Skinner |

William Skinner, planter of Calvert County, sold Clarke Skinner, planter of Calvert County on 12 Aug 1702: The Lord Baron of Baltimore did grant at St. Mary's on 23 Jun 1680 to James Nuthall 300 acres in the woods on the west side of the Patuxent River called *Hatchett*; James Nuthall and his wife Margaret sold the land to Robert Skinner 8 Mar 1686; Robert Skinner gave the land to his 3rd son William Skinner; William sold 111 acres of this land to his brother, Clarke Skinner for an unspecified amount of money; endorsed by Elizabeth Skinner
(Prince George's Col. Land Records, Liber C, folio 14a)

WILL of WILLIAM SKINNER, practitioner in physick, Calvert Co.; written 15 Apr 1738; probate 26 Jul 1738

To dau. Martha, sons James, Leonard, John and Joseph, personalty. Sons James' portion to include medical books, medicines, chirurgical instruments, etc., on condition that for 1 yr. after testator's death he shall administer or prescribe physic to any of his bretheren of sisters or their children without fee or reward

To 5 sons, viz. William, James, Leonard, John and Joseph and their hrs., entire real estate; residue of estate divided among all children

Ex.: Son John

Test: John Wood, Jno. Yoe, William Miller, Jr.
(Md. Cal. Wills, Vol. VIII, p. 251; Wills, Liber 21, folio 892)

Estate of William Skinner, Calvert Co.; value £784/18/6; 31 Aug 1738; 22 Dec 1738; next of kin: James Skinner, Leonard Skinner; Ex. John Skinner (Skinner, 23.481).

Estate of William Skinner, Calvert Co.; value £238/3/8; 18 Apr 1745; 10 May 1745; next of kin: James Skinner, Leonard Skinner; admnx. Elizabeth Skinner (Skinner, 30.415).

Hunting Creek Hundred 1782: Elizabeth Skinner owned 150 acres *Taney's Right*, 62 acres *Scrap*, 121 acres *Reserve*, 26 acres *William's Purchase*, *Water Mill* and 10 slaves. John Skinner owned *Newington* of 94 acres and 8 slaves; Robert Skinner owned *Taney's Delight* of 56 acres and 3 slaves; and Samuel Skinner owned 1 horse.

4-1 Martha Skinner; mentioned in 1718 will of grandmother Mary Mackall

4-2 William Skinner, Jr.; d. ca 1745; m. ?Elizabeth _____; owned 2 slaves in Hunting Creek Tax List of 1733; appr. estate of Joseph and Martha Gardiner 1735 (18.445; 21.156)

William Skinner, Charles Co.; £238.3.8; 18 Apr 1745; 10 May 1745; next of kin: James Skinner, Leonard Skinner; admn. Elisabeth Skinner (30.412).

    42-1 John Skinner; inherited a slave and 100 a. part of *Hunt's Chance* in Anne Arundel Co. from 1764 will of his uncle John Skinner and one of the residuary legatees

    42-2 William Skinner; one of the residuary legatees in 1764 will of uncle John Skinner

4-3 James Skinner; physician; m. ?Ann _____; children from his brother John's will and land records:

    43-1 ?James Skinner; believed to have been the oldest child; mother named Ann

30 Mar 1794 James Skinner and Thomas Gray sold Abraham Lowe 157 1/2 acres, part of *Chance* and *Bussey's Orchard* for £236; Ann Skinner, widow of James H. Skinner gave up her dower rights to same for 5s on 21 Mar 1794 (Book 1, folio 125 and 127, Calvert County Land Records)

James Skinner owned 200 acres of *Border Enlarged* and *Reserve* in Hunting Creek Hundred 1782 (History of Calvert County)

    43-2 Samuel Skinner; one of the residuary legatees of uncle John Skinner, along with his brothers Gabriel and Arthur

    43-3 Gabriel Skinner

    43-4 Arthur Skinner

4-4 Leonard Skinner; d. ca 1758; ?m/1 Susanna _____; ?m/2 Elizabeth _____: he was creditor in estate of John Allton in 1750 (44.225).

    44-1 Nathaniel Skinner; inherited clothing from 1764 will of his uncle John Skinner; and residuary legatee

    44-2 William Skinner; same as Nathaniel

44-3 Leonard Skinner; one of the residuary legatees of uncle John Skinner

Leonard Skinner, Calvert Co.; £67.6.7; 2 Aug 1758; 23 Aug 1760; next of kin: James Skinner, Joseph Skinner; admn. Elizabeth Skinner (70.258).

4-5 John Skinner; d. 1764; m. [52-5] Amelia Skinner; d/o Henry Skinner and Elizabeth Greenfield; he was next of kin in estate of Thomas Ross 1757 (73.12); admn. estate of George Wyley of Anne Arundel Co. 1751 (74.214); creditor estate of Jacob Stallings (98.212), estate of Richard Lewin (75.316) and estate of Samuel Wells (79.26); Benjamin Rogers, exec. estate of John Skinner; the lot in Lower Marlboro mentioned in his will is also mentioned in Calvert Co. Land Records (folio 295); children from will:

        45-1 Elizabeth Skinner
        45-2 Ann Skinner
        45-3 ?Orpha Skinner

WILL of JOHN SKINNER, Calvert Co., merchant; written 16 Feb 1764; probate 29 ___ 1764

To nephew John Skinner, son of bro. William, a slave and 100 a. of land, pt. of *Hunt's Chance*, lying in Anne Arundel Co., where Benjamin French now lives

Whereas I have taken up a mortgage granted by nephew William Skinner, to Charles Grahame, my will is that exs. allow him, sd. Wm. Skinner, 10 years without any interest to redeem same

Desire debt due me from bro. James Skinner, be forborn, providing he educates his eld. son in the Latin tongue

Debts due me from bro. Joseph Skinner, be forborn, provided he pays same to his 4 eld. daus., to be divided amongst them

To Susanna Skinner, widow of dec'd bro. Leonard, use of certain slaves

To nephews Nathan and William Skinner, sons of bro. Leonard, clothing

To the male children of my 4 bros., whether sd. bros. are dec'd or living, my clothing

To dau. Elizabeth Contee, half mansion house and lands, *Hall's Hills*, 776 a., which I bought of Elisha Hall; mill; tract, *Sneaking Point*, bought of Thomas Lingan; houses and lots in Lower Marlborough, bought of Roger Boyce

To dau. Ann Rogers, tract, *Hunt's Chance*, and *Broughton Ashly*, bought of John and Joseph Bickerton; *Hamilton's Part*, bought of sd. Bickertons and John Tucker; pt. of tract called *Lingan's Purchase*, bought of Philip Dowell; pt. of tract called *Hall's Hills*, 225 a., which I bought of James Kingsbury; and the improvements on the land now bequeathed to dau. Ann, are greatly impaired to those of dau. Elizabeth, give sd. dau. Ann Rogers, £250 money

To bros. James and Joseph Skinner, and their wives, a suit of mourning

To nieces, daus. of bro. Joseph, same

To James Stone, same, he to help adjust my books and accounts

£10 to buy religious books to be distributed by the Vestrys of All Saints and Christ Church Parishes, among the poor children of Calvert Co.

Give personal estate of every kind whatsoever to daus. Elizabeth Contee and Ann Rogers

Shd. some of the children die without issue, their pt. to the following: To William Skinner, son of bro. William; John Skinner, bro. to William; Samuel, Gabriel and Arthur Skinner, sons of bro. James; pt. of *Hall's Hills*, 225 a., to Joseph Skinner, son of bro. Joseph; Leonard Skinner, son of bro. Leonard; Nathaniel Skinner, son of bro. Leonard; Wm. Skinner, son of bro. Leonard

Exs: Son-in-law Theodore Contee, dau. Elizabeth Contee; son-in-law Benjamin Rogers, dau. Ann Rogers

Wit: Edward Johnson, James Stone, Margaret Popel

Came Dr. Edward Johnson, James Stone and Margaret Popel, witnesses, and state they saw testator John Skinner, sign his name to the will

(Md. Cal. Wills, Vol. XIII, p. 8; Wills, Liber 32, folio 45)

45-1 Elizabeth Skinner; m. Theodore Contee, b. 1736; d. ca 1764; s/o Alexander Contee and Jane Brooke; attorney; Theodore inherited *Wartinton* at Piscataway from the 1740 will of his father (Md. Cal. Wills, Vol. VIII, p. 131); no descendants of Theodore mentioned in his will or the 1779 will of his mother. Elizabeth inherited half mansion house and lands, 776 a. *Hall's Hills*; mill; *Sneaking Point*; house and lots in Lower Marlborough from 1764 will of her father; *Hall's Hills* later sold by her sister Ann and her husband, Benjamin Rogers.

WILL of THEODORE CONTEE of Calvert County; written 18 Apr 1764; probate 28 Jul 1764

Direct that my body be deposited in the vault to be built at the West end of my garden

Any debts due me to be paid to Messrs. James Russell and Mollison, merchants in London. For which purpose I do desire that all goods I may have remaining in my store at Lower Marlborough of my property at the time of my decease be immediately disposed of or sold and same remitted to aforesaid gentlemen

To Mother, £20 and mourning ring

To brothers John and Thomas and my sisters Jane, Catherine and Barbara to each and every of said mothers and sisters £10 and a mourning ring

To Samuel Harrison my store keeper and apprentice a suit of morning, my best saddle housing and briddle and £10

Whereas there is a balance of account stands on my book against Capt. Joseph Chilton of near £70 against which there out to be some credit for board, wages and some services done for me by his wife, Mrs. Sarah Chilton, my will is that the whole balance be released and acquitted

And to the two children of Mrs. Sarah Chilton, Margaret and Littleton, to each £5

To John Addison Smith, my wife's brother, a memorial of one of my best silver watch and a mourning ring

To my friend Charles Graham and Edward Gantt to each of them £20

To wife Elizabeth, residue of my estate

Exs: Wife, Elizabeth, Charles Graham and Edward Gantt

(Md. Cal. Wills, Vol. XIII, p. 31; Wills, Liber 32, folio 205)

Estate of Theodore Contee, Calvert Co.; value £2727.3.8; 10 Aug 1765; 16 Sep 1766; next of kin: John Contee, Thomas Contee; exs.: Elisabeth Contee (widow); Charles Grahame, Edward Grant, Gent. (Inv. Prerog. Ct., 89.141).

Across the Years in Prince George's County states that Theodore Contee married "an Elizabeth Smith of Calvert Co." The will of Theodore Contee mentions wife Elizabeth and "John Addison Smith, my wife's brother." This would seem to confirm that John Addison Smith had a sister who married Theodore Contee.

The will of John Skinner written 16 Feb 1764 calls his dau. Elizabeth Contee and his son-in-law Theodore Contee. Theodore's will was written 2 months later names his wife Elizabeth. This would appear to confirm that Elizabeth Skinner was his wife at the time his will was written.

John Addison Smith was the s/o Richard Smith and Elinor Addison of Calvert Co. The 1732 will of Richard Smith makes no mention of a daughter named Elizabeth (Md. Cal. Wills, Vol. VI, p. 254). John Addison did have sisters named Rachel and Rebecca, one of whom might possibly have been a first wife of Theodore Contee.

Investigation of the wills of family members shows the following relationship between Elizabeth Skinner and John Addison Smith: Ann Skinner, sister of Elizabeth, m. Benjamin Rogers, b. ca 1740; s/o William Rogers and Sarah Gill. Sarah Rogers, sister of Benjamin, m. John Addison Smith.

45-2 Ann Skinner; m. Benjamin Rogers, b. 28 Aug 1740 St. Paul's Parish; s/o William Rogers (1704-1761) and Sarah Gill (d. 1792). Benjamin and Ann sold *Hall's Hills* to Thomas Chaney who sold 56 a. to William Chaney 23 Sep 1797 (Calvert Co. Land Records). Benjamin was a vestryman of St. Paul's Church 1762-1764, 1771 and 1772; their children from church records:

452-1 Eleanor Rogers, b. 3 Jun 1764
452-2 William Rogers, b. 13 Sep 1765

45-3 ? Orpha Skinner; m. [52-3] Elisha Skinner (Skinner notes)

4-6 Joseph Skinner; owned 50 acres *Orchard*, 108 acres *Chance*, 98 acres *Dodson's Reserve* and 9 slaves in Hunting Creek Hundred in 1782; creditor in estate of John Marquis 1750 (44.224); will of his brother John states he had several daughters

4-7 Mary Skinner; inherited £3 in 1715 will of grandmother Mary Mackall

4-8 Elizabeth Skinner; m. Joseph Wilkinson; d. ca 1735; Elizabeth appears in the Tax List of 1733 in Hunting Creek Hundred; plantations called *Godsgrace* of 120 acres and *Stoakley* of 70 acres (A History of Calvert County); children:

48-1 Elizabeth Wilkinson
48-2 Joseph Wilkinson, Jr.; d. 1763; m. Betty Heighe; their children:

482-1 Gen. Joseph Wilkinson; m. Barbara Mackall, youngest daughter of Gen. James John Mackall; held rank of Major in County Militia at outbreak of Revolution; appointed General in War of 1812; represented Calvert Co. in the Lower House of the Assembly in 1790; Register of Wills of Calvert Co. 1798-1820; owned 50 slaves in 1800

482-1 Gen. James Wilkinson; d. 1825 Mexico City; m. Ann Biddle of Philadelphia. His family was in New Orleans when he died and descendants still live there. He was a Gen. in the Continental Army; commanded troops on the s.w. frontier against Indian tribes; drove the British out of Alabama in the War of 1812 and in charge of the invasion of Canada in the final year of the war. James studied medicine in Philadelphia

WILL of JOSEPH WILKINSON, merchant, Calvert Co.; written 25 Apr 1734; probate 15 Jul 1735

To brother-in-law John Skinner, personalty

To wife, extx., dau. Elizabeth and son Joseph, each 1/3 personal estate; should wife die brother-in-law John Skinner to act as ex. and guardian to children

Test: John Smith, Posths. Thornton, Roger Boyce, Alexander Lawson

(Md. Cal. Wills, Vol. VII, p. 146; Wills, Liber 21, folio 425)

Joseph Wilkinson, Calvert Co.; £1,414.13.10: 18 Sep 1764; 6 Mar 1765; next of kin: James Skinner, Joseph Skinner; admn. Betty Wilkinson (relict) (86.308).

5. Adderton Skinner, b. ca 1677, age ca 60 in 1737; age ca 68 in 1747 (Md. Deponents); d. ca 1756 Calvert Co.; m/1 Priscilla Skinner (Skinner notes); m/2 Rebecca _____; d. ca 1760; 1733 lived at *The Reserve* in Hunting Creek Hundred and owned 7 slaves jointly with his brother Robert; inherited *The Reserve* jointly with William by 1714; served in Lower House of Maryland Legislature; surveyor and planter; Major in Calvert Co. Militia; children:

| | |
|---|---|
| 5-1 Frederick Skinner | 5-5 Robert Skinner |
| 5-2 Henry Skinner | 5-6 Sarah Skinner |
| 5-3 Maryland Skinner | 5-7 Dorcas Skinner |
| 5-4 Major Skinner | 5-8 Ann Skinner |

*Note: A Skinner descendant states there were two Adderton Skinners. Being unable to prove this, all the information found for an Adderton Skinner has been listed as belonging to Adderton, s/o Robert. This Adderton gave his age as ca 68 years on 5 May 1747 and his undated will was probated in 1756.*

Adderton and William appraised the estate of James Bussey in 1701 (21.61); Adderton, William and Robert in 1701 list of debts of Hugh Jones minister of Christ Church (21.182); trustee of will of Bigger Head of Calvert Co. 1713; he and bro. Wm. appointed guardian of son of Wm. Sturney in 1714; wit will of Catherine Sturney in 1716 (Md. Cal. Wills, Vol. IV, p. 24, 35, 63); Adderton was a member of the Assembly in 1725; held 60 acres *Blind Tom* in 1729; deputy surveyor 1731; one of the supervisors of the 2nd building of Christ Church in 1735; held 500 ac. *Miller's Folly*, adjoining *The Reserve*, in 1740; held *Jerusalem* and 143 acres *German Quarter Enlarged* in 1747; held *Charles Gift* in 1750 and in 1753 had a total of 1422 acres of land.

Rebeckah Skinner and Basil Brooke were named as next of kin to Sarah Brooke of Calvert Co. in 1752 (51.50). Was Rebecca's maiden name Brooke?

WILL of ADDERTON SKINNER, Calvert County, probate 20 Nov 1756
Children: Henry, dec'd, Maryland, Major, Robert
Grandsons: Robert, Richard, and Clement Skinner, sons of son Robert Skinner
Tract: *Millar's Folly* on Long Branch, earlier called Friers Spring Branch
Wit: Thomas Talbott (Quaker), Wm. Allnutt, James Allnutt
Mary Skinner, dec'd        (Md. Cal. Wills, Vol. XI, p. 151; Wills 30.208)

WILL of REBECCA SKINNER, Calvert County; written 18 Oct 1757; probate 23 Apr 1760
To dau. Sarah Skinner, and son Major Skinner, slaves
Remainder of my thirds to be equally divided between Major Skinner and Dorcas, Maryland
Wit: John and Joseph Talbott        (Md. Cal. Wills, Vol. XII, p. 14; Wills, 31.70))

5-1 Frederick Skinner; m. ? Ann Stuart of Virginia; served under Gen. Lafayette, entertained him at *The Reserve* and visited him at his home in France; taxed on 13 slaves in Hunting Creek Hundred in 1782; Lieutenant under Capt. John Brooke in the Calvert County Militia (Hist. of Calvert Co.); his children:

> 51-1 Henry Skinner; d. 22 Jun 1819
> 51-2 John Steuart Skinner

1782 Frederick Skinner in Upper Hundred of The Cliffs owned 493 acres called *Angelica, Mears, Addition* and 5 slaves; in Hunting Creek Hundred Frederick Skinner owned 13 slaves (History of Calvert County).

7 Sep 1786 Frederick Skinner sold one undivided one-half of a mill called *Cypress Mill* with 6 1/4 acres, with Skinner retaining the other half
(Calvert County, MD Early Land Records)

4 Jul 1816 land on a branch of Hunting Creek was sold; one of the boundaries was described as "running to the mill branch at Ann Skinner's and intersecting with James Skinner (Calvert County, MD Early Land Records)

> 51-1 Henry Skinner; d. 22 Jun 1819; m. Eddyville, KY to Aurelia Lyons; d. 1831; her father was a member of Congress; Henry was a Regular Army Surgeon stationed ca 1810 at Ft. Massac, IL; children:
>
> 511-1 Beulah L. Skinner
> 511-2 Frederick H. Skinner, b. 22 Jun 1815 Eddyville, KY

*Marylanders to Kentucky* gives a different lineage for Henry Skinner taken from *Kentucky Biography and Genealogy*, Vol. 4. These publications state that Henry Skinner was a native of Baltimore, a physician, and son of Frederick Skinner who was born in England in 1750 and came to America where he married a Miss Stuart of Virginia and settled in Baltimore.

> 51-2 John Steuart Skinner

John Steuart Skinner rode his horse to Washington to warn Pres. James Madison that the British were sailing troops up the Patuxent during the War of 1812; in retaliation, the British burned the Skinner house at *The Reserve* on the night they marched overland from their ships and attacked Prince Frederick. John Skinner accompanied

Francis Scott Key aboard the British warship where he was inspired to write *The Star Spangled Banner* (A History of Calvert County).

John S. Skinner of Baltimore purchased *St. Leonard's* for $5,160 from James John Pattison (Calvert Co. Land Records); sold *St. Leonard's* for $6,600 to John G. Mackall (Calvert Co. Land Records).

5-2  Henry Skinner; d. ca 1750; m. Elizabeth Greenfield; d/o James Greenfield; granddau. of Thomas Greenfield and Martha Truman; owned 5 slaves in Hunting Creek in 1733 Tax List; believe he was the father of the following children:

| | |
|---|---|
| 52-1  Henry Skinner | 52-5  Amelia Skinner |
| 52-2  Frederick Skinner | 52-6  Walter Skinner |
| 52-3  Elisha Skinner | 52-7  Benjamin Skinner |
| 52-4  Mary Skinner | 52-8  Truman Skinner |

Henry Skinner, Calvert Co.; £1,276.6.6; 29 Apr 1750; 20 Jun 1753; next of kin: Adderton Skinner, Maryland Skinner; admn. Elisabeth Skinner (54.157).

52-1  Henry Skinner; d. ca 1763; no descendants

WILL of HENRY SKINNER, Calvert Co., planter; written 18 Dec 1762; probate 3 Jan 1763
After decease of mother Elizabeth Skinner, give to bro. Frederick Skinner, land whereon mother now lives called *Scraps* and *Reserve*
To bro. Elisha Skinner, 3 tracts lying in Calvert Co., called *Blind Tom*, *Fanney's Right* and *Addition*
To sisters Mary and Amelia Skinner, all lands that have descended to me from grandmother Rebecca Skinner, widow of Adderton Skinner
All personalty to bros. Walter and Benjamin Skinner
Exs: Mother Elizabeth Skinner, and bro. Truman Skinner
Wit: Leonard Hollyday, John Barnes, Ellis Slater
(Md. Cal. Wills, Vol. XII, p. 171: Wills, Liber 31, folio 843)

Estate of Henry Skinner of Calvert Co.; value £247/7/6; 13 Apr 1763; 15 Oct 1763; next of kin: Benjamin Skinner, Amelia Skinner; exs. Elisabeth Skinner (widow), Truman Skinner (82.18).

52-2  Frederick Skinner; m. Margaret Johns (Skinner notes)

522-1  Margaret Johns Skinner; m. Peter Wood

52-3  Elisha Skinner; ? m. [45-3]Orpha Skinner; d. by 1764; d/o John and Amelia Skinner (Skinner notes)

WILL of ELISHA SKINNER, Calvert Co.; written 3 Sep 1765; probate 1 Nov 1765
Mentions: Benjamin Skinner, Uncle Major Skinner
Bros: Henry, Truman, Frederick and Walter Skinner
Sisters: Amelia, Mary and Elizabeth Skinner
Tracts: *Blind Tom, Tanney's Right*
Ex: Truman Skinner
Wit: William and John Skinner, Benjamin Grover (Wills, Liber 33, folio 378)

52-4  Mary Skinner
52-5  Amelia Skinner; m. [4-5] John Skinner
52-6  Walter Skinner; d. by 1781 (Pr. Geo.'s Co. Probate Records)
52-7  Benjamin Skinner
52-8  Truman Skinner, b. ca 1737; d. by Oct 1780 (Pr. Geo.'s Probate Records); m. 3 Dec 1772 cousin Priscilla Skinner, sister-in-law to Gov. Johnson (Skinner notes); he was 1st Major in Jan 1777 when Col. Robert Tyler marched his Upper Battalion of militia to reinforce Gen. Washington in New Jersey; later became Lt. Col. (Prince George's Heritage); creditor estate of James Truman Greenfield in 1761 (75.202); Justice in 1775/6; children from Skinner notes:

528-1  Priscilla Skinner; m. Notley Maddox (Skinner notes)
528-2  Elizabeth Greenfield Skinner; m. Maj. Stephen Stuart Johns

>   5282-1  Margaret Johns; m. Benjamin Skinner; their third dau. Margaret J. Skinner Wood wrote the Skinner notes quoted in this section

5-3  Maryland Skinner; d. ca 1759; m. unknown; ? children:

53-1  Priscilla Skinner; m. 3 Dec 1772 [52-8] Truman Skinner
53-2  Maryland Skinner; 2 Mar 1802 paid £100 and 20,000 lbs. of tobacco to John Waring of Prince George's County for part of 3 contiguous tracts, *Taney's Delight, Taney's Right,* and *Blind Tom*

(Calvert Co. Land Records). A Maryland Skinner "ran a vessel" to Liverpool, England (Skinner notes); this might have been his son.

Maryland Skinner, Calvert Co.; £124.15.3; 6 Nov 1759; 12 Aug 1762; next of kin: Sarah Skinner, Dorcas Skinner; admn. Benjamin Johnson (78,268).

5-4  Major Skinner; d. ca 1762; unmarried

Major Skinner, Calvert Co.; £216.0.6; 16 Jan 1762; 30 Jan 1762; next of kin: Sarah Skinner, Dorcas Skinner; admn. Henry Skinner (75.280).

5-5  Robert Skinner; m. unknown; in 1733 tax list of Hunting Creek as owner of 7 slaves jointly with Adderton Skinner; children:

    55-1  Robert Skinner
    55-2  Richard Skinner
    55-3  Clement Skinner

Did Robert Skinner marry a daughter of Priscilla (Hitchins) Johns Beckett? The 1766 will of Sarah Skinner, sister of Robert, names the above males and Mary Anne, Priscilla, Margaret and Sarah Skinner as nieces and nephews. These same females are listed as grandchildren of Priscilla Beckett.

Would Priscilla, granddaughter of Priscilla Beckett, be the Priscilla Skinner who m. [52-8] Truman Skinner?

Priscilla Beckett of Calvert Co., d. between 15 Jan 1766 and 21 Jun 1766; she named her children Mary Johns and Kensey Johns; her grandchildren: Elizabeth and Kensey Johns; children of Mary: Elizabeth Frazier, Priscilla, Margaret, Sarah and Mary Ann Skinner. (Md. Cal. Wills, Vol. XIII, p. 108); Richard Skinner and Kensey Johns were next of kin; William Harriss and Mary Johns were exs. (99.103).

Priscilla Hitchins, b. 12 d. 6 mo. 1690; d. 24 d. 3 mo. 1766, age ca 76; m/1 Richard Johns; d. ca 1719 Calvert Co.; Richard's will names wife Priscilla, eldest son Richard, son Abraham and children; mentions plantations *Triller* and *Letchworth's Chance* (Md. Cal. Wills, Vol.. IV, p. 22).

The list of children of Richard Johns and Priscilla from the Clifts Monthly Meeting includes Richard (eldest), Abraham and Mary Johns, 5th dau. b. 29 d. 1 mo. 1719.

Priscilla m/2 John Beckett (1); he may have been the John who d. ca 1758 Calvert Co. (Md. Cal. Wills, Vol. XI, p.230). This will mentions his son John Beckett (2) who d. ca 1765/6, wife Elizabeth (Md. Cal. Wills, Vol. XIII, p. 108); Elizabeth m. George Gantt by 16 Dec 1766 when his probate was filed; value £1,325.13.3; next of kin Robert Skinner, Richard Skinner; exs. George Gantt, Elizabeth Gantt (104.247).

55-1 Robert Skinner

55-2 Richard Skinner; owned 145 acres *Miller's Folly*; 1 slave Upper Hundred of The Cliffs in 1782; next of kin estate of Priscilla Beckett, Calvert Co. 6 Sep 1766 (99.103).

552-1 Richard Skinner, Jr. of Prince George's Co. on 10 Apr 1815 sold part of several tracts in Calvert County: *Taney's Delight*, *Taney's Right*, and *Blind Tom* to Aquilla Ross for $2,014,76 and another part of these same tracts to Benjamin Buckmanster for $1,044.70; Richard Skinner's land also mentioned in folio 493 (Calvert County Land Records)

55-3 Clement Skinner; owned 160 acres *Miller's Folly*, *Whittle's Rest*; 2 slaves in Upper Hundred of The Cliffs 1782

5-6 Sarah Skinner; d. 1766; unmarried

WILL of SARAH SKINNER, Calvert Co.; written 7 Feb 1766; probate 10 Jul 1766
Nephews and nieces: Robert, Richard, Clement, Mary Ann, Priscilla, Margaret and Sarah Skinner
Sisters: Dorcas and Ann Skinner
Tracts: Land in Calvert Co. left by her father in his will
Wit: Benj. and Janney Johnson, Wm. Skinner    (Wills, Liber 34, folio 87)

5-7 Dorcas Skinner; alive 1757
5-8 Ann Skinner; may have d. young

Portions of the above material from the research of Judge James Trabue, and the following Skinner notes which were found at a flea market and given to me. Some of the notes were written on 1894 order sheets of the Dingee & Conard Company of West Grove,

Pennsylvania, a nursery and seed company. Part of the notes are said to be an "Extract from Wilkinson's Memoirs."

### EXCERPTS from SKINNER NOTES

Robert Skinner and Ann his wife emigrated from England to the province of Maryland and settled in Calvert Co. where he died in 1686 leaving a widow and four sons, Robert, Clark, William and Adderton and two daughters, M. Cary (Mary), who married Joseph Letchworth, and Martha who married Thomas Greenfield.

Unidentified Family Bible no dates:
Robert Skinner, Gent., m. Ann, Widow of Thomas Truman, Gent.
Adderton Skinner, m. Priscilla Skinner
Henry Skinner, m. Elizabeth Greenfield
Benjamin Skinner, m. Henrietta Smith
Elisha Skinner, m. Orpha Skinner
Benjamin Skinner, m. Margaret Johns; their child:
Margaret Johns Skinner; m. Peter Wood

Truman Skinner was the son of above Henry Skinner. Priscilla Skinner was the sister-in-law* to Gov. Johnson and sister to Maryland Skinner who ran a vessel to Liverpool, England.

Truman Skinner was Colonel in the Revolution. He was born in 1737 and married his cousin Priscilla Skinner Dec 3rd 1772. There are her Wedding Slippers and we also have her broach which belonged to her mother Priscilla, also to her mother Priscilla. Col. Truman Skinner died about four years after the Declaration of Independence 1780 leaving two daughters: Priscilla afterwards married to Notley Maddox and my mother's mother, Elizabeth Greenfield, married to Major Stephen Stuart Johns. Their daughter, Margaret, married Benjamin Skinner whose third daughter Margaret J. Skinner Wood is now writing the history of the kid slippers for her oldest daughter, Mary Stuart Wood who married W. H. Yoe.

Brookwood                                    December 1st 1894

[* Thomas Johnson (ca 1732-1819), the first governor of Maryland after the Revolution m. 16 Feb 1766 Anne Jennings, b. 8 May 1745; d/o Thomas Jennings and Rebecca Sanders who m. 17 Jul 1732. Thomas was Chief Clerk of the Land Office and commissioner of Anne Arundel Co. who d. 26 Aug 1759 intestate, survived by his wife. (All Hallow's Prish Records; Md. Gazette; Prerogative Ct. Records. 70.356; History of Calvert Co.). Unknown if or how Priscilla Skinner fit into this family.]

## Stephen West

Stephen West, Sr. was b. by 1682 at Horton, Buckinghamshire, England, and emigrated to Maryland ca 1711 (Courtesy - Michael L. Marshall). He was buried 11 Jan 1752 in All Hallow's Parish Church yard.

Stephen West, Sr., b. by 1682; d. 8 Jan 1752; bur. 11 Jan 1752 All Hallow's Church Yard; s/o John West, Gent., of Horton Parish, county of Bucks; m/1 21 Aug 1712 Elizabeth Maccubin; bur. 18 Dec 1725 All Hallows; m/2 28 Apr 1726 All Hallow's Parish Martha Hall, b. 27 Oct 1708 St. James Parish, Anne Arundel Co.; d. 8 Apr 1752; d/o Rev. Henry Hall and Mary Duvall; came to Maryland ca 1711; innkeeper of London Town children from All Hallow's Parish:

Children of m/1:
1. Mary West, b. 1714
2. Priscilla West, b. 1716
3. Robert West, bapt. 1719
4. Elizabeth West, b. 1721
5. Eleanor West, b. 1723

Children of m/2:
6. Stephen West, b. 1727
7. Mary West, b. 1729
8. Mary Magdalene West, b. 1731
9. John Henry West, b. 1733
10. Rebecca Ann West, b. 1735
11. Martha West, b. 1738
12. Ann West, b. 1741
13. John West
14. Elizabeth West, b. by 1750

These are to certify whom concern That the bearer hereof St. West son of John West of the parish of Horton in the County of Bucks, Gent, was born and educated in our said Parish of Horton and that during the time he was amongst us he was always modes in behaviour sober and civill in his life and conversation, a frequenter of the Church of England as now be...law established, and generally....our Neighbourhood and that he never was married or contracted to any...to our knowledge and that we do give this testimonial to no other than to do him Justice. Witness our hands this first day of August Dom 1711 (Mareen Duvall of Middle Plantation).

WILL of STEPHEN WEST, Anne Arundel Co.; written 3 Jan 1751; probate 14 Aug 1752
To dau. Priscilla Smith, 1 slave and £20, to be delivered to her so that
    Richard Smith, her husband, shall not receive any benefit from same
To daus. Elianor Lyles, Martha West and Ann West, slaves and £20

To dau. Mary West, slaves
To dau. Elizabeth, 2 slaves and £20
To granddau. Elianor Austin, grandson Henry Austin, granddau. Priscilla Smith, granddaus. Martha Lyles, Barbara Lyles and Priscilla Lyles, grandson William Lyles, £5
To cousin Ann Caton, £20
To son Stephen West, after decease of wife Martha West, land, but if sd. son die before his mother, then I bequeath that she have full possession of estate [this bequest from *Mareen Duvall of Middle Plantation* differs from the one abstracted in *Maryland Calendar of Wills*]
Exs. wife and son Stephen
Wit: Wm. Chapman, James Dick, Wm. Chapman, Jr., Samuel Chapman
(Md. Cal. Wills, Vol. X, p. 226: Wills, Liber 28, folio 353)

1. Mary West, b. 30 May 1714; Mary and her sisters, Priscilla and Elizabeth, were heirs of Robert Wood of Anne Arundel Co. written 1727 (Md. Cal. Wills, Vol. VI, p. 170)

2. Priscilla West, b. 12 Apr 1716; m/1 William Pearce; m/2 7 Oct 1736 Henry Austin; d. by 1743; m/3 Richard Smith; the will of Henry Austin of Calvert Co. written 18 Jan 1743 mentions grandchildren Henry and Elinor Austin, son and dau. of Henry Austin, dec'd (Md. Cal. Wills, Vol. IX, p. 44).

   2-1 Elianor Austin, b. 15 Sep 1737; bapt. 23 Apr 1738
   2-2 Henry Austin
   2-3 Priscilla Smith, b. 27 Dec 1743

3. Robert West, bapt. 19 Sep 1719; Robert does not appear in some histories of this family; but he is listed in All Hallow's Parish as a child of Stephen and Elizabeth

4. Elizabeth West, b. 15 Apr 1721; m. Anthony Beck, mariner

5. Eleanor West, b. 22 May 1723; m. William Lyles; children from will of grandfather West:

   5-1 Martha Lyles
   5-2 Barbara Lyles
   5-3 Priscilla Lyles
   5-4 William Lyles

6. Stephen West (2), b. 23 Jul 1727 London Town, Anne Arundel Co.; d. 3 Jan 1790 Baltimore; m. 8 Mar 1753 Hannah Williams; d. ca 1815; d/o Capt. Richard Williams, mariner of England, and his wife Christian _____ who m/2 George Gordon (Md. Cal. Wills, Vol. X, p. 216); known as Stephen West, Esq., a wealthy merchant of Upper Marlboro, Prince George's Co.; records suggest he may have been rather ruthless in his business dealings; Martha inherited 1/2 of her father's estate from his 1738 will; see *Mareen Duvall of Middle Plantation* for documentation of his life in Prince George's Co.; children:

    6-1 Christian Hannah West; left slaves in 1765 will of step-grandfather Judge George Gordon with her mother to have use of slaves but her father to have no interest in them
    6-2 William Henry West
    6-3 John Stephen West; m. 26 Nov 1794 Anne Pue
    6-4 Joseph West
    6-5 Mary West
    6-6 Harriet West
    6-7 Rachel Sophia West; m. Benjamin Oden
    6-8 Richard Williams West; m. Maria Lloyd

7. Mary West, b. 6 Jul 1729

8. Mary Magdalene West, b. 19 Sep 1731; m. 29 Mar 1752 Richard Moore; children:

    8-1 Richard Moore, b. 22 Jan 1753
    8-2 Hannah Moore, b. 19 Oct 1754
    8-3 Stephen West Moore, b. 16 Aug 1756
    8-4 Samuel Preston Moore, b. 14 Sep 1758

9. John Henry West, b. 2 Sep 1733; bapt. 23 Oct 1733

10. Rebecca Ann West, b. 10 Feb 1735/6; bapt 15 Jul 1736

11. Martha West, b. 13 Dec 1738; m. [115-3] John Dorsey Lawrence

12. Ann West, b. 19 Aug 1741

13. John West, b. _ Feb __;

14. Elizabeth West, b. before 1750; m. James Stone

Relationships from the will of William Hall of Elk Ridge, Anne Arundel Co.; written 13 Nov 1767; probate 6 Sep 1770 (Md. Cal. Wills, Vol. XIV, p. 156):

Stephen West, nephew, and his sons:
  William Henry West
  John Stephen West
  Stephen West
Elizabeth West, niece
Stephen West, nephew, dau.:
  Christiana Hannah West
Mary West, kinsman
Henry Hall, nephew, and his sons:
  2nd son Henry Hall and his son Henry
  3rd son William Hall
  4th son Nicholas Hall
Henry Hall, brother, and son:
  William Hall
Martha Lawrence, niece, and her daus.:
  eld. dau. Ann West Lawrence
  Susanna Lawrence
Elizabeth Dorsey, niece, and her children:
  William Henry Dorsey
  brothers and sisters
Ann Griffith, niece, and children:
  Rachel Griffith
  brothers and sisters
Benjamin Hall, brother, and son:
  Williams Hall
Henry Hall, brother, and unnamed daus.
John Hall, brother, and children:
  Martha Hall
  Elizabeth Hall
  Ann Hall
  Mary Magdalene Hall
Martha Hall, kinsman
Mary Hall, dec's, m. _____ Smith
Henry Hall, cousin, and sons:
  Nicholas Hall
  William Hall

## Thomas Letchworth

The earliest land record found for this family was the patent granted Thomas Letchworth 22 May 1657 for *Letchworth* in Calvert County (Hienton Map). *A History of Calvert County* states he was a Puritan settler who acquired 200 acres of land on the Upper Cliffs in 1652 which included the cypress swamp at the head of Battle Creek called *Letchworth's Cypress*. This great cypress swamp is now a Registered Natural Landmark.

On 26 Apr 1658 *Mount Pleasant* of 290 acres was patented to Thomas Letchworth; it bounded land of James Berry and Fendall's land in the area which became Prince George's Co. (Liber A, folio 7 and 133; Liber C, folio 160 and 168).

He was a member of the Lower House of Assembly during the Puritan regime in the 1660s and a Justice of Calvert County. He obtained a grant of 1,100 acres called *Letchworth's Chance*, located on Plum Point Road, for transporting 11 settlers including Michael and John Taney. This plantation was later owned by Richard Johns, who purchased half of the plantation in 1676 from Joseph, son of Thomas Letchworth, and Richard Chew owned the other half. He was also granted *Letchworth's Hills*, later called *Harwood and Letchworth*. His Calvert County land was sold and his children acquired *Brooke Court Manor* in Prince George's County (A History of Calvert County).

Thomas may have had a brother, father or uncle named Joseph who d. in Prince George's County prior to 12 Nov 1700 when his inventory was recorded in the Prerogative Court. The appraisers were George Nailor and William Watson (20.89). The account of his estate was filed 3 Aug 1703 in Prince George's County by Robert Skinner, administrator; value £16/6/6; £19/2/0 (24.35).

Thomas apparently died by 1678 as a deposition of Ninian Beale made in Calvert County in 1678 mentions "Widow Letchworth" (Md. Deponents).

Thomas Letchworth, b. est. 1620s; d. by 1678; and his wife Elizabeth \_\_\_\_\_; alive 1698 (son's will); the following children identified by land records and *A History of Calvert County*:

1. Joseph Letchworth, adult 1676    3. Ann Letchworth
2. Thomas Letchworth, b. by 1668    4. ?____ Letchworth

1. Joseph Letchworth, b. est. ca 1655; d. ca 1713 Prince George's Co.; m. by 1685 to Mary Skinner, b. est ca 1664-1670; d/o Robert Skinner. On 16 May 1687 Joseph patented *The Joseph and Mary* adjoining *Brook Court Manor* in that portion of Calvert Co. which became Prince George's Co. (Hienton Map); he inherited 1/2 of the 1,100 acres called *Letchworth's Chance* granted his father in 1663 and he sold it to Richard Johns in 1676. Samuel Chew obtained the other half of the plantation. The will of Robert Skinner, written 8 Mar 1685, mentions dau. Mary Letchworth. Wording in this will indicates Mary was recently married and had not had her first child. Known child:

1-1 Thomas Letchworth, b. after 1676

Was there also a son named Joseph who d. ca 1700? There is no mention of him in the *Index to Probate Records of Prince George's Co.*, but the following records appear in Skinner's *Maryland Inventories and Accounts*::

Joseph Letchworth, Prince George's Co.; inv. #350; 25 Jun 1700 (20.89)
Joseph Letchworth, Prince George's Co.; £16/6/6; £19/2/0; 3 Aug 1703; admn. Robert Skinner (24.35).

Joseph Letchworth sold 570 acres of land [410 acres by re-survey] to Ignatius Craycroft 14 May 1694 (Calvert Co., Liber R, folio 214 & Prince George's, Liber C, folio 191).

Prince George's County Court of Sep 1696: Attachment against the goods and chattles of Joseph Letchworth for 390# of tobacco debt and 454# of tobacco cost of suit; said attachment obtained in Calvert County. The suit had not been heard by the court of Sep 1697 and the attachment was against the "estate" of Joseph Letchworth in the court of Nov 1697 (folio 258).

The court record of Nov 1697 (folio 258) states that a steer in the possession of John Dunkin appraised at 800# of tobacco was attached and 190# of tobacco in the hands of Thomas Greenfield, sheriff. In the case following, Thomas Greenfield, admn. of Richard Charlett, plt., against Joseph Letchworth, def.; total debt of 1,717# of tobacco; "the said Joseph Letchworth as the said John Dunkin though sollemly called came not nor either of them, etc."

26 Aug 1707 Ignatius Craycroft, Gent. of Prince George's Co., gave Charles Diggs, husband of Sophia Craycroft, dec'd., a tract of land purchased from Joseph Letchworth 14 May 1694 (Calvert Co., Liber R, folio 214) containing 410 acres according to resurvey now in possession of Diggs (Land Records, Liber C)

WILL of JOSEPH LETCHWORTH, Calvert Co.; written 30 May 1696; probate 23 Oct 1713
To son Thomas, ex., at 20 years, and hrs., entire estate, real and personal. Should he die without issue, sd. estate to pass to mother, Eliza. Letchworth, widow, and both of devisees afsd. dying without issue, brother-in-law Robert Skinner to inherit estate
Test: Thos. Tarcey, Abel Enion, Thos. Earle, Eliza. Taney
(Md. Cal. Wills, Vol. III, p. 243; Wills, Liber 13, folio 536)

1713, 15 Feb; Joseph Letchworth, deceased (Inv., BB.1.206)

The above will was accidentally abstracted incorrectly as the will of Thomas Letchworth in the *Maryland Calendar of Wills*. Examination of the will at the Maryland State Archives in 1992 by F. Edward Wright, shows that it was the will of Joseph Letchworth. The second error in the abstract is that the will was not witnessed by Joseph Letchworth, but rather witnessed in the presence of Joseph Letchworth, the testator. It was easy to see how this latter error was made, but close examination revealed that it was an error.

1-1 Thomas Letchworth, b. by 1685/6; d. ca 1722; m. Elizabeth Magruder; d. after 1753; d/o Alexander Magruder; she m/2 Edward Truman; d. ca 1729 Prince George's County, Elisabeth Truman, extx.. (Inv. of Prerog. Ct. and Prince George's Probate Court). Did she then m/3 Robert Whitaker? The will of Alexander Magruder written in 1739 mentions his daughter Elizabeth Whitaker and leaves land to Robert Whitaker and wife Elizabeth (Md. Cal. Wills, Vol. IX, p. 67); Robert Whitaker, wife Elizabeth, d. ca 1753 in Prince George's Co.; Thomas inherited cow and calf from 1685 will of his grandfather Robert Skinner. Children from his will:

11-1 Thomas Letchworth; b. after 1703
11-2 Joseph Letchworth; b. after 1703
11-3 Anne Letchworth
11-4 Mary Letchworth
11-5 Elizabeth Letchworth

Thomas Letchwich of Calvert Co. sold Roger Boyd two parcels of land, *Blue Coat* and *Joseph and Mary* in Prince George's Co. bounding the Letchworth plantation; 1 Nov 1710 (Liber F, folio 69).

Thomas Letchworth of Prince George's Co. and Roger Boyce of Calvert Co. sold Levin Covington for £305 two tracts of land; 465 acres of *Brooke Court* and 240 acre part of *Joseph and Mary* (Liber F, folio 168).

Thomas Letchworth and his wife (unnamed) of Prince George's Co. sold to Charles Digges of Charles Co. a tract of 140 formerly sold by the father of Thomas Letchworth to Ignatius Craycroft; 24 Nov 1714 (Liber F, folio 423).

WILL of THOMAS LETCHWORTH, Prince George's County; written 14 Mar 1721; probate 21 Jun 1722
To son Thomas and Hrs., dwelling plantation *Joseph and Mary* and personalty at age of 18
To son Joseph and Hrs., 200 acres of *Brook Court Mannor* and personalty
To 3 daus. Anne, Mary and Elizabeth and their hrs., 250 acres of *Two Friends* (now in Charles Co.) equally. Shd. both sons die without issue, dau. Anne to have dwelling plantation. Shd. daus. die without issue, survivors to divide portion of dec'd
To wife, extx., and children, residue of estate equally. Sale of part of *Joseph and Mary* and part of *Brook Court* to Levin Covington confirmed
Overseers: Levin Covington and Leonard Holliday
Test: Nath. Magruder, Paul Rawlence, Benj. Walles
Note: 26 Nov 1722, Widow Elizabeth Letchworth claims her thirds
(Md. Cal. Wills, Vol. V, p. 123; Wills, Liber 18, folio 18)

Estate of Thomas Letchworth, Prince George's County; value £61/0/10; 15 Mar 1722; next of kin: Alexander Magruder (father-in-law) (Inv. Prerog. Ct., 8.87).

Estate of Thomas Letchworth, Prince George's Co.; value £195/16/1; 26 Nov 1722; next of kin: Alexander Magruder (father-in-law); extx. Elisabeth Letchworth (Inv. Prerog. Ct., 9.150).

18 May 1725 - Edward Truman recorded a statement regarding the plantation now in possession of Edward Truman who married the widow of Thomas Letchworth, who, by his will, left his sons, Thomas and Joseph Letchworth, a tract of land called *Brooke Court* of 200 acres; the uppermost part of the tract to Joseph and the lower most part to Thomas. /s/ Benj. Wallis, Owen Ellis (Prince George's Co. Land Records, Liber F, folio 633).

Estate of Edward Truman, Prince George's Co.; value £390/18/7; next of kin: Alexander Magruder, Robert Whitaker' admn. Elizabeth Truman (Inv. Prerog. Ct., 15.270).

2. Thomas Letchworth (2); nothing definite could be determined from the available records regarding this Thomas. A 1714 land record states he had a wife who was unnamed.

*A History of Calvert County* states that the first Thomas Letchworth had two sons, Thomas and Joseph, and two daughters, Ann who married Robert Skinner and an unnamed daughter who married John Taney.

Documents quoted under the Skinner family show Ann Mackall's 3rd husband was Robert Skinner (2) and she had previously been married to John Taney. Since Robert was her 3rd husband, it seems reasonable that he had been previously married also.

3. Ann Letchworth; m. ?Robert Skinner; who m/2 Ann Mackall

4. ? ____ Letchworth; m. ? John Taney

### LAND RECORDS

7 Nov 1695 Richard Edwards of Calvert Co., sold John Mills of Calvert Co. 40 acres on the west side of the north branch of the Patuxent River all the tract originally laid out to Thomas Letchworth bounded by *Fendall's Spring* (Land Records, Liber A, folio 7).

2 Nov 1697 Richard Edwards sold to Peter Scamper 150 of the 190 acres called *Mount Pleasant* originally patented to Thomas Letchworth 26 Apr 1658 (Land Records, Liber A, folio 133).

23 Feb 1705 John Mills sold Henry Bottelor a 40 acre part of a tract laid out for Thomas Letchworth (Land Records, Liber C, folio 160).

15 Jul 1706 John Mills sold Charles Walker 50 acres of the uppermost of a tract of 150 acres laid out on the west side of the Patuxent in the North Branch for Thomas Letchworth who sold to John Tate, dec'd; his son sold to John Milles; bounded by *Mount Pleasant* (Land Records, Liber C., folio 168).

28 Feb 1711 Thomas Letchworth, planter of Prince George's Co. and Roger Boyce (?Boyd) of Calvert Co. sold Levin Covington of Somerset Co., Gent., 139 acres of marsh, 101 acres of high land part of *Joseph and Mary* and 465 acres part of *Brooke Court*. Boyce rec'd £325 and Letchworth £30. No wife of Letchworth acknowledged deed. (Land Records, Liber F, folio 168)

24 Nov 1714 Thomas Letchworth (2) and his unnamed wife of Prince George's Co. sold Charles Digges of Prince George's Co. a tract of land sold by Thomas Letchworth (1) to Ignatius Craycroft and now in possession of Charles Diggs (Land Records, Liber F, folio 423).

8 Nov 1718 William Mills sold Samuell Barshear the westernmost part of a tract called *Letchworth* taken up by Thomas Letchworth of Calvert County on the west side of the Patuxent on (Land Records, Liber I, folio 159).

22 Jul 1719 Robert Mills sold William Smith 50 acres of land laid out for Thomas Letchworth on the North Branch on the west side of the Patuxent (Liber I, folio 237).

28 Jul 1719 Thomas Letchworth signed a bill of exchange (Land records, Liber I, folio 567).

## MARIARTY

Families bearing this surname descend from the O' Muircheartaigh sept, whose territory was in western County Kerry in Corkaguiney and Trughanacmy baronies around Castlemain harbour. Until the population movement of the present century 90 per cent of the Moriarty families in Ireland were still living in County Kerry and that county still houses the majority of the name in the country (Irish Family Names, Brian de Breffny).

### EDWARD MERIARTE

According to Donald P. Moriarty II, Edward Meriarte, the immigrant, arrived in Maryland ca 1676 from Killarney, Ireland (Louisiana Genealogical Register, Mar 1991). Since so many variations of the name were found, spelling in this document is, in most cases, as it was found in the records.

Edward Meriarte, b. Ireland; d. ca 1687/8 Anne Arundel Co., MD; m. Honor _____; d. ca 1700/1. Records of All Hallow's Parish, Anne Arundel Co., MD state "Honour Mariarttee, widow of Edward, bur. 8 Oct 1700." This conflicts with the date of 5 Mar 1701 given by *Maryland Calendar of Wills* as the date her will was written. Children of Edward and Honor from wills:

1. Daniel Meriarte, b. ca 1676
2. Edward Meriarte
3. Margaret Meriarte
4. Elizabeth Meriarte
5. Rachel Meriarte

Edward Mariarte, planter of Anne Arundel County sold 175 acres of the 500 acre *Covill's Folly* on 12 Dec 1676; lying on Flat Creek Branch of South River, near head of South River; Honor Mariarte released dower. *Covill's Folly* was laid out for Ann Covill, widow; Edward purchased the tract from Ann Mott, alias Lambert. Ann's husband was probably a Huguenot as the Covill name, with a variety of spelling, is French. Some members of the de Coville family who fled France during the reign of Francis I had changed their name to Caldwell by the time they landed in

New Castle, DE in 1727, after almost 100 years in Scotland and County Donegal, Ireland. In 1675 land of Edward Mariarte was located on ridge near Patuxent River adjoining 171 acres of Friend's Choice (Abstracts of Land Records, Anne Arundel Co., p. 79 &135; Caldwell Family History).

WILL of EDWARD MERIARTE, Anne Arundel Co., will written 16 Nov 1687; probate 4 Jun 1688:
To sons Daniel and Edward at 21 years of age, and heirs, 170 acres Friend's Choice
To daus. Margaret, Eliza: and Rachel, personalty, and land afsd. jointly in event of death of sd. sons without issue
To wife Honor, extx, personalty
Overseers: Edward Ser___ett, Solomon Sparrow, Richard Tidings
Test: Jos. Owen, Wm. White, Mary Williams, Jno. Elsey
(Md. Cal. Wills, Vol. II, p. 32; Wills, Liber 6, folio 16)

WILL of HONOR MARRIARTE; written 5 Mar 1701; probate 25 Apr 1701
To son Daniel, ex., Honor Stafford and daus. Margaret and Eliza:, personalty
To son Edward, 1/2 of estate, real and personal
To dau. Rachel, residue of estate, real and personal
Test: Jno. Garterell, Math. Hond, Isaac Potts, Jas. Mowatt
(Md. Cal. Wills, Vol. II, p. 207; Wills, Liber 11, folio 21)

Account of Honor Mariarte, Anne Arundel Co.; £297/1/3; £131/7/9; 18 Aug 1703; legatee: Mrs. Rachell Lawrence; Ex. Daniel Marriarte (24.42).

1. Daniel Maryartee, b. ca 1676; age 41 in 1717 Anne Arundel Co. (More Md. Deponents); d. ca 1724/6; m. Elinor ?Beall; d. 1726 Anne Arundel Co.; purchased 23 Jan 1698 *Maiden's Dowery* of 700 acres in the freshes of the Patuxent River, Prince George's Co. from Ninian Beall (Liber A, folio 173); sold 100 acres of *Maiden's Dowery* 27 Feb 1713 to Edward Mariarte and another part of the same land to Patrick Hepburn in 1720; Elinor acknowledged deeds (Land Records of Prince George's Co.); Mrs. Elinor Mariarte owed estate of James Beall of Prince George's Co. 23 Nov 1735 (Md. and Va. Colonials); Daniel served on juries and wit. documents 1703-1708 (Abstracts of Land Records, Anne Arundel Co., Vol. II); children from will and All Hallow's Parish:

1-1 Ninian Mariarte, b. 1701
1-2 Elinor Mariarte, b. 1704
1-3 Ann Mariarte, b. 1707
1-4 Thomas Mariarte, b. 1710
1-5 Arden Mariarte, b. 1711
1-6 Margaret Mariarte

WILL of DANIEL MARIARTE, Gent., Anne Arundel Co.; written 18 Jan 1724/5; probate 21 Feb 1726
To wife Elinor, 100 acres *Clark's Folly* of 300 acres on the south end of *Darnell's Grove*, at her decease to sons Ninian and Arden equally
To son Ninian and hrs., 100 acres at n. end of afsd. tract
To son Arden and hrs., residue of afsd. tract; shd. either son die without issue, survivor to inherit portion of dec'd; shd. both die without issue, sd. land to 3 daus. Elinor, Anne and Margarett and their hrs. equally
To 2 sons afsd., 88 acres *Piney Hedge* on east branch of Potomac
To wife and 5 children afsd., personal estate equally
Test: Joseph Richardson, Sarah Richardson, Mary Powell, Ester ?Idle
Exs.: Wife and son Ninian (Md. Cal. Wills, Vol. VI, p. 43; Wills, Liber 19, folio 270)

Estate of Capt. Daniell Mariartee of Anne Arundel Co.; £161/2/4; 17 Apr 1727; 10 May 1727; next of kin Eleanor and Ninian Mariarte
(Inv. Prerog. Ct., Liber 12, folio 437)

1-1 Ninian Maryarte, b. 31 Dec 1701; bapt. 15 Mar 1702; d. ca 1748; m. 8 May 1735 Prince George's Co. to Jane Griffin who must have predeceased Ninian; no known children

Ninian Mariarte and Henry Odell languishing prisoners in Prince George's Co. Jail; no details; 1731 thru Jul 1732.
Ninian Mariate and Henry Odell signed administrative bond 25 Nov 1736 estate of Thomas Odell for estate of Sarah Sprigg Peerce Combs.
Ninian Mariate mentioned in will of Osborn Sprigg.
(Maryland & Virginia Colonials, Doliante)

WILL of NINIAN MARIARTE, Prince George's Co., written 10 Dec 1748; probate 3 Feb 1748/9
To. Mr. Osburn Sprigg, 150 acre tract *Darnall's Grove* now called *Charlesses Folley*
Wit: James Edmonston, Tho. Hilleary, Thos. Belt, Wm. Chittam
(Md. Cal. Wills, Vol. IX, p. 194)

1-2 Elinour Maryarte, b. 12 Aug 1704; bapt. 15 Sep 1704
1-3 Ann Mariarte, b. 11 Jan 1707; bapt. 7 Mar 1707
1-4 Thomas Maryarte, b. 2 Jan 1710; bapt. 25 Aug 1711; bur. 21 Jul 1711

1-5   Arden Maryarte, bapt. 8 Apr 1711
1-6   Margaret Mariarte

2. Edward Maryartee; bur. 20 May 1718; m. 5 Feb 1705 Rachell Grey; she m/2 on 21 May 1719 William Chiffen; (William and Rachell had a daughter, Elianor Chiffin, b. 2 May 1720); Rachell was probably the d/o Rachel Grey (bur. 15 Jan 1705 All Hallow's Parish) who was widow of John Grey; Edward's estate record mentions only servants, appraisers and approvers (Inv. Prerog. Ct., Liber 3, folio 137); Edward served on juries and wit. documents 1703-1708 (Abstracts of Land Records, Anne Arundel Co., Vol. II); Maryarte children of Edward and Rachel from All Hallow's Parish:

2-1   Edward Maryarte, b. 14 Mar 1706; bapt. 30 Mar 1707; d. by 23 Apr 1741; shipwright; m. 17 Feb 1736 Baltimore Co., MD to Sarah Hanson; d/o Benjamin Hanson and wife Sarah; Sarah Meriarte m/2 21 Apr 1742 to John Garrettson, b. 17 Feb 1706; s/o Garrett and Elizabeth Garrettson; 1736 will of Benjamin Hanson calls dau. Sarah Garrettson and mentions granddaughter Rachel Meriarte (Baltimore Co. Families); the estate settlement of Benjamin Hanson in 1737 names Sarah Tayman (his mother) and Edward Mariorte as next of kin (Inv. of Prerog. Ct., Liber 22, folio 547); John Mariarte and Rachel Chifin next of kin in estate settlement in Baltimore Co. in 1741 (Inv. of Prerog. Ct., Liber 26, folio 37); known child:

21-1   Rachel Meriarte, b. 25 Mar 1739; m. 7 Sep 1758 James Gallion, Jr., b. 9 May 1736; d. ca 1774/5; s/o James Gallion and Phoebe Johnson; children from Harford Co. census of Harford Lower Hundred and *Baltimore County Families*; Rachel appears in census age 34:

211-1   Priscilla Gallion, b. 5 Aug 1759
211-2   Sarah Gallion, b. ca 1761
211-3   Abariller Gallion, b. ca. 1764
211-4   Pheobe Gallion, b. ca 1766
211-5   Martha Gallion, b. ca 1769

211-6 George Gallion, b. ca 1771
211-7 Mary Gallion, b. ca 1773
211-8 Rachael Gallion, b. ca 1775

Estate settlement of James Gallion, Jr. in Harford County; Samuel and Nathan Gallion next of kin; admnx. Rachel Gallion; value £273/6/7; 16 Jun 1775; 2 Dec 1775 (Inv. of Prerog. Ct., Liber 120, folio 226).

Phebe Gallion, widow and mother of James, was in the same area of Harford County when the census was taken 30 Aug 1776. Several of her children were living with her and she owned 11 Negroes.

2-2 John Maryarte, b. 3 Mar 1708; bapt. 15 May 1709; d. ca 1741 Anne Arundel Co.; Rachel and Eleanor Chiffen next of kin (Inv. of Prerog. Ct., Liber 26, folio 481; Liber 27, folio 93)
2-3 Rachell Maryarte, b. 27 Feb 1712; bapt. 8 Oct 1712; m. 5 Dec 1733 All Hallow's Parish to Nehemiah Covington; he was probably from the Eastern Shore family who also owned land in Prince George's County
2-4 Margaret Maryarte; bapt. 21 May 1719

3. Margaret Mariarte, b. by 1687; d. ca 1739; m. ca 1690 Thomas Sprigg (2); b. ca 1659; d. ca 1736/9; s/o Thomas Sprigg (1) and Catherine (Graves) Roper (Doliante); Thomas inherited plantation and remaining land of *Northampton* and *Kellering*, also 1/3 of 500 a. patent in *Manor of Collington* from 1704 will of his father (Md. Cal. Wills, Vol. III, p. 48); children not in order of birth:

3-1 Thomas Sprigg (3); d. ca 1726; m. Margery Wight; d. ca 1783; d/o Capt. John Wight and Ann Greenfield; Margery m/2 Col. Joseph Belt
3-2 Edward Sprigg, b. ca 1697; d. 30 Nov 1751; m/1 26 Apr 1720 to Elizabeth Pile; d/o Dr. Richard Pile; m/2 Mary Belt; d/o Col. Joseph Belt and Hester Beall
3-3 Osborn Sprigg, b. ca 1707; m/1 Elizabeth Morris; m/2 11 Jul 1727 Rachel Belt, b. 13 Dec 1711; d/o Col. Joseph Belt and Hester Beall

3-4 Priscilla Sprigg, b. ca 1700; d. after 1734; m. 22 Aug 1716 Ralph Crabb, b. ca 1694 Calvert Co.; d. 1734 Prince George's Co.; descendants to Clark and Henry Co., KY

3-5 Margaret Sprigg; m/1 26 Sep 1717 Francis King; m/2 as 2nd wife of Richard Keene

3-6 Eleanor Sprigg; m. Henry Wright

3-7 Elizabeth Sprigg; d. Nov 1781; m/1 Josiah Wilson, Jr.; d. 1727; m/2 1734 Turner Wooten, a widower

Margaret Sprigg, Prince George's Co.; £175.3.6; 14 Apr 1740; 22 Jul 1740; next of kin: Edward Sprigg, Thomas Sprigg; admn. Osborn Sprigg (25.93).

4. Elizabeth Mariarte; d. 1725 Prince George's Co.; m/1 Mathias Clark (Louisiana Genealogical Register); prob. s/o Matthias Clark and Elizabeth \_\_\_\_\_; d. 10 Feb 1702; m/2 ca 1713 Robert Levett of Beverly, Yorkshire; children from will and St. James Parish:

4-1 Margaret Clark, b. 13 Dec 1684; bapt. 25 Jun 1685

4-2 John Clark, b. 13 Jun 1686; bapt 11 Aug 1691

4-3 Webber Clark, b. 1 Mar 1690; bapt. 11 Aug 1691

Deed of Gift; Matthias Clarke, Anne Arundel Co., millwright, for fatherly affection gives to his son, Webber Clark, one bay mare and colt; 13 Jul 1706; /s/ Matthias Clark (mark) (WT2.368).

4-4 Ruth Clark; m. 1716 Anne Arundel Co. to Joseph Williams, b. 10 Feb 1691; s/o Benjamin and Ruth Williams

    44-1 Ruth Williams, bapt. 18 May 1718 All Hallow's Parish

    44-2 Margarett Williams, b. 13 Sep 1722; bapt. 3 Nov 1723 All Hallow's Parish

4-5 Elizabeth Clark, b. 22 Jul 1705; bapt. 19 Aug 1705; bur. 5 Dec 1706

4-6 Elizabeth Clark or Levitt; m. \_\_\_\_\_ Duskin

4-7 Robert Clark or Levitt

4-8 John Clark or Levitt; b. after 1707

Thomas Tench, Esq., Mathias Clarke, millwright, and Eliza his wife, sold 100 acres called *Warburton Square*, part of *Forest of Dann*, on 11 Jun 1706 for £60 to Abraham Symons (WT2.411).

12 Aug 1713; Benjamin Lawrence of Anne Arundel County, planter, binds himself to Robert Levitt, merchant of England for £300 to insure the marriage between Robert Levett and Elizabeth Clarke, widow, sister-in-law of Benjamin; Elizabeth made Deed of Gift of all her goods and debts in Maryland to Benjamin Lawrence in trust for her children; June Court of 1714 (Prince George's County Land Records, Liber F, folio 368)

WILL of ELIZABETH LEVETT, widow, Prince George's Co.; written 22 Sep 1725; probate 25 Nov 1725

To son Robert, all testator's interest in estate in Beverly, Yorkshire, due her as relict of Robt. Levett

To son John, personalty and £150 at age of 18

To dau. Elizabeth Duskin, bro. Daniel Mariartee, sister Margarett Sprigg and Col. James Haddock, personalty

To daus. Margarett and Ruth Clark, residue of estate

Exs. Col. James Haddock and dau. Margarett Clark

Test: Josiah Wilson, Margaret Dick, Lingan Wilson

(Md. Cal. Wills, Vol. V, p. 204; Wills, Liber 18, folio 416)

5. Rachel Mariarte; m/1 6 day 11 mo. 1701/2 to Benjamin Lawrence; d. by 27 Mar 1721 Baltimore Co.; m/2 by 13 Sep 1726 to Thomas or John Norwood; m/1 children listed with Lawrence family

## WILLIAM MARIARTE

William Mariarte, b. ca 1701; age 44 in 1745 Prince George's Co. (Md. Deponents). Nothing more was located.

## ABRAHAM CHILDS

Abraham Child of Anne Arundel County d. ca 1738. His will mentions no wife or children and his 206 acres of *Eagleton's Range* was left to Abraham Sevell and Philip Howard.

Abraham Child wit. will of James Warner of Anne Arundel Co. in 1673 and an Abraham Childs wit. will of Christopher Hall of Kent Co. in 1674 (Md. Cal. Wills, Vol. I). Were they the same person?

Abraham Childe, ex. of will of Henry Sewell of Anne Arundel Co. written 1691 (Md. Cal. Wills, Vol. II, p. 207); wit. will of Thomas Browne, Sr., Anne Arundel Co. 1714/5 (Md. Cal. Wills, Vol. IV, p. 31); wit. will of Joseph Smith, Sr. 1722 (Md. Cal. Wills, Vol. V, p. 107); will of Alexander Stuart written 1730 mentions land bought of Abraham Childs (Md. Cal. Wills, Vol. VI, p. 202).

4 Nov 1665; Abraham Child wit. land of George Yate (p. 73); 9 Nov 1672; wit. deed (p. 40); 2 Jun 1684; Abraham Child wit. deed (p. 77); 12 Aug 1685; Abraham Child, Anne Arundel Co., planter; purchased 206 acres called *Eagleston's Range* (p. 61); 15 Nov 1694; land of Abraham Chiles mentioned in deed (p. 73) (Abstracts of Anne Arundel Co. Land Records, Vol. I).

2 Jan 1703; Abraham Child wit. deed of gift (p. 100)
13 Nov 1705; deed describes original patent to Abraham Child 10 Sep 1683; tract called *Childton* on s. side of Ann Arundel River; 40 acres; sold to Richard Owens 4 Jun 1686; etc. (p. 12).
(Abstracts of Anne Arundel Co. Land Records, Vol. II)

Will of ABRAHAM CHILD, Anne Arundel Co.; 11 Jan 1736/7; 22 Apr 1738
To Abraham Sevell, Philip, son of Philip Howard and their hrs., 206 a.

---

To John Leatherwood, William Smith, Jr. and James Moore, Jr., personalty
Ex. Richard Hampton
Test: Samuel Leatherwood, William Smith, Jr., James Moore
(Md. Cal. Wills, Vol. VII, p. 239; Wills, Liber 21, folio 856)

## Henry Child

Henry Child (1), b. ____ England; d. ca 1740 MD; m. ____; d. by 1702 England; no wife mentioned in his will indicating that if he m/2 in Maryland, she was deceased by 1740; presumably all the children were b. England; children from will:

1. Henry Child (2)
2. Cephas Child
3. Mary Child; m. Richard Lewin
4. Sarah Child; m. John Sanders
5. Ruth Child; m/1 John Wilson; m/2 Henry Roberts
6. Rachel Child; m. William Wilson
7. Ann Child; m. Solomon Birckhead
8. ? John Childs of Prince George's Co.
9. ? William Childs of Anne Arundel Co.

From Monthly Meeting Minutes, 1677-1771 of West River, the Clifts, Patuxent, and Herring Creek: Henry Child, lately from England with divers of his children, produces certificate showing unity with Friends and clearness from engagement of marriage; 1 d. 11 mo. 1702 (Quaker Records of Southern Maryland).

5 Oct 1702; Henry Child, yeoman, Anne Arundel Co.; purchased 100 acres *Smithfield* at Herring Creek and 50 acres of *Scantley* from James Kingsbury, surgeon, for £200 (WT2.111).

WILL of HENRY CHILD, Anne Arundel Co.; 20 Jun 1731; 4 Jun 1740
To son Henry and hrs., land testator bought from James Kingsbury
To son Cephas and hrs., 1,000 acres bought of William Penn of
  Pennsylvania
To dau. Sarah Sanders, extx., and hrs., land bought of Nathan Rigbie
To daus. Ruth Robins and Rachel Wilson, grandsons Christopher
  Birchhead, Francis Lewin, and John Sanders, and grandaus. Ann Sharp,
  Ann Lewin and Sarah Lewin, personalty
Test: Joseph Richardson, Joseph Galloway (Quaker) and William Fowrd
(Md. Cal. Wills, Vol. VIII, p. 83; Wills, Liber 22, folio 178)

Henry Childs; Anne Arundel Co.; £907.15.3; 5 Dec 1740; 24 Jan 1741; next of kin: Henry Childs, Lewis Lewin; ex. Sarah Sanders (Quaker); (26.319)

1. Henry Child, Jr. (2), b. England; d. ca 1736; m. 20 Nov 1709 West River to Margaret Preston; d. 1719; d/o John Preston; she m/2 7 Jun 1737 Jerome Plummer; following will of John Preston confirms marriage of Margaret and Henry; children:

    1-1 Cassandra Child  1-6 Ann Child
    1-2 Elizabeth Child  1-7 Cephas Child
    1-3 Margaret Child  1-8 William Child
    1-4 Ruth Child    1-9 Lurana Child
    1-5 Henry Child

Henry Child: Certificate to Western Virginia; 22 d. 1 mo. 1705/6
Henry Child: Presents paper condemning himself for seeking a wife not educated in the way of truth; 23 d. 10 mo. 1709 (Quaker Records of So. Md.)

Will of JOHN PRESTON, Anne Arundel Co.; 19 Aug 1719; 18 Dec 1719
To son William and dau. Margaret Childe, 5s
To dau. Elizabeth Trott and hrs., dwelling plantation *Bersheba*; shd. she die without issue, sd. plantation to pass to son William and dau. Margaret Childe, equally
Ex.: Son-in-law Thomas Trott
Test: Henry Childe, Jr., John Brown, Wm. Ludwigg, Mary Skinbnor
      (Md. Cal. Wills, Vol. IV, p. 217; Wills, Liber 15, folio 241)

Indenture; 19 Sep 1724; 17 Feb 1724; Henry Child, Jr. of Anne Arundel Co. purchased a tract of land called *Dear Bought* for £117 on the Western Branch of the Patuxent from Epharim Gover of Calvert County; containing 212 acres; acknowledged by Mary Gover, wife of Epharim (Land Records, Liber I, folio 613).

Henry Childs, Jr., Anne Arundel Co.; £980/8/6; 25 Jun 1736; 18 Aug 1736; next of kin, William Wilson, Nathaniell Smith; admx. Margret Childs (21.426).

14 Nov 1738; Account of Henry Childs mentions payment to the following who married daughters of Henry Childs: Nathan Smith, John Sanders, Micajah Plummer; mentions minors Ruth, Henry, Ann, Cephas, William and Lawrence [Lurana] (16.325).

[Note: The following Cassandra has been called Cassandra Elizabeth in some family histories. The will of [4.] Sarah Sanders calls Elizabeth dau.-

in-law and other records appear to prove that Elizabeth and Cassandra were two different daus. of Henry Child, Jr.]

1-1 Cassandra Child, b. 1713 St. James Parish; d. by 16 Feb 1785 Anne Arundel Co.; m. 11 d. 2 mo. 1735 Nathan Smith, b. ca 1694; d. 25 Nov 1751; s/o Nathan Smith and Elizabeth Coale; children:
        11-1 Lurana Smith
        11-2 Mordecai Smith
        11-3 Margaret Smith
        11-4 Daniel Smith
        11-5 Hester Smith

WILL of NATHAN SMITH, Calvert Co.; oral declaration 24 Nov 1751; probate 7 Apr 1752
Richard Crosbey and John Elliet, being sworn, state that they were with Nathan Smith the night before he died, and that he desired them to take notice that his will was that his wife shd. be possessed with all his estate during her widowhood, after his debts were paid
Son Mordica, might have the great table, chest of drawers and slaves
To dau. Margett, Negro Ned
Rest of estate to his children (unnamed)
Signed: John Smith
Wit: Richard Crosbey and John Elliet
        (Md. Cal. Wills, Vol. X, p. 204; Wills, Liber 28, folio 270)

WILL of CASSANDRA SMITH, Calvert Co.; 7 Oct 1775; 16 Feb 1785
To son Daniel Smith, *Welch Poole*
To grandau. Ann Taneyhill
To grandson Morecai Plummer, s/o dau. Hester
To dau. Hester, negro woman Nell
To grandson Mordecai Plummer, negroes
To grandau. Ann Taneyhill, Negroes
To dau. Margaret Hinman, 5s
To dau. Lurana Tanyhill, 5s
Sons: Mordecai Smith, Daniel Smith
Dau: Hester Plummer
Wit: Plummer Ijames, Joseph Williams, Bazil Barry, John Ijames
        (Wills, Box S, folio 78)

11-1 Lurana Smith, b. ca 1736 Calvert Co.; m. John Taneyhill; s/o Philip Taneyhill; known children:

> 111-1 Leonard Taneyhill, b. ca 1757 Calvert Co.; m. 3 Oct 1778 Ann Anly
> 111-2 John Taneyhill, Jr., b. ca 1758 Calvert Co.; m. Eleanor Sunderland
> 111-3 Eleanor Taneyhill, b. ca 1760
> 111-4 Cassandra Taneyhill; m. [19-2] John Zachariah Child
> 111-5 Mordecai Taneyhill, b. ca 1767; d. ca 1837; m. Eliza Stone
> 111-6 Thomas Taneyhill, b. ca 1770 Calvert Co.
> 111-7 William Taneyhill, b. ca 1774
> 111-8 Hannah Taneyhill, b. ca 1775; m. William C. Fowler

11-2 Mordecai Smith, b. 9 Dec 1737; d. after 1775; m. before 1775 Phoebe Finch, b. 3 Nov 1740 Calvert Co.; d. after 1777; d/o Capt. William Finch, Jr. and Priscilla _____; Mordecai disowned 25 d. 5 mo. 1764 (Quaker Records of So. Md.); children:

> 112-1 Fielder Bowie Smith, b. 14 Nov 1775 Calvert Co.; d. 20 Jun 1844 Smithville, Calvert Co.; m/1 23 Jun 1802 Sarah Plummer of Prince George's Co.; m/2 Lucy Middleton Smith; d/o William Smith of Georgetown
> 112-2 Mordecai Finch Smith, b. 25 Nov 1777 Calvert Co.; d. 10 Jul 1835; m/1 8 Feb 1810 Jane M. Boswell; m/2 Ann Wheeler Kent

England: Will of Phoebe Finch; 8 Sep 1756; 18 Feb 1757; To granddaughter Phoebe Finch, if in Potenxent, MD £20; residuary legatee and sole executrix, my dau., Elizabeth Higginson (Md. Gleamings in England - Bowie)

> 11-3 Margrett Smith; was this the Margaret Smith who obtained certificate to Pennsylvania 29 d. 11 mo. 1754?; m. _____ Hinman
> 11-4 Daniel Smith; was this the Daniel Smith who was disowned 25 d. 9 mo. 1767 for "debauching a young woman"?
> 11-5 Hester Smith; m. [1(10)-3] Joseph Plummer; d. 1789

1-2 Elizabeth Child; d. before 18 Jul 1774; m. 1st cousin [4-1] John
  Sanders, Jr.; s/o Sarah Child and John Sanders, Sr.; children under
  father's family
1-3 Margaret Child; m. [1-8] Micajah Plummer; no known children
1-4 Ruth Child, b. after 1717; d. ca 1794; m. [5-7] Plummer Ijams; d.
  ca 1792; children listed under father's family
1-5 Henry Child (3), b. ca 1721; age 35 in 1756; Quaker; age 46 in
  1768 Anne Arundel Co. (Md. Deponents); d. 11 Sep 1772, killed by
  lightning at his plantation, part of *Anne Arundel Manor* (Md. Gazette);
  m. by 1742 Jemina Pottenger, b. after 1719; d. Jan 1785 Anne
  Arundel Co.; d/o Samuel Pottenger and Elizabeth Tyler; 31 Jan
  1742 sold for £60 2 tracts of land in Calvert Co. on the Patuxent
  River called *Archer's Hay*; his wife Jemina waived dower rights
  (Anne Arundel Gentry); inv. 8 Dec 1772; acct. 13 Aug 1777; final acct. 1
  Oct 1778; in 1776 Jemima was in St. James Parish, Anne Arundel
  Co. with 4 white boys, 2 white girls and 3 slaves (census); Jemima
  assessed 1783 on Lyon's Creek, *Portland Manor*; children not in
  order of birth:

  15-1 Samuel Childs           15-6 Joseph Childs
  15-2 William Childs          15-7 Mary Childs
  15-3 John Childs             15-8 Susannah Childs
  15-4 Cephas Childs           15-9 Elizabeth Childs
  15-5 Henry Childs

In the abstract of the will of Henry Childs in Vol. XIV, *Maryland Calendar of Wills* son William is not named, "brother Henry" is a rather ambiguously phrased, and *Wickham* and *Pottengers Discovery* are listed as two plantations. The following abstract of the will is from the records of Anne Arundel County.

WILL of HENRY CHILDS, *Portland Manor*, Anne Arundel Co.; 12 Dec
  1767; 6 Oct 1772
To Henry Childs, son of Cephas, *Smithsfield*; if Henry dies without heirs,
  then to his brother William
To my brother William Child
To son Henry, *Thomson Pasture*, Frederick Co.
To son John, part of *Thomson Hopyard*, Frederick Co.
To son William, *Wickham and Pottengar's Discovery* in Frederick Co.
To son Samuel, *Gowry Banks* in Anne Arundel Co.

To son Cephas, 40 acres of *Portland Manor*; 60 acres of *His Lordship's Manor*; if Cephas die without issue, then to Joseph
To wife Jemima, Negro woman Easter, boy Joe
Ex.: Jemima
Wit: Gerard Hopkins (Quaker), Benjamin Brasshears, Jonathan Brasshears, Francis Murphe (mark)  (Anne Arundel Wills, Liber 38, folio 827)
10 Oct 1772; Jemima gives up ex. to Samuel and William

WILL of JEMIMA CHILDS, widow of Anne Arundel Co.; 20 Dec 1784; 26 Jan 1785
To son Cephas Childs, household goods
To son Joseph Childs, household goods
To dau. Susanna Childs; Negro woman Easter, age ca 35, household goods
To dau. Mary Gott, negro man Joe, age ca 25 years
To Cephas and Joseph, remainder of estate
To remaining children, nothing more than what they have already
Exs.: sons Cephas and Joseph
Wit: Isaac Owens, Samuel Sheckell, Sam Ward, Jr.
(Wills, Anne Arundel Co., Book TG1:34, p. 241)

15-1 Samuel Childs, b. by 1750; d. by 30 Apr 1782 Anne Arundel Co.; m. 22 May 1770 St. James Parish, Anne Arundel Co. to [17-2] Sarah Childs; in 1772 he was ex. of Henry Childs; 1776 census St. James Parish shows Samuel head of household with 1 white woman, 1 white girl, 2 white boys; 7 slaves

15-2 William Childs, b. by 1750; d. will filed 13 Jan 1818 Montgomery Co., MD; m. 13 Dec 1781 Prince George's Co. to Mary Willett; will filed 22 Apr 1819 Montgomery Co.; 1776 St. James Parish, no dependents; 1800 census Montgomery Co. age 45+; children from his will:

152-1 Elizabeth Childs
152-2 Eleanor Childs
152-3 Joseph Childs
152-4 Cephas Childs
152-5 Mary Childs
152-6 Enos Childs
152-7 William Childs
152-8 Henry Childs
152-9 Edmond P. Childs

15-3 John Childs, b. by 1755; d. ca 1800/10 Anne Arundel Co.; m/1 on 7 Jan 1778 St. James Parish, Anne Arundel Co. to Ann Owens, d/o Isaac Owens and Priscilla Norman; in 1790 & 1800 census Anne Arundel Co.; children from estate settlement of her uncle Thomas Owens (Chancery Case 3875, Anne Arundel Co. 1815) and will of Elizabeth Childs:

153-1 Isaac Childs; d. 1815; m. 28 Feb 1810 Elizabeth Deale; d/o Samuel Deale
153-2 Elizabeth Childs; d. 1818; unmarried (Will, Anne Arundel Co., Box C, folio 32)
153-3 Ann Childs; m. 3 Mar 1816 Benjamin Sunderland
153-4 Rebecca Childs
153-5 Susan Childs

15-4 Cephas Childs, b. by 1760; d. by Oct 1804 Anne Arundel Co.; m/1 21 Jun 1785 Ann Welsh; d/o Robert Welsh; m/2 4 Apr 1801 Martha P. Elson; 1783 assessment Lyons Creek, *Child's Addition*; 1790 and 1800 census; admn. bond and inv. 1804; final acct. and distribution 1807 Anne Arundel Co.; children of m/1 listed in estate settlement, all b. Anne Arundel Co.:

154-1 Henry Childs, b. ca 1786; d. after 1807; m. 16 Feb 1809 Sotterly, St. Mary's Co. to Mary Tottle
154-2 Ann E. Childs, b. aft. 1786; d. after 1819; m. 4 May 1819 Leo Fenwick
154-3 John Childs, b. ca 1790; d. 1 Dec 1845; m. 7 Jan 1818 Sophia Drury
154-4 Benjamin Childs, b. 1 Jan 1794; bapt. 13 Jul 1794 St. James Parish; d. 30 Jul 1837 Baltimore; m. 12 May 1818 Annapolis to Elizabeth Monroe
154-5 Samuel Childs, b. ca 1796; d. ca 1833 Charles Co.; m. 4 May 1824 Prince George's Co. to Elizabeth Lamar

15-5 Henry Childs, b. by 1767; d. 1777/84 ? Montgomery Co.; inherited Frederick Co. land from 1767 will of Henry Childs; 2 Henry Childs as taxable in 1777 Montgomery Co.

15-6 Joseph Childs, b. by 1767; d. ca 1817; m. 20 May 1793 Prince George's Co. to Eleanor Soper (Pr. Geo.'s Co. Marriage Records); assessment 1783 Lyons Creek, Anne Arundel Co.; children from distr. of estate by Eleanor Childs 15 Nov 1817 (JG#3, folio 61):

156-1 Jonathon Childs
156-2 Nathan Childs
156-3 Juliana Childs
156-4 William Childs
156-5 Mary Childs
156-6 Henry Lloyd Childs

15-7 Mary Childs, b. after 1767; d. after 1784 ; m. 5 Sep 1783 Anne Arundel Co. to Ezeckial Gott

15-8 Susanna Childs, b. 22 Aug 1769; d. 10 Sep 1843 Anne Arundel Co. (tombstone); m. 7 Nov 1789 to Robert Carr; mentioned in 1784 will of Jemima Childs

15-9 Elizabeth Childs, b. 1 Oct 1749; d. 22 Apr 1824 Meade Co., KY; m. 7 Dec 1770 St. James Parish, Anne Arundel Co. to her cousin Jonathon Simmons, b. 1 Oct 1740 Prince George's Co. (Simmons Bible); d. 22 Apr 1824 Mead Co., KY; s/o Richard Simmons and Susanna Pottenger; children born St. John's Parish, Prince George's Co.:

159-1 William Simmons, b. by 1782
159-2 Samuel Simmons, b. 2 Jun 1772; d. by 8 May 1820; m. 26 Sep 1797 Bruckner Co., KY to Elizabeth Scott
159-3 Richard Simmons, b. ca 1773; d. after 1797; m. 19 Sep 1797 Sophia Hart
159-4 Susannah Simmons, b. 7 Sep 1775; d. after 1821; m. Richard Welch 5 Jun 1793 Prince George's Co.
159-5 Robert Simmons, b. ca 1779; d. after 1802; m. 18 Sep 1802 Chloe Chenowith
159-6 Henry Childs Simmons, b. by 1780; d. after 1800 KY; m. Elizabeth _____
159-7 Cephas Simmons, b. by 1780; d. after 1800; m. 8 May 1800 Synthia Shain

159-8 Jonathon Simmons, b. 2 May 1781; d. after 1810; m. 11 Jan 1810 Mary Troutman
159-9 Joseph Simmons, b. 2 Feb 1783; d. after 1806; m. 8 Jul 1806 Charity Scott
159-10 Tyler Simmons, b. by 1793; d. after 1813; m. 16 Feb 1813 Margaret Woods
159-11 Enos Simmons, b. by 1800; d. after 1819; m. 29 Jul 1819 Alice Scott
159-12 Elizabeth Simmons; d. after 1824

1-6 Ann Child, b. after 1717; d. by 1763; ? m. Samuel Purnell; d. ca 1761; widow Ann Purnell (Test. Papers 38.254)

Estate of Samuel Purnell, Anne Arundel Co.; £72/8/5; 2 Mar 1763; next of kin: Robert and John Pottinger; admn. Henry Child (80.332).

1-7 Cephas Childs, b. after 1717; d. before 15 Jun 1768 Anne Arundel Co.; m. Susannah _____; d. after 1778; Cephas' estate admn. by his brother Henry who died in 1772; son Henry takes over in 1773 and he d. in 1778; Sarah, widow of Henry, takes over in 1777 and estate settled in 1778; children listed in orphans court; all children b. Anne Arundel Co.:

Cephas Child, Anne Arundel Co.; £268/3/3; 8 Jun 1768; 26 Aug 1768; next of kin, William Child, Susannah Child; admn. Henry Child (99.93).

17-1 Henry Childs, b. before 1750; d. before 11 Jul 1778; m/1 Mary Scrivener; m/2 1770 St. James Parish to Sarah Scrivener; Henry adm. of Cephas Childs (Acct., L. 68, f. 290); Sarah adm. of Henry's estate 1778 (Box 1, f. 19, EV#1, f., 81); she m/2 10 Dec 1778 John Holliday; children from guardian bonds:

171-1 Elizabeth Childs, b. ca 1772; d. after 1788; m. 13 Sep 1788 Richard Parrott
171-2 Cephas Childs; m. 25 Dec 1794 Phoebe Tannihill
171-3 Mary Childs, b. 25 Dec 1776; d. after 1792; m. 10 Dec 1791 Joseph Bryan Dailey

17-2 Sarah Childs, b. before 1755; d. after 1783; m. 22 May 1770 St. James Parish to [15-1] Samuel Childs
17-3 Benjamin Childs, b. before 1761; d. after 1781; m. 18 Oct 1781 St. James Parish to Mary Roberts
17-4 Elizabeth Childs, b. bef. 1768; d. after 1778
17-5 Martha Childs; d. after 1778
17-6 Ann Childs; d. after 1778;
17-7 _____ Childs (f); ? m. William Larkin bef. 10 Aug 1778 when he signed receipt for Cephas Childs' estate
17-8 William Childs, b. ca 1768; d. after 1778 (Orphans Ct., MHR 9524)

Cephas Child of Anne Arundel Co.; £268/3/3; 8 Jun 1768; 26 Aug 1768; next of kin: William Child, Susannah Child; admn. Henry Child (99.93).

1-8 Lurana Childs, b. after 1717
1-9 William Childs, b. after 1728; d. by 1777; m. Anne Arundel Co. to Elizabeth _____; d. by 1792; William Childs, orphan of Henry, 12 Jun 1749 chose Nathan Smith as guardian (Judgments ISB #1, f. 197); next of kin to [1-7] Cephas Childs in estate settlement of 1768; 17 Dec 1777 Inv. Anne Arundel Co.; Elizabeth Childs, admn (EV#1, f. 49); children from mother's estate:

19-1 Elizabeth Childs
19-2 John Zachariah Childs, b. bef. 1766 Anne Arundel Co.; d. before 1797 Anne Arundel Co.; m. [111-1] Cassandra Taneyhill, b. ca 1765 Calvert Co.; d. bef. 1800 Anne Arundel Co.; d/o Lurana Smith and John Taneyhill

192-1 William Childs, b. 1786 Anne Arundel Co.; m. 5 Feb 1812 Elizabeth Fisher
192-2 Lurana Childs, b. ca 1788 Anne Arundel Co.; d. ca 1806 Anne Arundel Co.; m. 6 Mar 1805 George Scrivener; Lurana found in guardian records 1800-1803 (JG#1, f. 253, 258, 288 & Ct. Min. 4802, F, 101).
192-3 John Childs, b. 1789 Anne Arundel Co.; d. 21 Mar 1815 Annapolis (Md. Gazette); m. 3 Feb 1812 Annapolis to Mary Anne Hyde; John found in guardian bonds 1800-1810; guardians were Anne Child and Isaac Simmons (Box 47, f. 46; Box 97, f. 98).

192-4 Levy Childs, b. 1792 Anne Arundel Co.; d. after 1807
192-5 Cassandra Childs, b. 1794 Anne Arundel Co.; d. ca 1826 Calvert Co.; m. 22 Jan 1817 MD Somerset Bowen; Cassandra found in guardian bonds 1800-1810; guardians were Anne Child and Isaac Simmons (Box 47, f. 46; Box 7, f. 98).

19-3 Mary Childs; m. 18 Mar 1784 Lewis Fisher
19-4 Cephas Childs, b. by 1774; d. by 10 Jun 1806 Anne Arundel Co.; m. 28 Jun 1786 Sarah Miles, b. ca 1770; d. after 1818; children b. Anne Arundel Co.:

194-1 Obediah Childs, b. by 1790; d. after 1855 Albany, IN
194-2 Mordecai Childs, b. by 1790; d. 28 Nov 1825 Floyd Co., IN; m. 29 Feb 1820 Floyd Co., IN to Anna Kendall
194-3 Mary Ann Childs, b. ca 1790; d. after 1820; m. 1807 George Scrivener; no children
194-4 Elizabeth Childs, b. after 1796; d. after 1817
194-5 Ann Childs, b. after 1796; d. after 1817
194-6 Sarah Childs, b. after 1796; d. after 1817
194-7 Sophia Childs, b. after 1796; d. after 1817
194-8 Elijah Childs, b. after 1796; d. after 1817; no children

19-5 Ann Childs; m. 22 Feb 1784 Isaac Simmons; child:

195-1 George Simmons, b. ca 1788; d. 1837; m. Nov 1816 Marianna Ewell Weems (1798-1839)

19-6 Eleanor "Nelly" Childs; m. 25 Sep 1792 Ebenezer Plummer
19-7 Sarah Childs; m. 1794 Abel Hill
19-8 Barbary Childs

2. Cephas Child, b. England; m. ca 1717 Bucks Co., PA to Mary Atkinson (IGI); he inherited land in Pennsylvania purchased from William Penn; children born Plumstead Twp., Bucks Co., PA (IGI):

2-1 Henry Child, b. 22 Jan 1717; d. by 1725 PA
2-2 Cephas Child, b. 30 Oct 1718; d. ca 1727 PA
2-3 John Child, b. 10 Jun 1720; d. by 1730 PA
2-4 Isaac Child, b. 1 Mar 1722; d. by 1734 PA

2-5 Abraham Child, b. ca 1724
2-6 Henry Child, b. 1 Jan 1725
2-7 Cephas Child, b. 18 Jan 1727; d. by 1768
2-8 John Child, b. 14 Jun 1730
2-9 Isaac Child, b. 14 Mar 1734

3. Mary Child, b. by 1689 England; d. by 1731; m. ca 28 d. 10 mo. 1705 Richard Lewin; d. by 1761; he m/2 after 1731 Sarah Purnell; d. ca 1776 Anne Arundel Co. (Will, 41.226); d/o John and Mary Purnell and widow of Daniel Smith (___-1728); Smith children were Daniel, Elizabeth and Alice; Mary Purnell, widow of John, m. Josias Towgood (___-1734); will of Mary Towgood mentions eldest dau. Sarah Lewin (Md. Cal. Wills, Vol. X, p. 88); children from Anne Scrivener Agee:

3-1 Mary Lewin, b. by 1715; d. ca 1772 Anne Arundel Co.; m. ca 1732 John Scrivener, b. ca 1709 St. James Parish, s/o Richard Scrivener and Mary Burck; children:

31-1 Richard Scrivener, b. 26 Jan 1733 St. James Parish; d. 1762
31-2 John Scrivener, b. 22 Dec 1735 St. James Parish; d. 1762; m. Elizabeth ?Deale
31-3 Francis Scrivener, b. ca 1742; d. 1797; m/1 ? Elizabeth Simmons; m/2 25 Nov 1794 [32-2] Eleanor ?Ward; widow of Richard Lewin and Samuel Robertson
31-4 William Scrivener; d. 1796
31-5 Elizabeth Scrivener; d. 1809; m/1 Absolom Warfield, b. 30 Apr 1733; d. ca 1767 (Wills, 36.118); s/o Alexander Warfield and Dinah Davidge; m/2 by 30 Jan 1769 George Snell; Absolom apparently died shortly after his marriage and left no children; he settled in Frederick Co. and possessed *Bear Garden* and *Spring Garden*; his estate was settled in Anne Arundel Co. 2 May 1768 naming Azel and Davidge Warfield as next of kin and Elisabeth Warfield as extx. (96.158).

3-2 Lewis Lewin; d. by 1764; m. Elizabeth _____; d. Baltimore Co. 1794; children from will, distribution of estate of Lewis, Jr., and St. James Parish:

32-1 Mary Lewin, b. 4 Oct 1736; m. William ?Simmons
32-2 Richard Lewin, b. 27 Sep 1738; d. by 10 Oct 1771 (AA Co. Inv., TG#1, f.130); m. Eleanor ?Ward; d/o Benjamin Ward and Elizabeth; Eleanor m/2 10 Feb 1773 to Samuel Robertson; she m/3 25 Nov 1794 to [31-3] Francis Scrivener
32-3 Ann Lewin, b. 2 Feb 1740/1; d. by 1791; m. John Carter
32-4 Elizabeth Lewin, b. 9 Jan 1742/3; d. by 1791
32-5 Sarah Lewin, b. 20 Dec 1744; m. 4 Apr 1780 Samuel Sudler
32-6 Henrietta Lewin, b. 4 May 1747; m. John Steele
32-7 Margret Lewin, b. 13 Mar 1748/9; bapt. 5 Sep 1749; m. John Deale
32-8 Lewis Lewin, Jr.; d. by 1785; distribution of estate lists siblings and mother Elizabeth (Inv. Box 9, folio 54; dist. JG#1, folio 22).
32-9 Samuel Lewin; m. 27 Aug 1775 Mary Lane
32-10 Francis Lewin; d. by 1791; m. 1 Mar 1778 Peter Clark
32-11 Christiana Lewin; m. ca 1775 St. James Parish Jacob Brice

WILL of LEWIS LEWIN, Anne Arundel Co.; 26 Jul 1764; 20 Sep 1764
To wife Elizabeth, furniture; if wife remarries, estate to youngest children
To son Richard, 150 acres land, part of *Birched Lott* where James Smith now lives
To 2nd son Lewis, land between branch called Shew's Mill Branch and the main branch where Skinner's Mill now stands being part of tract called *Maidstone* and part of *Meekine Hill*
To 3rd son Samuel, dwelling plantation
To dau. Christian, 50 acres part of *Burkhed's Lot*; if no heirs to dau. Sarah and hrs.
To my several children by names, as a legacy to each child, slaves: Richard, Henrarita, Margaret, Lewis, Francis and Christian, 1 slave each; Sarah and Samuel, 2 slaves each
Ex. Wm. Simmond, Jr.
Wit: Lewis Lewin, Samuel Robertson (Quaker), Francis and Thos. Whittington  (Md. Cal. Wills, Vol. XIII, p. 42; Wills, Liber 32, folio 261)

3-3 Francis Lewin, b. by 1731; d. by 1761; did not sign papers for father's estate
3-4 Ann Lewin, b. by 1731; m. Anne Arundel Co. to John Griffith
3-5 Sarah Lewin; m. William Johnson

4. Sarah Child, b. England; d. ca 1754; m. by 1731 John Sanders; d. by 1748; known child:

    4-1 John Sanders, b. by 1731

Will of SARAH SANDERS, Anne Arundel Co.; 4 d. 2 mo. (April) 1748; 19 Apr 1754

To grand-son Henry Childs Sanders, plantation I live on being the late dwelling of my dec'd father Henry Childs, after decease of his father, John Sanders; if said grand-son dies before age 21 without issue, plantation to be sold and money divided with my 4 grand-children: Ann Sanders, Sarah, Elizabeth and Edward, or the survivors of them
To grand-son Henry Childs Sanders, £10, furniture
To grand-dau. Ann Sanders, certain slaves
To grand-dau. Sarah Sanders, certain slaves
To grand-dau. Eliz. Sanders, certain slaves
To grand-son Edward Sanders, certain slaves
To dau-in-law Elizabeth Sanders, £10
To cousin Richard Lewin, son of my nephew Lewis Lewin, £5
Ex. son John Sanders
Wit: D. Noones [David Weems], Lewis Lewin, Cephis Child
                    (Md. Cal. Wills, Vol. XI, p. 21; Wills, Liber 29, folio 102)

Sarah Sanders, Anne Arundel Co.; £659/7/9; 28 May 1754; 12 Nov 1754; appraised by D. Weems, Nehemiah Birckhead; next of kin Lewis Lewin, William Simmons, Jr.; ex. Elisabeth Sanders (Quaker) (57.443).

4-1 John Sanders, b. by 1718; d. ca 1754; m. by 1738 1st cousin [1-2] Elizabeth Childs, b. ca 1718, age 47 in 1765; children from mother's will:

    41-1 Henry Childs Sanders, b. between 1727 & 1748; was this the same person: reference to scandalous practice of Henry Sanders, disowned 24 d. 6 mo. 1763 (Quaker Records of So. Md.)

    41-2 Ann Sanders, b. by 1748; d. ca 1788 Anne Arundel Co. (Wills, JG#1, F48)

    41-3 Sarah Sanders, b. by 1748; m. Samuel Maynard; children:

        413-1 Elizabeth Maynard
        413-2 Ann Maynard

41-4 Elizabeth Sanders, b. by 1748; m/1 31 ___ 1772 St. James Parish to Knighton Simmons, b. 1 Mar 1745/6 St. James Parish; d. ca 1774; s/o George Simmons and Margaret; m/2 21 Dec 1775 St. James Parish to William Hayes

41-5 Edward Sanders, b. by 1748; m. ___; known child:

415-1 John Sanders

41-6 John Sanders; b. after 1748; not named in grandmother's will

John Sanders appr. estate of Rev. John Lang, Anne Arundel Co.; 1 May 1749; 5 Jul 1749 (39.187); John Sanders creditor estate of James Trott, Anne Arundel Co.; 16 Feb 1748; 11 Aug 1749 (40.47); appr. estate of Sarah Robertson, Calvert Co., 16 Mar 1751; 26 Jun 1752 (48.544)

John Sanders, Anne Arundel Co.; £421/0/8; 8 May 1754; 12 Nov 1754; appr. D. Neemes, Nehemiah Birckhead; next of kin, Lewis Lewin, William Simmons, Jr.; admx. Elisabeth Sanders, Quaker (57.445).

WILL of ELIZABETH SANDERS, Anne Arundel Co.; 1 Dec 1773; 18 Jul 1774
To son Henry Childs Sanders, 1s
To dau. Ann, dwelling house and 50 acres, also slaves and personal property
To dau. Sarah Maynard and granddaughters Elizabeth Maynard and Ann Maynard
To dau Elizabeth Simmons
To son Edward Sanders; to grandson John Sanders not yet 21, s/o Edward
To son John Sanders
Ex. dau. Ann
Wit: Marmaduke Wyvill, James Trott, Isaac Simmons (Wills, Box S, folio A)

Estate of Elisabeth Sanders, Anne Arundel Co.; £575/5/3; 22 Aug 1774; 30 Aug 1774; next of kin: E. Simmons, William Maynard; ex. Ann Sanders (119.94).

Balance and Final Distribution, Estate of Eliza Sanders; 15 Oct 1775; Ex. Ann Sanders; receipts from: Elizabeth Simmons, John Sanders, Edward Sanders, Edward Sanders for his son John, Samuel Maynard, husband of Sarah and Samuel Maynard, father of Ann and Elizabeth (Liber 7, folio 35)

5. Ruth Child, b. England; m/1 12 Nov 1714 West River to John Wilson (3); d. ca 1723; m/2 16 Jul 1724 All Hallow's Parish to Henry

Roberts (called Robins in her father's will); acct. of Henry Roberts 7 May 1725 (6.322); no known children

John Wilson, Anne Arundel Co.; £107/13/2; 12 Mar 1723; next of kin: Henry Child, Jr., and William Wilson; admx. Ruth Wilson (8.292).

John Wilson (1), (ca 1630-1690); came to Md. ca 1656 with John Burrage and Gerard Hopkins; owned *Burrage* and 1,000 acres *Friendship* in Baltimore Co.; his son John Wilson (2) (ca 1665-1702); his sons were John Wilson (3), Joseph Wilson (to Harford Co.) and William Wilson (Baltimore County Families).

Was this the Henry Roberts who, after the death of his wife Anne, m. Ruth after the death of John Wilson? Henry Roberts, b. after 1662; s/o Andrew Roberts and Jane Hopkins of Anne Arundel Co. (Md. Cal. Wills, Vol. I, p. 106); m. 10 Dec 1699 to Anne Hopkins; d/o Gerard Hopkins; their children were Sarah Roberts, bur. 21 Jul 1711, John Roberts, bapt. 29 Mar 1711, Henry Roberts, bapt. 10 Sep 1712 (Anne Arundel Church Records). In 1706 John Chapell wrote a will leaving his estate to Anne Roberts, wife of Henry Roberts, and her son John Roberts; this will also mentions her sister Mary who m. Thomas Wells and her sister Thomasin who m. John Welch (Md. Cal. Wills, Vol. IV, p. 17).

6. Rachel Child, b. England; mi(1). 8 d. 2 mo. 1715 William Wilson; s/o John Wilson and Margaret Kidd; d/o William and Margaret Kidd of Calvert Co. (Md. Cal. Wills, Vol. II, p. 64); children:

6-1 John Wilson
6-2 Benkid Wilson
6-3 William Wilson
6-4 Henry Wilson

7. Ann Child, b. England; d. 27 Aug 1708 Anne Arundel Co.; m. ca 21 d. 2 mo. 1704 Solomon Birckhead; d. ca 1742; in Talbot Co. by 1717 when he wit will of Andrew Skinner (Md. Cal. Wills, Vol. IV, p. 150); children:

       7-1 Christopher Birckhead
       7-2 Ann Birckhead

Solomon Birckhead was probably the son of Christopher Birckhead whose will made in England and probated Anne Arundel Co. 26 May 1676 mentioning only son Nehemiah (Md. Cal. Wills, Vol. I, p. 171). The will of Abraham Birkehead written 7 Jan 1684, probate 1685, mentions land bought of brother Christopher and names contingent legatees as nephews Nehemiah, Eleazer and Solomon Birkehead (Md. Cal. Wills, Vol. I, p. 161).

Will of SOLOMON BIRCKHEAD, Talbot Co.; 31 May 1741; 3 May 1742
To dau. Ann Sharp, 320 a. pt. of *Little Brisstoll*, at her death to pass to her son Birckhead (Sharp)
To grandson Christopher (Birckhead), 400 acre part of *Little Bristoll* where his mother now lives
To grandson Solomon (Birckhead), dwell. plan. and residue of real estate
To grandchil. Peter, Birckhead and Ann Sharp, Christopher
To grandson Solomon (Birckhead), dwell. plan. and residue
To dau. Ann Sharp and child. of son Christopher, residue of personalty, that share last named to be delivered to their mother Ann for their maintenance
Trustee for child. of son Christopher, John Dickinson
Ex.: Son-in-law Dr. Wm. Sharp
Test: Jno. Dickinson, Samuel Sharp (Quaker), Ann Birckhead
(Md. Cal. Wills, Vol. VIII, p. 175; Wills, Liber 22, folio 481)
Note: At date of probate of will, Ann Birckhead signed as Ann Sharp, wife of Samuel

Solomon Birchhead; Talbot Co.; £28.222; 19 Mar 1742; 27 Oct 1743; next of kin: Solomon Sharp, John Dickenson; admn./ex. William Sharp (Quaker); (28.222)

7-1 Christopher Birckhead, b. 17 d. 11 mo. 1705, 5th day of week ca 6 a.m. (Quaker Rec. of So. Md.); d. ca 1740 Talbot Co.; s/o Solomon and Ann; m. 1729 Ann Harrison; she m/2 on 2 Jun 1741 Samuel Sharp; d. ca 1745; m/3 4 Feb 1747 William Troth, Jr.; d. ca 1748; m/4 _____ Brooke; m/5 Daniel Powell; [the Powell, Troth and Sharp families (Quakers) of the Eastern Shore were related by marriage (Md. Cal. Wills, Vol. I, p. 188; Vol. VI, p. 221)]; children:

71-1 Christopher Birckhead  By her m/2: 71-4 Peter Sharp
71-2 Solomon Birckhead  By her m/3: 71-5 _____ Troth
71-3 Rachel Birckhead  By her m/4: 71-6 Harrison Brooke

Christopher Birchhead; Talbott Co.; £532.5.9; 26 Aug 1740; 3 Dec 1740; next of kin: Solomon Birchhead, William Sharp; admn/ex. An Birchhead (Quaker) (25.357)

Will of SAMUEL SHARP, Talbot Co., planter; 19 May 1743; 8 Apr 1745
To wife Ann Sharp, my estate. Written on back: Talbot Co., Ann, the wife of Wm. Troth, being one of the people called Quakers, made her solemn affirmation and declared she saw Samuel Sharp, dec'd, write his name to the within will; John Dickenson, being one of the people called Quakers, made his affirmation, and declared he was acquainted with sd. Samuel Sharp, dec'd; Thomas Barnett, Jr. made oath who states he was acquainted with the sd. Samuel Sharp; the widow made her election
(Md. Cal. Wills, Vol. IX, p. 142; Wills, Liber 25, folio 267)

WILL of ANNE POWELL, Talbot Co., widow of Daniel Powell; 13 Jul 1758; 5 Aug 1758
Children: Christopher Birkhead, Peter Sharp and Harrison Brooke (my 3 children)
Grandchildren: Henry, William and Ann Troth; Elizabeth Macmanus (Macmans)
Ex. Christopher Birkhead
Wit: Daniel Dickinson (Quaker), Daniel Maynadier, John Flood
(Md. Cal. Wills, Vol. XI, p. 209; Wills, Liber 30, folio 533)

71-1 Christopher Birckhead; next of kin to Peter Sharp 1769
(115.70)
71-2 Solomon Birckhead; d. ca 1754; unmarried

Will of SOLOMAN BIRCKHEAD, Talbot Co.; 10 Dec 1753; 8 Jan 1754
To bro. Christopher Birckhead, lands lying in above said county, known by name of *Little Bristole*; 2 slaves
To nephew Henry Troth, 1 slave
To niece Elizabeth Troth, 1 slave
To sister Rachel Birckhead, slaves
To mother Ann Brooke, 1 slave
Ex. mother
Wit. Wm. Dickinson, Wm. Cary, Pierce Jones
(Md. Cal. Wills, Vol. XI, p. 9; Wills, Liber 29, folio 38)

71-3 Rachel Birckhead; unmarried 1753; ? m. Pollard Edmondson; Rachel Edmondson next of kin to Peter Sharp 1769 (115.70)

71-4 Peter Sharp, Jr.

71-5 William Troth; m. \_\_\_\_\_ \_\_\_\_\_; children:

715-1 Henry Troth; called nephew in 1754 will of Solomon Birckhead; called grandchild in 1758 will of Anne Powell
715-2 Elizabeth Troth; called niece in 1754 will of Solomon Birckhead; called grandchild in 1758 will of Anne Powell
715-3 Ann Troth; called grandchild in 1758 will of Anne Powell

71-6 Harrison Brooke

7-2 Ann Birckhead, b. 18 d. 10 mo. 1707 (Quaker Rec. of So. Md.); d/o Solomon and Ann; d. after 1748; m. Dr. Wm. Sharp; d. 1748; she m/2 1749 Michael Hacket (Md. Marriages); children:

72-1 Peter Sharp            72-4 William Sharp
72-2 Birckhead Sharp        72-5 Henry Sharp
72-3 Ann Sharp

Will of WILLIAM SHARP, Talbot Co., surgeon; 13 Apr 1748; 21 Dec 1748
To wife Ann Sharp, my lands on the south side of Island Creek called *Rattle Snake Point, Saxon's Neck, Eason's Lot, Fancy Conjure, Sharp's Addition* and the enclosure, until son William is of age 21
At decease of wife, I give son Peter Sharp, sd. lands on the north side of the creek, *Morefields Adventure* and *Dines Point*
To son Henry Sharp, tract; in default of hrs., give sd land to son William
To dau. Ann Sharp, 1 slave
Mentions: my 5 children: Peter, Birkhead, Wm., Henry and Ann Sharp
Exs. wife Ann Sharp and son Peter Sharp
Wit: Francis Chaplin, Samuell Mulliken, Sarah Webb (Quaker)
(Md. Cal. Wills, Vol. IX, p. 188; Wills, Liber 25, folio 510)

Dr. William Sharp, Talbot Co.; £928/19/1; 27 Feb 1748; 4 Nov 1749; next of kin: Solomon Sharp, Ann Sharp; Ex.: Ann Hacket, wife of Michael Hacket (41.309).

72-1 Peter Sharp; d. ca 1752 Talbot Co.; unmarried

WILL of PETER SHARP, Talbot Co.; 14 Oct 1751; 9 Jun 1752
To bros. William and Henry Sharpe, all money I have in hands of Michel Hackett, as well for commission on the estate on my dec'd father; remainder pt. of father's estate to be equally divided between them
To uncle Solomon Sharp, son of Solomon Sharp, slaves, in token of love I have for his sd. father
To sister Nancy Sharp, 2 tracts devised me by my father called *Morefield* and *Adventure* and 38 a. I bought of John Padison
To bros. William and Henry
Ex.: Uncle Solomon Sharp
Wit: Edmnd. Delahuntey, Philip McManus, Obediah James
(Md. Cal. Wills, Vol. X, p. 225; Wills, Liber 28, folio 350)

Peter Sharpe of Talbot Co.; £378/7/6; 22 Aug 1752; 22 Sep 1752; next of kin: William Sharp, Michael Hackett; admn. ex. Solomon Sharp (Quaker) (51.42).

Solomon Sharp apparently died intestate and unmarried between 1752 and 1754; next of kin Richard and William Sharpe (58.330). The appraisers of his estate were Tristram Thomas and Thomas Stevens, the same persons who appraised Peter's estate. Ann Cox was the admnx. of both estates which were filed consecutively in Talbot Co.

Peter Sharpe, Talbot Co.; £51/8/9; 30 Aug 1754; 26 Oct 1754; next of kin: Anne Hackett, William Sharpe; admn. Ann Cox, wife of Powell Cox (Quaker) (58.344).

72-2 Birckhead Sharp; d. ca 1771; m. Margaret _____; he appraised several estates in Talbot Co.; known children:

    722-1 William Sharp
    722-2 Nancy Sharp
    722-3 Margaret Sharp
    722-4 Mary Sharp
    722-5 Catharine Sharp
    722-6 Elisabeth Sharp
    722-7 Lydia Sharp
    722-8 Unborn child

WILL of BIRCKHEAD SHARP, Talbot Co.; written 1 Feb 1771; probate 26 Mar 1771
To wife Mary, Ex.
Children: William, Nancy, Margaret, Mary, Katharine, Elizabeth, Lydia, unborn child.
Brother: William
Tract: *Bristol*
Wit: Thomas Martin, Jr., Howell Powell, Stephen Bodle
(Md. Cal. Wills, Vol. XIV, p. 164; Wills, Liber 38, folio 215)

Birkhead Sharp, Talbot Co.; £427/13/3; 6 May 1771; 10 Aug 1773; next of kin: Samuel Sharp, Nancy Sharp; daus. Margaret, Mary, Catharine, Elisabeth, Lydia; ex. Margaret Sharp (115.18).

72-3 Ann "Nancy" Sharp; ? m. Powell Cox; Quaker
72-4 William Sharp, b. after 1727
72-5 Henry Sharp

8. ? John Child of Prince George's County, d. ca 1750; m/1 Sarah \_\_\_\_\_; m/2 on 31 Dec 1730 Queen Anne Parish to Elizabeth DuMolin, b. 8 Jan 1706/7; d. after 1751; d/o Dr. Gabriel DeMilliane and Ann Young who m. 31 Jan 1704 Christ Church, Calvert Co.; John and Elizabeth Childs were exs. of the will of Ann Demilane 12 Jun 1733 (L. 11, f. 701); children from his will:

   8-1 Elizabeth Child, b. 1711/2
   8-2 Henry Child
   8-3 Gabril Child
   8-4 John D'Million Child, b. 1732
   8-5 Ann Child, b. 1733/5
   8-6 Cassandra Child

 Elizabeth, 2nd wife of John, may have been the dau. of Ann Demiliane, Queen Anne Parish, Prince George's Co., whose will was written 13 Oct 1730 and probated 5 Feb 1730. Her entire estate was left to her two daughters, Ann and Elizabeth (Md. Cal. Wills, Vol. VI, p. 174).
 John Child wit. will of Mary Read in 1732 (Md. Cal. Wills, Vol. VII, p. 2); wit. will of Robert Beal 1740 (Md. Cal. Wills, Vol. VIII, p. 87); wit. deed of gift from David Swearingen to Samuel Swearingen enrolled 5 Apr 1718 (Liber F, folio 31).

5 Mar 1719 John Childe purchased a tract of land containing 117 acres called *Spitefull* in Prince George's Co., part of tract called *Remainder of Truman's Choice* (Liber F, folio 292). John Child one of the admns. of the estate of Sarah Odell of Prince George's Co. (Inv., Liber 12, f. 129).

Will of JOHN CHILD, Prince George's Co.; 10 Apr 1750; 27 Jun 1750
To dau. Elizabeth Wess (?Webb), 5s money
To son Henry Child, 5s current money
To wife Elizabeth Child, tract called *Newfoundland* and 100 acres called *Orphan's Gift*, to hold during her widowhood; after marriage or decease, my will is that I give afsd. tracts to son Gabrial Child
To wife 1/3 personal estate; stock; desire is that wife shall enjoy use of personal estate during her widowhood; same to be divided, at her decease, between 3 children: Gabril, Ann and Cassandra Child
Wit. Samuel Brasshear, Jacob Henderson, Morda. Jacob
(Md. Cal. Wills, Vol. X, p. 97; Wills, Liber 27, folio 330)

John Child, Prince George's Co.; £77/9/7; 24 Sep 1750; 28 Aug 1751; ex. Elisabeth Child (47.288)

8-1 Elizabeth Child, b. 11 Feb 1711/2 Queen Anne Parish; d/o John and Sarah; m. 19 Nov 1734 Thomas Webb

   81-1 Thomas Webb, b. 18 Sep 1736

8-2 Henry Child
8-3 Gabrial Child
8-4 John D'Million Child, b. 25 Nov 1732; s/o John and Elizabeth
8-5 Ann Child, b. 13 Jan 1733/4 Queen Anne Parish; d/o John and Elizabeth
8-6 Cassandra Child

9. ? William Childs; m. 9 Feb 1715/6 St. Anne's Parish Anne Arundel Co. to Mary Cook; was he possibly disowned for marrying outside the meeting?

## BOARMAN

The following persons are shown to have come into Maryland according to *Early Settlers of Maryland*, Skordas:

    Capt. William Boarman, transported prior to 1650 (5.56)
    Mary Boreman, transported 1661 (4.609)
    Richard Boreman, transported 1640 (1.63,128)
    Richard Boreman, transported 1637-40, Servant (ABH.101)
    Robert Boreman, transported 1671 (16.435)
    Sarah Boreman, transported 1651, wife of William (Q.33)
    Sarah Linle, transported 1650 (5.56)
    Sarah Lindle, transported 1651 (ABH.245)

### TWO WILLIAM BOARMANS

According to the excellent research of Mary Louise Donnelly, a Capt. William Boarman died in St. Mary's County in 1674 (Court TP#6:333). One of the appraisers of the estate was Richard Edelen; two of whose children later married Boarmans (Charles Co. Gentry). *Abstracts of the Prerogative Courts of Maryland* does not contain any information regarding this estate. Thomas Richard Gardiner states in his book on the Gardiner family that "a will of Capt. William Boarman was discovered showing a date of probate of 1684" (no documentation). He makes no comment on the contents of the will which is not abstracted in *Maryland Calendar of Wills*.

Donnelly notes that a William Bowman (? Boarman) was brought into the Province of Maryland in 1640 by Capt. Giles Brent (Patent 1:171). On 4 Feb 1651 William Boarman made a deposition regarding his being employed to kill cattle in Jun 1650 for Giles Brent on Kent Island (10:150-156). These two documents possibly refer to the same person. Do they also refer to the William Boarman who d. in St. Mary's County in 1674?

### WILLIAM BOARMAN

William Boarman was in the colony of Maryland by 1645. On 28 May 1650 he gave his age as 20 years when he made a deposition in which he described an incident which took place aboard a ship riding in St. Inegoes Creek five years previously (10:12). Thus he was b. ca 1630 in England. William was taken prisoner in Port Tobacco in 1645 during an uprising and in 1655 he "confessed" in court that he was "borne and bred" a Roman Catholic (10:426-427). Donnelly states he lived with the Jesuits when he was 15 years old. The evidence presented by Donnelly suggests he came from a Catholic family in England and was sent to the colony in the charge of Jesuit priests.

On 9 Feb 1648 William Boarman was on a jury at St. John's (4:470). Would an 18 year old have been eligible for jury duty? In 1649 a William Boarman was a wit in a court case (4:532). In 1662 Capt. William Boarman claimed 100 acres for his own immigration prior to 1650 (5:56).

The following children will be numbered according to the premise that William Boarman (1630-1708) was married to Sarah Linle, Mary Mathews and Mary Jarboe. There is no doubt there were two men named William Boarman in the province at this time and the possibility exists that these marriages are not all of the same man.

m/1: Sarah Linle was transported into the province in 1650 (5.56) and Sarah Lindle in 1651 (ABH.245) according to Skordas. On 17 May 1658 William Boarman rec'd 300 acres on the east side of the fresh run of Nangemy Creek adjoining land of Job Chandler for transporting his wife and 4 able men (Charles Co. Court Records, Liber A, folio 160) Sarah Linle is said to be the wife referred to in this document. An indenture dated 10 Nov 1658 from William Boarman of St. Mary's Co., Gent., to Richard Trew, boatwright, for 300 acres on the east side of the easternmost branch of Nangemy Creek was signed by William and Sarah Boarman (Charles Co. Court Records, Liber C, folio 120). This land, located near Portobacco, was sold by Trew to Andrew Watson 26 Feb 1661 and Watson of Stafford Co., VA sold it to Gerrard Brown 10 Nov 1668 (Charles Co. Land Records, Liber D, folio 37).

Children of William Boarman and Sarah ?Linle:
1. William Boarman, b. ca 1654
2. Sarah Boarman, b. ca 1656
3. George Boarman, b. ca 1658
4. Mary Boarman, b. ca 1660
5. Benjamin Boarman

m/2 Mary Matthews by 1674; on 4 Aug 1674 Capt. William Boarman and Mary his wife sold William Hatton a tract formerly called *Thompson's Rest* on the east side of Piscataway River and north side of Piscataway Creek of 1,000 acres resurveyed and named *Boarman's Content* (Charles Co. Land Records, Liber F, folio 25); the will of Thomas Mathews of Charles County written 9 Jan 1675 mentions dau. Mary, wife of Capt. Boarman (Md. Cal. Wills, Vol. I, p. 176).

    Child of William Boarman and Mary Matthews:
    6. Anne Boarman, b. ca 1675

m/3 by 1686 Mary Jarboe; d. 1739 (WRC#1:396, 406-7 - Donnelly); d/o John Jarboe of Dijon, France, and his wife Mary Tettershall. The will of Lt. Col. John Jarboe written 4 Mar 1664 mentions land which had already been given daughter Mary Jarboe (Md. Cal. Wills, Vol. I, p. 89). The will of Mark Cordea, St. Mary's Co., written 27 Mar 1685 mentions Mary, dau. of Col. Jarboe, deceased (Md. Cal. Wills, Vol. I, p. 159).

William Boarman, b. ca 1630, would have been ca 57 years old in 1687 when the child, Benedict Leonard Boarman, was born to William and Mary Boarman. Gardiner and Donnelly both list 5 more children born to this couple, the last in 1701. He would have been 71 years old in 1701.

    Children of William Boarman and Mary Jarboe:
    7. Elizabeth Boarman
    8. Benedict Boarman, b. ca 1687
    9. John Baptist Boarman, b. ca 1689
    10. Mary Boarman
    11. Clare Boarman
    12. Francis Ignatius Boarman, b. ca 1701

Donnelly, Gardiner and *Marriages and Deaths in St. Mary's County* all state that Mary Jarboe married by 1686 to Maj. William Boarman, b. ca 1630. Mary Jarboe Boarman m/2 by 1711 John Sanders, d. 1730 (I & A, 328.247).

WILL of WILLIAM BOARMAN, Charles Co.; written 16 May 1708; probate 17 Jun 1709

To "the intent that my son may be remembered after I depart this life at the most holy Sacrifice of the altar"...

To wife Mary personal estate and 1/2 dwelling plantation, *Boarman's Rest* during her life; wife to pay dau. Clare £10 due from debt of Ephram Leverton of North Carolina

To son Benedict and hrs., dwelling plantation, *Boarman's Rest*, provided he keep in repair the Chapell (Catholic) which is on the place; failing which, sd. plantation to pass to next heir; and personal estate

To son John Baptist and hrs., tract *Lanterman* and rents which shall be due from Edward Benson living on sd. land; and personal estate

To son Francis Ignatius and hrs., part of *St. George's Rest*, formerly belonging to Robert Green; and personal estate

To daus. Mary and Clare, personal estate and 400 acres whereon my negro Quarter is, being part of the manor

To dau. Ann Brookes and her hrs., 500 acres to be taken up by executrix

Equally to wife and 2 sons, Francis Ignatius and John Baptist, all stock of hoggs and cattle

Remainder of "goods" to be divided between 3 sons and my wife

In event of death of sons John Baptist or Francis Ignatius during minority or without issue, survivor to inherit deceased's portion, and both dying without issue or during minority, their estate to revert to son Benedict and hrs., and the latter dying during minority or without issue, his lands to pass to other two sons afsd. and hrs.

Overseers: son Benedict, Benjamin Hall, Raphael Neale

Wit: Joseph Pile, John Mudd, John Wathen

Proven at Port Tobacco in Chandler Town

Codicil: 17 Jan 1708 bequeaths 65 a. of *Lanterman* to Thomas Hagan, Sr. to correct acreage error made on former sale to Hagan; Capt. Benjamin Hall and Wm. Boarman to determine

    (Md. Cal. Wills, Vol. III, p. 140; Wills, Liber part 2-12, folio 108; Donnelly)

WILL of MARY SANDERS, Charles County; written 12 Mar 1739; probate 17 Dec 1739

To sons Benedict, John Baptist and Francis Boarman, exs., personal estate

To daus. Mary Sly, Elizabeth Hamoxly and Clare Shirbin, personalty

To priest that buries testator and the poor, personalty

Test: Nathan Roseman, Thomas Ash

    (Md. Cal. Wills, Vol. VIII, p. 58; Wills, Liber 22, folio 119)

1. William Boarman (2), b. ca 1654; d. 1720; age 60 in 1714 Charles Co. (Md. Deponents); s/o William Boarman (1) and Sarah ?Linle; m/1 by

1683 Jane Neale, d/o Capt. James Neale and Anne Gill. The will of James Neale, written 37 Nov 1683, mentions grandchild Jane Boarman, daughter of William and Jane Boarman (Md. Cal. wills, Vol. I, p. 131); account of James Neale in 1706 shows distribution to Jane Boarman (26.193). The will of Henrietta Maria (Neale) Lloyd, written 6 Apr 1697, mentions sister Jane Boarman (Md. Cal. Wills, Vol. II, p. 117). The will of Anne Neale, widow of James Neale, written 28 Jun 1697 does not mention dau. Jane but does mentions grandchildren, viz. William Boarman's child. (Md. Cal. Wills, Vol. II, p. 138). William m/2 Mary Pile; d/o Joseph Pile whose estate calls her wife of William Boarman, Jr. (26.192); Mary was given 110 acres of *Baltimore's Gift* in will of her father (Md. Cal. Wills, Vol. II, p. 49).

Accounting of estate of Joseph Pile of St. Mary's Co. shows distribution of 1/5 of estate to William Boarman who married Mary, his daughter; 11 Oct 1701 (21.149).

Children of Wm. and Jane:
1-1 Jane Boarman, b. by 1681/4
1-2 William Boarman, b. ca 1685
1-3 Henrietta Boarman, b. ca 1687
1-4 Ann Boarman, b. ca 1689
1-5 Sarah Boarman, b. ca 1691

Children of Wm. and Mary:
1-6 Joseph Boarman
1-7 Jane Boarman
1-8 Thos. James Boarman, b. ca 1703
1-9 Mary Boarman, b. ca 1705

Mr. Gardiner lists a James Boarman (1687-1715), s/o William Boarman and Jane Neale; m. ca 1710 Mary Jane Thompson; d/o William Thompson and Victoria Matthews; their children: Mary, b. 1711, James, b. 1713. Mr. Gardiner further states that Mary Boarman, b. 1711; d. 1769; m. by 1733 to William Bowling (d. 1789) and had John, William, Joseph, Francis, Mary and Thomas Bowling.

WILL of WILLIAM BOARMAN, SR., Charles County; written 8 Apr 1720; probate 23 May 1720

To son William personalty and land bet. the _____ run, and Thomas Jamson's great run that his mill stands on, reserving the use of wife Mary, dwelling plantation and use of necessary lands during life, at her decease to return to son William and hrs.

To son Joseph, tract ___ bet. lines of son-in-law Marsham Warran and son Josua Guibert (for desc. see will) and personalty

To son Thomas James, tract beginning at foot of run and running to line of Mannor _____ and personalty

To dau. Sarah, personalty, £20 absolutely, and use of orchard with 60 a. where Betty Prockter lives, while unmarried

To dau. Jean, personalty, 30 a. in hands of cousin Thomas Turner, absolutely, and use of 60 a. from her brother Joseph's tract while unmarried

To dau. Mary, personalty, £40 absolutely, and use of 60 a. of her bro. Thomas James' tract while unmarried

To sons Joseph and Thomas James, tract bet. son-in-law Josua Giurbert's and Joseph's great run, equally. The upper pt. with plantation where John Glass lives to son Joseph. Sd. sons to be of age at 18, shd. either die during minority, deceased's portion to survivor; shd. both die and without issue, their lands to 3 daus., viz. Sarah, Jane and Mary, equally

Wife Mary extx. and residuary legatee.

Test: William Hunter, Philip Dorey, Joseph Routhoume
(Md. Cal. Wills, Vol. V, p. 10; Wills, Liber 16, folio 67)

Estate of William Boarman; Value: £399/12/2; Dated: 27 Jun 1720; 18 Aug 1720; appraisers: Thomas Jameson, Richard Eglin (?Edelen); next of kin: John Pile, Benjamin Boarman; extx: Mary Boarman (4.235)
Second entry:
Value: £49/16/0; Dated: none listed; appraisers: Thomas Jameson, Richard Edelen; next of kin: Benedict Boarman, Francis Ignatius Boarman (5.101)

WILL of MARY BOARMAN, Charles County; written 20 Feb 1732/3; probate 27 Nov 1733

To daus. Jane Neale and Mary Gardiner, Thomas Leconby and the poor, personalty

To son Thomas James, ex., and residuary legatee

Test: William Boarman, John Bowling
(Md. Cal. Wills, Vol.. VII, p. 50; Wills, Liber 20 folio 842)

Children of William and Jane:

1-1 Jane Boarman, b. ca 1681 (Gardiner); b. by 1684 (Donnelly); unmarried

1-2 William Boarman, b. ca 1685; d. ca 1729; m. Monica Turner; d. by 1729; the will of her father, Thomas Turner, written in St. Mary's County on 31 Oct 1696 left her personal estate and 300 acres of St. Dorothy's on the west side of St. Clement's Bay (Md. Cal. Wills, Vol. II, p. 123); their children:

    12-1 William Boarman
    12-2 James Boarman
    12-3 Elizabeth Boarman

WILL of WILLIAM BOARMAN, Charles County; written 26 Feb 1728/9; probate 30 Jun 1729
To son William and hrs., St. Dorothy's, Clement's Bay, St. Mary's Co.; pt. of tract had from father, beginning at branch bet. plan. where mother-in-law _____ now dwells and Elizabeth Procters; and personalty
To son James and hrs., pt. of tract had from father, including dwell. plan. and plan. where mother-in-law now lives (for desc. see will); 50 a. Coventry; and personalty
To dau. Elizabeth, personalty. Tract nr. uncle Benjamin's to be sold and proceeds invested for sd. dau.
To cousin Raphael Neal, Jr., personalty
To 3 child. \_\_\_\_, int. in any other lands and residue of personalty
Exs.: Sons afsd.
Test: Rev. George Thorold, Raphael Neale, Theophilus Grew
                              (Md. Cal. Wills, Vol. VI, p. 118; Wills, Liber 19, folio 727)

William Boarman, Charles Co.; £9.3.0; 6 Nov 1730; 26 Feb 1730; next of kin: Francis Ignatius Boarman, Thomas James Borman; exs. William Boarman, James Boarman (16.108).

    12-1 William Boarman, b. ca 1710; d. ca 1767; age 32 in 1742 Charles Co. (Md. Deponents); m. Winifred Edelen; d/o Richard Edelen (Charles Co. Gentry); children from his will:

        121-1 William Boarman
        121-2 Mary Anne Boarman
        121-3 Edward Boarman

WILL of WILLIAM BOARMAN, Charles Co.; written 26 Mar 1765; probate 6 Apr 1767
To wife Winnifred Boarman, extx., dwelling plantation; at her decease, to son Wm. Boarman
Dau. Mary Ann Boarman; son Edward Boarman
To Marshall Queen, 25 a. for his dwelling house and orchard
Wit: H. Hawkins, Henry Boarman, Hugh Kerrick
                              (Md. Cal. Wills, Vol. XIII, p. 182; Wills, Liber 35, folio 333)

121-1 William Boarman; m. [19-7] Elizabeth Gardiner, b. ca 1745; d/o Mary Boarman and Luke Gardiner; child:

    1211-1 Cornelius Boarman, b. ca 1762 Charles Co.; d. ca 1810 KY

121-2 Mary Anne Boarman; Mr. Gardiner states that Mary E. Boarman, d/o William and Winifred; m. Richard Gardiner, b. ca 1747 (19-8); s/o Luke Gardiner and Mary Boarman; Mary Anne inherited *The Hope* of 250 acres from the will of her grandfather, Richard Edelen, written 16 Jul 1760 (Md. Cal. Wills, Vol. XII, p. 53).

121-3 Edward Boarman; an Edward Boarman, Sr., legatee and ex. of will of John Gardiner of Charles Co. written 5 Dec 1764; Henry Boarman, wit.; mentions daughters Mary and Monica Gardiner (Md. Cal. Wills, Vol. XIII, p. 66).

12-2 James Boarman
12-3 Elizabeth Boarman

1-3 Henrietta Boarman, b. ca 1687; m. ca 1705 Marsham Waring, b. ca 1680 Prince George's Co.; s/o Basil Waring and his m/2 to Sarah Marsham; Marsham m/2 Eleanor Hill; d/o Clement Hill and Ann Darnall; Eleanor m/2 2nd wife of Col. Leonard Hollyday and m/3 Dr. Murray of Cambridge, MD (Bowie); from the 1713 will of his grandfather, Richard Marsham, he inherited 1/5 of 1040 acres of *Enclosure* and 400 acres *Mt. Pleasant*, 300 acres *The Exchange*, residue of *Marsham's Rest*, 150 acres *Barron Point*; Henrietta, if widowed, to have use of land during her widowhood; then to grandson Richard Marsham Waring (Md. Cal. Wills, Vol. III, p. 240); children from his will:

    13-1 Richard Marsham Waring, b. ca 1706
    13-2 Sarah Waring
    13-3 Basil Waring, b. ca 1711
    Child of m/2:
    13-4 Ann Waring, b. ca 1732

The will of Richard Marsham of Prince George's Co. quoted by Bowie (Liber 1, folio 69) does not exactly agree with the abstract by Cotton (Md. Cal. Wills, Vol. III, p. 240). The children of Marsham Waring, except for Ann, are mentioned.

WILL of MARSHAM WARING, gent., Prince George's Co.; written 12 Mar 1730; probate 20 Oct 1732

To wife Eleanor, certain personalty and use of dwell. plan. for one year, at expiration of that time to live at Mount Pleasant and to have use of 1/2 the land during widowhood, with the 48 a. bought of William Smith, bequest not to be taken for her right of dower; and 1/3 part of household stuff

To daus. Sarah and Ann, certain personalty, and each 1/3 of personal estate after certain legacies are deducted; portion of dau. Ann to be in care of Clement Hill until she arrives at age of 16

To son Basil and hrs., 300 a. of Hearts Delight on w. branch of Patuxent, bou. of Thomas Brooke; also 38 a. Brooke Land, adj. to afsd. tract; 300 a. Indian Field near Zachia Swamp, Charles Co.; 96 a. Bryan Dayley, adj. to same; certain personalty and 1/3 of personal estate

To son Richard Marsham, ex., and hrs., 48 a. bou. of William Smith, after decease of his mother; and certain personalty

To Peter Davis, £5

Overseers: Clement Hill, Charles Sewell

Test: Ann Watton, James Haddock, Clement Hill, Jr., James Haddock Waring    (Md. Cal. Wills, Vol. VI, p. 233; Wills, Liber 20, folio 450)

13-1 Richard Marsham Waring, b. ca 1706 Prince George's Co.; d. ca 1743; s/o Marsham and Henrietta; m. ca 1732 Elizabeth Hawkins; d/o Henry Holland Hawkins and Joan Greenfield (Bowie); children:

131-1 Richard Marsham Waring, Jr., b. ca 1733; d. 1766
131-2 Henry Waring, b. ca 1735
131-3 Basil Waring; d. ? young
131-4 John Waring, b. ca 1739; d. ca 1813; m. Henrietta Maria Hall; d/o Francis Hall and Dorothy Lowe

WILL of RICHARD MARSHAM WARING, Prince George's Co.; written 17 Aug 1743; probate 1 Sep 1743

To son Richard Marsham, dwell. plan., *Marsham's Rest*, *The Exchange*, *His Lordship's Favor*, *Barren Point*, 458 a. Mt. *Pleasant* purchased from William Smith by test. father
To son Henry, 500 a. *Jamaica* on w. side of Potomac River
To son John, 496 a. being part of *The Exchange* which test. bought from William Murdock
To son Basil, house and lot in Upper Marlboro
To bro. Basie, sisters Sarah, Anne Holliday, Martha Hawkins, and Francis and bro. Henry Hawkins, personalty
To wife, Elizabeth, 1/3 personal estate, life int. in dwell. plan. Slaves to be sold to pay debts owed in England and Maryland, chil. to remain with their mother and be educated in the Catholic Church
Test: Charles Neal, Sarah Neal, Abraham Cox, William Steward
(Md. Cal. Wills, Vol. VIII, p. 227; Wills, Liber 23, folio 219)

13-2 Sarah Waring; d/o Marsham and Henrietta
13-3 Basil Waring, b. ca 1711; d. 15 Apr 1793; s/o Marsham and Henrietta; m/1 ca 1736 Henrietta Maria Digges; d. 1737; m/2 ca 1753 Susannah Darnall, b. ca 1723; d. 19 Jan 1806; d/o Henry and Henrietta Maria Darnall (Bowie); his children:

Child of m/1:
133-1 Henrietta Maria Waring, b. ca 1737; m. _____ Walker
Children of m/2:
133-2 Marsham Waring, b. 4 Jun 1754; m. ____; child:

1332-1 Marsham Waring, Jr., b. ca 1794; d. 15 Oct 1860

133-3 Elizabeth Waring, b. 28 Jun 1756; d. 9 Aug 1808; m. 5 Jan 1782 Bernard O'Neil

1333-1 Mary O'Neil
1333-2 Elizabeth O'Neil; d. 1804

133-4 Anne Waring, b. 18 Jul 1758; d. 9 Mar 1802; m/1 6 Apr 1779 Jesse Wharton of St. Mary's Co.; d. May 1788; m/2 Dr. Joseph Hall of *Locust Grove*, Montgomery Co.
133-5 Henry Waring, b. 19 Apr 1762; d. 11 Oct 1835; m./1 Henrietta Hall, b. ca 1773; d. 14 Feb 1795; m/2 8 Oct 1805 Millicent Brooke

133-6 Eleanor Waring, b. 15 Jun 1764; d. 11 Oct 1842; m. 8 Oct 1798 Henry Brooke; d. 1819

Child of m/2:

13-4 Ann Waring; d/o Marsham and Eleanor; m. step-brother Thomas Hollyday; d. ca 1767; m/2 Walter Cooke

Thomas Hollyday, Prince George's Co.; £1198.16.4; 6 Apr 1767; 26 Apr 1767; next of kin: L. Hollyday, Mary Waring; extx. Mrs. Ann Hollyday (91.324).

1-4 Ann Boarman, b. ca 1689; m. Joshua Guybert; her father's will written 1720 calls him son-in-law; Joshua Guybert of St. Mary's Co.; deposition of John Jee in 1757 mentions William Boarman whose dau. m. Joshua Guibert (F#3 50.495).

Joshua Guibert, wife Elizabeth, d. ca 1713; names children Thomas, Matthew, Joshua, Mary, Elizabeth Carberry (formerly wife of Thomas Turner), and Ann Blackston, wife of John Blackston; left *Tower Hill* in Charles Co. to son Joshua (Md. Cal. Wills, Vol. III, p. 252); Joshua Guibert of St. Mary's Co., wife Jane, d. 1743; children named Elizabeth, Anne, Joshua, Susannah Goode, and Mary Woodward (Md. Cal. Wills, Vol. VIII, p. 254).

John Blackistone and Ann Guibert had a son, John, who m. Eleanor Dent of Calvert Co., d/o Col. George Dent and Anne Harbert (Chas. Co. Gentry).

1-5 Sarah Boarman, b. ca 1691; this family is "iffy" as not much proof was found; Gardiner states she m. 1707 Charles Co. to Thomas Higdon; he may have been John Higdon; child:

15-1 William Higdon

A John Higdon gave a deposition in 1683, age ca 25. The John Higton, wife Menesenca, who d. in Charles Co. in 1723 names the following children: John, Charles, Benjamin, Thomas, William and Mary Sims (Md. Cal. Wills, Vol. V, p. 138). The William Higdon, Sr. who gave his age as 50 on 29 Aug 1758 mentioned his father, John, living 35-36 years ago (Chas. Co. Dep., Barnes). Other depositions by William give his age as 58 in 1767, 70 in 1178, and 71 in 1779, consistent with a 1708/9 date of birth.

15-1 William Higdon, b. ca 1709; d. after 1779; m. 1732 [8-8] Jane Boarman; d/o Benedict Leonard Boarman and Ann Brooke; children b. Charles Co.(Gardiner:):

151-1 Benjamin Higdon, b. 11 Dec 1733; m. 1754 Amelia Downing
151-2 William Higdon, b. 21 Feb 1735
151-3 Benedict Leonard Higdon, b. 6 Aug 1740
151-4 Ignatius Higdon, b. 12 Aug 1741; m. 8 Feb 1781 Elizabeth Taylor
151-5 Susannah Higdon, b. 25 Jun 1743
151-6 Martha Higdon, b. 13 Nov 1745
151-7 Clare Higdon, b. 2 Feb 1748

Children of Wm. and Mary:
1-6 Joseph Boreman; d. 1730; unmarried

WILL of JOSEPH BOARMAN, Charles Co.; written 26 Dec ____; probate 13 Apr 1730
To bro. Thomas James Boarman and hrs., entire real estate
To Thomas Bucknan and Peter Attwood, personalty
To mother Mary Borman, extx., residue of personal estate
                    (Md. Cal. Wills, Vol. VI, p. 148; Wills, Liber 19, folio 891)

1-7 Jane Boarman; m/1 in 1716 2nd w/o James Neale; d. ca 1730/1; s/o James Neale and Elizabeth Lord; m/2 Capt. Joseph Lancaster; James Neale dau. by his m/1 named Elizabeth Neale; Jane mentioned in 1683 will of her grandfather James Neale; children of Jane and James Neale from his will:

17-1 James Neale
17-2 Jane Neale
17-3 Mary Ann Neale

WILL of JAMES NEALE, Charles County; written 7 Jan 1730/1; probate 8 Mar 1730

To son James and hrs., entire real estate, including *Woollestan Mannor*, 1/2 thereof to be reserved for use of wife Jane during her life; and personalty at age of 21; he dying during minority or without issue, all lands to pass to 2 daus. Jane and Mary Ann and their hrs.
To dau. Eliza. and hrs., land in St. Mary's Co. had with former wife, her mother; and personalty at age of 16 or marriage
To daus. Jane and Mary Ann, personalty at age of 16 or marriage
To wife Jane, extx., residue of personal estate
Test: Raphael Neale, John Lancaster, Bennett Hoskins
(Md. Cal. Wills, Vol. VI, p. 181; Wills, Liber 20, folio 160)

1-8 Thomas James Boarman, b. ca 1703; d. 1785; m. Jane Edelen; d/o Richard Edelen; Gardiner says he m/2 1767 to Susanna Semmes; d/o Marmaduke and Henrietta Semmes of Charles Co.; 1772 will of Marmaduke and 1774 will of Henrietta Semmes mention dau. Susannah Boarman (Wills, Liber 40, folio 294); children from *Charles County Gentry*, wills, and *Chronicles of St. Mary's*:

18-1 Jane Boarman
18-2 Thomas Boarman; his grandfather Richard Edelen deeded him a portion of *Boarman's Manor* 12 Feb 1747 (Chas. Co. Gentry)
18-3 Raphael Boarman; inherited cattle from "upper quarter" of Grandfather Edelen
18-4 Sarah Boarman; her grandfather Richard Edelen deeded her a portion of *Boarman's Manor* 12 Feb 1747 (Chas. Co. Gentry)
18-5 Mary Boarman; m. Charles Boone; she inherited 180 acres *Boarman's Manor* from 1760 will of grandfather Richard Edelen (Md. Cal. Wills, Vol. XII, p. 52); children from *Chronicles of St. Mary's*::

185-1 James Boone
185-2 John Boone
185-3 Walter Boone
185-4 Charles Boone
185-5 Henrietta Boone
185-6 Ann Boone
185-7 Sarah Boone
185-8 Eleanor Boone
185-9 Catherine Boone; m. _____ Green

18-6 Thomas Boarman

The will of Richard Edelen of Charles Co. written 16 Jul 1760 (Md. Cal. Wills, Vol. XII, p. 52-54), calls Raphael Boarman his grandson. This will also devises to "grand-dau. the wife of Charles Boon and dau. of Thomas James Boarman, 180 acre part of *Boarman's Manor.*"

1-9 Mary Boarman, b. ca 1705; m. 1723 Luke Gardiner; s/o Luke Gardiner and Elizabeth Slye; children from Gardiner:

        19-1 John Gardiner, b. ca 1724
        19-2 Mary C. Gardiner, b. ca 1729
        19-3 Susannah Gardiner, b. ca 1733
        19-4 Joseph Gardiner, b. ca 1736
        19-5 Jane Gardiner, b. ca 1740
        19-6 Luke Gardiner, b. ca 1743
        19-7 Elizabeth Gardiner, b. ca 1745
        19-8 Richard Gardiner, b. ca 1747

19-1 John Gardiner, b. ca 1724; d. 11 Feb 1765; m. _____; children from his will:

191-1 Mary Gardiner
191-2 Monica Gardiner

WILL of JOHN GARDINER, Charles Co.; written 5 Dec 1764; probate 26 Feb 1765
To Edward Boarman, all those Negroes in possession of Thomas Matly (?), John Paptis Matly (?John Baptist Mattingly) of St. Mary's Co. and Benedick Spalding of Calvert Co., that appears to be due me. Account to be settled by William Bowling and Joshua Sanders. Balance to be applied to debts and balance to two daus. Mary Gardiner and Monica Gardiner
Wit: Thomas Bowling, Jr., Henry Boarman
                        (Md. Cal. Wills, Vol. XIII, p. 66; Wills, Liber 33, folio 111)

19-2 Mary C. Gardiner, b. ca 1729

19-3 Susannah Gardiner, b. ca 1733

19-4 Joseph Gardiner, b. ca 1736

19-5 Jane Gardiner, b. ca 1740; m. ca 1764 Richard Mudd; d/o Thomas Mudd and Ann Gardiner

19-6 Luke Gardiner, b. ca 1743
19-7 Elizabeth Gardiner, b. ca 1745; d. by 28 Jul 1780; m. ca 1762 St. Mary's Co. to [121-1] William Boarman; s/o William Boarman and Winifred Edelen
19-8 Richard Gardiner, b. ca 1747; m/1 1780 Mary E./Anne Boarman [121-2]; d/o William Boarman and Winifred Edelen; m/2 ca 1803 KY Sarah _____; children:

    198-1 William Gardiner, b. 1782 Charles Co.; d. 1831 Jefferson Co., KY
    198-2 Richard J. Gardiner, b. 1784 Charles Co.; d. 1829 Washington Co., KY

2. Sarah Boarman, b. ca 1654/6; d. ca 1685; d/o Capt. William Boarman and Sarah Linle; m/1 Thomas Matthews, Jr.; d. ca 1675/6 while a soldier on an expedition to Susquehannock Fort; s/o Thomas Matthews (d. 1676) and his m/1 Hester _____; brother of Mary Matthews Boarman, Sarah's step-mother; Thomas inherited part of a 700 a. tract on Mattawoman Branches from his father's will (Md. Cal. Wills, Vol. I, p. 176); they lived on the 450 a. *Hall's Place* which Sarah was given by her father; Sarah m/2 on 1 Aug 1678 as 2nd wife of Thomas Mudd, b. ca 1647; d. ca 1696/7; age ca 34 in 1681 Charles Co. (Md. Deponents); he m/3 Ann Mathews; half-sister of his wife Sarah's first husband; children:

| Children of her m/1: | Children of her m/2: |
|---|---|
| 2-1 Ignatius Mathews | 2-4 Barbara Mudd, b. ca 1678/9 |
| 2-2 Sarah Mathews | 2-5 Thomas Mudd (2), b. ca 1679/80 |
| 2-3 Mary Mathews | 2-6 Sarah Mudd, b. ca 1682 |
| | 2-7 Henry Mudd, b. ca 1686 |

    The will of Thomas Mudd mentions dau. Sarah who is listed by Gardiner as a child of Sarah Boarman. The name Sarah suggests she is a daughter of Sarah Boarman, but some family histories list her as a child of Ann Matthews. A third possibility is that she is Sarah Matthews raised by Thomas Mudd.

Oral WILL of THOMAS MATTHEWS, St. Mary's Co.; probate 1676
To wife (unnamed) and child. (unnamed), entire estate, real and personal; ex.: not named
Wit: Robert Greene, William Boarman, Jr.
(Md. Cal. Wills, Vol. I, p. 185; Wills, Liber 5, folio 163)

WILL of THOMAS MUDD, Charles Co.; written 12 Oct 1696; probate 11 Mar 1696/7
To wife Ann, *Hall's Place* during life
To son Thomas, sd. plantation at decease of wife and land in dispute bet. testator and Maj. Boreman; also 650 a. *Brierwood*
To son Henry, *Boreman's Reserve*
To son George, 400 a. part of *Cannarvan*, bought of Capt. Jos. Pile
To son John, 180 a. *St. Catherine's* bought of Edmond Nugent, and 250 a. residue of *Cannarvan* afsd.
In event of death of any son or sons without issue, lands to pass in natural succession to male hrs.
To dau. Julian[a] Clarke and hrs., 120 a. *Jarviss*
To dau. Barbara and hrs., 200 a. *Mudd's Rest*
Sons Henry and George to be taken in charge by their brother-in-law, Thomas Clarke
Wife Ann and son Thomas afsd. joint exs.
Residue of estate to be divided among wife and child., viz., Thomas Henry, George, John, Barbara, Sarah, Jane and Ann Mudd. Child. to be of age at 18 yrs.
Overseers: Son Thomas Clarke and brother William Boarman
Test: Wm. Howell, Wm. Burman, Jno. Brookes
(Md. Cal. Wills, Vol. II, p. 120; Wills, Liber 7, folio 265)

Children of Sarah Boarman and Thomas Matthews, Jr.:
2-1 Ignatius Mathews
2-2 Sarah Mathews
2-3 Mary Mathews
Child of Thomas Mudd and Julianna Gardiner:
[1] Juliana Mudd; m. Thomas Clarke
Children of Sarah Boarman and Thomas Mudd:
2-4 Barbara Mudd, b. ca 1678/9; d. ca 1710; unmarried
2-5 Thomas Mudd (2), b. ca 1679/80; age ca 52 in 1731 Charles Co. (Md. Deponents); d. ca 1761; m/1 Rebecca Wright; m/2 Cassandra Warburton (Gardiner); children from his will:

25-1 Henry Mudd
25-2 Richard Mudd
25-3 Luke Mudd
25-4 Mary Mudd; m. _____ Johnson
25-5 Thomas Mudd
25-6 Ignatius Mudd
25-7 Joseph Mudd
25-8 Francis Mudd

WILL of THOMAS MUDD, Charles Co.; written 2 Feb 1760; probate 12 Aug 1761
To son Henry Mudd, land called *Devil's Nest*, out of a tract of land called *Boarman's Reserve*, but desire my bro. Henry Mudd, to have plantation he now dwells on, with all land adjoining on that side of the branch next to sd. plantation
To sons Richard and Luke Mudd, all remaining pt. of land on south side of *Devil's Nest*
To son Richard Mudd, some slaves, etc.
To son Luke Mudd, one slave, etc.
To dau. Mary Johnson, one slave
To my children, Thomas, Ignatious, Joseph and Francis, all remaining personal estate equally divided
Wit: Wm. Hagan, Sr., Ignatius Gardner, Richard R. Bevin
(Md. Cal. Wills, Vol. XII, p. 94; Wills, Liber 31, folio 482)

Estate of Thomas Mudd, Charles Co.; value £351/9/3; 10 Nov 1761; next of kin: Richard Mudd, Luke Mudd; ex.: Henry Mudd (Inv. Prerog. Ct., 76.246).

2-6 Sarah Mudd, b. ca 1682 (Gardiner)
2-7 Henry Mudd, b. ca 1686, age 36 in 1722 deposition in Charles County (Md. Deponents); d. ca 1736; m. Elizabeth _____; d. ca 1763; children from their wills:

27-1 Elizabeth Mudd; m. Ignatius Simpson
27-2 Thomas Mudd
27-3 Mary Mudd; m. \_\_\_\_\_ Bevens
27-4 Sarah Mudd; m. _____ Wathen
27-5 Henrietta Mudd; m. _____ Clements

27-6 Henry Mudd
27-8 Monica Mudd
27-9 Bennett Mudd

279-1 Ezekiah Mudd

27-10 Ellinder Mudd

On 3 Jul 1755 Henry Mudd requested a resurvey of *Boarman's Reserve* which states that the land "was originally granted Maj. William Boarman, being deceased, the 10th day of October 1686" (Test. Proc., 6:333- Gardiner). Donnelly states *Boarman's Reserve* of 588 acres was patented to William Boarman 2 Nov 1685 (Patent ND#2:199)

WILL of HENRY MUDD (Mood); written 20 Jun 1736; no date of probate
To wife Elizabeth, extx., and 4 youngest child., viz., Henry, Monaca, Bennett and Ellinder, personalty
To dau. Elizabeth Simson, son Thomas, daus. Mary Bevens, Sarah and Heneretter, personalty
Test: Charles Farrall, Ignaus Simson, Ignasious Hagun
(Md. Cal. Wills, Vol. VII, p. 191; wills, Liber 21, folio 663)

Estate of Henry Mudd, Charles Co.; value £169/0/4; 1 Nov 1736; 15 Dec 1736; next of kin: Thomas Mudd, Ignatius Simpson; admnx.: Elisabeth Mudd (Inv. Prerog. Ct., 22.142).

WILL of ELIZABETH MUDD, Charles Co.; written 25 May 1761; probate 19 Sep 1763
To son Bennett Mudd, one slave
To sons Thomas and Henry Mudd, 1s
To dau. Mary Bidden, one slave
To dau. Sarah Wathen, furniture
To grand-son Ezekiah Mudd, son of Bennett, slaves
To Elizabeth Ann Salsbury, some slaves; in case she dies without issue, sd. slaves to dau. Mary Bibben; leave sd slaves in her care until Elizabeth Ann Salsbury arrives at age
To dau. Henrieta Clements, one hogshead of tobacco
Wit: John Green, Edward Edelin
(Md. Cal. Wills, Vol. XII, p. 206; Wills, Liber 31, folio 996)

Children of Thomas Mudd and Ann Matthews (Gardiner):
[1] George Mudd; d. ca 1715; unmarried
[2] John Mudd, b. ca 1692; m. Susannah Smith
[3] Jane Mudd; m. John Craycroft and Nicholas Brent

3. George Boarman, b. ca 1658; d. ? young; ? never married; according to Donnelly he is mentioned when his father deeded land to him (S#1:110) and in a deposition made in 1681 by his brother-in-law, Thomas Mudd (Md. Deponents).

4. Mary Boarman, b. ca 1660; d/o William Boarman and Sarah Linle; m. Robert Green; s/o Thomas Green; an interesting account of Thomas Green, boyhood friend of Leonard Calvert and second governor of Maryland, can be found in *The Flowering of the Maryland Palatinate*. His relationship to Thomas Green who m. Mary Boarman has not been examined by me; their children from Donnelly:

4-1 Thomas Green, b. ca 1683
4-2 Elizabeth Green
4-3 Mary Green
4-4 Sarah Green
4-5 William Green, b. 28 Dec 1694
4-6 Robert Green; d. 1749
4-7 James Green

4-1 Thomas Green, b. ca 1683; m. Tecla Shircliff; d/o William Shircliff and Mildred Thompson; she wit. the will of Alexander Hamilton 14 Jan 1730/1 (Md. Cal. Wills, Vol. VI, p. 177).

4-2 Elizabeth Green; m. Alexander Hamilton; d. ca 1730 Charles Co.; children from his will:

42-1 John Hamilton
42-2 William Hamilton
42-3 James Hamilton
42-4 Patrick Hamilton
42-5 Mary Hamilton

WILL of ALEXANDER HAMILTON, planter, Charles Co.; written 14 Jan 1730/1; probate 20 Feb 1730
To wife, extx., dwell. plantation during life, and personal estate absolutely; sd. wife to giver certain personalty to dau. Mary at marriage
To 4 sons, viz. John William, James, and Patrick, real estate equally; John, the eldest, to have his choice and to be for himself 1st Dec. next, son

William the following Dec., and the rest as they come of age; sd. 4 sons to pay youngest son Samuel certain personalty after age 21

Test: Richard Combes, Tecla Green, Gilbert Canty

(Md. Cal. Wills, Vol. Vi, p. 177; Wills, Liber 20, folio 138)

Estate of Alexander Hamilton of Charles County; 20 Apr 1731; 15 May 1731; value £74/4/5; next of kin: minors; extx. Elisabeth Hamilton (Inv. Prerog. Ct., 16.156).

4-3 Mary Green; m. John Thompson
4-4 Sarah Green; m. Patrick Atee
4-5 William Green, b. 28 Dec 1694
4-6 Robert Green, d. 1749
4-7 James Green; m. Charity Hagan

5. Benjamin Boarman; s/o William Boarman and Sarah ?Linle; in 1717 deed he and John Baptist Boarman rec'd payment in tobacco for squirrel heads (1#2:34 - Donnelly); mentioned in will of his nephew William (Md. Cal. Wills, Vol. VI, p. 118).

6. Ann Boarman, b. ca 1675; d/o Capt. William Boarman and Mary Mathews; m. 1695 to Leonard Brooke; d. 1718; s/o Baker Brooke and Ann Calvert and the grandson of Leonard Calvert (Donnelly); children:

6-1 Elinor Brooke; d. 1760
6-2 Ann Brooke; m/1 William Neale; m/2 by 1757 [8.] Benedict Leonard Boarman, her first cousin
6-3 Jane Brooke
6-4 Charles Brooke; d. by 1 Jul 1761; unmarried

WILL of LEONARD BROOKE, gent., St. Mary's Co.; written 1 Nov 1716; probate 2 Apr 1718

To dau. Elinor and hrs., *Hardshift*

To dau. Jane and hrs., *Haphazard* always providing that 150 a. of sd. land be excepted for use of the plan. now thereon, and sd. plan. for the use of two daus., Jane and Ann, and their hrs.

To dau. Ann and hrs., tract of land lying in fork of the creek that runs to Col. Henry Lowe's landing

To son Charles and hrs., residue of real estate and personalty. Residue of personal estate to four child. afsd. and delivered to them as they arrive at maturity

Shd. any of afsd. child. die during minority and without issue, their share in est. to pass to survivors. Shd. all afsd. child. die before attaining majority or without issue, estate, real and person, to be equally divided bet. cousins Richard and Leonard Brooke

Exs.: Bro.-in-law Raphael Neale and cousin Richard Brooke

Test: Chas. Hutton, Thos. Ashton, Thos. Dillon

(Md. Cal. Wills, Vol. IV, p. 131; Wills, Liber 14, folio 486)

7. Elizabeth Boarman, b. ca 1689 (Gardiner); d. after 1741; d/o William Boarman and Mary Jarboe; m/1 Joseph Pile (1688-1724) according to Donnelly; s/o Capt. Joseph Pile and Mary Turner; m/2 1726 Francis Hammersley; d. 1745; s/o Francis Hammersley and Margaret Brandt of Stafford Co., VA; owned *Barbadoes*, an island in the Potomac River near Georgetown, now known as Roosevelt Island (Donnelly); he m/2 Mary _____; The will of Elizabeth's mother, Mary Sanders of Charles Co., written 12 Mar 1739, calls her Elizabeth Hamozly (Md. Cal. Wills, Vol. VIII, p. 58). The will of Joseph Pile written 15 Jun 1724 names overseer "Brother John Parnham." An undocumented and unsigned family history (quoted in Volume I) states that Joseph Pile (d. 1724) m. Elizabeth Parnham and that the children were from this marriage. Therefore Elizabeth Boarman may have been a second wife. Joseph's will written and probated in 1724 names wife Elizabeth and the following 5 children (Md. Cal. Wills, Vol. V, p. 176). The question remains unresolved as no absolute proof has been found by me. Pile children from his will; mother undetermined:

7-1 Ann Pile
7-2 Elizabeth Pile
7-3 Mary Pile
7-4 Joseph Pile
7-5 Bennett Pile

Children from Elizabeth's m/2 to Francis Hammersley (Donnelly):

7-6 William Hammersley
7-7 Basil Hammersley; d. 1771
7-8 Francis Hammersley

8. Benedict Leonard Boarman, b. ca 1687; d. ca 1757; age ca 58 in 1745 Charles Co. (Md. Deponents); s/o William Boarman and Mary Jarboe; m. [6-2] Anne Brooke, his first cousin; d/o Leonard Brooke and [6.] Ann Boarman; 7 Aug 1727 Benedict purchased *Asenton* or *Assington* on the east side of Zachiah Swamp from Richard Edelen (Chas. Co. Gentry); children from will:

8-1 Mary Boarman
8-2 Benedict Leonard Boarman
8-3 Richard Basil Boarman
8-4 George Boarman
8-5 Joseph Boarman
8-6 Catherine Boarman
8-7 Elinor Boarman
8-8 Jane Boarman

6 Apr 1722 Benedict sold *Hardshift* lying in Zachiah Swamp to Richard Edelen for 5,000 lbs. of tobacco; Anne, his wife, waived Dower (Chas. Co. Gentry).

WILL of BENEDICT LEONARD BOARMAN, Charles Co.; written 28 Jul 1754; probate 11 Mar 1757
To wife Anne Boarman, dwelling house and plantation; [if she should marry 1/3 for her natural life]
To sons Benedict Leonard Boarman, Richard Basill Boarman, George Boarman, and Joseph Boarman, all the land I now possess
To Benedict Leonard Boarman, plantation he now lives on, [pt. of *Boarman's Rest*]
To son Richard Basill Boarman, plantation where Quarter is, being pt. of *Boarman's Rest*, pt. of *Inlargment*
To son George Boarman, piece of land known as *Standfords Field*, being pt. of *Boarman's Rest*, part of *Assenton* and *Boarman's Inlargement*
To Joseph Boarman, plantation I now live on after his mother's decease
If any of my three daus. should be unmarried after their mother's decease, Mary Boarman, Eliner Boarman, Jane Boarman, that they shall have 100 acres, 25 a. from each of my sons' part
To wife a mulatto man Stephen
To dau. Catharine Gardiner Negro girl name Winnifret. Remainder of Negroes to be divided amongst my 5 children George Boarman, Joseph Boarman, Mary Boarman, Eliner Boarman and Jane Boarman
To sons Benedict Leonard Boarman and Richard Basill Boarman, each 5s
Wife, extx.
Wit: Marsham Queen, Igns. Doyne, Wm. Matthews
(Md. Cal. Wills, Vol. XI, p. 163; Wills, Liber 30, folio 277)

8-1 Mary Boarman, b. by 1713; legatee in 1713 will of her grandfather, Richard Marsham of Prince George's Co. (Md. Cal. Wills, Vol. III, p. 240). Gardiner says she was b. 1717; d. 1780

8-2 Benedict Leonard Boarman; b. ca 1723; d. ca 1791; m. 1744 Elizabeth Jenkins; d/o Thomas Jenkins and Ann Middleton (Gardiner); children:

  82-1 Charles Boarman; m. Mary Edelen; d/o Philip Edelen and Jane Gardiner; Charles was on of the exs. in the final accounting in 1803 (AK 11, folio 194 - Charles Co. Gentry); daughters inherited slaves from the 1793 will of Jane Edelen:

    821-1 Elizabeth Boarman
    821-2 Jane Boarman

  82-2 Monica Boarman; d. by 1809; m. John Edelen (17__-1803); s/o Edward Edelen and Susannah Wathen; children (Chas. Co. Gentry):

    822-1 James Edelen
    822-2 Leonard Edelen, b. ca 1783; d. 1823; priest
    822-3 Walter Edelen
    822-4 Robert Edelen; m. Mary Catherine _____
    822-5 John M. Edelen
    822-6 Elizabeth Hester Edelen; m. Basil Smith
    822-7 Elizabeth Cecilia Edelen; m. John C. Gardiner
    822-8 Wilfred Edelen

  82-3 Catherine Boarman; m. Richard Gardiner; their son:

    823-1 Joseph Benedict Gardiner; m. 14 Apr 1793 Dorothy Edelen

  82-3 Ann Boarman; m. Ignatius Gardiner
  82-4 Leonard Boarman, Jr.

To clear a title on 31 Jan 1794, John and Monica Edelen, Henry and Catherine Gardiner, Ignatius and Anne Gardiner of Charles Co. conveyed to Joseph Boarman, s/o Leonard, *Boarman's Rest, Calvert*

*Hope* and *Hardship*; 1/2 of the land conveyed by Leonard Boarman, father of Catherine Gardiner, Monica Edelen and Ann Gardiner, to his son Leonard Boarman, Jr., by deed 13 May 1785 (Chas. Co. Gentry).

8-3 Richard Basil Boarman, b. 1720; d. 27 Jul 1792; m. 1740 Anne Gardiner; d/o Clement Gardiner and Eleanor Middleton; the will of Eliner Gardiner, St. Mary's Co., written 28 Jan 1760 mentions dau. Ann Boarman and dau. Mary Boarman (Md. Cal. Wills, Vol. XII, p. 2)

8-4 George Boarman, b. 1715; m. 1738 Mary Gardiner; d/o Clement Gardiner and Eleanor Middleton (Gardiner); children from will:

    84-1 Benedict Boarman
    84-2 Aloysius Boarman
    84-3 Elizabeth Boarman
    84-4 Elenor Boarman
    84-5 Mary Boarman

WILL of GEORGE BOARMAN, Charles Co.; written 7 Apr 1768; probate 5 Jul 1768
To wife Mary Boarman, one working Negro over and above a third part
To son Benedict Boarman several parcels of land which I now live on called *Boarman's Rest*
To son Aloysus Boarman, part of tract in St. Mary's Co. called *Rich Lands* which I bought of my brother Richard Boarman
Remainder of estate to my five children, Benedict, Aloysius, Elisabeth Eleanor and Mary Boarman
Extx: Wife Mary
Wit: Leonard Boarman, Elenor Boarman, Jane Boarman
                (Md. Cal. Wills, Vol. XIV, p. 48; Wills, Liber 36, folio 491)

8-5 Joseph Boarman; d. prior to 1760 (Donnelly); Gardiner says he d. 1777

8-6 Catherine Boarman, b. ca 1727; d. 1780; m. 1750 Richard Gardiner; s/o Luke Gardiner and Ann Craycroft; Gardiner says she was the youngest child; their children:

    86-1 John Francis Gardiner
    86-2 Joseph Benedict Gardiner; m. 14 Apr 1793 Dorothy Edelen; d/o Richard Edelen and Sarah Harrison (Chas. Co. Gentry)
    86-3 Charles Llewelyn Gardiner

8-7 Elinor Boarman; d. ca 1795; unmarried in 1790 census
8-8 Jane Boarman; Donnelly says d. ca 1779; unmarried; Gardiner says she was b. 1715; m. 1732 to William Higdon; s/o Thomas Higdon and Sarah Boarman

9. John Baptist Boarman, b. ca 1689;d. ca 1750; s/o William Boarman and Mary Jarboe; Donnelly says he m. Elizabeth Lancaster; d/o John Lancaster and Elizabeth Neale; *Charles County Gentry* states Barton Warren's 2nd wife "by whom no issue resulted was the Catholic lady Elizabeth, widow of John Boarman, and dau. of Richard and Ann Maria (Neale) Edelen (Court Record, Liber B no. 2, folio 340, La Plata);" the widow Elizabeth m/2 Barton Warren; d. 1757; his will names wife Elizabeth and Warren children (Md. Cal. Wills, Vol. XI, p. 163). The will of [9-1] Henrietta (Boarman) Thompson mentions her grandfather, Richard Edelen, and his will mentions granddaus. Elizabeth, Corry and Mary Lancaster (Md. Cal. Wills, Vol. XII, p. 52).

9-1 Henrietta Boarman, b. ca 1720
9-2 Richard Bennett Boarman, b. ca 1722
9-3 Joseph Boarman, b. ca 1733
9-4 Raphael Boarman, b. May 1736
9-5 Richard Boarman, b. Dec 1743

On 12 Nov 1718 John Baptist Boarman sold *Lanterman*, excepting 60 acres Maj. Wm. Boarman devised to Thomas Hagan, to Richard Edelen which Edelen willed to his son and grandson. Elisabeth Boarman waived her dower rights (Chas. Co. Gentry).

WILL of JOHN BOARMAN, Charles Co.; written 25 Apr 1747; probate 15 Aug 1750
To wife Elizabeth Boarman, tract purchased of Chas. Smoot, whereon I now live, and after her decease to son Richard Boarman
To sons Joseph and Raphael Boarman, pt. of *Colbert's Hope*; also 70 a. tract in Zachiah Swamp near the old bridge called *Hazard*
To dau. Henaritta Tomson, pt. of tract *Simpson's Supply*, 150 a. provided she makes my son Joseph Boarman satisfaction for 50 a.
To wife Eliza. Boarman, Negroes Charles, Harry, Richard, Ann and Elizabeth
To sons Joseph, Raphael and Richard, 7 Negroes: Jane, Samuel, James, Lydda, Samuel, William and Judah

If my wife should marry then my son Bennett Boarman and Richard
Tomson should be guardians to my 3 sons. That my sons Joseph and
Raphael at age of 16 should live with Richard Tomson to learn his
trade
To son Bennett Boarman, 1s.
To dau. Henritta Tomson, 1s.
Wit: William Hamersly, Benja. Newton, Joseph King
(Md. Cal. Wills, Vol. X, p. 105; Wills, Liber 27, folio 368)

WILL of ELIZABETH WARREN, Charles County; written 3 Jul 1769; probate
4 Mar 1771
To son Richard Boarman, *Widow's Discovery*
To sons Joseph Boarman and Raphael Boarman
To dau. Henrietta Thompson
To grandchildren Elizabeth Thompson, Jane Thompson, Baltis Thompson
To great-granddau. Anne Bradford, dau. of Eleanor Bradford
Wit: Edward Edelen, John Smoot, Charles Bradley (Wills, Liber 38, Folio 231)

9-1 Henrietta Boarman, b. ca 1720; d. ca 1772; m/1 Thomas
Jenkins; d. ca 1740; m/2 Richard Thompson; Gardiner states she
had a Jenkins son who d. in his teens; children from Henrietta's
will and the will of grandmother Elizabeth Warren:

91-1 Elizabeth Thompson; in Warren will
91-2 Jane Thompson; mentioned in Warren will
91-3 John Baptist Thompson; called Baltis in Warren will; in
mother's will
91-4 Henrietta Thompson; in mother's will
91-5 Anna Maria Thompson; called Ann in mother's will
91-6 Richard Walbert Thompson; mentioned in both wills
91-7 Raphael Thompson; in mother's will; Gardiner gives name as
Rachel

Estate of Thomas Jenkins, Charles Co.; 25 Feb 1740; 3 Jan 1741; value
£274/14/4; next of kin: Edward Jenkins, Mary Jenkins; admnx. Henrietta
Jenkins (Inv. Prerog. Ct., 26.439).

Will of HENERITTA THOMPSON, Charles Co.; written 20 Mar 1772;
probate 1 May 1772

Children: John Baptis Thompson, Heneritta Thompson, Ann
  Thompson, Richard Walbert Thompson, Raphael Thompson
Tract: land give me by my grandfather Richard Edelin in St. Mary's Co.
Ex.: son-in-law Raphael Brooke
Wit: Joseph Thompson, Sopha Leigh, Henrietta Brook
(Md. Cal. Wills, Vol. XIV, p. 219; Wills, Liber 38, folio 650)

9-2 Richard Bennett Boarman, b. ca 1722/4; d. ca 1758; m. 1744 Mary Ann (Neale) Hoskins; d. 1792; he and Mary Ann sold *Simkin* to Richard Edelen 23 Oct 1752; and on 24 Oct 1757 he sold 138 acres *Simpson's Supply* to Edelen; Mary waived dower rights (Chas. Co. Gentry); 1743 will of Raphael Neal mentions Hoskins children of "dau. Mary Boarman (once Hoskins);" will of Bennet Hoskins appoints "father Raphael Neale" as ex. (Md. Cal. Wills, Vol. VII, p. 77); estate names John Lancaster and William Neale as next of kin (18,297); children from Richard's will and Gardiner:

92-1 Raphael Boarman
92-2 Eleanor Boarman; m. _____ Bradford; she inherited a slave from 1760 will of Richard Edelen (Chas. Co. Gentry)

  922-1 Anne Bradford; mentioned in 1769 will of Grandmother Warren
  922-2 Polly Bradford
  922-3 Nancy Bradford

92-3 Elizabeth Boarman; m. Richard Neale
92-4 Richard Bennett Boarman; d. 1785; unmarried
92-5 Mary Ann Boarman, b. 11 Jan 1754

WILL of RICHARD BENNETT BOARMAN, Charles Co.; written 14 Sep 1752; probate 8 Jul 1758
To wife Mary Ann Boarman, half of my dwelling plantation being part of three tracts called *Calvert Hope*, *Boarman's Rest* and *Boarman's Low Ground*
To brothers Joseph Boarman and Raphael Boarman my rights to the land left to them by my father John Baptist Boarman
To wife Mary Ann Boarman, Negroes
To dau. Ellender Boarman, Negroes
To dau. Elizabeth Boarman, Negroes

To son Raphael Boarman, Negroes

To son Richard Bennet Boarman; tract I now live upon being part of *Calvert Hope, Boarman's Rest* and *Boarman's Low Ground*; also Negroes

To son Raphael Boarman, pt. of tract called *Calvert Hope*, the plantation whereon Thomas Reed formerly lived, also part of tract called *St. George's*, 110 a., also tract in possession of Richard Thompson whereon James Short now lives and Thomas Warren, 150a.

All the rest of personal estate to my four children, Raphael, Elender, Elizabeth, and Richard Bennet Boarman

Wit: Fran. Parnham, Samuel William Abbot, Guy Cornish, Edward Edelin (Md. Cal. Wills, Vol. XI, p. 219; Wills, Liber 30, folio 593)

Note: The conflicting following information regarding the marriage of Joseph Boarman has not been resolved. Newman states that it was [9-3] Joseph, s/o John Baptist, who m. Jane Cordelia Edelen, while Gardiner states this Joseph m. Mary Bowling. Considering the following census record it appears that [9-3] Joseph was m. to Mary in 1776. The wills of her family show that Joseph Boarman was m. to Jane Cordelia Edelen in 1794 and 1808. Therefore, it appears at this time, from the evidence located, that the husband of Jane Cordelia was [94-1] Joseph, the grandson of John Baptist Boarman.

9-3 Joseph Boarman, b. ca 1733; m. 1756 Mary Bowling; d/o William Bowling and Mary Boarman (Gardiner); the 1776 census of St. John's and Prince George's Parish, Prince George's Co. shows a Joseph Boarman age 44; Mary age 40; males age 21, 18, 15, 10.

93-1 Richard Bennett Aloysius Boarman, b. ca 1761; m. Eleanor Pile (Gardiner)

9-4 Raphael Boarman, b. 13 May 1736; d. 1781; m. 1758 Eleanor Neale; d/o Wm. Neale and Ann (Gardiner); child:

94-1 Joseph Boarman, b. ca 1760; d. by 1810 Charles Co.; m. ca 1780 Jane Cordelia Edelen; d/o Richard Edelen and Sarah Stonestreet; children from wills; the 1794 will of Christopher Edelen, brother of Jane Cordelia, left slaves to his sister Cordelia Boarman and named his brother-in-law, Joseph Boarman as ex. (Wills, T no. 1, folio 351); dates from Gardiner:

941-1 Anna Maria Boarman, b. ca 1781
941-2 Raphael Harris/ Horace Boarman, b. ca 1782
941-3 Caroline Matilda Boarman
941-4 Catherine Anamentia Boarman, b. ca 1787; d. ?young

On July 15 1808 Jane Cordelia Boarman's three spinster sisters, Anna, Elizabeth Anamenta and Mary Verlinda Edelen, made their wills in Prince George's County which were all 3 probated 28 Apr 1815. These wills named their sister Jeanne Delia Boarman and her four children, Catherine Anamentia, Anna Maria, Raphael Harris and Carolina Matilda Boarman (Pr. Geo's Probate, TT1, 117, 118; Charles Co. Gentry).

9-5 Richard Boarman, b. 3 Dec 1743/4; d. 6 Oct 1785; wit 1765 will of Elizabeth Jameson of Charles Co. (Md. Cal. Wills, Vol., XIII, p. 143)

10. Mary Boarman; d. ca 1744; d/o William Boarman and Mary Jarboe; m/1 2nd w/o John Gardiner (1677-1717); m/2 Gerard Sly (d. 1733); eldest s/o Capt. Gerard Slye and Jane.

Donnelly states that the children of both wives of John Gardiner and Gerard Slye were raised as brothers and sisters.

    Children of John Gardiner and his m/1 Susanna Barton:
      [1] John Gardiner
      [2] Clement Gardiner
      [3] Richard Gardiner
      [4] Susannah Gardiner; ? m. _____ Key
      [5] Elizabeth Gardiner; m. John Miles
      [6] Mary Gardiner; ? m/1 _____ Neal; ? m/2 _____ Lancaster
    Children of John Gardiner and m/2 Mary Boarman:
(10)-1 Wilfred Gardiner; d. by 1744; unmarried
(10)-2 Anne Gardiner; m. _____ Neale
(10)-3 Henrietta Maria Gardiner*
    Children of Gerard Slye and his m/1 Sarah Vansweringen:
      [1] Ann Slye; m. Francis Ignatius Boarman
      [2] Susannah Slye; m. Charles Craycroft
      [3] Jane Slye
Children of Gerard Slye and m/2 Mary Boarman:
(10)-4 Henrietta Marie Slye*; m. _____ Plowden
(10)-5 George Slye; m. Clare Neale

\* The will of John Gardiner mentions daughter Henrietta Maria and the will of Gerrard Slye mentions daughter Henrietta. Donnelly states Henrietta Maria Slye was the d/o Gerard Slye; she does not mention Henrietta Maria Gardiner.

WILL of JOHN GARDINER, gent., St. Mary's Co.; written 13 Oct 1717; probate 9 Dec 1717

To sons John and Clement and hrs., *Hillaley*, son John to have 100 a. more than son Clement. Should sons John and Clement die without issue, the sd. tract *Hillaley* to pass to 2 sons Rich. and Wilfraid and hrs.

To son John personalty

To Charles Smith, John Hayes and Edw. Hall and their hrs., 2 tracts, *Gardiner's Grove* and *Addition of Gardiner's Grove*. There being no patent granted for sd. tracts, testator directs wife Mary to obtain patent for them in her own name for use of sd. Smith, Hayes and Hall

To wife Mary, extx., personalty, 1/2 dwel. plant., *Cannon Neck*, during life. The sd. tract of land, *Cannon Neck*, to be equally divided at her decease between two sons, Rich. and Willfraid and hrs.

Residue of personal estate divided between wife and child., 4 sons, John Clement, Rich., and Willfraid and 5 daus., Susannah, Elizabeth, Mary, Ann and Henrietta Maria; wife to accept afsd. legacies in lieu of her thirds.

Test: Thos. Williams, John Reid, John Atkinson, Dorothy Smith

(Md. Cal. Wills, Vol. IV, p. 128: Wills, Liber 14, folio 470)

WILL of GERRARD SLYE, gent., *Bushwood*, St. Mary's Co.; written 23 Jul 1733; probate 23 Nov 1733

To wife Mary, extx., 1/2 personal estate absolutely

To child., viz., Henrietta, George and Elizabeth, other half of personal estate

To daus. Mary Neale, Susannah Key, Ann Boarman and Susannah Craycroft, each a ring

To dau. Jane, personalty, some of which des. as in possession of Philip Key. Testator directs that 62 a. *Wee Bit* and 150 acres of *Bushwood Lodge* be sold in order to discharge debt to Mr. Henry Neale of about £40

To dau. Henrietta, 100 a. *Piper Hill* now in possession of Philip Syllavin, during life

To dau. Elizabeth, 100 a. now in possession of Richard Raper, during life

To son George and hrs., 1/2 *Bushwood*, the other half to wife Mary during her life, at her decease to son George and hrs. Also all other lands in

Province, or in Colony of Virginia. Wife to have liberty to bring up child, in religion she thinks most fit
Test: Thomas McWilliams, Philip Dorey, Ann Gardener
(Md. Cal. Wills, Vol. VII, p. 48; Wills, Liber 20, folio 833)

WILL of MARY SLYE, St. Mary's Co.; written 10 Dec 1744; probate 7 May 1744
Mentions priest, Mr. Livers; dau. Mary Lancaster; dau. Henrietta Plowden; dau. Anne Neale; granddau. Mary Neale, Jr.; Mary Miles; son George Slye
Wit: Arnold Livers, Jr. (Jesuit Priest), Philip Key, Anne Carroll
(Wills, Liber 24, folio 163- Donnelly)

(10)-1 Wilfred Gardiner; d. by 1744; unmarried

WILL of WILFRED GARDINER, St. Mary's Co.; written 9 Sep 1743; probate 6 Jun 1744
To bro. George Sly and to Philip Key, Bennet Neale, son of Anthony, and negro Harry _____, personalty
To mother Mary Sly, residue of personal estate
To sisters Mary Lancaster and Anne Neal, Canoe Neck and Hellelewy
Exs.: John Lancaster, Henry Neal
Test: William Mills, Richard Roper, Thomas Hopkins
(Md. Cal. Wills, Vol. VIII, p. 271; Wills, Liber 23, folio 528)

(10)-2 Anne Gardiner: m. _____ Neale
(10)-3 Henrietta Maria Gardiner; may have died young or may be same person as [(10)-4]
(10)-4 Henrietta Marie Slye; m. _____ Plowden
(10)-5 George Slye; m. Clare Neale

WILL of GEORGE SLYE, St. Mary's Co.; written 21 May 1773; probate 20 Jun 1773
To poor relations: £100
To Rev. Mr. Lewes, for mission £100
To niece: Miss Jean Craycroft, one negress
To nephew: Wilfred Neale, all the money he owes me
To 3 nephews: Henry Neale, Nicholas Craycroft and Nancy Craycroft, £25 each
To sister: Plowden, all the money she owes me
To wife: Clare Slye, extx., two acres of land with small Chapel on it; she to make over land to John Shileck of Frederick County if he pays

£141/6/8, with interest, also another tract to John Milford and Christopher Hiders provided they pay my ex. £195 with interest; also one other tract to be made over to Nicholas Stulls of Frederick Co. provided he pay £5000, also two tracts of land to my wife, *Stones Rest* and *Lincey* bought of Samuel Green and his wife, also 1/3 personal estate and real estate to her

To: Child or children my wife goes with, residue of estate real and personal if they or it have no heirs to my nephew Edward Plowden, land I live on provided he give to his two brothers land that belonged to his father. My wife to bring up child but if she died she to appoint a guardian for it

N. B. If my child die personal estate to my sister Plowden's children

Test: Wm. Hamersly, John Diggs, Francis Hamersly (Wills, Liber 39, folio 350)

11. Clare Boarman, b. ca 1695 (Gardiner); d. 1747; d/o William Boarman and Mary Jarboe; m/1 Richard Brooke d. ca 1719; s/o Baker Brooke and Katherine Marsham; m/2 Dr. Richard Sherburn; d. by 1747

>  (11)-1 Richard Brooke
>  (11)-2 Baker Brooke
>  (11)-3 Nicholas Sherburn

WILL of CLARE SHIRBURN, St. Mary's County; written 21 Feb 1745; probate 6 Aug 1747

To sons Richard Brooks and Baker Brooks Shirburn, cooper kettle and furniture

To Nicholas Shirburn, rest of estate, ex.

Wit: John Miles          (Md. Cal. Wills, Vol. IX, p. 122; Wills, Liber 25, folio 152)

(11)-1 Richard Brooke; d. 1755; m. Monica Gardiner; d. 1772; d/o Clement and Eliner Gardiner, d. 1760 (Md. Cal. Wills, Vol. XIV, p. 2); she m/2 Henry Queen (1729-1768); child from her will:

> (11)1-1 Ann Brooke; m. _____ Hill
>
>> (11)11-1 Henry Hill

WILL of HENRY QUEEN, St. Mary's Co.; written 21 Dec 1767; probate 2 Feb 1768

To my two sisters, Catherine Edlin and Sarah Jameson, both living in Charles Co., tract of land in Prince George's Co. called *Pinner*

To brother Samuel Queen's son Edward Queen, 5s
To sister-in-law Margret Mewthis, suit of mourning
To dau.-in-law Clear Brooke, tract called *Hardship* being part of *Delebroke Manner* where James Jones now lives; 2/3 of Negro woman Sarah
To brother-in-law Walter Pye, tract in Cob Neck, being part of *Wolleston Mannor* lying on Cockeols Creek know by the name of *Shaws*; also tract in St. Mary's Co., being part of land called *St. Johns*; also tract where James Jones now lives being part of *Dillebrooke Mannor* known as *Hardship* after the death of my dau-in-law Clare Brooke if she die without issue
That you should give two of my brother Saml. Queen's children that you think most deserving, 80£
To wife use of tract known as *Hardship* and other real estate
Extx: wife (Monica Queen)
Wit. Richd. Boarman, Clement Hill, Jr., John Smith
(Md. Cal. Wills, Vol. XIV, p. 32; Wills, Liber 36, folio 336)

WILL of MONICA QUEEN, St. Mary's Co.; written 24 Nov 1772; probate 1 Dec 1772
To dau: Ann Hill, 5s
To grandson: Henry Hill, 1/3 part of estate but if he die before 21 years of age, said part of estate to my two sisters, Ann and Mary Boarman; they to have 1/3 of estate each
To the poor, 500 lbs. of tobacco
Richard Boarman, ex.
Wit: John Smith, Basil Smith                (Wills, Liber 39, folio 33)

(11)-2  Baker Brooke; d. 1756; m. Mary _____; no children

WILL of BAKER BROOKE, St. Mary's Co.; written 13 Feb 1756; probate 3 Mar 1756
To wife Mary Brooke, all my land during her life and after her decease to be divided among my brother Richard Brooke's children
To said brother's children, Negro woman Ann and two children Heney and Monica
To nephew Richard Shirburn, Negro
To godson Thomas Craycroft and goddau. Elizabeth Gardiner, each to have ewe and lamb
Remaining person estate to wife Mary Brooke
Wit: Richard Boarman, Joseph Routhorn, Elizabeth Fowler
(Md. Cal. Wills, Vol. XI, p. 123; Wills, Liber 30, folio 45)

Estate of Baker Brooke, St. Mary's Co.; 18 Mar 1756; value £528/15/6; next of kin: Richard Boarman, Nicholas Shierburn; extx.: Mary Brook (Inv. Prerog. Ct., 61, 315).

(11)-3 Nicholas Sherburn

(11)3-1 Richard Shirburn mentioned in will of uncle Baker Brooke

12. Francis Ignatius Boarman, b. ca 1701; d. 1743; age 41 in 1742 Charles Co. (Md. Deponents); s/o William Boarman and Mary Jarboe; m. Ann Slye; d/o Gerard Slye and Sarah Vansweringen (Donnelly); children from his will:

>   (12)-1 Ignatius Gerard Boarman, b. 9 Nov 1728; d. 1799
>   (12)-2 William Boarman; d. ca 1730
>   (12)-3 Francis Boarman, b. ca 1732
>   (12)-4 John Boarman, b. ca 1734; ?d. young

WILL of IGNATIUS BOARMAN, gentleman, Charles Co.; written 19 Jun 1743; probate 15 Mar 1743
To sons Gerard, William, Francis, and John, entire estate at 18 yrs., they not to have liberty to dispose of it until they reach 21
Ex.: Richard Brook, Willeford Gremer
Test: William McPherson, Jr., Mary Walley, Thomas Johnson, Jr.
(Jameson)      (Md. Cal Wills, Vol. VIII, p. 259; Wills, Liber 23, folio 446)

(12)-1 Ignatius Gerard Boarman; m. Susanna Sewell; d/o Mary Sewell; Gerard Boarman. Gent., sold *Green's Rest* and a portion of *Boarman's Manor* to Edward Edelen 6 Feb 1767; wife Susannah waived dower rights (Chas. Co. Gentry); will of Mary Sewell of Charles Co. names daus. Dorothy and Susanna Boarman; son-in-law Gerrard Boarman; Boarman grandchildren: Ann, Basil Smith, Henry and Ignatius
(12)-2 William Boarman
(12)-3 Francis Boarman; m. Batris _____; d. by May 1773; children from St. Andrew's, Leonardtown:

>   (12)3-1 John Boarman, b. 8 Oct 1758
>   (12)3-2 Francis Ignatius Boarman, b. 14 Mar 1762
>   (12)3-3 Sarah Boarman, b. 1 Mar 1764

WILL of FRANCIS BOARMAN, St. Mary's Co.; written 12 May 1773; probate 1 Jul 1773

Part of my estate to be sold to pay my debts and the money and residue of estate to be disposed of as follows:

To 3 children: John, Francis Ignatius and Sarah Boarman, residue of estate equally

My 3 orphan children to be in the care of the following persons:

Son, Francis Ignaitus Boarman to Mr. George Slye

Son, John Boarman to Mr. Richard Boarman

Daughter, Sarah Boarman to Mrs. Henrietta Plowden

Ex.: Enoch Fenwick

Test: Timothy Bowes, Raphael Thompson   (Wills, Liber 39, folio 352)

(12)-4 John Boarman


Special References:

DONNELLY, MARY LOUISE; *Major William Boarman, Charles County, Maryland (1630-1709)*

GARDINER, THOMAS RICHARD; *Gardiner, Generations and Relations, Volume II*

NEWMAN, HARRY WRIGHT; *Charles County Gentry*

## NUTHALL

The earliest surviving record of John Nuthall who died 1667 at *Cross Manor*, St. Mary's County, was found in the wills of his grandmother Margaret _____ Taynter Nuttall Joslin, d. 1619, and her last husband, Thomas Joslin of Rocheford, County Essex, who d. 1606.

Margaret's son, James Nuthall, gentleman, of Rocheford and Hockley, Essex County, England; d. 1637; m. Jane Wiseman; d. 1622; their children:

(1) Thomas Nuttall, b. ca 1600; of Rocheford, Essex Co., England, yeoman; who received a license from the office of the Bishop of London to marry Elizabeth Letton, spinster, of Basseldon, in the same county on 6 Nov 1622

(2) James Nuttall, b. ca 1602; attended Oriel College, Oxford, from 11 Apr 1617 to 23 Jun 1623, receiving his BA in 1620 and MA 23 Jun 1623

(3) Mary Nuttall, b. ca 1603; marriage license to John de Cerf, bachelor, 27, clerk of St. Katherine's Coleman, London; issued with the consent of her father, James Nuttall, gentleman, on 3 Feb 1628/9

(4) Charles Nuttall; may be the same person as Charles Nuthall, gentleman, who was living at Staple Inn, London, Dec 1641; he is possibly the ancestor of the Talbot County family of John and Elijah Nuttall

(5) Martha Nuttall, b. ca 1613; marriage license to Richard Wythe, gentleman, bachelor, 28 of St. Martin-in-the-Fields, London issued 21 Oct 1637; both of her parents said to be deceased; it is possible Martha and Frances were twins

(6) Frances Nuttall, b. ca 1614; license to marry Richard Bouchier of Little Stainbridge, gentleman, 27 May 1635 at Canewden, Essex; part of the bond paid by James Nuttall of Rocheford, gentleman. Richard Bouchier was the 3rd son of Sir James Bourchier of Little Stainbridge and the younger brother of Elizabeth Bourchier Cromwell, wife of Oliver Cromwell, the Lord Protector of England

(7) John Nuttall (Nuthall), b. ca 1618; d. 1667 Cross Manor, St. Mary's County, Maryland

Extensive research has been done on the Nuthall family whose name is spelled in a variety of ways in both England and the colonies. Nelson Nuttall and his son, Lindsay Nuttall, of Bloomington, Indiana, have compiled impressive information on the ancestry of the Nuthall and allied families in England as well as documenting the Nuthalls of the Maryland and Virginia colonies. They are currently working on the Talbot Co. ancestry of their ancestor Elijah Nuttall and other Nuttalls of the Eastern Shore. They have graciously given permission for their research to be used in this chapter on the Nuthall family.

In her book *Maryland and Virginia Colonial*, Sharon J. Doliante quotes extensive documentation on the life of John Nuthall and his descendants in Virginia and Maryland. There is some differences of opinion between these researchers which mainly centers on the letter written in London, 16 Aug 1644 by Jonathan Phillips to his brother in Virginia which states "Remember my kind respects to Mr. Nuthall and tell him his father, mother & sister are all in good health". Nelson and Lindsay Nuttall do not believe "Mr. Nuthall" is the John Nuthall who settled on *Cross Manor* in St. Mary's County. It is their opinion, backed by research in England, that John Nuthall of *Cross Manor* was not the son of the London merchant of the same name. John Nuthall of *Cross Manor* was not old enough to have a male child old enough to be called "Mr." in 1644. This John Nuthall was himself in England with his wife, the former Elizabeth Bacon, and step-daughter, Priscilla Holloway, at the time the letter was written.

Priscilla Holloway, step-daughter of John Nuthall, married William Stevens who transported John Cissell to Maryland. Stevens assigned the land rights for transporting the group that included John Cissell to Andrew Skinner of Talbot County.

## JOHN NUTHALL of ST. MARY'S COUNTY

John Nuthall was born in England ca 1618. He died in St. Mary's County, Maryland, between June 5 and October 10, 1667 at *Cross Manor*; inventory of his estate is listed in *Maryland and Virginia Colonials*. The first documentation of his presence in Virginia was found in Northampton County, Virginia, from the deposition of Capt. William Jones on 18 Jul 1664:

> ...about 35 to 36 years ago while trading with the Indians on Chesapeake Bay near the Pokomoke River, found Nutwell, a boy and servant who had run away from his master Hugh Hays (of Accowmacke Co. on the Eastern Shore); Capt. Jones traded a hoe to the Indians for the boy and, strapping him to the hallyards, returned him to Hays...(Maryland and Virginia Colonials, Doliante)

Hugh Hays, a neighbor of the Nuthall family in England, was transported to Maryland by his cousin William Stone, third governor of Maryland. He could not have been in the colonies with an indentured servant in the 1620s, as some sources state, because of his age. He was born ca 1609 and English law forbade anyone under 24 from holding an indentured servant. Therefore the above deponent is probably mistaken about how many years had passed since the incident of finding John Nuthall occurred.

John Nuthall apparently began to learn some of the their language during his time with the Indians as he is later documented as an Indian interpreter licensed to trade with the Indians on what is now the Eastern Shore of Maryland.

### MARRIAGES OF JOHN NUTHALL

m/1   In Jun 1642 in England John Nuthall married Rebecca Bright of Great Warley, Essex Co.; d/o Robert Bright

m/2   In Jan/Feb 1644 in Northampton Co., VA John Nuthall married Elizabeth Bacon, b. ca 1609 England; d. 1653/60; widow of Dr. John Holloway of Northampton County, VA; her child by her m/1 was Priscilla Holloway

1. Elinor Nuthall
2. John Nuthall, Jr. (2)
3. James Nuthall
4. Elias Nuthall

In the latter part of 1651 William and Elizabeth Gaskins accused Elizabeth Nutthall of adultery. They were found guilty of slander in the court of Northampton and subjected to fines and severe lashings (Northampton Wills, Deeds and Orders).

m/3  12 Sep 1660, Hungar's Parish, Northampton Co., VA John Nuthall married Jane Johnson who d. by 1663

John made several trips back to England during his lifetime which were undoubtedly business related. One source calls him a "noted ship captain and trader to Virginia and Maryland".

In 1643 he gave testimony regarding a death which had taken place on board a vessel in Maryland waters. Although he obviously traveled to Maryland in his capacity as trader, it is well documented in Northampton County records that he was living in Virginia as late as 1661. On 9 Aug 1661 John Nutthall "of Northampton County, Virginia, now being in England" purchased two manors, *Cornewalleys Crosse* of 2,000 acres and *St. Elizabeth's* also of 2,000 acres, plus 200 acres of land on St. Inigoes Creek called *Nuthall*, all in St. Mary's County, along with servants, goods, chattels, cattle and other things, from Thomas Cornwallis and Penelope his wife who were also in England at the time of the sale. Payment was to be made in installments to Cornwallis who had apparently returned to England to live. Lindsay Nuttall has also done considerable research in England on the Cornwallis connection with the Nuthall family.

*Cornwallis Cross* of 2,000 acres in St. Inegoes Hundred was surveyed 9 Sep 1639 for Thomas Cornwallis; possessed in 1707 by William Herbert (Rent Rolls of 1704 & 1707). *St. Elizabeth's*, surveyed 9 Sep 1639 for Thomas Cornwallis in St. Inigoes Hundred, is listed in 1704 as having 200 acres (Chronicles of St. Mary's) and in the 1707 rent roll as 2,000 acres (Wilson Cary Miles Collection). 1,500 acres of *St. Elizabeth's* was held by Mary VanSwearingen in 1707 and 500 acres by William Bladen. *Nutthall*, 200 acres, was surveyed in 1654 for Thomas Cornwallis and called *Town Land, Cross Town Land*, and *Cross Neck*, lying mostly within the bounds of *St. Mary's Hill Freehold* in St. Mary's Hundred; held in 1707 by Elizabeth Baker (Rent Rolls). Cornwallis was also granted 4,000 acres called *Resurrection Manor* in Resurrection Hundred in 1650 (Chronicles of St. Mary's County, vol. 21, no. 5).

*Early Settlers of Maryland*, Skordas, reflects the applications for land made by John Nutthall for bringing himself and his children to the colony of Maryland: John Nutthall, immigrated 1663; James Nutthall, transported 1663, son of John; John Nutthall, transported 1663, son of John (Liber 5, folio 343). Daughter Elinor was transported by Capt. Edward Peerce prior to 1670 (Liber 12, folio 576). No land was ever requested for son Elias.

Two others of the name Nuthall were transported into Maryland according to Skordas: Arthur Nuthall came to Maryland as a servant in 1674 (Liber 18, folio 168 and Liber 5, folio 233); Nicholas Nuthall was transported in 1676 (Liber 15, folio 383). An Arthur Nutthall was a legatee in the will of William Burk of Calvert County written 10 Dec 1666 (Wills, Liber 1, folio 279).

Records relating to the inventory and distribution of the estate of John Nutthall of *Cross Manor* are found in the Archives of Maryland, although he left no will. His children are proven by two documents cited by Doliante: 1 Sep 1668 identifies John, James and Elinor as his children; 22 Nov 1671 claim of the 4th child, Elias, is recognized.

1. Elinor Nuthall, b. ca 1645 Northampton Co., VA; d. ca 1700/4 Prince George's County, MD; m. ca 1667/8 as second wife of Thomas Sprigg, b. ca 1630, age ca 35 in 1665 and ca 64 in 1694; d. ca 1704; he m/1 VA to Catherine (Graves) Roper. Elinor was transported to Maryland by Capt. Edward Peerce; date unknown, but prior to her marriage to Thomas Sprigg as she is listed as Elinor Nuthall on the application Edward Peerce made 15 Jun 1670 for 1,050 acres of land for transporting 21 people; children:

Children of Thomas Sprigg and Catherine:
[1] Nathaniel Sprigg, b. ca 1651 Northampton Co., VA
[2] Samuel Sprigg, b. ca 1653 Northampton Co., VA
[3] Sarah Sprigg, b. ca 1655 Calvert Co.; d. ca 1736; m/1 John Pearce, Jr.; b. ca 1650-1655; d. ca 1687-1700; m/2 Enoch Combs
[4] John Sprigg, b. ca 1656/7 Calvert Co.; d. ca 1700; unmarried
[5] Thomas Sprigg (2), b. ca 1659/60 Calvert Co.; d. ca 1736-9; m. Margaret Mariarte, b. by 1687; d. ca 1739; Bowie says he was s/o Eleanor; Doliante cites a VA document which she says proves he is the s/o of Catherine

Children of Thomas Sprigg and Eleanor (births estimated):
1-1 Elias Sprigg (Christopher Johnson); b. ca 166_ Calvert Co.; named for his uncle Elias Nuthall; d. by 1704
1-2 Elizabeth Sprigg, b. ca 1671; m/1 Robert Wade; m/2 William Penson
1-3 Mary Sprigg, b. ca 1673; d. 27 Jan 1694; m. Thomas Stockett
1-4 Eleanor Sprigg, b. ca 1675; d. after 1741; m. 2nd wife of Thomas Hillery
1-5 Martha Sprigg, b. ca 1677; m/1 Thomas Prather; m/2 Stephen Yoakley
1-6 Ann Sprigg, b. ca 1679; m. Phillip Gittings

Will of THOMAS SPRIGG, SR., Prince George's Co.; written 9 May 1704; probate 29 Dec 1704
To son Thomas, ex., plantation and land of *Northamton* and *Kellering* which have not been disposed of; also 1/3 of patent 500 a. in *Manor of Colington*
To dau. Martha Prather and hrs., 1/3 of residue of 500 a. lying near Jonathan Prather's
To dau. Oliver Nutthall residue of afsd. patent lying near Jonathan Prather's
To Thomas Stockett, grandson Thomas Stockett, Oliver Stockett, and each of sd. Thos. Stockett's child., to daus. Elizabeth Wade and her child., Ann Gittens and her child., Oliver Nutthall and her child, and Martha Prater and her child., personalty
To daus. afsd., residue of estate; division to be made by Sam'l Magruder, Sr., Edward Willett and John Smith at Mattapany
In event of death of son Thomas, sons-in-law ___ Wade, Philip Gittens and Thomas Prater to assume executorship

Test: Thomas Lucas, Sr., Thomas Lucas, Jr., Dorothy Lucas
(Md. Cal. Wills, Vol. III, p. 48; Wills, Liber 3, folio 443)

[For descendants of these lines see *Maryland and Virginia Colonials*.]

2. John Nuthall (2), b. Mar 1648 Northampton Co., VA; d. 1714 St. Mary's County, MD; he made at least one marriage to Barbara _____ according to Doliante, but since no grandchildren were named Barbara, it is questionable as to whether she was the mother of John, his only known son. Barbara Nuthall died prior to 1714 as she is not mentioned in the will of her husband. John was transported into Maryland with his father ca 1661 and land was claimed for his transport by his father in 1663. John was bound to William Burke of Calvert County who "gave him one whole year of his time" 16 Dec 166 (Doliante). John Nuttell, Sr. is mentioned in accounting of the estate of John Wilson 17 May 1707 (26.319). According to several documents found in St. Mary's County, he made his living as an innkeeper.

2-1 John Nuthall (3)

WILL of JOHN NUTTHALL, SR., Gent.; St. Mary's Co.; written 22 Nov 1713; probate 28 Sep 1714:

To grandson Breant Nuthall, at age 21, and granddaughter Elinor Nuthall, at 16 years, personalty.

To son John, executor, residue of estate, real and personal and reversionary legatee in event of death of either grandchild aforesaid during minority

Test: Edmund Plowden, Thomas Sprigg, Dorothy Ashe
(Md. Cal. Wills, Vol. IV, p. 18: Wills, Liber 13, folio 728)

The value of the personal estate was £184/12/6. Wit: Edmd. Plowden, Elinor Nuthall, Wm. Combes (Inv. & Acct., Liber 36b, folio 21 & Doliante,)

The Edmund Plowden whose name appears in the above records was the s/o George Plowden and Margaret Brent. Margaret and Mary Brent, wife of [2-1] John Nuthall (3), were sisters of William Brent of Stafford County, VA. The Plowden family owned at least part of *Resurrection Manor* which was patented by Thomas Cornwallis in 1650 for 4,000 acres in Resurrection Hundred.

2-1 John Nuthall (3), b. ca 1671 MD; d. by 9 Nov 1714 St. Mary's Co.; s/o John Nuthall (2); m/1 by Rev. Nicholas Gulick ca 1693 to Mary Brent, b. VA; d/o Giles Brent, Jr. (1652-1679) of Stafford Co., VA; m/2 ca 1699 to Eleanor Sprigg Hilleary; d. by 1760; d/o Thomas Sprigg (1) and Eleanor Nuthall; widow of Thomas Hilleary (Marriages and Deaths St. Mary's Co.). After the death of John (3), Eleanor m/3 ca Mar 1727/8 Rev. George Murdock. The will of James Nuthall states that his brother John (2) had a son named John. No record found to date of a will for John Nuthall who m. Eleanor Sprigg Hilleary. In the will of John Nuthall (1), two grandchildren are mentioned, Brent and Elizabeth. Since these names do not appear in the will of his brother James and since John Nuthall (3) m. Mary Brent, it is assumed they were children of this John (3); who was the executor of his father's will. On 8 Dec 1720 an Elenor Nuthall witnessed the will of Philip Gittings of Prince George's County (Wills, Liber 16, folio 172).

     21-1 Brent Nuthall
     21-2 Elinor Nuthall
     21-3 Priscilla Nuthall
     21-4 Elizabeth Nuthall
     21-5 Mary Nuthall

Deed, 25 Jun 1700; from John Nutthall of St. Mary's Co., Planter, to Thomas Sprigg, Jr. of Prince George's Co., Gent.; for £50 all of a 250 acre tract at the head of Western Branch in Prince George's Co. Said tract was bequeathed by Thomas Hillary, late of Calvert Co., deceased, in his will dated 2 Feb 1697, to his wife Elinor who, after his death, married the said John Nutwell (sic). The tract was originally part of a tract called *Three Sisters*; /s/ John Nuttwell (sic); wit: Meriton, Josias Towgood (Prince George's Co. Land Records, Liber A, folio 218)

Deed, 26 Mar 1701; from John Nuttwell of St. Mary's Co., planter, and wife Elinor, to Thomas Sprigg, Jr. of Prince George's Co., Gent.; for £50 a 250 acre part of the tract called *Three Sisters* in Prince George's Co. at the head of Western Branch; said tract having been bequeathed by Thomas Hillary, late of Calvert Co., deceased, by will dated 2 Feb 1697, to said Elinor who was then his wife; /s/ John Nuttwell, Jr., Elinor Nuttwell (mark); wit: Rob't Bradley, Rob't Wade (Pr. Geo.'s Co. Land Records, Liber A, folio 354)

Deed, 26 Mar 1701; from Thomas Sprigg, Jr. of Prince George's Co., Gent. to Maj. Walter Smith of Calvert Co., Gent.; for £61 a 250 acres part of *Three Sisters* in Prince George's Co. at the head of Western Branch; said land was formerly bequeathed by Thomas Hillery in his will dated 2 Feb 1697, to Elinor his wife, who after his decease, married John Nuttwell; said tract was conveyed to said Thomas Sprigg, Jr. by John Nuttwell and wife Elinore, 26 Mar 1701; wit: Rob't Bradley, Rob't Wade; ackn'd: Thomas Sprigg, Jr. and wife Margarett, 26 Mar 1701 (Land Records, Liber A, folio 357)

John Nutthall, Jr., witnessed the will of William Hutchings, St. Mary's Co., 29th Nov 1708 (Wills Part 2 - Liber 12, folio 65)

> 21-1 Brent Nuthall, b. Oct 1697; d. after 1758; m. Elizabeth (aka Ann) King; (\_\_\_\_ - 1762); d/o Charles King of St. Mary's Co.; children:
>
>> 211-1 Mary Brent Nuthall
>> 211-2 Margaret Brent Nuthall
>> 211-3 ?Charles Nuthall; d. Great Mills 1846

Brent Nuthall paid excess liquor taxes between 1758 and 1760 indicating he was selling liquor at that time. He and his wife Elizabeth were apparently operating a tavern in the Great Mills area of St. Mary's County.

The will of Charles King, probate 1739, appears to disinherit Elizabeth as the last statement is "To dau. Neuthall, 1s" after disposing of several large tracts of land to the other children and stating "certain personalty to be divided among 6 children" Residue of estate to be divided among 5 children" (Md. Cal. Wills, Vol. VIII, p. 22). Probate of Charles King's estate does not mention Elizabeth or her husband (Inv. Prerog. Ct., 24.543).

This appears to indicate that Charles King did not approve of the marriage of his daughter and Brent Nuthall. The rather unusual "deed" filed in Somerset County by Brent Nuthall on 18 Sep 1759 and quoted on a following page suggests that there might have been some irregularity regarding their marriage. Investigation regarding Brent Nuthall is not complete.

The following records are from the 1717 lawsuit brought by Brent Nuthall in an attempt to gain possession of *Cross Manor*:

> Charles, Lord Baltimore appointed Thomas Truman Greenfield, James Bowles, and Henry Peregrine Jowles of Saint Maries County to examine evidence touching the birth or lineage of Edmund Plowden and Brent Nuthall.
>
> Deposition 3 Aug 1717 of the Reverend Nicholas Gulick aged about seventy years or thereabouts:
> About twenty four years ago deponent did joining together in the Holy State of Matrimony Mr. John Nutthall, Jun of St. Mary's County and Miss (Mrs.) Mary Brent of Stafford County in the Collony of Virginia according to the cannon and civil laws of the land (Maryland Chancery Records, Vol. III, p. 361).
>
> 3 Aug 1717 deposition of Susan Evans, about 65 years or thereabouts, that 20 years come Oct., deponent was sent for as a mid-wife to Mrs. Mary Brent sister to Margarett Brent and wife to Mr. John Nutthall, Junior and at the house of said Nutthall brought to bed the said Mrs. Mary Brent the wife of said Nutthall with a man child who is now a man and known by the name of Brent Nutthall and further deponent saith that she always understood that the aforesaid Mrs. Mary Brent wife of the said Nutthall and Mrs. Margerett Brent wife of Mr. George Plowden, late of St. Mary's County, deceased was own sisters to Mr. William Brent of Stafford County in the Collony of Virginia who lately died in great Britain and further deponent saith that the said Brent Nutthall is the only surviving son of the said Mrs. Mary Brent, wife of said John Nuthall, junior.
>
> 6 Aug 1717 Commissioners took deposition of Mr. Leonard Brooke of All Faiths Parish he was formally present and did see Mr. George Plowden and Mrs. Margarett Brent, sister of Mr. William Brent married and Mr. Edmund Plowden has always been reputed as the legal issue of such marriage.  (Maryland Chancery Records, Vol. III, p. 361)

Charles Absolute Lord and Proprietary of the Province of Maryland and Avalon Lord Baron of Baltimore: To Capt. John Baker and Mr. Michaell of Saint Maries County Gent Greetings Know Yee that we have nominated and appointed you to be our commissioners to examine evidence concerning Mr. Brent Nuthalls title to a certain tract of land lying in Saint Maries County aforesaid called *Cross Manor* Wee therefore require you that at such time and place as to you shall seem convenient you cause to come before you all such evidence as shall be to you named by the said Brent Nuthall aforesaid concerning his title to the land aforesaid and that you examine them and every of them on their corporale oaths to be by you administered to them on the holy Evanglish touching their knowledge and remembrance in the premisses and that reducing into writing their several depositions you send the same together with this our commission under your hands and seals with all convenient speed to us in our high court of chancery there to be recorded in petuari (?) rei memoriam Witness our trusty and well beloved William Holland Evess (?)Chancellor of Maryland keeper of the Great Seale thereof the first day of October in the fifth year of our dominion anno dom 1720.

By Virtue of the commission hereto annexed to us the subscribed (?) directive we have called before us the several evidences following and taken their depositions in the presence of Vitus (?) Herberts (?) a party concerned therein viz....

The Deposition of Robert Clarke of Saint Maries County aged about seventy one years who being sworn of the Holy Evangelist of Almighty God deposeth that he very well knew John Nuthall the Elder the grandfather of Brent Nuthall and that the said John Nuthall and this deponent on comparing ages together told this deponent that he the said John was of the same age with this deponent save that the said John was as much older than this deponent as from March tile November this deponent being seventy one years of age the fifth of November next and that he had heard that the said John Nuthall the grandfather [?father] sold the land called *Cross Manor* and the he heard he was under the age of twenty one years when he sold it and that he endeavored to recover it again and insisted on his nonage but could not that thereupon the said Nuthall would have appealed to England but that the then Lord Baltimore forbid any ship from carrying him out of the Province as he has heard. And further saith not.

The depositions of Levina Twisden of Saint Maries County aged about seventy one years who being sworn as aforesaid deposseth that she knew John Nutthall the great grandfather of the said Brent and that when she came into the country which was about fifty four years agoe the said John the great grandfather lived on the land called the *Cross Manor* where on he died about fifty three years ago last July and that she heard that John Nuthall the grandfather sold the land soon after the death of the said John the great grandfather and that he sold it for a suit of cloathes horse bridel and sale and that she heard this from the neighbors but not from the said John Nuthall that sold it. And further this deponent saith not.

The deposition of William Johnson of Saint Maries County aged about fifty two years who being sworn on the holy Evangelist of Almighty God deposses that he hath heard that when John Nuthall the grandfather of Brent Nuthall sold the land called *Cross Manor* he under the age of twenty one years and that after the said John Nuthall endeavord to get his land again but that the then Lord Baltimore in favour to Mark Corder his former cook prevented him from recovering but how he heard not And further saith not.

Sworn before us this eighth day of October Anno Dom 1720

William Combs of Saint Maries County aged about fifty years who being sworn deposses that he heard and was told by John Nuthall the grandfather of Brent Nuthall that the said John's father left him at age to do for himself when he came to age eighteen years of age but that before he arrived at twenty-one years of age he had never a foot of land left or to that effect but how the said John disposed of it this deponent knoweth not.

Charles Calvert of Saint Maries County, Gentleman, aged about fifty-nine years of age swears that he was told by one Robert Large who as he said had waited on Walter Hall, but first severed the first part of his time with John Nuthall the great grandfather of the said Brent Nuthall that the said Walter Hall bought the land that the said Nuthall's held from John Nuthall the grandfather of the said Brent and when the said John last named was under age and this deponenth's father William Calvert quarrelled with the said Hall about it because he had cheated the same John and bought his land from him when he was under age and this deponent further saith that he had heard his father and mother say the same or that purpose but particularly his mother very often and this deponent further saith that he hath been told by the said John Nuthall the grandfather that he was under age when he sold his land to Walter Hall and further that he has heard he sold his lands for ordinary expenses (Maryland Chancery Records, Vol. III, p. 748-750).

Brent Nuthall witnessed will of Isaac Nobel of Somerset County in 1731 (Wills, Liber 20, folio 522)

*Somerset* To all whom these presents shall come Greeting Know Ye that I Brent Nutthall of Somerset County in the Province of Maryland as well for and in consideration of the Great Love and Affection which I bear to my Dear and well beloved wife Elizabeth Nutthal and also for divers other good causes and considerations are heretoe moving have given and granted and by these presents Do give grant and confirm unto the said Elizabeth Nutthall all and singular my goods Chattles, Leases, Reversions, Debts Ready Money Household Stuff and all other my substance whatsoever moveable and immoveable quick and Dead of what kind and Nature Soever the same are and in what place & places Soever the same be either in my Possession or in Custody of any Person or Persons whatsoever. To have and to Hold all and Singular the afsd. granted Premises unto the said Elizabeth Nutthall and her heirs and Assigns forever to her and their own proper use and behoof forever without any manner of Challenge Claim or Demand from me
(p. 24) Any other Person or Persons whatsoever for me or authorized or precured by me And without Any money or other thing to be yielded therefore unto me the said Brent Nutthall or my heirs and of the said Brent Nutthall all and Singular the above granted premises to the said Elizabeth Nutthall her heirs and Assigns to the use afsd. Against all Persons whatsoever do and will warrant and for ever defend by these presents And further know ye that I the said Brent Nutthall have put the said Elizabeth Nutthall in possession of all and Singular the afsd. granted premises by the Dive___ of the Sum of five shillings unto her the Said Elizabeth Nutthall in Witness whereof I have hereunto Set my Hand and Seal this Eighteenth day of September in the Year of our Lord God One thousand Seven Hundred fifty and nine
/s/ Brent Nutthall (seal)
Sealed and Delivered it being first interlined between the first

& Second Lines with the words of Somerset County in the Province of Maryland; In Presence of us Ben Burridger, William Rencher, John Ballard

Be it Remembered that on the eighteenth day of September in the year of our Lord God thousand Seven Hundred fifty and nine came before me the Subscriber one of his Lordships Justices of the ____ for the County of Somerset Brent Nutthall and acknowledged the within Deed together with the Delivery of the within granted premises according and agreeable to an Act of the Assembly in that case made and provided
before me ____ Jones
Recorded in Liber 6, folio 23 on the Eighteenth Day of September Anno Dom One thousand Seven hundred fifty and Nine; Thomas Hayward

WILL of ELIZABETH NUTTHALL, St. Mary's Co., written 13 Jun 1762; probate 23 Dec 1762:
To daughter Mary Atkinson one bed and furniture; 1/2 of pewter and pots
To daughter Margaret Brent Nuthall one good bed and furniture and half the pewter and pots; largest tea kettle; red cloak and "cubbard" and set of tea ware
To granddaughter* Araminta Nuthall one good bed and furniture to be kept by my daughter Margaret Nutthall till she arrives to age 16 or day of marriage
To granddaughter Ann Nuthall one good bed and furniture to be kept by my daughter Margaret Brent Nuthall till she is 16 or day of marriage
Exs: daus. Mary Brunt Atkinson and Margarett Brunt Nutthall
(Wills, TA-1, p. 440 & Liber 31, folio 870)

* The copy of this will in St. Mary's County calls Araminta granddaughter while the copy of the will in Annapolis calls her daughter. There is no way to be absolutely positive which is correct, but she was most likely a granddaughter.

The estate inventory of Elisabeth Nuthall 21 Dec 1762 St. Mary's Co.; value £22/0/7 names Mary Brent Nuthall and Joshua Atkinson as executors with Charles King and Susanna Daffin as next of kin. [This Charles King would undoubtably be the brother of Elizabeth King Nuthall. Susannah Daffin was her sister Susannah King who m/1 Wm.

Daffin and m/2 after 1740 to George Daffin] (Inv. Prerog. Ct., Liber 81, folio 288).

211-1 Mary Brent Nuthall, m. by 1762 Joshua Adkinson

Mary Brent Adkinson, b. 25 Aug 1759; d/o Joshua and Susanna Adkinson; granddau. of Brent Nuthall who was the s/o Mary Brent; sister of William Brent, Esq. (St. Andrew's Parish records)

211-2 Margaret Brent Nuthall; believed to have married a Roach; ?marriage not recognized as one was Protestant and the other Catholic; ?illegitimate children; no father listed on church record for Ann; only mother's name

2112-1 ?Araminta Nuthall, b. by 1762
2112-2 Ann Roach, b. 28 Feb 1761 St. Andrew's Episcopal; m. by license 29 Sep 1782 Robert Hammitt Breeden" St. Andrew's Episcopal records

211-3 ?Charles Nuthall

21-2 Elinor Nutthall, b. ?by 1700; m/1 Baruch Williams, Jr.; d. by 24 Jul 1724; s/o Baruch Williams and Mary Hillery; m/2 John Pratt; 20 Jan 1742 indenture from Elinor Pratt, innkeeper, to Richard Duckett, planter, and husband of her sister, Mary, for £20 a tract of 66 acres being part of *Sprigg's Request* given by Elinor Murdock (her mother) to Elinor Pratt (Doliante); their children:

212-1 Baruch Williams; d. ca 1753; m. Lucy _____; she wit. the will of Edward Sprigg of Prince George's Co. written 30 Nov 1751 (Md. Cal. Wills, Vol. X, p. 195); no known children

WILL of BARUCH WILLIAMS, Prince George's Co.; written 20 Apr 1753; probate 13 Jul 1753
To wife Lucy Williams, land where I live, and that tract called *Addition to Bacon Hall*
Wit: John Sprigg, H. Belt, Jr., Richard Harwood, Jr.
(Md. Cal. Wills, Vol. X, p. 273; Wills, Liber 28, folio 504)

212-2 Mary Williams, b. 19 Jan 1717/8

Nov 1729; Mary Williams, dau. of Baruch Williams, aged 12, is admitted in her proper person in Court to choose her Guardian and accordingly makes choice of Rev. Mr. Murdock who accepts guardianship; court orders guardian give security at March Court next for the said Mary's estate (P 272).

    212-3  Hilleary Williams, b. 27 Dec 1719; not mentioned in the Orphans Court; may have d. young

    21-3  Priscilla Nuthall; m. 12 Dec 1723 Queen Anne's Parish, Prince George's Co. to Robert Lyles; children:

        213-1  Zachariah Lyles
        213-2  Hillary Lyles

WILL of ROBERT LYLES, planter, Calvert Co.; written 28 Feb 1733; probate 22 Mar 1733
To 2 sons Zechariah and Heleary and their hrs., entire real estate; to be of age at 18 years
Wife Priscilla, extx.
Test: Henry Austin, Henry Austin, Jr., John Richardson
                  (Md. Cal. of Wills, Vol. VII, p. 72; Liber 21, folio 28)

    213-1  Zachariah Lyles
    213-2  Hillary Lyles; d. ca 1769; m. Lucy Bowie, b. ca 1738; d/o James and Martha Bowie; children:

        2132-1  Priscilla Bowie Lyles; m. 17 Jan 1779 Wiseman Clagett
        2132-2  Zachariah Lyles; killed in the Revolution
        2132-3  James Lyles; Pvt., 2nd. Reg, Maryland Line

Will of HILLIARY LYLES, Prince George's Co.; written 26 Apr 1769; probate 28 Jun 1769
Children: Priscilla, Zachariah and James
Exs: Friends Henry Brooke and George Frazier Magruder
Wit: Joseph Sprigg, Enoch Magruder, Thos. Pindell
                  (Md. Cal. Wills, Vol. XIV, p. 101; Wills, Liber 37, folio 339)

Hiliary Lyles; Prince George's Co., £188/0/8; 7 Jun 1769; next of kin W. Bowie; exs. Henry Brookes and George F. Magruder (102.30).

Hilliary Lyles, Prince George's Co.; £69.7.11; 6 Oct 1770; 17 Jan 1771; next of kin: Edward Sprigg, Jr.; exs. Henry Brookes, George Fraser Magruder (105.265).

21-4 Elizabeth Nuthall; m. 17 Feb 1725/6 Queen Anne's Parish, Prince George's Co. to John Smith Prather, b. after 1693 as he not yet 18 in 1710/1; d. 1763; inn holder s/o Martha Sprigg and Thomas Prather; m/2 William Deakins; s/o John Deakins (Md. Cal. Wills, Vol. VIII, p. 260); their children:

      214-1 Josiah Prather, b. 1727
      214-2 Martha Prather, b. 1730
      214-3 Jeremiah Prather, b. 173_
      214-4 Eleanor Prather, b. 173_
      214-5 Aaron Prather, b. 173_
      214-6 Elizabeth Prather; b. 174_
      214-7 Rachel Prather, b. ca 1742
      214-8 Zachariah Prather, b. ca 1745

Will of JOHN SMITH PRATHER, Prince George's Co.; written 14 Jul 1763; probate 3 Sep 1763

To son Jeremiah Prather, 110 acres in Frederick Co., being pt. of tract called *Deer Park* and *Bear Garden Enlarged*

To son Zachariah Prather, pt. of tracts called *Deer Park* and *Bear Garden Enlarged*, 310 acres, after his sister Rachel Prather has her first choice

To dau. Eleanor Beall, £20 money

To grand-son John Smith Prather, son of Josiah Prather, dec'd, £20 money

To dau. Rachel Prather, slaves. Son Jeremiah, and daus. Martha Odell and Rachel Prather

Extx.: Wife Elizabeth Prather

Wit: Thomas Hilliary, William Deacon, Thomas Chittam
                        (Md. Cal. Wills, Vol. XII, p. 206; Wills, Liber 31, folio 999)

Inventory of the estate of John Smith Prather in Prince George's County lists Jeremiah Prather, Jr. and Zachariah Prather as next of kin with Elisabeth Prather as extx. (Inv. Prerog. Ct., Liber 83, folio 151).

The list of creditors of the estate of John Smith Prather includes a large number of the families living near Bennett's Creek in the area of the present day line between Frederick and Montgomery Counties (Doliante, p. 723).

214-1 Josiah Prather, b. 21 Dec 1727 Queen Anne Parish; d. 1755 Frederick Co.; m. Jane Deakins; family moved to NC; child:

2141-1 John Smith Prather; inherited £70 and a gray horse called Pompey from grandfather's will

Josiah Prather, Frederick Co.; £13.17.5; 20 Jun 1755; next of kin Isaac Prather, James Odell; admn. John Smith Prather (61.13).

214-2 Martha Prather, b. 20 Apr 1730 Queen Anne Parish; m/1 James Odell; m/2 Robert Lazenby

214-3 Jeremiah Prather, b. 17 Jul 173_ Queen Anne Parish; inherited from father part of *Deer Park* and *Bear Garden Enlarged* "convenient" to 200 acre part of these tracts previously given him; went to Montgomery Co., KY

214-4 Eleanor Prather, b. 2 Apr 173_ Queen Anne Parish; m. Joseph Beall, b. ca 1719/20; d. ca 1800 Frederick County, MD (Doliante)

214-5 Aaron Prather, b. 173_ Queen Anne Parish; d. young

214-6 Elizabeth Prather, b. 23 Sep 1740

214-7 Rachel Prather

214-8 Zachariah Prather; ml. 2 Mar 1778 Prince George's Co. Rosamond Callahan (Brumbaugh); inherited from father remainder of *Deer Park* and *Bear Garden Enlarged* of 310 acres

21-5 Mary Nuthall; m. 13 Nov 1729 Queen Anne Parish to Richard Duckett, Jr., b. 11 Feb 1704; 6 Feb 1728/9 George Murdock and Elinor gave Mary Nuthall 100 acres of *Sprigg's Request*; Richard Duckett m/2 2 Jun 1735 Elizabeth Williams; their children from *Across the Years in Prince George's County*:

215-1 Richard Jacob Duckett
215-2 son, b. 17 Mar 1733
215-3 Eleanor Duckett
215-4 Martha Duckett
215-5 Rachel Duckett
215-6 Charity Duckett
215-7 Thomas Duckett
215-8 Baruch Duckett
215-9 Ann Duckett
215-10 Jacob Duckett
215-11 Isaac Duckett

WILL of RICHARD DUCKETT; written 12 Sep 1785; probate 29 Sep 1788
To sons Richard, Thomas, Baruch Duckett
To son Isaac, land and plantation where I live, *Spriggs Request* and *Duckett's Addition*
Mentions sons Jacob and Richard Jacob Duckett
Residue divided among my children and grandchildren:
  Jacob, Isaac, Richard, Martha Hall, Anne Hall, Rachel William, Eleanor Lyles, and my grandchildren by my daughter Charity Boyd
Exs.: Son Isaac and wife Elizabeth
Wit: John Duvall, Robert Wheeler, Zach. McCally  (T.1, 266)

    215-1 Richard Jacob Duckett, b. 12 Apr 1732 Queen Anne Parish; d. ca 1803; m. Martha Waring, b. 20 Jan 1735; d/o Thomas Waring (1710-1762); granddau. of Capt. Basil Waring (1683-1733); their children:

        2151-1 Mary Duckett, b. 6 Jan 1756; m. Oct 1785 Belt Mullikin
        2151-2 Martha Duckett, b. 7 Oct 1759
        2151-3 Jane Duckett, b. 9 Oct 1761; m. 1794 Stephen Waters
        2151-4 Lucy Duckett, b. 26 Oct 1763; m. 11/13 Nov 1790 Zephaniah Athey
        2151-5 Thomas Waring Duckett, b. 9 Oct 1765
        2151-6 Elizabeth Duckett, b. 12 Jul 1767
        2151-7 Ann Duckett, b. 5 Jun 1770; m. 20 Jun 1791 Thomas F. Bowie
        2151-8 Basil Duckett, b. 26 Mar 1772; m. 13 Feb 1798 Sophia Mullikin; d/o Sophia and Belt Mullikin

WILL of RICHARD J. DUCKETT; written 9 Apr 1803; probate 21 May 1803
To son Basil, all real estate, except 1 room in my dwelling house, with a fire-place; to 2 single daughters, Lucy and Ann, as a residence, as long as they remain single, then to my son Basil; also to him £100
To daughters Lucy and Ann each, £100; to Elizabeth Soper £100
Residue of personal estate to Basil, Mary Mullikin, Martha Hall, Lucy Duckett, Elizabeth Soper, Ann Duckett, Richard, Basil and Stephen Waters, sons of Stephen Waters by my daughter, Jane. Residue divided between the 6 children above
Wit: Baruch and Richard Duckett, Jr., Jos. Cross   (T.1,552, W.M.)

215-2 son b. 17 Mar 1733 Queen Anne Parish
215-3 Eleanor Duckett, b. 25 Dec 1737; m. 10 Apr 1779 Thomas Lyles
215-4 Martha Duckett, b. ca 1738
215-5 Rachel Duckett, b. ca 1739; m. 1774 Col. Thomas Williams, b. ca 1739; d. 1785; their children:

    2155-1 Elizabeth Williams
    2155-2 Eleanor Williams
    2155-3 Elisha Williams
    2155-4 Rachel Williams

215-6 Charity Duckett, b. 6 Jan 1743; m. 24 Mar 1757 Thomas Boyd

    2156-1 Richard Duckett Boyd, b. 28 Dec 1757

215-7 Thomas Duckett, b. 26 Mar 1744; m. Priscilla Bowie, b. ca 1750; d. 1786
215-8 Baruch Duckett, b. ca 1745; d. 1810; m. 11 Jan 1783 Mary Bowie Beanes
215-9 Ann Duckett, b. ca 1750; m. 15 Mar 1764 William Hall of Pleasant Grove
215-10 Jacob Duckett, b. 23 Oct 1751; m. 1799 Mary Meek Clagett; d/o Thomas Clagett and widow of Patrick McElderry
215-11 Isaac Duckett, b. ca 1753; d. 1823; physician; m. Mary Bowie

3. James Nuthall (1), b. ca 1649; probate 12 Jun 1685; m. Mrs. Mary Bolton, a widow with two sons, John and James Bolton, who were not 21 years old in 1685 according to the will of James Nutthall. Mary's first husband may have been the John Bolton who is mentioned in wills (no county) in 1663 and 1670 (Md. Cal. of Wills, Vol. I). It appears that James Nuthall died before his father, thus is not mentioned in his father's will. No trace was found of his daughters to date, but his son James appears in several

documents. Why was he not mentioned in the will of his grandfather?

    3-1 James Nuthall (2)
    3-2 Eliza: Nuthall
    3-3 Mary Nuthall

13 Aug 1679 James Nutthall patented *The Hatchett* in that part of Calvert County which became Prince George's Co. (Hienton Map).

Mar 1711; William Willson, son-in-law [?step-son] to William Hill, dec'd, age 15 years came into court and was bound to James Nuttwell till age; ye said James obliging himself to give him a years schooling (G.43).

WILL of JAMES NUTTHALL, no county; written Apr 1685; probate 12th Jun 1685
To wife Mary, execx, 1/5 of personalty
To son James, all land and l/5 of personalty
To dau. Eliza:, 1/5 of personalty, at 16 yrs. of age
To dau. Mary, 1/5 of personalty, at 16 yrs. of age
To wife's 2 sons, John and James Boulton, 1/5 of personalty at 21 yrs. of age
To John, son of brother John Nutthall, 200 A, residue of lands to daus. and stepsons of testator, sd. son James dying during minority
Test: Hanna Cosden, Jas. Dossey, Philip Ryan   ( Wills, Liber 4, folio 111)

3-1 James Nuthall (2), b. ca 1675/83

In 1710 James Nutwell witnessed the will of William Hill in Prince George's County (Wills, Liber 13, folio 183); in 1715 he witnessed the will of Joseph Grear of the same county (Wills, Liber 14, folio 100). James was one of the appraisers of the estate of John Gittings of Calvert Co., undated but with the filings of 1678 (Inv. Prerog. Ct., 6.4).

3-2 Eliza: Nuthall; not yet 16 in 1685

3-3 Mary Nuthall; not yet 16 in 1685

4. Elias Nuthall; d. ca 1677; m. Elizabeth Beckwith; d/o George Beckwith and Frances Harvey; Elias was a servant in Virginia in 1671 when his father's estate was divided and he wished to use

his part to purchase his freedom; 6 Dec 1671 his brothers proposed to purchase Elizabeth Bradshaw, servant, and send her to Virginia for Elias' release and would pay more tobacco if necessary. Elias moved to Talbot Co. ca 1688.

31 Dec 1678 Ellias Nuthall in list of debts for estate of Richard Chillman (Inv. Prerog. Ct., 5.382-404).

9 Oct 1679 Elias Nuttall in list of debts for estate of John Garnish (Inv. Prerog. Ct., 6.547).

28 Apr 1679 accounting of the estate of George Beckwith of Calvert County mentions two unnamed orphans; Elias Nutalls as husband of an orphan ( Inv. Prerog. Ct., 6.46).

22 Apr 1680 Elias Nuthall is on the list of receivers of the estate for Richard Chilman (Inv. Prerog Ct. 7a.39).

10 Aug 1686 "due from" Elias Nutthall in accounting of estate of Peter Joy of Calvert Co. (Inv. Prerog. Ct., 9.134).

17 Apr 1689 Elias Nutwell listed as runaway in the list of debts in the accounting of the estate of Daniell Clocker of St. Mary's County (Inv. Prerog. Ct., 10.232).

## GOVER

The Gover family held land in the late 1600s in Anne Arundel County. At least part of the family belonged to the Quaker Meetings. Descendants moved about in Anne Arundel, Baltimore, Harford, Calvert and Prince George's Counties using the same given names every generation, thus making it very difficult to determine the relationships.

*Abstracts of Land Records, Anne Arundel County, Maryland, 1662-1703* documents the following records:

Special Court 13 Mar 1709 at Annapolis: Ephraim Gover was one of the persons present to record deeds, etc., relating to the former burnt records.

4 Jan 1677; Francis Holland and Margarett his wife to Robert Gover 100 acres, part of 950 acres *Broughton Ashley*; recorded at the request of Robert Gover.

4 Jan 1677; Francis Holland, Sr. of Herring Creek, Anne Arundel Co. and wife Margarett to Robert Gover, Herring Creek, bricklayer; for 3,000 lbs. of tobacco, 100 acres of *Browton Ashley* of 950 acres; recorded at the request of Ephraim Gover.

24 May 1684; Francis Holland and wife Sarah to Robert Gover; 50 acres, part of the 950 acre *Browton Ashley*; adjoining Robert Gover; called recorded at request of Ephraim Gover.

6 Mar 1692; bond between William Holland and Robert Gover, bricklayer for £100. Arbitration regarding a parcel of land on Herring Creek known as *Broughton Ashley* next to Robert Gover's land called *Gover's Ferrying* and *Gover's Adventure*; recorded at the request of Ephraim Gover.

11 Jun 1694; Robert Orme, Calvert Co. planter, and wife Sarah to Robert Gover, Anne Arundel County, bricklayer; for £30; one half part of *Knighton's Purchase* of 197 acres; recorded at request of Robert Wood who owned half of the land with Robert Orme.

*Side-Lights on Maryland History: Gover's Venture*, 295 acres, surveyed 31 Aug 1678 for Robert Gover

## Robert Gover

Robert Gover (1); d. ca 1700 Anne Arundel Co.; bur. 4 d. 2 mo. 1700; m/1 unknown, d. by 1699; he may have been the Robert Gover who stated intention to marry Susanna Billingsley on 8 d. 10 mo. 1699 (Quaker Records of So. Md.); children from will:

1. Robert Gover
2. Samuel Gover
3. Ephraim Gover

WILL of ROBERT GOVER, Anne Arundel County; written 11 Nov 1699; probate 6 May 1700
To eld. son Robert and hrs., 100 a., part of *Boughton Ashly* and 295 a. dwelling plantation, *Gover's Adventure*
To 2nd son Samuel and hrs., 1/2 of *Gover's Ferrying* and 100 a. part of *Knighton's Purchase*
To young. son Ephraim at majority and hrs., residue of *Gover's Ferrying* and 167 a. *Gover's Addition*, Calvert Co.
3 sons afsd., exs., and residuary legatees of estate
Test: Saborne Tucker, Jno. Stephens, Robt. Wood, Thos. Hughs
(Md. Cal. Wills, Vol. II, p. 196; Wills, Liber 6, folio 364)

Account of estate of Robert Gover, the elder; Anne Arundel Co.; £246.14.8; 29 Apr 1703; exs.: Samuel Gover (Quaker), Ephraim Gover (Quaker), Elisabeth Ward (widow of Robert Gover, Jr.) wife of John Ward (Quaker) (23.55).

WILL of SUSANNAH GOVER, widow, Calvert Co.; written 2 Sep 1723; probate 14 Mar 1723
To dau. Rebecca Birckhead, extx., personalty; and to her husband, 20s
To 2 grandsons Abraham and Eleazar Birckhead, personalty
To 6 grand-daus., residue of estate
Test: John Pearson, Jno. Beckett, Thos. Chambers
(Md. Cal. Wills, Vol. V, p. 159; Wills, Liber 18, folio 233)

Estate of Susanna Gover, Calvert Co.; value £92/15/0; 5 Apr 1724; 27 Jun 1724; next of kin: Abraham Birckhead, Ann Birckhead; Exs/admns. Richard and Daniel Talbott (Inv. of Prerog. Ct., 10.81).

Robert Gover (assumed to be Robert, the elder) and John Sollers appraised several estates in Anne Arundel Co. Robert is also found in the several lists of debts in the Prerogative Court Records.

Francis Billingsley d. ca 1695 in Calvert Co.; his will names his wife Susanna and dau. Rebecca Birckhead (Md. Cal. Wills, Vol. II, p. 104). Quaker records show Robert Gover married Susanna Billingsley shortly after writing his will in 1699. When he died several months later, there was no provision for Susanna in his will. Her will, probated 23 years later, mentions only her daughter Rebecca and Rebecca's family.

By 1699, all of Robert Gover's children would have been grown and therefore this last marriage was undoubtedly one of convenience with perhaps a pre-marital agreement as his estate went to his children and her estate to her child and Susanna did not stay in Anne Arundel County on the Gover plantation, even though she never remarried.

Robert (1) or (2) was named in a deed from Samuel Chew on 18 Mary 1699 for 1 1/4 acres for the building of a Quaker meeting house adjoining *Smith's Delight* (WT1.68).

1. Robert Gover (2); d. 1700; s/o Robert; m. 5 Dec 1695 Elizabeth Cotton; d. ca 1749; she m/2 20 Feb 1700/1 Anne Arundel Co. to John Ward; d. ca 1736; Robert inherited 100 acres of *Boughton Ashley* and 295 a. *Gover's Adventure* from father's will and died shortly thereafter; the entire 195 acres of *Gover's Adventure* left by Robert (1) to his son, Robert (2), was willed by his brother Samuel to Samuel's eldest son in 1744; child from will:

    1-1 Rachel Gover, b. ca 1697

Richard Thornberry binds himself to Robert Gover, bricklayer for £100, 10 May 1694. He also agrees to abide by arbitration regarding the claim to a parcel of 40 acres on Herring Creek (WT1.195).

27 Aug 1701; arbitration report from John Sollers, Richard Johns, Richard Harrison and William Turner concerning 40 acres on Herring Creek, part of a tract known as *Broughton Ashley*. First award, on the westernmost side of cleared and tended ground of the west bounds of Richard Thornberry and the land to the west of the land deemed to belong to Robert Gover, Sen. Secondly, award that Richard Thornberry pay to Robert Gover sum of 400# tobacco upon his now dwelling plantation in part of the charges of the law

suit. Lastly that Gover and Thornberry give to each other upon demand all manner of law suits, trespasses and damages that might be concerning these lands (WT2.196).

WILL of ROBERT GOVER, Anne Arundel Co.; written 6 May 1700; probate 7 Sep 1700
To dau. Rachel and unborn child at majority, entire estate
Extx: Wife Eliza: In event of death of child. afsd. sd. wife to have entire estate until the year 1710, at which time it is to pass to pass to brothers Samuel and Ephraim and their hrs.
Test: Robt. Wood, Jno. Stephens, Jno. Cole Speagle, Thos. Hughs
(Md. Cal. Wills, Vol. II, p. 201; Wills, Liber 6, folio 393)

Inventory of Robert Gover, Jr.; £246.14.8; 5 Oct 1700 (20.92).

Account of the estate of Robert Gover, the younger; Anne Arundel Co.; £266.14.7; £33.6.6; 29 Apr 1703; extx.: Elizabeth Ward (relict), wife of John Ward (23.42).

1-1  Rachel Gover, b. 16 Apr 1697

Bond, 14 Aug 1707; John Ward, Robert Ward and Edward Ward, Anne Arundel Co., planters, are bound to Rachel Gover, orphan of Robt. Gover, Jr., Anne Arundel Co., Gent., in the sume of £487.14; this obligation is void if John Ward pays Rachell Gover £243.17 when she come of age (WT2.521).

The estate of John Ward and the will of Elizabeth Ward make no mention of Rachel; unknown if Eleanor Franklin was unborn child mentioned in Elizabeth Ward's will or if she was a child of John Ward.

John Ward, Anne Arundel Co.; £576.2.9; 3 Jun 1736; 5 Nov 1737; next of kin: Robert Ward, Richard Ward; admn. Elisabeth Ward (Quaker) (22.23).

Will of ELIZABETH WARD, Anne Arundel Co., widow; written 7 Jul 1748; probate 27 Oct 1749
To son Robert Ward, furniture
To dau. Eleanor Franklin, clothing
Child. hereafter named: Eleanor Franklin, Richard Ward, Samuel Ward, Joseph Ward and Benjamin Ward, equally at my decease
Ex: Son, Richard Ward
Wit: Richard Stallings, William Tucker, Elizabeth Keys
(Md. Cal. Wills, Vol. X, p. 51; Wills, Liber 27, folio 89)

2. Samuel Gover (1); d. 1744; Quaker; m. 1706 Elizabeth Roberts; d. ca 1764; intention to marry 14 d. 4 mo. 1706 and 12 d. 5 mo. 1706 (Clifts Monthly Meeting); inherited half of *Grover's Ferrying* and 100 acres of *Knighton's Purchase* from father's will; Samuel was executor of the 1711 will of John Stephens of Anne Arundel Co. which mentions his son, Samuel Gover, Jr. (Md. Cal. Wills, Vol. III, p. 198); children from wills and Quaker records:

    2-1 Samuel Gover, b. 1707    2-6 Benjamin Gover, b. 1716
    2-2 Robert Gover, b. 1708    2-7 Ephraim Gover, b. 1718
    2-3 Elizabeth Gover, b. 1710    2-8 Richard Gover, b. 1720
    2-4 Cassandra Gover, b. 1712    2-9 Rachell Gover, b. 1722
    2-5 Priscilla Gover, b. 1714    2-10 Phillip Gover, b. 1726

Deed 27 Apr 1703; from John Emerton, Anne Arundel Co., planter, to Samuell Gover, Anne Arundel Co., planter; for £35 part of a tract of land called *Emerton's Range*, lying adjacent to: land of John Griffin; land of Samuel Chew; *Boughton Ashley*, lately sold by Col. William Holland to Samuel Gover; near the now dwelling plantation of Samuel Gover; containing 50 acres. Heretofore the estate and inheritance of Humphrey Emerton, father of John Emerton; release of dower by Mary Emerton (WT2.42).

Deed, 30 Aug 1703; recorded 2 Nov 1703; from William Holland, Anne Arundel Co., Esq., and Margaret, his wife, only daughter and heir of Francis Holland, the Elder, late of Anne Arundel Co., Gent., dec'd, to Samuell Gover, Anne Arundel Co., planter; 24 acre part of tract called *Broughton Ashly*, by line of Jno. Emerton and of Daniel Browne (WT2.87).

WILL of SAMUEL GOVER, Anne Arundel Co.; written 13 Dec 1743; probate 13 Oct 1744

To oldest son Samuel and hrs., 295 a. *Gover's Adventure* also land in Calvert Co. which testator bought from John Bagby

To eldest son Samuel and youngest son Philip and hrs., dwelling plantation, 200 a. *Gover's Firing* and 150 a. in Baltimore Co. which testator bought from John Bagby this being part of *Rapatta*

To son Ephraham, 250 a. of *Elberton* which testator bought from Lawrence Draper, 50 a. *Elberton* purchased from Samuel Griffin. He to pay to his cousin Elizabeth, at 21, (dau. of Robert), £20

To son Richard and hrs., 263 a. *Smith's Addition*, part of *Kenton's Purchase* on the line dividing properties of Robert Gover and Robert Wood and

*Expedition* in Calvert Co. He to pay to his cousin Priscilla at 21 yrs., dau. of Robert, £20

To 5th son Philip and hrs., residue of *Kenton's Purchase*, part of *Emerton's Range* which testator purchased from John Emerton, 24 a. which testator purchased from Col. Holland, part of land testator bought from \_\_\_\_ Brown and 50 a. of *Boughton Ashley* where John Waters lived

To bro. Ephraham and hrs., 50 a. *Boughten Ashley* which testator's father purchased from Francis Holland, Jr.

To sons and hrs., 1 a. *Hall's Hills* for warehouse. This never to be sold as long as there is one of that name in Maryland

To Elizabeth Lee, Cassandra Willson, Priscilla Willson, Robert and sons afsd., personalty

To wife \_\_\_; life interest in dwelling plantation and personal estate

Ex.: Sons Samuel, Ephraham, Philip and Richard

Test: Gerrard Ball, Robt. Gover, Quaker, William Evans

(Md. Cal. Wills, Vol. VIII, p. 279; Wills, Liber 23, folio 584)

Note: Widow refuses to abide by will and requests her legal thirds.

Estate of Samuel Gover, Anne Arundel Co.; value £694/4/6; 12 Feb 1744; 8 Oct 1745; next of kin: Ephraim Gover, Henry Wilson; exs. Ephraim Gover, Phillip Gover (Inv. Prerog. Ct., 31.306).

Will of ELIZABETH GOVER, Baltimore Co.; probate 31 Aug 1764

To dau. Elizabeth Lee, £10 to be paid to her by ex., within 3 years after my decease

To daus. Cassandra Wilson and Priscilla Wilson, £10

To son Ephraim Gover, and Elizabeth Wilson, wife of Ben Kid Wilson, and Priscilla Gover, 5s. money

To son Philip Gover, remainder of estate

Ex: Son Philip Gover

Wit: Samuel Harris, Richard Jones (?Johns), Quakers

(Md. Cal. Wills, Vol. XIII, p. 35; Wills, Liber 32, folio 229)

2-1 Samuel Gover (2), b. 30 d. 3 mo. 1707; d. 11 Mar 1744/5; Samuel, late of Herring Creek, Anna Hundred, \_\_\_\_ Co. m. 11 Nov 1742 Bush Creek to Hannah Webster; d. 8 mo. 1806; d/o Isaac (of Bush River, Baltimore Co.) and Margaret Webster; she m/2 20 d. 2 mo. 1749 Nathan Richardson of Baltimore; d. ca 1756; (Nottingham Quakers); Samuel inherited 150 acres *Rapatta* in Baltimore Co. from will of father; Hannah named in 1759 will of her father

Isaac (Md. Cal. Wills, Vol. XI, p. 248); she wit. Quaker weddings Baltimore Co. in 1759 and 1760; child from will:

21-1 Samuel Gover (3)

WILL of SAMUEL GOVER, Baltimore Co.; written 27 Apr 1744; probate 13 Mar 1744/5
To wife Hannah and son Samuel, entire estate, real and personal
Ex.: John Hanbury, merchant of London; Jacob Giles, merchant of Maryland, at present in London (Quaker)
Test: Mary Butcher, Mary Cox, Abraham Harman
(Md. Cal. Wills, Vol. VIII, p. 253: Wills, Liber 23, folio 401)
Note: 6 Jun 1744 exs. afsd. refuse to act, witnessed by John Shaw
Note: 11 Feb 1744/5 Hannah afsd. turns over the administration to her father Jacob (Isaac) Webster

Estate of Capt. Samuel Gover, Baltimore Co.; value £330/10/3; 6 Jul 1745; 8 Aug 1746; next of kin Hannah Gover, Ephramin Gover; admn. Isaac Webster, Quaker (Prerog. Ct., 33.34)

WILL of NATHAN RICHARDSON, Baltimore Co., written 7 Jan 1756; probate 5 Aug 1756
Wife: Hannah
Children by my 1st wife: Elizabeth, Sarah, William, Nathan, Daniel Richardson and Margaret Hill
Mother-in-law: Margaret Webster
Exs: Wife, Hannah Richardson, bro.-in-law Isaac Webster
Wit: Maj. Wm. Dallam, Dr. James MacGill, John Kidd, John Bond
(Quaker) (Md. Cal. Wills, Vol. XI, p. 136; Wills, Liber 30, folio 118)

Hannah Richardson, d/o John Webster, d. 8 m. 1806 (Nottingham Quakers). This is undoubtedly Hannah Webster, d/o Isaac. The will of Isaac Webster of Baltimore Co., written 9 Mar 1755, wife Margaret; names among his children: dau. Hannah Richardson and a son named Isaac Webster (Md. Cal. Wills, Vol. XI, p. 248).

2-2 Robert Gover, b. 19 d. 10 mo. 1708; d. ca 1737; this may have been the Robert Gover int. to marry 13 d. 2 mo. 1733 to the Elizabeth Johns who m/2 Robert Freeland; d. 1757; children:

Robert Gover, Calvert Co.; £217.12.5; 30 Sep 1737; 10 May 1742; creditor Benjamin Johns; next of kin Samuel Gover; admnx: Eliza Freeland (26.540).

22-1 Priscilla Gover, b. ca 1734; d. 1790; a certificate to Nottingham 28 d. 1 mo. 1757; unmarried

Will of PRISCILLA GOVER; written 31 Jan 1790; probate 6 Sep 1790
To Nephews, Benjamin Kidd Wilson and Henry Wilson, s/o Benjamin Kidd Wilson
To Samuel, Elizabeth, Gerard, Robert, Philip, Mary & Priscilla Gover, children of Philip Gover, deceased
Ex: Samuel Gover, Robert Gover
Wit: Mary Johns, Elizabeth Pusey, Ephraim Gittings Gover (AJ-2-251)

22-2 Elisabeth Gover, b. ca 1736; m. 26 d. 12 mo. 1755 Benkid Wilson (Quaker Rec. of So. Md.);

222-1 Benjamin Kidd Wilson; m. Elizabeth _____; she m/2 1796 to [2(10)-1] Samuel Gover, b. ca 1766; s/o Philip Gover
222-2 Henry Wilson

2-3 Elizabeth Gover, b. 13 d. 6 mo. 1710; m. 16 Jun 1730 James Lee, b. ca 1707; d. ca 1778 Harford Co.; s/o James Lee and Margaret _____ Wilson; census of Deer Creek Hundred 1776 show James Lee, Sr., age 72; Elizabeth, age 66; 24 Negroes and their 2 VanCleave grandchildren in household; children from *Baltimore County Families*:

23-1 Margaret Lee; m. 6 Feb 1752 John Paca, Jr., b. 14 Apr 1725; d. 1757; their children from his will and St. George's Parish:

231-1 Aquilla Paca, b. 30 Mar 1753
231-2 James Paca, b. 25 Oct 1754
231-3 John Stokes Paca, b. 22 Sep 1757

WILL of JOHN PACA, JR., Baltimore Co.; written 17 Sep 1757; 1 Dec 1757; probate 11 Feb 1758
Children: Aquilla, James and John Paca

To son John, plantation called *Mouls Success, Paca's Park* at head of Bush River, *Goldsmith's Hall, Gibson's Ridge, Paca's Enlargement, Stoney Ridge, Paca's Delight, Delph, Paca's Convenience,* and *Delph's Neglect*
Col. Wm. Hammond, Alexander Lawson, open my bank at Bush river and raise what iron ore they judge necessary to secure money to maintain and educate my 3 sons
Exs: Wife Margaret, friends John Paca, Robert Adair
Wit: Robert Pryce, Edward Hays, Dr. Benjamin Crockett
(Md. Ca. Wills, Vol. XI, p. 191; Wills, Liber 30, folio 435)

23-2 James Lee, b. 1 Mar 1733; d. infancy
23-3 James Lee (twin), b. 16 Oct 1735; m/1 unknown; m/2 1779 to Sarah Elliott; children:

    233-1 James Lee (4), b. 31 Aug 1756
    233-2 Richard Lee
    233-3 Corbin Lee

23-4 Samuel Lee (twin), b. 16 Oct 1735; m. Mary Hall; d/o Parker Hall; children:

    234-1 Parker Hall Lee, b. 14 Jan 1759; d. 1829
    234-2 James Lee, b. 10 Dec 1760; d. 1786; m. Milcah _____; he was a physician
    234-3 Priscilla Lee, b. 3 Sep 1762; m. George Presbury
    234-4 Mary Lee; m. John Moores
    234-5 Blanch Lee; m. William Welch
    234-6 Elizabeth Lee; m. Robert Gover
    234-7 Cassandra Lee; m. Robert Gover
    234-8 Margaret Lee; m. William Smithson

23-5 Mary Lee, b. ca 1739; m. Samuel Wilson
23-6 Elizabeth Lee; m. 12 Jul 1758 William Webb
23-7 Cassandra Lee, b. ca 1744; m. William Morgan, b. ca 1744; children from Deer Creek Lower Hundred census:

    237-1 Elizabeth Morgan, b. ca 1773
    237-2 Sarah Morgan, b. ca 1774
    237-3 Cassandra Morgan, b. ca 1775

Deer Creek Lower Hundred census 1776: William Morgan, age 32; Cassandria, age 32; Elizabeth, age 3; Sarah, age 1 1/2; Cassandria, age 1; 10 Negroes

    23-8 Josiah Lee; m. Sarah Chew Worthington
    23-9 Rachel Lee; m. 1766 Dr. Gideon VanCleave; their children with her parents in 1776 census of Harford Co.; both mentioned in will of Aquilla Paca, Jr. written 8 Nov 1783 (AJ-2-513_:

        239-1 Elizabeth VanCleave, b. ca 1767
        239-2 Mary VanCleave, b. ca 1768

2-4 Cassandra Gover, b. 30 d. 3 mo. 1712; m. 19 d. 7 mo. 1740 at Bush River to William Wilson, Jr.; moved membership from Nottingham to Gunpowder dated 1753 (Nottingham Quakers);

    24-1 Rachel Wilson, b. 19 Jun 1741
    24-2 William Wilson, b. 14 Nov 1747
    24-3 Gover Wilson, b. 3 Mar 1749/50
    24-4 Samuel Wilson, b. 11 Feb 1752/3; m. Mary _____, b. ca 1751; 9 Negroes in 1776 census of Susquehannah Hundred

Susquehannah Hundred census of 1776: William Wilson, age 56; Cassandra, age 65; 9 Negroes

2-5 Priscilla Gover, b. 11 d. 4 mo. 1714; m. 11 d. 10 mo. 1742 to Henry Wilson, b. ca 1721; rec'd into membership in Gunpowder Mtg. 27 d. 6 mo. 1753 by certificate from Nottingham; their children:

    25-1 Henry Wilson, b. 19 Jun 1747; m. Margaret _____; b. ca 1749; their children from census:

        251-1 Henry Wilson, b. ca 1772
        251-2 William Wilson, b. ca 1774
        251-3 Samuel Wilson, b. ca 1775

Bush Creek Lower Hundred census 1776: Henry Wilson, Jr., age 29; Margaret Wilson, age 27; Henry Wilson, age 4; William Wilson, age 2; Samuel Wilson, age 1; 6 Negroes; 1 servant

    25-2 Priscilla Wilson, b. 29 Oct 1749

25-3  Rachel Wilson, b. 9 Nov 1751
25-4  Elizabeth Wilson, b. 13 Mar 1754

Bush Creek Lower Hundred census 1776: Henry Wilson, Sr., age, 55; Pricilla, age 62; Casandra, age 13; 13 Negroes

2-6  Benjamin Gover, b. 17 d. 6 mo. 1716
2-7  Ephraim Gover, b. 18 d. 7 mo. 1718; d. ca 1770; m. Elizabeth Gittings, b. ca 1726; d/o Thomas Gittings and Elizabeth Redgrave; guardian of Robert Cook Baltimore Co. 1750; the widow Elizabeth in Deer Creek Lower Hundred, Harford Co. in 1776; children from will, census and church records:

27-1  Elizabeth Gover, b. 1741
27-2  Cassandra Gover, b. ca 1743
27-3  Ephraim Gover
27-4  Mary Gover, b. ca. 1746
27-5  Priscilla Gover, b. ca 1748
27-6  Margaret Gover, b. ca 1750
27-7  Rachel Gover, b. ca 1751
27-8  Samuel Gover, b. ca 1755
27-9  Gittings Gover, b. ca 1759
27-10  Robert Gover, b. ca 1761

The minutes of the Quaker meetings held alternately at West River - the Clifts and Patuxent - Herring Creek show that Ephraim Gover and family were given a certificate of removal to Nottingham on 19 d. 4 mo. 1747. A Samuel and Ephraim Gover witnessed a wedding at Bush River 11 d., 8 mo., 1741. On 11 d. 9 mo. 1742 Ephraim and known relatives witnessed the wedding of Samuel Gover to Hannah Webster. On 1 d. 3 mo. 1750 Ephraim and relatives witnessed the wedding of Benjamin Chew, Jr. and Cassandra Johns (Nottingham Quakers).

The birth of Elizabeth Gover, d/o Ephraim Gover and Elizabeth his wife on 7 Apr 1741 was recorded in St. George's Parish Register. He is also shown as a vestryman of St. George in 1762. On 6 Sep 1757 Ephraim was appointed one of the inspectors for Swan Town and Rock Creek warehouses according to the vestry records.

All indications I have found are that these records refer to the same Ephraim, yet, could a Quaker be a vestryman at St. George's Parish? Could a member of St. George's be a witness at a Quaker wedding? Later members of this family are also found in the baptismal records of St. George's.

Thursday, 10 Mar 1757: A Negro woman named "Fida", belonging to Ephraim Gover of Herring Bay, was tried and found guilty at the County Court for attempting to poison her master (Md. Gazette, no. 618).

Deed, 26 Feb 1705; from Richard Thornberry, heretofore of Anne Arundel Co., planter, now resident in Westmoreland Co., VA, to Ephraim Gover, Anne Arundel Co., planter; 50 acres, part of a tract called *Broughton Ashly*, formerly belonging to Francis Holland, dec'd; and the remaining part of 200 acres, part of the tract which Richard Thornberry purchased from Francis Holland, the other part being sold by Richard Thornberry to John Chappell, 50 acres. Adjacent to the land now in possession of John Ward, adjacent to Well's land and Stirling's land, all of which premises are now in occupation of John Prichard (WT2.306).

Ephraim Gover of Calvert Co. sold a tract called *Elberton* to Wm. Allnut on 19 Sep 1724 (B'more Co. Families).

WILL of EPHRIAM GOVER, Baltimore Co.; written 8 Dec 1769; probate 3 Mar 1770
Wife: Elizabeth
Children: Samuel, Ephraim, Gettins, Robert, Mary, Cassandra, Margaret, Priscilla, Rachel
Tract: *Elberton*, left me by my father's will, and *The Sting*
Extx: Wife Elizabeth
Wit: William Hopkins, John Worthington, Samuel Wilson
(Wills, Liber 37, folio 455)

Estate of Ephraim Gover, Baltimore Co.; value £1018/5/4; 16 Apr 1770; 19 Sep 1770; next of kin: Cassandra Gover, Mary Hopkins; extx: Elizabeth Gover (Inv. Prerog. Ct., 105.82).

Estate of Ephraim Gover, Baltimore Co.; value £36/15/2; 21 Jun 1773; list of debts; extx., Elizabeth Gover (Inv. Prerog. Ct., 111.417).

27-1 Elizabeth Gover, b. 4 Apr 1741 St. George's Parish; m. 9 d. 2 mo. 1769 to Joseph Hopkins; s/o Joseph and Ann Hopkins; both of Deer Creek

27-2 Cassandra Gover, b. ca 1743; age 33 in 1776 census living with her mother; m. 10 d. 3 mo. 1785 Deer Creek to Samuel Harris; s/o Samuel and Margret Harris

27-3 Ephraim Gittings Gover; m. 31 Jan 1793 Harford County to Elisabeth Gover

27-4 Mary Gover, b. ca 1746; m. 8 d. 6 mo. 1769 to Samuel Hopkins; s/o Philip and Elizabeth Hopkins; Deer Creek records; children from census:

    274-1 Elizabeth Hopkins, b. ca 1770
    274-2 Ephraim Gover Hopkins, b. ca 1771
    274-3 Phillip Hopkins, b. ca 1773
    274-4 Samuel Hopkins, b. ca 1775

Census of Deer Creek Hundred, Harford Co.; census 1776; Samuel Hopkins, age 30; Mary age 30; Elizabeth, age 6; Ephraim Gover, age 5; Phillip, age 3; Samuel, age 1; 3 Negroes

27-5 Priscilla Gover, b. ca 1748; age 28 in 1776 census living with her mother; d. ca 1790

27-6 Margaret Gover; m. 9 d. 1 mo. 1772 Winston Smith Dallam; s/o Richard Dallam, dec'd, and Frances; Deer Creek Meeting

    276-1 Francis Dallam, b. ca 1772
    276-2 Elizabeth Dallam, b. ca 1774

Census of Deer Creek Lower Hundred 1776: Winston Dallam, age 27; Margaret, age 26; Francis, age 4, Elizabeth, age 2; two workers; 2 Negroes

27-7 Rachel Gover; m. 19 d. 5 mo. 1774 to William Cox, Jr. ; Deer Creek Meeting

    277-1 Mary Cox; b. ca 1775
    277-2 William Cox; 3 mos. old when 1776 census taken

Census of Deer Creek Lower Hundred 1776: William Cox, Jr., age 25; Rachel, age 25; Mary, age 1; William, age 3 mos.

27-8 Samuel Gover, b. ca 1755
27-9 Gittings Gover, b. ca 1759
27-10 Robert Gover, b. ca 1761; age 15 in Susquehannah Hundred census of 1776 in household of Gidian Pervail

2-8 Richard Gover, b. 20 d. 9 mo. 1720

2-9 Rachell Gover, b. 28 d. 9 mo. 1722

2-10 Philip Gover, b. 7 d. 8 mo. 1726; d. by 1791; s/o Samuel Gover and Elizabeth Roberts; inherited part of *Repatta* in Baltimore Co. from father's will; m. int. 30 d. 6 mo. 1761 to Mary Hopkins, b. ca 1734 (census); d/o Gerard Hopkins; he took Oath of Fidelity in Harford Co. in 1778; circumstantial evidence of given names of the children, geographical location and the following information indicate that this is the family of Philip; children from census records and 1790 will of Priscilla Gover:

2(10)-1 Samuel Gover, b. ca 1766; m. 3 d. 11 mo. 1791 Ann Hopkins; d/o Joseph and Elizabeth Hopkins; both of Harford Co.; m/2 on 22 Jul 1796 Elizabeth Wilson, widow of [222-1] Benkid Wilson of Baltimore Co., dec'd, Benjamin and Henry Wilson, sold Samuel, s/o Philip Gover of Harford County, land in Calvert Co. for £300 including *Aldermason*, part of *Smith's Addition*, 203 a., part of *Hilton's Purchase*; adjoining land mentioned in 1743 will of Samuel Gover of Anne Arundel Co.; also part of *Expedition* in Calvert Co.; recorded 9 Dec 1811 (Calvert Co. Land Records).

Deer Creek Monthly Meeting, 22 d. 9 mo. 1791; Samuel Gover, son of Philip and Mary Gover, deceased, intends to marry Ann Hopkins, d/o Joseph and Elizabeth Hopkins, who were present, "but as they are in a degree between 1st & 2nd cousins, friends at the preparative meeting advised against it" and the matter will be looked into further (Quaker Records of No. Md.).

2(10)-2 Elisabeth Gover, b. ca 1767; disowned 26 d. 7 mo. 1792 for holding her fellow creatures in a state of bondage (Deer Creek)

2(10)-3 Gerard Gover (twin), b. ca 1769

2(10)-4 Robert Gover (twin), b. ca 1769; Robert of Harford County sold interest in *Gover's Venture*, *Smith's Addition*, *Knighton's Purchase*, *Expedition*, *Emmerton's Range*, *Broughton Ashley*, and *Aldermason* in Anne Arundel and Calvert Cos. to Abraham Jarrett for $1,500; 21 Jun 1810 (Calvert Co. Land Records).

2(10)-5 Phillip Gover (twin), b. ca 1771

2(10)-6 Hennery Gover (twin), b. ca 1771

2(10)-7 Mary Gover
2(10)-8 Priscilla Gover, b. ca 1773

The birth of Phillip is shown as 1726 in *Quaker Records of Southern Maryland* from the West River Meeting. On 28 d. 1 mo. 1746 Elizabeth Gover and son Philip were given certificate of removal to Nottingham.

The vestry proceedings of St. George's of 27 Jul 1756 and 19 Jun 1759 include Philip Gover in the list of bachelors. He is shown as a bachelor over age 25 in the list of 17 Jun 1757 of Susquehannah Hundred. In 1760 Phillip Gover and Mary Hopkins were among the witnesses at a Quaker wedding at Deer Creek.

The West River Meeting records show Philip Gover and Mary Hopkins were married 11 d., 8 mo., 1761. The vestry proceedings of St. George's of 13 Jul 1762 state that his name no longer is on the tax list for bachelors, apparently confirming this is the same person.

The census of 1776 gives his age as 57 (b. ca 1719) while the Quaker records say he was b. in 1726.

Philip Gover and Richard Johns inventories the estate of Margaret Barnes in 1756. Tract of land called *Repulta* was owned by the Barnes family (B'more Co. Families).

3. Ephraim Gover, b. ca 1682/3; age 56 in 1738/9, 63 in 1745, age 73 in 1756 Anne Arundel Co. (More Md. Deponents); s/o Robert (1); inherited residue of *Gover's Ferrying* and 167 a. *Gover's Addition*; int. to marry Mary Harper on 15 d. 4 mo. 1705 and 3 d. 5 mo. 1705; children from his will:

        3-1 Robert Gover
        3-2 Ephraim Gover
        3-3 Mary Gover

19 Sep 1724 Epharim Gover of Calvert County sold 212 acres of *Dear Bought* on the Western Branch of the Patuxent to Henry Child, Jr. of Anne Arundel Co. for £117; Mary, wife of Epharim acknowledged deed (Land Records of Pr. Geo's Co., Liber I, folio 613).

WILL of EPHRAIM GOVER, Anne Arundel Co.; written 20 Mar 1757; probate 21 Apr 1756 (sic)
Children: Robert, Ephraim and Mary

Land in Baltimore, Anne Arundel, Calvert and Prince George's Counties
Friend: Wm. Sandsbury
Exs: Robert and Ephraim
Wit: John Carr, Robert Wood, Wm. Parlitt
(Md. Cal. Wills, Vol. XI, p. 206; Wills, Liber 30, folio 518)

Estate of Ephraim Gover, Anne Arundel Co.; value £591/10/11; 24 May 1758; 20 Feb 1759; next of kin: Philip Gover, Ephraim Gover; admn.: Robert Gover (Inv. Prerog. Ct., 66.132).

3-1 Robert Gover; d. ca 1762; m. Sarah _____; children from will:

    31-1 William Gover    31-6 Rachel Gover
    31-2 Robert Gover    31-7 Jane Gover
    31-3 Samuel Gover    31-8 Margaret Gover
    31-4 Sarah Gover    31-9 Elizabeth Gover
    31-5 Mary Gover    31-10 Hannah Gover

WILL of ROBERT GOVER, Calvert Co.; written 27 Jun 1762; probate 12 Aug 1762
To eldest son William Gover, tract called *Dineurk*; 60 a. part of a tract called *Exchange*, on Patuxent River
To 2nd son Robert Gover, pt. of tract laying in Calvert Co., called *Archer Hate* (*Archer Hays*) on side of Patuxent River; pt. of tract called *Gover's Meddow*; all pt. of tract called *Gauss Purchase*
To 3rd son Samuel Gover, pt. of tract called *Gover's Fearon* in Anne \_\_\_\_ Co.; tract lying in Calvert Co. called *Gover's Addition*
Whereas I have a right by my dec'd father Ephraim Gover's will, to sundry lands after death of my bro. Ephraim Gover and sister Mary Gover, that after death of bro. Ephraim, and sister Mary, in case they shd. die without issue, all my lands afsd. I give to daus: Sarah, Mary, Rachel, Jane, Margaret, Elizabeth and Hannah Gover, equally
To wife Sarah Gover, extx., 1/3 of lands
Wit: William Hammond, Samuel and Mary Robertson
(Md. Cal. Wills, Vol. XII, p. 141; Wills, Liber 31, folio 697)

Robert Gover, Calvert Co.; £267.17.10; 18 Oct 1762; 22 Nov 1762; extx: Sarah Gover (Quaker) (79.160).

31-1 William Gover; inherited *Dineurk (Dunkirk)* and *Exchange* from 1762 will of father; the 1782 tax assessment in Lyons

Creek Hundred, Calvert Co., shows William owned 120 acres of *Dunkirk* with 1 male over 16 and a total of 3 white inhabitants

William Gover of Prince George's County for £250 purchased 125 acres in Calvert Co. called *Harnisham* from John Brooke who holds as sheriff of Calvert County; William then sold Robert Gantt 125 a. *Harnisham* on 20 Feb 1796 for £234 (Calvert Co. Land Records).

    31-2 Robert Gover; inherited part of *Archer Hays, Gover's Meadow* and *Gauss Purchase* from 1762 will of father.

The 1782 tax assessment in Lyons Creek Hundred, Calvert Co., shows Robert owned 189 acres of *Archer Hays, Griffith's Pasture* and *Turner's Place*; 1 male over 16; 4 white inhabitants.

Robert sold Theodore Hodgkins land called *Turner's Pasture* on the south side of Turner's Creek on 6 May 1794 for £30. 23 Mar 1795 Robert Gover purchased part of *Archer Hays* near the Patuxent River from William Sansbury for £40. On 1 Dec 1797 Robert sold 40 a. called *Tune* to Thomas Simson for £45. (Calvert Co. Land Records)..

Calvert County land records also show that the residence and property of 250 acres on the Patuxent River of Capt. Robert Gover, deceased, being part of *Archer's Hays, Turner's Pasture, Gover's Meadow* and *Gough's Purchase*, was sold for £2,400 on 26 Jan 1816 by Gassaway Pindell and his wife, Sarah, and Samuel Gover of Anne Arundel County. The family burial ground of Capt. Gover of 1/4 acre was excluded.

    31-3 Samuel Gover; inherited part of *Gover's Fearon* (*?Gover's Ferrying*) in Anne Arundel Co. and *Gover's Addition* in Calvert Co.
    31-4 Sarah Gover
    31-5 Mary Gover
    31-6 Rachel Gover; ? same person: Rachel Gover; m. Thomas Allen and disowned 29 d. 3 mo. 1765 (Quaker Records of So. Md.).

Estate of Thomas Allen, Calvert Co.; Value £13/11/9; 11 Dec 1772; 30 Nov 1773; next of kin: Hannah Hanest, Jane Gover; admn: Martin Morris, Rachel Allen (Inv. Prerog. Ct., 114.18).

31-7 Jane Gover
31-8 Margaret Gover
31-9 Elizabeth Gover
31-10 Hannah Gover

WILL of ROBERT GOVER, Calvert Co.; written 27 Jun 1762; probate 12 Aug 1762
To eldest son William Gover, tract called *Dineurk*; 60 a. part of a tract called *Exchange*, on Patuxent River
To 2nd son Robert Gover, pt. of tract laying in Calvert Co., called *Archer Hate* (*Archer Hays*) on side of Patuxent River; pt. of tract called *Gover's Meddow*; all pt. of tract called *Gauss Purchase*
To 3rd son Samuel Gover, pt. of tract called *Gover's Fearon* (*Gover's Ferrying*) in Anne ____ Co.; tract lying in Calvert Co. called *Gover's Addition*
Whereas I have a right by my dec'd father Ephraim Gover's will, to sundry lands after death of my bro. Ephraim Gover and sister Mary Gover, that after death of bro. Ephraim, and sister Mary, in case they shd. die without issue, all my lands afsd. I give to daus: Sarah, Mary, Rachel, Jane, Margaret, Elizabeth and Hannah Gover, equally
To wife Sarah Gover, extx., 1/3 of lands
Wit: William Hammond, Samuel and Mary Robertson
(Md. Cal. Wills, Vol. XII, p. 141; Wills, Liber 31, folio 697)

3-2 Ephraim Gover
3-3 Mary Gover

## JOHN GOVER

On 20 Aug 1689 John Gover was one of the signers of *Declaration of Calvert County for not Choosing Burgesses til October*. This document shows there was an adult John Gover in Calvert County in 1689. His relationship, if any, to Robert Gover (d. 1700) of Anne Arundel County is unknown. John does not appear as a given name in the descendants of Robert Gover.

Land Records of Prince George's County from 1692 to 1727 do not show any land for a John Gover. Plantations listed on the Hienton map do not show any original grants in those portions of Calvert and Charles Counties which became Prince George's County for a Gover. The Court Records of 1696 to 1699 do not mention a Gover. Nothing appears in the Probate Court records of Prince George's County until 1778.

Since the 1882 fire of the Calvert County Court House destroyed the land records, nothing is available for Calvert County prior to the two books in the Archives at Annapolis which start with the year 1785.

In 1757 John Gover married Elizabeth Duvall in Queen Anne Parish. He might have been a descendant of the John in Calvert County in 1689.

### JOHN GOVER and ELIZABETH DUVALL

John Gover, b. ca 1731; m. 15 Dec 1757 Queen Anne Parish, Prince George's Co. to Elizabeth Duvall, b. 15 May 1738 at Pleasant Grove, Prince George's Co.; d. after 1799; d/o Samuel Duvall (1707-1775) and Elizabeth Mullikin; 1773 will of Samuel Duvall, s/o Mareen the younger and Elizabeth, named his dau. Elizabeth Gover (Mareen Duvall of Middle Plantation). John Gover took the Oath of Fidelity in Prince George's Co.

St. John's & St. George's Parish, Prince George's Co., 1776; John Gover, age 45; males ages 6 and 2; Elizabeth, age 40; females age 16, 13, 8

### ROBERT GOVER and SARAH

Robert Gover, Calvert County, value £267/17/10; 18 Oct 1762; 22 Nov 1762; extx. Sarah Gover (Quaker) (Inv. of Prerog. Ct., 79.160).

The following family from the West River Meeting records appears to be the same family as that of [3-1] Robert, son of Ephraim Gover and Mary Harper, until the 1762 will of [3-1] Robert Gover is taken into consideration. In that will Robert states his eldest son was William, 2nd son Robert and 3rd son Samuel. This does not fit the dates of birth of the following children.

Although there is much similarity in the two families, the following children are listed together in *Quaker Records of Southern Maryland* as if they are children of the same Robert and Sarah.

1. Ephraim Gover, b. 5 d. 11 mo. 1744; d. ca 1778; admn. Francis Gover; Prince George's Co.

2. Sarah Gover, b. 28 d. 1 mo. 1745; m. and disowned 29 d. 11 mo. 1765
3. Mary Gover, b. 25 d. 6 mo. 1746
4. Rachel Gover, b. 14 d. 3 mo. 1747
5. Ephraim Gover, b. 10 d. 10 mo. 1748
6. Hannah Gover, b. 5 d. 8 mo. 1750
7. William Gover, b. 18 d. 2 mo. 1752; m. 28 d. 12 mo. 1786 to Sarah Cowman, b. 9 d. 2 mo. 1764; d. by 1813; d/o John and Sarah Cowman of Anne Arundel Co.

   7-1 Sarah Gover, b. 2 d. 11 mo. 1787
   7-2 Mary Cowman Gover, b. 24 d. 2 mo. 1789; m. 23 d. 12 mo. 1813 at Indian Springs to Gerard Hopkins of Anne Arundel Co.; s/o Joseph Hopkins and his dec'd wife, Elizabeth Hopkins
   7-3 William Alexander Gover, b. 16 d. 2 mo. 1791
   7-4 Augustus Frederick Gover, b. 18 d. 1 mo. 1793
   7-5 Elizabeth Gover, b. 22 d. 12 mo. 1794
   7-6 Margaret Gover, b. 10 d. 9 mo. 1796
   7-7 John Gover, b. 17 d. 3 mo. 1798
   7-8 Eliza Gover, b. 31 d. 5 mo. 1800
   7-9 Ann Maria Gover, b. 1 d. 8 mo. 1802
   7-10 Caroline Gover, b. 4 d. 9 mo. 1804; m. Tues. last. near the Head of South River to Theodore Williams (Md. Gazette, 25 Jul 1822).
   7-11 Robert Gover, b. 1 d. 1 mo. 1806

8. Robert Gover, b. 17 d. 10 mo. 1753
9. Jean Gover, b. 3 d. 3 mo. 1755
10. Margarett Gover, b. 23 d. 3 mo. 1757
11. Elizabeth Gover, b. 22 d. 9 mo. 1759

## COWMAN

Joseph Cowman, b. ca 1696; d. 3 Oct 1753; mariner of the City of London; m. 5 d. 1 mo. (Mar) 1723/4 at West River Meeting Sarah (Galloway) Hill; widow of Henry Hill (Md. Cal. Wills, Vol. V, p. 172); Joseph brought certificate from Monthly Meeting of Paslow Cragg in Cumberland to Maryland; Capt. Joseph Cowman, Anne Arundel Co., made deposition 1741, age ca 45 (Md. Deponents); Sarah was the sister of Richard Galloway whose will calls her "Sarah Cowman, sister"; will wit. by Joseph Cowman (Md. Cal. Wills, vol. VI, p. 237-8); Sarah Galloway; d/o Samuel and Ann Galloway; m. 9 d. 1 mo. (Mar) 1720/1 West River to Henry Hill, Jr.; children:

1. Joseph Cowman, b. 1732
2. Ann Cowman, b. 1733
3. Mary Cowman, b. 1735
4. John Cowman, b. 1737

11 Feb 1728/9, Joseph Cowman arrived from London on *Champion of London* (Md. Gazette, no. LXXIV)

3 Jul 1729, departure of *Champion of London*, Joseph Cowman, master for London (Md. Gazette, no. XCV)

12 Dec 1750, Joseph Cowman at West River reports a strayed or stolen gelding (Md. Gazette, no. 294)

Will of JOSEPH COWMAN, West River, Anne Arundel Co.; written 25 Dec 1752; probate 5 Nov 1753

To wife Sarah Cowman, sons Joseph and John Cowman, daus. Ann and Mary Cowman, slaves

To son John Cowman, land lying in Cumberland Co., Parish of Dissington in Great Britain; to son John and hrs., tract *Cowman's Manor* on Bush Creek in Frederick Co., MD; tract called *Catch as Catch Can*; *He That Gets The Said Land Is The Best Man*, lying in said county

Balance to wife Sarah, and my 4 children

Exs: wife and son Joseph

Wit: Lewis Stockett, John Ramsay, Philip Hall, Eliza. Tidings

(Md. Cal. Wills, Vol. XIV, p. 286; Wills, Liber 28, folio 553)

Capt. Joseph Cowman, age 59, died yesterday "of the Dropsy." He will be buried next Saturday at the West River Meeting House (Md. Gazette, #439, 4 Oct 1753).

Joseph Cowman, Anne Arundel Co.; £1591.3.0; 20 Mar 1754; 17 Oct 1743; next of kin: Samuel Galloway, John Cowman; ex. Joseph Cowman (Quaker) (60.32).

Joseph Cowman, Anne Arundel Co.; £117.0.10; list of debts (60.55).

1. Joseph Cowman, b. 8 d. 8 mo. 1732; m. 4 d. 4 mo. (Apr) 1754 Elizabeth Snowden; d/o Richard Snowden; Joseph Cowman, Jr. called nephew in 1752 will of Joseph Galloway which also mentions "Mary Plummer, sister of my wife"; Elizabeth Cowman, called dau. in 1763 will of Richard Snowden, inherited *Snowden's Manor Enlarged* (Md. Cal. Wills, Vol. XII, p. 184).

   1-1 Richard Cowman, b. 17 d. 1 mo. 1755
   1-2 Joseph Cowman, b. 13 d. 4 mo. 1757
   1-3 Elizabeth Cowman, b. 1 d. 7 mo. 1759
   1-4 Samuel Cowman, b. 26 d. 7 mo. (Jul) 1762
   1-5 John Cowman, b. 30 d. 3 mo. (Mar) 1765
   1-6 Sarah Cowman, b. 16 d. 11 Mo. 1769

   30 May 1754, Joseph Cowman, ex. of estate of Capt. Joseph Cowman, late of Anne Arundel Co., regarding estate settlement (Md. Gazette, no. 473)
   6 Mar 1755, Joseph Cowman has a stray steer at his plantation near West River in Anne Arundel Co. (Md. Gazette, no. 513)
   3 Jul 1760, Joseph Cowman, at his store near West River, has goods for sale just imported from London by Capt. Joseph Richardson in the *Two Sisters* (Md. Gazette, no. 791)
   6 Aug 1761, Joseph Cowman has a stray horse at his plantation near West River (Md. Gazette, no. 848)
   3 Sep 1761, Joseph Cowman, at his store near West River in Anne Arundel Co., will sell, for the benefit of the insurers, damaged goods from Capt. Joseph Richardson's ship *Friendship*; Joseph Galloway also has damaged goods for sale at Cowman's store (Md. Gazette, no. 852)

2. Ann Cowman, b. 1 d. 8 mo. 1733; m. int. 26 d. 9 mo. 1760 Joseph Gill
3. Mary Cowman, b. 24 d. 12 mo. 1735

4. John Cowman, b. 24 d. 4 mo. 1737 Anne Arundel Co.; m. Sarah
_____; 8 Jan 1761 John Cowman in Anne Arundel Co. has a
stray mare at his plantation (Md. Gazette, no. 818); 4 Mar 1761, John
Cowman will see land at Arthur Charlton's house in Frederick
Town, containing 540 acres called *Catch as Catch can, he that gets
the Land is the best Man.*" It will be shown by Westall Ridgely
who lives near the land (Md. Gazette, no. 826)

  4-1 Joseph Cowman, b. 8 d. 9 mo. 1758; d. 14 Dec 1808; m. 23 d.
2 mo. (Feb) 1786 at Indian Springs to Mary Snowden; d/o
Samuel and Elizabeth Snowden of Prince George's Co.;
children from Sandy Spring

    41-1 Elizabeth Cowman, b. 29 d. 12 mo. 1786
    41-2 Sarah Cowman, b. 28 d. 5 mo. 1789
    41-3 Gerard Cowman, b. 9 d. 11 mo. 1791; d. "Tues. morning" from *Md. Gazette* of 14 Feb 1833
    41-4 Samuel Snowden Cowman, b. 9 d. 2 mo. 1794
    41-5 John G. Cowman, b. 22 d. 4 mo. 1796
    41-6 Mary Cowman
    41-7 Joseph Cowman, b. 22 d. 5 mo. 1801

  4-2 Mary Cowman, b. 18 d. 4 mo. 1760; m. 31 d. 10 mo. (Oct)
1775 Samuel Thomas; s/o Richard of Frederick Co.
  4-3 Gerrard Cowman, b. 6 d. 5 mo. 1762; d. 31 d. 12 mo. 1789;
age 26; lived South River; bur. Indian Spring
  4-4 John Cowman, b. 10 d. 4 mo. 1764; m. 16 Apr 1793 to Mary
Plummer; lived South River

    44-1 John Cowman, b. 27 d. 3 mo. 1794
    44-2 Gerard Cowman, b. 17 d. 4 mo. 1796
    44-2 Sarah Cowman, b. 12 d. 7 mo. 1798
    44-4 Joanna P. Cowman, b. 12 d. 8 mo. 1800
    44-5 Mary Cowman, b. 2 d. 4 mo. 1803

  4-5 Sarah Cowman, b. 9 d. 2 mo. 1766
  4-6 Margaret Cowman, b. 22 d. 5 mo. 1769

4-7 Ann Cowman, b. 24 d. 7 mo. 1771; m. 22 d. 11 mo. (Nov) 1792 at Indian Springs to Thomas Norris; s/o Thomas
4-8 Elizabeth Cowman, b. 12 d. 3 mo. 1774; m. 1 d. 12 mo. 1796 at Indian Springs to Samuel Snowden
4-9 Richard Cowman, b. 13 d. 9 mo. 1777

## CORRECTIONS and ADDITIONS
## to
## Early Families of Southern Maryland, Volume I

### CECIL

p. 19 - [1-2] Samuel W. Cecil, b. 23 Mar 1719 MD; m. ca 1745/50 Rebecca White, b. 20 Aug 1723 Queen Anne Parish, Prince George's Co.; d/o Benjamin White and Ann Hilliard [b. 10 Oct 1701] who m. 1 Feb 1722/3 Queen Anne Parish; children of Benjamin and Ann from the records of Queen Anne Parish, Prince George's County

1. Rebecca White, b. 20 Aug 1723
2. Lettice White, b. 12 Dec 1726
3. Margaret White, b. 29 Jul 1729
4. Rachel White, b. 25 Feb 1730
5. Mary Ann White, b. 24 May 1733
6. William White, b. 29 Jul 1735
7. John White, b. 17 Jan 1739
8. Sarah White, b. 5 Oct 1741
9. Benjamin White, b. 1745

BENJAMIN WHITE who married ANNE HILLIARD

Contrary to the information in the many publications about this family, including my own work, the Benjamin White who married Anne Hilliard was not a descendant of Guy White as proven by the following information recorded under the White family. The list of taxables of Patuxent Hundred, Prince George's Co. taken in 1733 shows there were two Benjamins in the county at that time (Black Books).

Benjamin who married Anne Hilliard could have been an immigrant, although his name does not appear in the long list of Whites in *Early Settlers of Maryland*. Or he might have been a descendant of the James White who patented *Eglington* plantation 18 Apr 1670 in that portion of Calvert County which became Prince George's County (Hienton Map).

In 1742 Benjamin Hall petitioned the Court of Prince George's County regarding the boundaries of the plantation called *Eglington*. Depositions were taken as to the ancient boundary. One of the deponents was Benjamin White age 47 [b. ca 1695]. Was he the one who m. Ann Hilliard?

### JAMES WHITE

James White (1); d. ca 1673 Anne Arundel Co.; m. Susanna _____; d. by 1684 Anne Arundel Co.; she m/2 by 1674 to John Waters; John m/2 Elizabeth Giles and became a Quaker; children of James and Susanna:

    1. Margaret White
    2. Elizabeth White
    3. James White (2), b. after 1654

WILL of JAMES WHITE, Anne Arundel Co.; 29 Dec 1672; 21 Jul 1673
To dau. Margaret and hrs., 300 ac, *Eglinton*
To dau. Eliza: and hrs., sd land in event of death of dau. Margaret without issue
To son James, dwelling plantation at 18 yrs. of age
Extx. Wife Susanna
Wit: John Stansby, Samuel Lane, Robt. Lockwood
                      (Md. Cal. Wills, Vol. I, p. 74; Wills, Liber 1, folio 550)

1. Margaret White; inherited *Eglington* from 1673 will of father
2. Elizabeth White; m. by 1685 John Brown of Calvert County; Elizabeth was contingent legatee if Margaret dies without heirs; John Brown conveyed *Eglington* to Gabriel Parrott of Anne Arundel Co. 10 Jan 1685 by indenture in Calvert Co. records. When this land was patented to James White, it was located on the west side of a branch of the Patuxent River then either in Calvert or Baltimore County, now Prince George's (Prince George's Co. Land Records, Liber F, folio 113).
3. James White (2); b. after 1654

        3-1 James White, Jr. (3)

James White, West River, Anne Arundel Co., bought *Fordstone* from Thomas Ford 23 May 1670; rerecorded at request of Samuell Galloway (WH4.1).

James White, son and heir of James White, late of Anne Arundel Co., on 12 Mar 1687 sold Daniel Longman *Fordstone* and 50 acres on Herring Creek Swamp called *Addition*, patented to James White 17 Sep 1666 (WH4.4).

James White, cooper of Anne Arundel Co., 14 Apr 1686 sold land lying in Herring Creek Swamp, part of possession of James White, deceased, father of said James White, to John Waters; rerecorded by Eliza Waters [2nd wife of John Waters whose first wife was the widow of James White (1)] (WH4.38).

3-1 James White, Jr. (3)

James White, Jr. (3) wit. will of William Ray, Sr., Frederick Co. 1760 (Md. Cal. Wills, Vol. XII, p. 24).

p. 36 - Records show that Philip Cecil, Jr. (3) married an Elizabeth; circumstantial evidence of the middle name of their eldest daughter suggests her name was Elizabeth Thomas; no proof of this has been found to date. Some descendants of this line question that this [23-1] Philip Cecil was the son of [2-3] Philip Cecil. It is possible that [2-3] and [23-1] are the same person, or that [23-1] had no relationship to this family.

## EVANS

p. 89 - Lewis Evans, b. ca 1650; d. 1690/1; m. ca 1674 Lois Gongo; d/o Anthony Gongo and Faith ?Wilson; Lois m/2 ca 1690/1 Christopher Vernon, b. after 30 Jul 1663; d. ca 1724/5; bur. 11 Dec 1724 St. Dunstan, West, London, England; see Christopher Vernon wills at the end of this segment on the Evans family; children:

Children of Lois & Lewis Evans:
1. Elizabeth Evans
2. Sarah Evans
3. Catherine Evans
4. Ann Evans

Children of Lois & Chris. Vernon:
5. Ephraim Vernon, b. 18 Feb 1691/2
6. William Vernon, b. 23 Jan 1693/4
7. Loys/Lucy Vernon, b. 1 Oct 1697
8. Thomas Vernon, b. 27 Jan 1701/2
9. Ann Vernon

Anthony Congoe (? Gongo) was the sole legatee of John Peart of Anne Arundel Co. in his will of 1668 (Md. Cal. Wills, Vol. I. p. 44); the 1694 will of Faith Gongo, Anne Arundel Co., mentions dau. Lois, wife of Christopher Vernon (Md. Cal. Wills, Vol. II, p. 67).

Estate of Lewis Evans, planter of Anne Arundel Co.; £224/5/0; 10 Dec 1690; 5 Jun 1691; bequests: dau. Elisabeth Evans, dau. Sarah Evans; dau. Katherine Evans; dau. Ann Evans; on of the trustees was Samuel Griffin of Calvert Co.; Anthony Congee (? Gongoe) in list of debts (11A.13 1/2).

1. Elizabeth Evans, b. ca 1674-1690; d. ca 1757-62; m/1 19 Aug 1708 St. James Parish to Francis Anctill; s/o Francis Anctill who d. ca 1675 (Md. Cal. Wills, Vol. I, p. 118); m/2 Moses Faudrie; d. ca 1729; children:

   1-1 Francis Anctill
   1-2 George Anctill
   1-3 Barnaby Anctill; d. ca 1733 St. Mary's Co.; m. Elizabeth _____; his will written 21 Feb 1732, probated 12 Apr 1733, mentions wife Elizabeth and cousin Jean Thompson; no mention of children (Md. Cal. Wills, Vol. VII, p. 11).

WILL of MOSES FAUDRY (Faudrie), planter, Herring Creek, St. James Parish, Anne Arundel Co.; 31 Aug 1728; 22 Apr 1729
To wife Elizabeth, extx., entire estate
Test: John Elliot Brown, William Vernon
(Md. Cal. Wills, Vol. VI, p. 135: Wills, Liber 19, folio 809)

[A James Fawdrie d. in St. Mary's Co. and Barnaby Anktill was one of the appraisers; 3 Dec 1729 (15.277)]

WILL of [ELIZABETH] FODORY, Calvert Co.; 8 Sep 1755; 17 Sep 1762
To sister Katherine Thornbury, slaves
To Zachariah MacCubin, £5
To Leowis Stephens, son of John and Rachel Stephens, slaves; slaves to be divided amongst all the sd. John Stephens other children, then living
To Ann Vernon, £3; to Elizabeth Vernon, £3
To Sarah Jones, £5; to Rachel Stephens, £5
To Catherine Thornbury and hrs., remaining pt.
Exs: Sister Catherine Thornbury, and friend Zachariah MacCubin
Wit: John Carr, Joseph Mumford, Ephraim Gover

There were letters of administration granted on this estate several months before this will was found by Clement Smith, Deputy Comry. of Calvert Co. (Md. Cal. Wills, Vol. XII, p. 156; Wills, Liber 31, folio 769)

2. Sarah Evans, b. ca 1680-90; m. Samuel Griffith, Jr. (see Griffith corrections and additions)
3. Catherine Evans, b. ca 1680-90; d. by 1768; m. John Clark, b. 13 Jun 1686 Anne Arundel Co.; s/o Mathias Clark and Elizabeth ?Webber; Catherine m/2 William Thornbury; d. 1750

   3-1 Elizabeth Clark; m. William Scrivener, b. 7ber 1713 At. James Parish Anne Arundel Co.; s/o Richard Scrivener and Mary Burck; known child:

   31-1 John Scrivener; d. 1812 Montgomery Co., MD; m. Elizabeth Purnell; d/o Richard Purnell, Jr. and Mary Pickering; d. 1802 Montgomery Co.

   3-2 Lois/Lewsey Clark; m. John Carr; children from Thornberry will; Lewsey appears to be a nickname for Lois as the two are used interchangeably in family records:

   32-1 William Carr; b. by 1750
   32-2 Elizabeth Carr; b. by 1750; m. ____ Lambeth
   32-3 Catherine Carr
   32-4 Ann Carr; m. ca 1770 John Hilliday

WILL of WILLIAM THOURNBURY, Anne Arundel Co.; written 22 Dec 1746; probate 6 Jul 1750
Wife Catharine Thornbury
That cousin William Vernon, have delivered him at the age of 18 with the profits it shall gain after the decease of my wife
Leave to 2 sons-in-law William Scrivener and John Car
If cousin Wm. Vernon shd. die without hrs., then all the before bequests be divided bet. all the child. of dau.-in-law Lewsey Car's children
To dau.-in-law Elizabeth Scrivener and hrs., 2 slaves, but in default of hrs. to dau.-in-law Levies Car, Negroes Jenny and Moll
To Wm. Car, son of John and Lewsey Car, Negro Pris
To Elizabeth Car, dau. of John and Lewsey Carr, Negro Janney
Wit: Ephraim Gover (Quaker), James Pickering
(Md. Cal. Wills, Vol. X, p. 88; Wills, Liber 27, folio 277)

Estate of William Thornbury of Anne Arundel Co.; £901/17/6; 12 Oct 1750; 9 Mar 1750; extx. Katharine Thornberry (44.419).

WILL of CATHERINE THORNBURY; 24 Dec 1767; 23 Nov 1768
To grandson John Scrivener (son of William Scrivener) plantation *Kequotan's Choice* and negro Jack, formerly property of Richard Scrivener, Sr.
To grandson William Carr plantation *Jerico*
To granddau. Elizabeth Lambeth, negro
To granddau. Catherine Carr, negro
To granddau. Ann Carr, negro
To Susanna Weems, dau. of David Weems, negro
All other to be divided between children of deceased daughters Eliz and Lois, John Scrivener, son of Elisha, one-half; and the children of my daughter Lois the other half
Ex.: John Scrivener and Wm. Carr
Wit: William Child, William Parret, Thomas Parret (Wills, Liber 39, folio 655)

Estate of Catharine Thornbury of Anne Arundel Co.; £394/6/6; 1 Dec 1768; 10 Mar 1769; next of kin: John Carr, John Scrivener; ex. William Carr (99.339).

4. Ann Evans; b. ca 1680-90; m. Aug 1717 Benjamin Battee, b. 24 May 1695 All Hallow's Parish, Anne Arundel Co.; d. ca 1741; s/o Ferdinando Battee and Elizabeth ____; Ann Battee next of kin to William Vernon 1740 (25.390); children:

  4-1 Elizabeth Battee; m. Thomas Sherbutt; children from St. James Parish, Anne Arundel Co.:

   41-1 Ann Sherbutt, b. 2 Feb 1738
   41-2 Mary Sherbutt, b. 12 Dec 1740
   41-3 Elizabeth Sherbutt, b. 4 Feb 1742
   41-4 Benjamin Batty Sherbutt, b. 2 Apr 1744
   41-5 John Sherbutt, b. 25 Jun 1746
   41-6 Sarah Sherbutt, b. 10 Oct 1750
   41-7 Thomas Sherbutt, b. 3 May 1752

  4-2 Ann Battee

WILL of BENJAMIN BATTEE, planter of Anne Arundel Co.; 2 Jan 1741; 25 May 1741
To wife, Ann, extx., life interest in dwell. plan., and 1/3 *Hopewell.* At her death to be divided between daus. Elizabeth Sherbutt and hrs. and Ann and hrs.
To daus. Elizabeth Sherbutt and Ann *Coles Point* and *Coles Quarter* belonging to testator as hr. at law of Mary Keely, widow of John
To grandchild. Ann and Mary Sherbutt, personalty
Testator desires that in case bro. Ferdinando or his hrs. dispute the division of property made by exs. of father Ferdinando, that father's will shall stand
Test: John Franklin, Abraham Simmons, Isaac Simmons
(Md. Cal. Wills, Vol. VIII, p. 146; Wills, Liber 22, folio 393)

5. Ephraim Vernon, b. 18 Feb 1691/2; bapt. 11 Jun 1704 Herring Creek St. James Parish; d. ca 1761 Port Vernon Plantation, Brunswick, NC; m/1 ____; m/2 ca 1723 Richmond, VA to Ann Smith Lucas; m/3 ca 1751 Brunswick, NC to Ann "Nancy" Gott

6. William Vernon, b. 23 Jan 1693; bapt. 11 Jun 1704 Herring Creek; d. ca 1740; m/1 27 Nov 1733 Anne Arundel Co. to Mary Brown; m/2 by 1735 to Sophia _____; child::

    6-1 Anne Vernon, b. 4 Oct 1735 St. James Parish

    William Vernon, Anne Arundel Co.; £66/15/0; 24 Jun 1740; 12 Mar 1740; next of kin: Thomas Vernon, Ann Battee; adm. Sophia Vernon (25.390).

    It appears that Sophia had an illegitimate son named John b. either 19 Jan or 28 Mar 1748/9 recorded in St. James Parish.

7. Loys/Lucy Vernon, b. 1 Oct 1697; bapt. 11 Sep 1698 Herring Creek; d. bur. 27 Sep 1718; although one record calls her Loys and another Lucy, it appears that this is the same person

8. Thomas Vernon, b. 27 Jan 1701/2; d. Bladen, NC after 1758; next of kin to William Vernon 1740 (25.390)

9. Ann Vernon; d. ca 1773 Bertie, NC; m/1 ca 1722 Capt. George Martin, mariner; d. ca 1734; m/2 ca 1735 Joseph Anderson

## Christopher Vernon

The will of Christopher Vernon, planter, written 8 Dec 1724, probated in London 1 Jan 1724[5] was accepted as the final will of Vernon who leaves nothing to his children (Md. Cal. Wills, Vol. V, p. 192).

Ephraim Vernon was in possession of Christopher Vernon's property after his death, so Christopher must have assigned the property to Ephraim prior to sailing for England.

The following will was entered for probate by the extx. Elizabeth Evans Anctill Faudrie was rejected by the September Term of the Prerogative Court.

### Unprobated Will of Christopher Vernon
#### Transcribed by Robert P. Carter, Charlotte, NC

WILL of CHRISTOPHER VERNON, planter of Herring Creek, St. James Parish, Anne Arundel Co.; 9 Jun 1724; entered for probate 26 Jul 1736; rejected

First, I recommend my soul into the hands of Almighty God The Giver thereof, my body to the Earth to be decently buried by my Executrix hereafter named, not allowing any pomp or vain expense. I appoint my just debt (which are few or none) to be paid by my said Executrix

Item - I give unto my two eldest children of my son Ephraim Vernon and to the heirs of their body lawfully begotten all my land where upon I now dwell. Being two tract (viz.) *Marshes Seat* and *Barwell's Plantation* with all the appurtenances there-to belonging. The eldest son to have his first choice of either of the said two plantations and at the age of one and twenty years, and my will and desire in that Ephraim Vernon and his wife, or the longer liver of them (if they are so minded) may live thereon and look after the same during their and either of their natural lives, but no ways sell, let or to farm let the whole or any part there-of, nor make any willful wast(e) and in any case Ephraim cannot compound his debts to come and live there-on. My further will and desire is that Elizabeth Amckill look after the same till the two children come at age and after the death of Ephraim Vernon and his wife and his two eldest children and their heirs my will is (that) my son Thomas Vernon and his heirs have and enjoy the same forever.

Item; As to my goods, chattels, and moveables in this Province of Maryland, my will is they be equally divided between my son Thomas Vernon and Agnes Martin and the two eldest children of my son

Ephraim Vernon, and the part belonging to the said Agnes Martin and Ephraim's children is to remain and be in the hands of Elizabeth Amsckill or her assignes till they come to age, and to prevent all future disagreement about Lois, my (prehensile) wife's third. Being well assured to the love and affection her daughter Elizabeth Amckstill leaves to her mother, and she, her mother, having sufficient of her own, and I having never enjoyed any share of her thirds, and because I was never married to her---she utterly denying to say the words at the intended solemnization of marriage (that she would honor and obey her husband) and hath verified and made true how stubborn and brutish (her) behaviour in all her actions, and poisoned me and to cover the same, poisoned two of her Negroes at the same time. One where-of died in less than a minute (after he never-the-less) by drinking water, also she hath these tenth of said last past (10 May 1724) separated her self so that here-by I utterly renounce the said Lois and solemnly say she was never married to me, nor shall have no right or title of Dower to any part of my estate, but in case it should so happen...being moved by the (misguidance of the Devil and an evil controlled lewd and corrupt justice--she should have her thirds allowed. She, the said Lois, shall have no part or share of any (of) my monies in London in the Kingdom of Great Britain. In March to hand there I having given the same away by deed of gift to my Aunt Ann Vernon, my brother John and wife and children and other relatives as by deed of gift if may more at large appear.

Item; I give and bequeath unto William Vernon and Ann Martin one shilling current money apiece and no more by cause they having by all ways and means grievously slighted me and utterly renounced by me as a parent.

Item; I give and bequest unto Elizabeth Amkstill and her heirs and assignes forever all these lots with their appurtenances on the Town Land which were excepted by James Maxwell in his conveyances from Thomas Tench, Esquire, from Nehemiah Birkhead, Sr., and from John Wilson, Senior and Junior.

Item, It is my will and desire that so much as Elizabeth Amkstill is any manner of ways indebted to me by bill, bond, exempt, or any other debt what-so-ever she shall not by any means be compelled to pay the same (unless she, the said Elizabeth Amkstill, happen to die before me) and the same is hereby given to her and she's discharged there from and for that it is not mentioned in my will how the portions allotted to my granddaughter Agnes Martin and Ephraim Vernon's two eldest children. If they or either of them happen to die in their minority (Elizabeth shall) have the same and (it) shall be disposed of afterwards. It is my will and desire that Elizabeth Amkstill shall have the share of any such child, decease, and bestow the same as she shall think fit among my children or their children, and lastly that the said Elizabeth Amkstill may the better perform her trust and duty in executing this my last Will and Testament - I constitute, make, and ordain her my sold executrix of this --my last Will and Testament and I do hereby utterly disallow, revoke and disavow all and every other former testaments, wills, legacies, and bequeaths and executors by me in any way and before named wills and bequeaths. Ratifying and confirming this and no other to be my last will and testament in witness where-of I have unto set my hand and seal this ninth day of June in the year of our Lord 1724.

Signed, sealed, published and endorsed by said Christopher Vernon to be his last will and Testament in the present of us who subscribed our names as witnesses there-to in the presence and sight of the executor: John Elliott Browne, Anthony Gott, John Gott, Thomas Nell (mark)
/a/ Christr. Vernon (seal)

## PILE

P. 118 - Joseph Pile, Jr.; see Volume II, p. 148, Elizabeth Boarman

## WHITE

p. 131 - Thomas Miles, whose will names his children, m/1 Ruth Jones and had 3 children: Thomas Miles, Jr., Elizabeth Miles [m. Samuel Roberts], and Sarah Miles [m. Samuel Plummer]. Thomas m/2 Elizabeth (Griffith) White, widow of Guy White, and had 2 children: John Miles [m. Mary ____], Rachel Miles [m. Thomas Hamilton].

The Benjamin White shown in Volume I of this series was not the son of Guy White. The following corrections have been made from the research of Mr. Ernest C. Allnutt, Jr. of Baltimore and Maj. Edgar Ray Luhn of Newville, PA.

p. 134 - [1-5] Benjamin White, b. ca 1702 Prince George's Co.; d. 1776-1782; m. by Mar 1739 Elizabeth Smith, b. ca 1713; d. ca 1784; d/o William Smith and his m/1 Jane Edmonston; their children were:

15-1 William White      15-6 Jane White
15-2 Elizabeth White    15-7 Eleanor White
15-3 Sarah White        15-8 Hester White
15-4 Nathan Smith White 15-9 Benjamin White
15-5 John White

The 1733 records of Patuxent Hundred show "Benjamin White, John Miles and 5 slaves" (Black Books). Benjamin White and Elizabeth Smith lived on the 200 acres of *Cool Spring Manor* he inherited from his father (Debt Books 1756-1772). Benjamin purchased land from John Evans 1739-1743 (Deeds, Liber BB, folio 303). Benjamin's portion of *Cool Spring Manor* inherited from his father was resurveyed 14 Oct 1754 for 200 acres called *White's Adventure* (Debt Book 1756-1772).

WILL of ELIZABETH WHITE, Prince George's Co.; written 15 Dec 1783; probate 20 Mar 1784
To dau. Jane, wife of Hezekiah Thomas, slave woman Bettie
To son William White, slave Charles
To son Benjamin White, desk plus shared slave man Jack
To dau. Elizabeth White, silver
To son John White, cattle, plus shared slave man Jack
To son Nathan Smith White, slave woman, Priss
To granddau. Mary White, dau. of my son William
To granddau. Elizabeth Smith Chiswell, slave
To niece Ann Cleland, slave
Residue equally with sons Benjamin and Nathan Smith White
Exs. Sons Benjamin White and Nathan Smith White
Wit: Joseph White Clagett, Samuel White Clagett
(Wills, Prince George's Co., Box 14, folder 72)

15-1 William White, b. ca 1740 Prince George's Co.; d. 3 Dec 1812 Prince George's Co.; m. by Dec 1783 Elizabeth Orme, b. ca 1738; d/o John Orme and Ruth Edmonston

15-2 Elizabeth White, b. ca 1741 Prince George's Co.; m. ca 1770 Frederick Co. to Archibald Allen, b. ca 1741 Frederick Co.

15-3 Sarah White, b. 2 Nov 1742 Prince George's Co.; d. 6 May 1816 Montgomery Co.; m. 22 Jul 1761 Prince George's Co. Edward Jones, b. 8 May 1737; d. 25 Nov 1790 Montgomery Co.; dates from headstone at Monocacy Cemetery

15-4 Nathan Smith White, b. 11 Oct 1743; d. 19 May 1823; m. ca 1785 Montgomery Co. Margaret Presbury Chiswell; d/o Stephen Newton Chiswell and Sarah Newton

15-5 John White, b. ca 1746 Prince George's Co.

15-6 Jane White, b. ca 1748 Prince George's Co.; m. 27 Jun 1780 Montgomery Co. Hezekiah Thomas, b. ca 1735 Charles Co.; d. ca 1790

15-7 Eleanor White, b. 29 Apr 1750 Prince George's Co.; d. 23 Mar 1831 Montgomery Co.; m. 11 Nov 1779 Montgomery Co. to Joseph Newton Chiswell, b. 2 Apr 1747; d. 1837 Montgomery Co.; s/o Stephen Newton Chiswell and Sarah Newton; Eleanor's birth from Chiswell Bible.

15-8 Hester White, b. ca 1751 Prince George's Co.; d. 8 Apr 1833; m. 1773 Pr. Geo.'s Co.; Alexander Whitaker, b. ca 1746; d. 1824

15-9 Benjamin White, b. ca 1752 Prince George's Co.; d. 1822 Montgomery Co.; m. 17 Dec 1790 Frederick Co. Rebecca Odell Chiswell; d/o Stephen Newton Chiswell and Sarah Newton

## ORME

p. 139 - The sons of George Ransom sold *The Wedge* in 1724 with no wife or wives signing dower rights

## DICKESON

p. 154 - John Dickeson m. prior to 1721 to Francis Clarvo; d/o Francis Clarvo, planter, Prince George's Co. (Md. Cal. Wills, Vol. V, p. 79).

p. 156 - [311-1] Thomas Dickerson was not a minister.

p. 160 - Elizabeth Dickeson m. ca 1713 John Virgin

## DOYNE

p. 161 - Robert Doyne came from Barbados in the party of Dr. Jesse Wharton; he m/1 Mary Stone, d/o Gov. William Stone and Verlinda Graves and widow of John Thomas; Robert m/2 Ann Burford; the 6 children listed were from the marriage between Robert and Mary Stone.

p. 171 - Jane Doyne, now wife of Ethelbert Doyne, was relict and extx. of estate of Peter Johnson in St. Mary's Co.; value £116.12.6; £1.16.2; dated 13 May 1707 (26.323). Thus Jane Sanders m/1 Peter Johnson; m/2 Ethelbert Doyne.

## GRIFFITH

p. 200 - [3-8] John Griffith; the will of Benjamin Griffith (p. 201) mentions 2 daus. of his brother John Griffith; it appears that an error was made and the John Griffis/Griffith who d. in 1750 is not the brother of Benjamin; according to Anne Scrivener Agee and further research, the following correction is made:

3-8 John Griffith, b. ca 1714 prob. Calvert Co., age 45 in 1759 (More Md. Dep.); d. ca 1764 Calvert Co.; m. Ann Lewin; d/o Richard Lewin and Mary Childs; children from Anne Scrivener Agee:

    38-1 Samuel Griffith
    38-2 Lewis Griffith; d. 13 Nov 1783 Anne Arundel Co.; m. 5 Dec 1769 All Hallow's Parish Susanna Stewart; disowned by Quakers 26 Mar 1770 because of his marriage
    38-3 Sarah Griffith, b. by 1751
    38-4 Millison Griffith
    38-5 ? Elizabeth Griffith, b. by 1751; d. by ?1764; mention in Benjamin's will

WILL of JOHN GRIFFITH, Calvert Co.; 21 Dec 1764; 28 Feb 1765
Wife Ann, extx.
Children: Samuel, Lewis, Sarah and Millison Griffith
Father-in-law: Richard Liven [Lewin]
Wit: John Miles, Robert Lyle, Joseph Smith
                (Md. Cal. Wills, Vol. XIII, p. 71; Wills, Liber 33, folio 161)

Estate of John Griffith, Calvert Co.; £173/17/0; 7 Mar 1765; 25 Jun 1765; next of kin: Lewis Griffith, Lewis Jones, Jr.; admn. Ann Griffith (88.38).

Estate of John Griffith, Calvert Co.; £65/2/8; 13 Oct 1666; next of kin: Lewis Griffith; admn. Ann Griffith (89.262).

The John listed as Griffith on p. 200 is listed in *Maryland Calendar of Wills* as Griffis or Griffith. Other documents have been found where Griffis and Griffith are used interchangeably. *Abstracts of the Inventory of the Prerogative Courts* by Skinner as follows:

Estate of John Griffis of Anne Arundel Co.; £115/12/10; 1 Apr 1751; 9 Sep 1751; next of kin: Edward Graffis, Thomas Marshall younger; admn.

Mary Hardesty, extx. of Henry Hardesty who was ex. of John Griffis (47.22).

p. 201 - [3-12] Barsheba/Bathshebey Griffith, b. ca 1739 (census); d. will dated 18 Feb 1800 Monongalia Co., VA; m. ca 1751 John Ferguson, b. ca 1725 (census); d. will dated 4 Dec 1793 same co.; children b. Prince George's Co., MD; children and grandchildren from a land record dated 29 Nov 1823 Monongalia County, Virginia (OS15-401); information on this line from J. Marlene Slack, San Marcos, CA:

3(12)-1 Catharine Ferguson, b. ca 1752; m. 29 Aug 1776 William Lanham, b. ca 1750; although the marriage date was given of 29 Aug 1777, the census taken 31 Aug 1776 shows William Lanham age 26, and Catherine his wife, age 24; an 18 year old female living in household

3(12)1-1 Verlinda Lanham
3(12)1-2 Alexander Lanham; d. ca 1809

3(12)-2 Rebecca Ferguson, b. ca 1756; d. ca 1823; m. 1 Oct 1777 Prince George's Co. 2nd wife of William Wilson, b. ca 1730; d. ca 1807 Monongalia Co., VA; he had 3 children from m/1 and 8 from m/2; family went to Virginia

3(12)-3 Ann Skinner Ferguson, b. ca 1760; m. 29 Aug 1777 Prince George's Co. Joseph Wilson

3(12)-4 Susannah Ferguson, b. ca 1762; m. 21 Apr 1781 Prince George's Co. Farquire McRae/McCray/McCrea; he operated a tavern in Morgantown, WV

3(12)4-1 Duncan F. McRae/McCray/McCrea
3(12)4-2 Susannah Maria McRae/McCray/McCrea; m. John Welling
3(12)4-3 Alexander McRae/McCray/McCrea

3(12)-5 Verlinda/Lydia Ferguson, b. ca 1765; bapt. 10 Aug 1766; m. 5 Jan 1783 Monongalia Co., VA Zephaniah Bell/Beall; d. by 1806

3(12)-6 John Ferguson, b. ca 1768; m. Elizabeth _____

3(12)-7 Margaret Ferguson, b. ca 1779; d. intestate Monongalia Co. ca 1799; never married; she inherited lower end of his land on Decker's Creek in Monongalia County, VA

Census of 1776, St. John's & Prince George's Parish, Prince George's Co.: John Fergusson, 51, 8 [? John]; Bershiba, 37, 20 [? Rebecca], 16 [? Ann Skinner], 14 [? Susannah], 11 [? Verlinda]; 2 Negroes

John Furguson and his wife Bathsheba of Monongahela, VA sold to David Carcaud for £200, land in Calvert Co.; 158 acres called *Turner's Place*, Griffin's and Gover's Pasture (Calvert Co. Early Land Records).

Will of John Ferguson [written] 4 Dec 1793; [probate 1796] mentions wife, Barsheba; Cath. Lanham, Ann Wilson, Rebecca Wilson, Susanna McCrea, Lydia Bell, Margaret, dau.; John son (West Virginia Estate Settlements, Monongalia Co., p. 73).

*West Virginians in the American Revolution* states Lt. John Ferguson moved to Morgantown, WV ca 1788 and operated a tavern. His widow Bathsheba appears on the Monongalia tithable lists for many years after her husband's death in 1796.

*The Monongalia Story* mentions Barsheba Ferguson whose slave, Will, was found guilty as accessory to the burning of a barn and his sentence was to be burnt on the hand and receive 30 lashes. Barsheba's daughter, Susanna McCrea was on the jury of 12 women of 16 Aug 1798 which convicted the slaves of burning the barn

BELT

p. 274 - Lucy Lawrence who m. John Belt (2) was the d/o Elizabeth (Talbott) Preston and her 2nd husband, Benjamin Lawrence.

PLUMMER

p. 293 - See Plummer family in this Volume which has been corrected with much new information added.

BOARMAN

p. 315 - This family has been corrected and added to in Volume II

# INDEX

Names are indexed under what appeared to be the most common spelling.

Abbott, Samuel William, 155
Adair, Robert, 193
Addison, Elinor, 79
  Thomas, 32
*Addition, The,* 55, 82, 83, 211
*Adventure,* 125
Agee, Anne Scrivener, 117, 221
*Aldermason,* 198
Aldridge, Wm., 57
Allen, Archibald, 219
  Rachel, 201
  Thomas, 201
Allnutt, Ernest C., Jr.,218
  James, 81
  William, 81, 196
Allton, Ann, 70
  Arthur, 70
  John H., 70
  John, 75
  Mariah, 70
  Rebecca, 70
  Samuel, 70
*Anchor-in-Hope,* 52
Anctill, Barnaby, 212
  Elizabeth, 212, 216, 217, 218
  Francis, 212
  George, 212
Anderson, Joseph, 23, 215
  Philemon, 23
  Stephen, Sr., 23
Andrew, Patrick, 66
Andrews, Hannah, 52
*Angelica,* 82
Anly, Ann, 109
*Anne Arundel Manor,* 2, 110

*Archer Hays,* 110, 200, 201, 202
Arnell, Richard, 42
Arnold, Ann, 58
Arthur, Benjamin, 53, 54
Ashcomb, Ann, 41, 61
  Nathaniel, 41, 42
  Samuel, 41, 42
  Winifred, 41
Ash/e, Dorothy, 169
  Thomas, 131
Ashton, Thomas, 148
*Assington,* 149
Atee, Patrick, 147
Athey, Zephaniah, 181
Atkins, Mary, 116
Atkinson, John, 157
  Joshua, 176, 177
  Mary Brent, 176, 177
  Mary, 176
  Susannah, 177
Attwood, Peter, 139
  Eleanor, 89
  Henry, 89, 178
  Henry, Jr., 178

*Barwell's Plantation,* 216
*Bacon Hall, Addition to,* 177
Bacon, Elizabeth, 164, 165
Bagby, John, 189
Bailey, Jane, 15
Baker, John, Capt., 173
  Elizabeth, 167
Ball, \_\_\_\_, 11
  Marian, 12
Ballard, John, 176

Ballinger, Ann, 14
　Cassandra, 9, 14
　Elizabeth, 14
　Hannah, 14
　Henry, 14
　Mary, 14
　Rachel, 14
　Samuel, 14
　Sarah, 14
　William, 1, 14
*Baltimore's Gift*, 132
Banfield, Nancy, 7
　Samuel, Jr., 8
Baptistyler, John, 32
*Barnes' Purchase*, 46
Barnes, Catherine, 38
　John, 83
　Margaret, 199
　Peter, 44
Barnett, Thomas, Jr., 122
*Barren Neck*, 43
*Barren Point*, 135, 137
Barry, Bazil, 108
Barshear, Samuell, 97
Barton, Susanna, 156
*Batchelor's Choice*, 19
*Batchelor's Choice, Addtn. to*, 19
Battee, Ann, 214, 215
　Benjamin, 214, 215
　Elizabeth, 214
　Ferninando, 43, 214, 215
*Beal's Pasture*, 7
*Beal's Pleasure*, 6
Beall, Eleanor, 99, 179
　Hariet, 22
　Hester, 102
　James, 99
　Ninian, 92
　Robert, 126
　Zephaniah, 222

Beanes, Mary Bowie, 182
*Bear Garden Enlarged*, 179, 180
*Bear Garden*, 117
*Beatty's Range*, 21
Beatty, Charles, 21
Beck, Anthony, 89
　Elizabeth, 37
　James, 37
Beckett, Elizabeth, 86
　John, 86, 186
　Priscilla Hitchins, 85
　Priscilla, 86
Beckwith, Elizabeth, 183
　George, 183
Beedle, Henry, 61
　Sophia, 42
*Beginning, The*, 31 32
Bell, Joseph, 24, 180
　Lydia, 222
　Zephaniah, 222
Belt, Elizabeth, 59
　H., Jr., 177
　Higginson, 59
　John (2), 222
　John, 59
　John, Jr., 59
　Joseph, 59, 60
　Joseph, Col., 102
　Leonard, 59
　Lucy, 59
　Margaret, 60
　Mary, 60, 102
　Nathan, 60
　Rachel, 102
　Sarah, 59
　Thomas, 100
　Tobias, Jr., 7
*Benjamin Addition*, 45, 44
*Benjamin's Favour*, 43
*Benjamin's Fortune*, 42, 43

# Index

Bennett, John, 6
Benton, Benjamin, Jr., 13
Berry, James, 92
Bersheba, 107
Besson, Hester, 55
Bevens, _____, 144
   Mary, 145
   Richard R., 144
*Beyond Far Enough*, 46
Bibben, Mary, 145
Bickerton, John, 77
   Joseph, 77
Bidden, Mary, 145
Biddle, Ann, 80
Bigger, John, 66, 68
Biggs, John Sr., 20
Billingsley, Francis, 187
   James, 61
   Susanna, 186, 187
*Birched Lott*, 118
Birckhead, Abraham, 122, 186
   Ann, 121, 122, 124, 186
   Christopher, 121, 122, 123, 106
   Eleazar, 122, 186
   Nehemiah, 119, 120, 122
   Nehemiah, Sr., 217
   Peter, 122
   Rachel, 122, 124
   Rebecca, 186, 187
   Solomon, 106, 121, 122, 124
Blackiston/e, Ann, 138
   John, 138
Bladen, William, 167
Blake, Thomas, 72
*Blind tom*, 81, 83, 84, 86
*Blue Coat*, 95
*Boarman's Content*, 130
*Boarman's Inlargement*, 149
*Boarman's Low Ground*, 154, 155
*Boarman's Manor*, 140, 141, 161

*Boarman's Reserve*, 143, 144, 145
*Boarman's Rest*, 131, 149, 150, 151, 154, 155
Boarman, Aloysius, 151
   Ann/e, 130, 132, 138, 142, 147, 149, 150, 151, 157, 161
   Anna Maria, 156
   Basil Smith, 161
   Benedict Leonard, 130, 139, 147, 149, 150
   Benedict, 130, 131, 133, 151
   Benjamin, 129, 133, 147
   Bennett, 153
   Caroline Matilda, 156
   Catherine Anamentia, 156
   Catherine, 149, 150, 151
   Charles, 150
   Clare, 130, 131, 159
   Cordelia, 155
   Cornelius, 135
   Dorothy, 161
   Edward, 134, 135, 141
   Edward, Sr., 135
   Eleanor, 149, 151, 152, 154
   Elizabeth, 130, 134, 135, 148, 150, 151, 152, 154, 155, 218
   Ellen, 155
   Francis Ignatius, 130, 131, 133, 134, 156, 161, 162
   George, 129, 145, 149, 151
   Gerard, 161
   Henrietta, 132, 135, 152, 153
   Henry, 134, 135, 141, 161
   Ignatius Gerard, 161
   Ignatius, 161
   James, 134, 135
   Jane Cordelia, 156
   Jane, 132, 133, 139, 140, 149, 150, 151, 152
   Jean, 133

Jeanne Delia, 156
John Baptist, 130, 131, 147, 152, 155
John, 161, 162
Joseph, 132, 133, 139, 149, 150, 151, 152, 153, 154, 155
Leonard, 150, 151
Leonard, Jr., 150, 151
Mary Anne, 134. 135, 154
Mary E., 142
Mary Jarboe, 130
Mary Matthews, 142
Mary, 128, 129, 130, 131, 132, 133, 135, 139, 140, 141, 146, 149, 150, 151, 154, 155, 156
Monica, 150
Raphael H., 156
Raphael, 140, 141, 152, 153, 154, 155
Richard Basil, 149, 151
Richard Bennett Aloysius, 155
Richard Bennett, 152, 154, 155
Richard, 128, 152, 153, 156, 160, 161, 162
Robert, 128
Sarah, 128, 129, 132, 133, 138, 140, 142, 143, 152, 161, 162
Susanna, 140, 161
Thomas James, 132, 133, 134, 139, 141
Thomas, 140, 141, 142, 143, 146, 147
William, 129, 131, 132, 134, 135, 138, 148, 149, 152, 156, 159
William, Capt., 128, 130, 142, 147
William, Jr., 143
William, Maj., 130, 145, 152
Winifred, 134, 135

**Bodle**, Stephen, 126
**Bolton**, James, 182, 183
John, 182, 183
Mary, 182
**Booker**, Martha, 49
Nancy, 49
**Boone**, Ann, 140
Catherine, 140
Charles, 140, 141
Eleanor, 140
Henrietta, 140
James, 140
John, 140
Sarah, 140
Walter, 140
*Border's Enlarged*, 70, 75
*Border, The*, 63, 64
**Bordley**, Thomas, 43
**Boreman**, see Boarman
**Bottelor**, Henry, 97
**Bouchier**, Richard, 163
*Boughton Ashley*, 77, 185, 186, 187, 189, 190, 196, 198
**Bowen**, Somerset, 116
**Bowes**, Timothy, 162
James, 178
Jartha, 178
Lucy, 178
Mary, 182
Priscilla, 182
Thomas F., 181
**Bowles**, James, 172
**Bowling**, Francis, 132
John, 132, 133
Joseph, 132
Mary, 132, 155
Thomas, 132
Thomas, Jr., 141
William, 132, 141, 155
**Bowsell**, Jane M., 109

**Boyce**, Caroline, 52
  Roger, 76, 80, 97
**Boyd**, Charity, 181
  Richard Duckett, 182
  Roger, 95, 97
  Thomas, 182
**Bradford**, \_\_\_\_, 154
  Anne, 153, 154
  Eleanor, 153
  Nancy, 154
  Polly, 154
**Bradley**, Charles, 153
  Robert, 171
**Bradshaw**, Elizabeth, 183
**Brandt**, Margaret, 148
**Brashear**, Benjamin, 111
  Samuel, 32, 127
  Jonathan, 111
**Breeden**, Robert Hammitt, 177
**Brent**, Giles, Capt., 128
  Giles, Jr., 170
  Margaret, 169, 172
  Mary, 170, 172, 177
  Nicholas, 145
  William, 169, 172, 177
**Brice**, Jacob, 118
*Bridge Hill*, 2, 3, 33, 37l, 39
*Brierwood*, 143
**Bright**, Rebecca, 165
*Bristol*, 126
**Brock**, Martha, 27
*Brooke Court Manor*, 92, 93, 95, 96, 97
*Brooke Land*, 136
**Brooke**, \_\_\_\_, 69, 122
  Ann/e, 122, 131, 139, 147, 149, 159
  Baker, 147, 159, 160, 161
  Basil, 81
  Charles, 147, 148
  Clare, 160
  Elinor, 147
  Harrison, 122, 124
  Henrietta, 154
  Henry, 138, 178, 179
  Jane, 77, 147
  John, 143, 201
  John, Capt., 82
  Leonard, 147, 148, 149, 172
  Mary, 160, 161
  Millicent, 137
  Raphael, 154
  Richard, 148, 159, 160, 161
  Sarah, 81
  Thomas, 136
*Brother's Partnership*, 46
**Brothers**, Nathaniel, 32
**Brown**, \_\_\_\_, 190
  Daniel, 14, 189
  Gerard, 129
  Isaac, 14
  James, 48
  John Elliot, 212, 218
  John, 107, 210
  Mary, 215
  Sarah, 14
  Susanna, 14
  Thomas, Sr., 105
*Browsley Hall*, 19, 28
**Brucebank**, Edward, 3
**Bruse**, Ann, 69
*Bryan Dayley*, 136
**Buckley**, Michael, 17
**Buckmanster**, Benjamin, 86
**Bucknan**, Thomas, 139
**Burck**, Mary, 117, 213
**Burford**, Ann, 220
**Burgess**, Grace, 12
  Joseph, 43

William P., 10
William, 61
Burke, William, 167, 169
Burket, Mary, 16
*Burkhed's Lot*, 118
Burman, William, 143
*Burrage*, 121
Burrage, John, 121
Burridger, Ben, 176
Burton, Benjamin, Lt., 59
*Bush Creek Mountain*, 9
*Bushwood Lodge*, 157
Bussee, ___, 67
*Bussey's Garden*, 70
*Bussey's Orchard*, 75
Bussey, James, 81
Butcher, Mary, 191
Buttner, Adam, 24

*Calendar*, 68
*Calf Pasture Branch*, 72
Callahan, Rosamond, 180
*Calvert Hope*, 150, 151, 154, 155
Calvert, Ann, 147
   Leonard, 146, 147
   William, 174
*Calverton Manor*, 19, 21
Cann, Mr., 64
*Cannarvan*, 143
*Cannon Neck*, 157
*Canoe Neck*, 158
Canty, Gilbert, 147
Carberry, Elizabeth, 138
Carcaud, David, 222
Carmole, Samuel, 7
Carmon, John, 18
Carr, Ann, 213, 214
   Catherine, 213
   Elizabeth, 213
   John, 200, 212, 213, 214

Lewsey, 213
Robert, 113
William, 213, 214
Carroll, Anne, 158
Charles, 35
Carter, John, 118
   Robert P., 216
Carvel, Nancy, 36
Cary, William, 122
Carycroft, Jean, 158
Cash, Dorcas, 5
   Mary, 5
*Catch as Catch Can*, 205, 207
Caton, Ann, 89
Cay, Jonathan, 71
Cecil, Elizabeth, 37
   Isaac, 69
   John B., 37
   Judge Joshua, 69
   Julia, 36
   Philip, 36
   Philip, Jr. (3), 211
   Samuel W., 209
   Samuel, 36
Chambers, Mary Lawrence, 49
   Rowland, 49
   Thos., 186
   William, 48
*Chance*, 63, 75, 79
Chandler, Job, 129
Chaney, Thomas, 79
   William, 79
Chapell, John, 121
Chapline, Anne, 31
   Elizabeth, 31
   Francis, 124
   Joseph, 30, 31
   Mary, 31
   Moses, 31
   William, 31

Chapman, Samuel, 89
  William, 89
  William, Jr., 89
Chappell, John, 196
*Charles Gift*, 81
Charles II, 43
*Charles' Folly*, 100
Charlett, Richard, 93
Charlton, Arthur, 207
*Cheney's Resolution*, 33, 35
Cheney, Elizabeth, 33, 34
Chenowith, Arthur, 12
  Chloe, 113
  John, 12
*Cherry Walk*, 39
Chettin, Will, 35
Chew, Benjamin, Jr., 195
  Samuel, 93, 189
  Sydney, 57
Chiffen, Eleanor, 101, 102
  Rachel, 102
  William, 101
*Child's Addition*, 112
Child, \_\_\_\_, 115
  Abraham, 105, 117
  Ann, 106, 107, 112, 114, 115, 116, 121, 126, 127
  Anne E., 112
  Barbary, 116
  Benjamin, 112, 115
  Cassandra Elizabeth, 107, 108
  Cassandra, 28, 116, 126, 127
  Cephas, 106, 107, 110, 111, 112, 114, 115, 116, 117, 119
  Edmond P., 111
  Eleanor, 111, 116
  Elijah, 116
  Elizabeth, 107, 108, 110, 111, 112, 113, 114, 115, 116, 119, 126, 127
  Enos, 111
  Gabriel, 1271, 126
  Henry (2), 106
  Henry (3), 110
  Henry Lloyd, 113
  Henry, 24, 106, 107, 110, 111, 112, 114, 116, 117, 126, 127
  Henry, Jr., 18, 107, 121, 199
  Isaac, 112, 116, 117
  Jemima, 111, 113
  John D'Million, 126
  John Zachariah, 109
  John, 106, 110, 112, 115, 116, 117, 126, 127
  Jonathon, 113
  Joseph, 110, 111, 113
  Juliana, 113
  Levy, 116
  Lurana, 107, 115
  Margaret, 18, 24, 107, 110
  Martha, 115
  Mary Ann, 116
  Mary, 106, 110, 111, 113, 114, 116, 117, 221
  Mordecai, 116
  Nathan, 113
  Obediah, 116
  Rachel, 106, 121
  Rebecca, 112
  Ruth, 38, 106, 107, 110, 120
  Samuel, 110, 111, 112, 115
  Sarah, 106, 110, 111, 114, 115, 116, 119, 127
  Sophia, 116
  Susan, 112
  Susanna/h, 110, 111, 113, 114
  William, 106, 107, 110, 111, 113, 114, 115, 127, 214
Childs, see Child
*Childton*, 105

Chillman, Richard, 183
Chilton, Joseph, Capt., 78
  Littleton, 78
  Margaret, 78
  Sarah, 78
Chiswell, Elizabeth Smith, 219
  Joseph Newton, 220
  Margaret Presbury, 220
  Rebecca Odell, 220
  Stephn Newton, 220
Chittam, Thomas, 179
  William, 100
Cissell, John, 164
Clagett, Joseph White, 219
  Mary Meek, 182
  Samuel White, 219
  Thomas, 182
  Wiseman, 178
Clargo, Francis, 220
*Clark's Folly*, 100
Clark, see Clarke
Clarke, Ann, 30
  Benjamin H., 28
  Daniel, 29
  Eliza, 104
  Elizabeth, 103, 104, 213
  Ellen, 10
  John, 103, 213
  Joseph, 71
  Juliana, 143
  Katharine, 65
  Lois, 213
  Margaret, 103, 104
  Mathias, 103, 104, 213
  Peter, 118
  Raymond, 68
  Robert, 103, 173
  Ruth, 103, 104
  Thomas, 143
  Webger, 103

Cleland, Ann, 219
Clements, _____, 144
  Henrieta, 145
Clinard, Philip, 36
Clocker, Daniell, 183
*Clover Hills*, 46
Coale, Elizabeth, 108
  Mary, 13
  William, 13, 16
Coder, Mary, 174
*Colbert's Hope*, 152
Cole, George, 68
*Coles Point*, 215
*Coles Quarter*, 215
Coller, William, 35
*Collington Manor*, 168
Colt, Ellen, 36
Combs, Enoch, 168
  Richard, 147
  Sarah Sprigg, 100
  William, 169, 174
Compton, Mathew, 7, 8
Congoe, Anthony, 212
*Conigochigee Manor*, 20, 21
Contee, Alexander, 77
  Barbara, 78
  Catherine, 78
  Elizabeth, 76, 77
  Jane, 78
  Theodore, 77, 79
  Thomas, 78
Cook, John, 40
  Mary, 127
  Phebe, 40
  Robert, 195
  Walter, 138
*Cool Spring Manor*, 219
Coope, George, 31
*Cooper*, 68
*Cope's Hill*, 30

Cordea, Mark, 130
Cornall, Elizabeth, 64
Cornish, Guy, 155
*Cornwallis Crosse*, 166
Cornwallis, Penelope, 166
   Thomas, 166, 167, 170
Cosden, Hanna, 183
Cotton, Elizabeth, 187
*Coventry*, 134
*Covill's Folly*, 98
Covill, Ann, 98
Covington, Levin, 95, 97
   Nehemiah, 102
*Cowman's Manor*, 205
Cowman, Ann, 205, 208
   Elizabeth, 205, 207, 208
   Gerard, 207
   Joanna P., 207
   John G., 207
   John, 204, 205, 206, 207
   Joseph, 205, 206, 207
   Joseph, Capt., 205, 206
   Joseph, Jr., 206
   Margaret, 207
   Mary, 205, 207
   Richard, 205, 208
   Samuel Snowden, 207
   Samuel, 205
   Sarah, 204, 205, 207
Cox, ___, 70
   Abraham, 137
   Ann, 70, 125
   John, 70
   Mary, 191, 197
   Mr., 69
   Powell, 125, 126
   William, 197
   William, Jr., 197
Crabb, Ralph, 103
Craycroft, Ann, 151

   Charles, 156
   Ignatius, 71, 93, 94, 95, 97
   John, 145
   Nancy, 158
   Nicholas, 158
   Sophia, 94
   Susannah, 157
   Thomas, 160
Cress, John, Sr., 20
Crichtealony, John, 18
Crockett, Benjamin, Dr., 193
   Hannah, 51
   Mary, 47
Cromwell, Elizabeth Bourchier, 163
   Oliver, 163
Crosbey, Richard, 108
*Cross Manor*, 163, 164, 165, 167, 172, 173, 174
*Cross Neck*, 167
*Cross Town Land*, 167
Cross, Jos., 181
Crum, Abraham, 19
Culick, Nicholas, Rev., 170
*Cumberland*, 44, 54
Cumming, Elizabeth, 48
Curtis, Thomas, 43
   John, 41
*Cypress Mill*, 82

Daffin, George, 177
   Susanna/h, 176
Dailey, Joseph Bryan, 114
Dallam, Elizabeth, 197
   Frances, 197
   Richard, 197
   Winston Smith, 197
Daniels, Jane, 16
Darnall, Ann, 135
   Henrietta Maria, 137

Henry, 137
Susannah, 137
*Darnell's Grove*, 100
**David**, Peter, 136
**Davidge**, Dinah, 117
**Davis**, Catharine, 13, 57
**Dawson**, Edward, 32
**de Coville**, family, 98
**Deacon**, William, 179
**Deakins**, Jane, 180
   John, 179
   William, 179
**Deale**, Elizabeth, 112, 117
   John, 118
   Samuel, 112
*Dear Bought*, 107, 199
*Debutt's Delight*, 19, 20, 21
**deCerf**, John, 163
*Deer Park*, 179, 180
*Defiance Resurveyed*, 46
*Delaware Bottom*, 47
*Delebroke Manor*, 160
*Delph's Neglect*, 193
*Delph*, 193
**Demilane**, Ann, 126
**DeMilliane**, Gabriel, Dr., 126
**Dent**, Eleanore, 138
   George, Col., 138
*Deserts, The*, 41
*Devil's Nest*, 144
**Dick**, James, 89
   Margaret, 104
**Dickerson**, Thomas, 220
**Dickeson**, Elizabeth, 220
   John, 220
**Dickinson**, Daniel, 122
   John, 122
   William, 122
**Digges**, Charles, 94, 95, 97
   Henrietta Maria, 137

   John, 159
**Dillon**, Thomas, 148
*Dines Point*, 124
*Dineurk*, see Dunkirk
*Disappointment*, 46
*Doden*, 2, 3, 33, 38, 39
*Dodson's Reserve*, 79
**Doliante**, Sharon J., 164
**Donnelly**, Mary Louise, 128, 162
**Dorey**, Philip, 133, 158
*Dorsey's Grove*, 43, 44, 47, 54
*Dorsey's Partnership*, 10
**Dorsey**, Achsah, 52, 53
   Amelia, 45, 46
   Ann, 45, 46
   Ariana, 11, 45, 46, 47, 53
   Basil, Jr., 47
   Benjamin Lawrence, 49
   Caleb, 52, 54, 57
   Catherine, 46
   Cordelia Harris, 47
   Edward, 46, 49
   Edward, Col., 54
   Edward, Jr., 44
   Elias, 48, 49, 50
   Elizabeth, 45, 46, 55, 91
   Evan, 50, 51
   Evan, Jr., 51
   Greenberry, 60
   Henrietta, 45, 46
   John, 43, 44, 45, 46, 50, 57, 60
   John, Jr., 44
   Joshua, 45, 46, 49
   Judge Basil, 47, 51
   Katherine, 45
   Levin Lawrence, 49
   Maria, 46, 47
   Mary Ann, 49
   Mary Snowden, 50
   Mary, 49

Matilda, 49
Michael, 45, 46
Nicholas, 53
Nimrod, 49
Patience, 49
Philemon, 45, 46, 47
Philemon, Capt., 45
Rachel, 46, 47
Rebecca, 52, 54
Ruth, 43, 48, 49
Sarah, 45, 46, 54
Susanna/h, 44, 46, 49, 51
Thomas, 48
Upton Lawrence, 51
Urith Owings, 49
Urith, 49
Vachel, 45, 48, 49
William Henry, 91
William, 54
**Dossey**, Jas., 183
**Dowell**, Philip, 77
**Downey**, Edwin, 53
    John, 53
    John, Capt, 53
**Downing**, Amelia, 139
**Doyne**, Ethelbert, 220
    Igns., 149
    Jane, 220
    Robert, 220
**Drake**, David, 22
    William, 21
**Drury**, Ann, 39
    Elizabeth, 38, 39
    Samuel, 38
    Sophia, 112
    William, 38
*Duchman's Imployment*, 32
*Duckett's Addition*, 181
**Duckett**, Ann, 180, 181, 182
    Baruch, 180, 181, 182

Basil, 181
Charity, 180, 182
Eleanor, 180, 182
Elizabeth, 181, 181
Isaac, 180, 182
Jacob, 180, 181, 182
Jane, 181
Lucy, 181
Martha, 180, 181, 182
Mary, 181
Rachel, 180, 182
Richard J., 29
Richard Jacob, 180, 181
Richard, 177, 181
Richard, Jr., 180
Thomas Waring, 181
Thomas, 180, 181, 182
**DuMolin**, Elizabeth, 126
*Dundee*, 3, 26, 28
*Dundee, Part of*, 3
**Dunkin**, John, 93, 94
*Dunkirk*, 200, 201, 202
**Duskin**, \_\_\_\_, 103
    Elizabeth, 104
*Duvall's Delight*, 35
**Duvall**, Benjamin, 38
    Elizabeth, 203
    John, 181
    Marsh Mareen, 36
    Mary, 88
    Samuel, 203
    Sarah, 37
    Susannah, 28

*Eagleton's Range*, 105
**Earle**, Thos., 94
*Eason's Lot*, 124
**Edelen**, Anna, 156
    Catherine, 159
    Christopher, 155

Dorothy, 151
Edward, 145, 150, 153, 155, 161
Elizabeth Anamenta, 156
Elizabeth Cecilia, 150
Elizabeth Hester, 150
James, 150
Jane Cordelia, 155
Jane, 140
John M, 150
John, 150
Leonard, 150
Mary, 150
Mary Verlinda, 156
Monica, 150, 151
Philip, 150
Richard, 128, 133, 134, 135, 140, 141, 149, 151, 152, 154, 155
Robert, 150
Walter, 150
Wilfred, 150
Winifred, 134, 142
*Eden*, 47
**Edmondson**, Pollard, 124
  Rachel, 124
  James, 100
  Jane, 218
  Ruth, 219
**Edwards**, Richard, 96, 97
**Eglin**, Richard, 133
*Eglington*, 210
*Elberton*, 189, 196
**Elder**, Honor, 43, 44
**Ellicott**, Andrew, 26
  John, 26
**Elliet**, John, 108
**Elliott**, Sarah, 193
**Ellis**, Owen, 96
**Elsey**, John, 71, 99
**Elson**, Martha P., 112

*Emerton's Range*, 189, 190, 198
**Emerton**, Humphrey, 189
  John, 189, 190
  Mary, 189
*Enclosure*, 135
**English**, Ann, 60
**Enion**, Abel, 94
**Erickson**, Gunder, 69
  Martha, 69
  widow, 69
**Evans**, Ann, 211, 212, 214
  Catherine, 211, 212, 213
  Eliner, 4
  Elizabeth, 211, 212
  John, 9, 17
  John, 219
  John, Jr., 4
  John, Sr., 4
  Lewis, 211, 212
  Sarah, 211, 212, 213
  Susan, 172
**Evess**, William Holland, 173
*Ewan upon Ewanton*, 43
**Ewen**, Ann, 61
  Elizabeth, 41, 61
  John, 61
  Richard, 61
  Richard, Jr., 61
  Richard, Maj., 61
  Sophia, 61
  Susanna, 61
*Ewings Addition*, 43
*Exchange, The*, 135, 137, 200, 202
*Expedition*, 31, 198

*Fancy Conjure*, 124
*Fanney's Right*, 83
*Farm, The*, 69
**Farquhar**, Allen, 16
  Caleb, 16

**Farrall**, Charles, 145
**Faudrie**, Elizabeth, 216
  Moses, 212
*Favour, The*, 43
*Fendall's Spring*, 96
**Fenley**, Robert, 37
**Fenwick**, Enoch, 162
  Leo, 112
**Ferguson**, Ann Skinner, 222
  Bathsheba, 222
  Catharine, 222
  John, 222
  John, Lt., 222
  Lydia, 222
  Margaret, 222
  Rebecca, 222
  Susannah, 222
  Verlinda, 222
**Finch**, Phoebe, 29, 109
  Priscilla, 109
  William, Jr., Capt., 109
**Fisher**, Elizabeth, 115
  John, 71
  Lewis, 116
**Flemming**, Caleb, 10
**Flood**, John, 122
**Fodory**, James, 212
*Food Plenty*, 8
**Ford**, Thomas, 211
*Fordstone*, 211
*Forest of Dann*, 104
*Forrest, The*, 30, 31
**Fouts**, Jacob, 20
**Fowler**, Elizabeth, 160
  William C., 109
**Fowrd**, William, 106
**Fox**, Elijah, 20
**Francis I**, 98
**Franklin**, Eleanor, 188
  John, 215
  Rachel, 39
**Frazier**, Elizabeth, 85
**Freeland**, Elizabeth, 192
  Robert, 191
**French**, Benjamin, 76
*Friend's Choice*, 99
*Friendship* (ship), 205
*Friendship*, 46, 68, 121

**Gaither**, Beale, 25
  Elenor, 25
  Elizabeth, 53
  Massey Ann, 25
  Susanna, 25
**Gallion**, Abariller, 101
  George, 102
  James, Jr., 101, 102
  Martha, 101
  Mary, 102
  Nathan, 102
  Pheobe, 101, 102
  Priscilla, 101
  Rachael, 102
  Samuel, 102
  Sarah, 101
**Galloway**, Ann, 205
  Elizabeth, 42, 56, 59
  Hannah, 61, 205
  Joseph L. Growden, 59
  Joseph, 58, 59, 106
  Lawrence Growden, 59
  Peter Bines, 58
  Richard, 41, 42, 43, 56, 58, 61, 62, 205
  Samuel, 18, 19, 42, 58, 205, 206
**Gantt**, Edward, 78
  Elizabeth, 86
  George, 86
  Robert, 201
  Thomas, 69

*Gardiner's Grove*, 157
*Gardiner's Grove, Addition to*, 157
**Gardiner**, Ann/e, 141, 150, 151, 156, 157, 158
  Catherine, 150, 151
  Charles Llewelyn, 151
  Clement, 151, 156, 157, 159
  Eliner, 151, 159
  Elizabeth, 135, 141, 142, 156, 157, 160
  Henrietta Maria, 156, 157, 158
  Henry, 150
  Ignatius, 144, 150
  Jane, 141, 150
  John C., 150
  John Francis, 151
  John, 141, 156, 149, 150, 151, 157
  Joseph Benedict, 151
  Joseph, 75, 141
  Julianna, 143
  Luke, 135, 141, 142, 151
  Martha, 75
  Mary C., 141
  Mary, 133, 135, 141, 151, 156, 157
  Monica, 135, 141, 159
  Richard J., 142
  Richard, 135, 141, 142, 150, 151, 156, 157
  Susannah, 141, 156, 157
  Thomas Richard, 128, 162
  Wilfred, 156, 157, 158
  William, 142
**Garnish**, John, 183
**Garrettson**, Elizabeth, 101
  Garrett, 101
  Jazar, 16
  John, 101
**Gartrell**, Aaron, 24

**Gaskins**, Elizabeth, 166
  William, 166
**Gassaway**, Ann/e, 56, 57
  Benjamin, 56, 57, 58
  Elizabeth, 56, 57
  Hannah, 56, 58
  James, 56, 57, 58
  John, 56, 58
  John, Capt., 55
  Lucy, 56, 58
  Margaret, 57
  Mary, 56, 57, 58
  N., 44
  Nicholas, 55, 56, 58
  Nicholas, Capt., 55
  Nicholas, Jr., 57
  Rachel, 56, 57, 58
  Richard, 56, 57, 58
  Robert, 56, 57, 58
  Sarah, 56, 57, 58
  Susanna/h, 56, 57
  Thomas, 56, 57, 58
*Gauss Purchase*, 200, 201, 202
**George**, Robert, 146
*German Quarter Englarged*, 81
**Gibbs**, Ann, 61
  Edward, 42, 60, 61
  Frances, 60
  Mary, 60, 61
  Nathaniel, 60
  William, 61
*Gibson's Ridge*, 193
**Giles**, Elizabeth, 210
**Gill**, Anne, 132
  Joseph, 205
  Sarah, 79
**Gillian**, Robert, 68
**Gilpin**, Thomas, 12
**Gittings**, Ann, 168
  Elizabeth, 195

John, 183
Philip, 168, 170
Thomas, 195
**Glass**, John, 133
*Godsgrace*, 79
**Godsgrace**, John, 68
*Goldsmith's Hall*, 193
**Gongo**, Anthony, 211, 212
  Faith, 212
  Lois, 211
*Good Prospect*, 69
**Goode**, Susannah, 138
**Gordon**, George, 90
  Judge George, 90
  Thomas, 6
**Gott**, Ann, 215
  Anthony, 218
  Ezeckial, 113
  John, 218
  Mary, 111
*Gough's Purchase*, 201
*Gover's Addition*, 186, 199, 200, 201
*Gover's Adventure*, 185, 186, 187, 189
*Gover's Ferrying*, 185, 186, 189, 199, 200, 201, 202
*Gover's Meadow*, 200, 201, 202
*Gover's Venture*, 185, 198
**Gover**, Ann Maria, 204
  Augustus Frederick, 204
  Benjamin, 189, 195
  Caroline, 204
  Cassandra, 189, 194, 195, 196
  Elizabeth, 188, 189, 190, 192, 195, 196, 197, 199, 200, 202, 203, 204
  Ephraim Gittings, 192, 197
  Ephraim, 107, 185, 186, 189, 190, 195, 196, 199, 200, 202, 203, 204, 212, 213
  Evans, William, 190
  Francis, 203
  Gerard, 192, 198
  Gittings, 195, 196, 197
  Hannah, 191, 200, 202, 204
  Henry, 198
  Jane, 200, 201, 202
  Jean, 204
  John, 202, 203, 204
  Margaret, 195, 196, 197, 200, 202, 204
  Mary Cowman, 204
  Mary, 107, 192, 195, 196, 197, 198, 199, 200, 202, 204
  Philip, 189, 190, 192, 198, 199, 200
  Priscilla, 189, 190, 192, 194, 195, 196, 197, 198, 199
  Rachel, 188, 189, 195, 196, 197, 198, 200, 201, 202, 204
  Richard, 189, 197
  Robert (1), 187
  Robert (2), 187
  Robert, 185, 186, 187, 188, 189, 190, 191, 192, 192, 193, 195, 196, 197, 198, 199, 200, 202, 204
  Robert, Capt., 201
  Robert, Jr., 188
  Samuel, 15, 186, 187, 189, 190, 192, 195, 196, 197, 198, 200, 201, 202, 203
  Samuel, Jr., 189
  Sarah, 185, 200, 201, 202, 203, 204
  Susanna, 186
  William Alexander, 204

William, 200, 201, 202, 203, 204
*Gowry Banks*, 110
**Graffis**, Edward, 221
**Graham**, Charles, 76, 78
**Graves**, Verlinda, 220
**Gray**, George, 13
  Thomas, 75
*Green's Rest*, 161
**Green**, _____, 140
  Charles, 66, 67
  Elizabeth, 64, 67, 146
  James, 146, 147
  John, 145
  Mary, 146, 147
  Robert, 131, 143, 146, 147
  Samuel, 159
  Sarah, 146, 147
  Tecla, 147
  Thomas, 146
  William, 146, 147
**Greene**, see Green
**Greenbury**, Chas., 56
**Greenfield**, Ann, 66, 102
  Elizabeth, 66, 76, 83, 87
  James Truman, 84
  James, 66, 83
  Joan, 136
  Martha, 65, 66
  Micjah, 66
  Thomas Truman, 66, 172
  Thomas, 64, 65, 66, 83, 87, 93
  Truman, 66
*Greenland*, 4, 5
**Greenup**, John, 6, 7
**Gremer**, Willeford, 161
**Grenfield**, Elizabeth, 66
**Grew**, Theophilus, 134
**Grey**, John, 101
  Rachel, 101

**Griffin**, Jane, 100
  John, 42, 189
  Samuel, 189, 212
**Griffis**, John, 221, 222
*Griffith's Pasture*, 201
**Griffith**, Ann, 91, 221
  Barsheba, 222
  Benjamin, 221
  Elizabeth, 5, 221
  Howard, Jr., 10
  John, 118, 221
  Lewis, 221
  Millison, 221
  Rachel, 91
  Ruth, 10
  Samuel, 71, 221
  Samuel, Jr., 73, 213
  Sarah, 221
**Groce**, Hester, 55
**Gross**, Adam, 22
**Grover**, Benjamin, 84
**Growden**, Grace, 59
  Lawrence, 59
**Guibert**, Anne, 138
  Elizabeth, 138
  Jane, 138
  Joshua, 132, 133, 138
  Mary, 138
  Matthew, 138
  Thomas, 138
**Gulick**, Nicholas, Rev., 172

**Hackett**, Ann, 124
  Michael, 124
**Haddock**, Edward, Col., 54
  James, 136
**Hagan**, Charity, 147
  Igansious, 145
  Thomas Sr., 131
  Thomas, 152

William, Sr., 144
**Hager**, Elizabeth, 51
  Jonathan, Capt., 51
  Jonathan, Jr., 51
**Haines**, Ruth, 10
*Hall's Hills*, 76, 77, 79, 190
*Hall's Inheritance*, 55
*Hall's Place*, 142, 143
**Hall**, Ann/e, 91, 181
  Benjamin, 91, 131, 210
  Benjamin, Capt., 131
  Christopher, 105
  Elisha, 76
  Elizabeth, 91
  Francis, 136
  Henrietta Maria, 136
  Henrietta, 137
  Henry, 91
  Henry, Rev., 88
  Isaac, 181
  Jacob, 181
  John, 91
  Joseph, Dr., 137
  Martha, 50, 88, 91, 181
  Mary Magdalene, 91
  Mary, 18, 69, 193
  Nicholas, 10, 91
  Parker, 193
  Philip, 205
  Richard, 68, 181
  Walter, 174
  William, 51, 91, 182
*Hamilton's Part*, 77
**Hamilton**, Alexander, 146, 147
  Elisabeth, 147
  James, 146
  John, 146
  Mary, 146
  Patrick, 146
  Thomas, 218

William, 146
**Hammersley**, Basil, 148
  Elizabeth, 131
  Francis, 148, 159
  William, 148, 153, 159
**Hammond**, Nathan, 21
  Rebecca, 54
  Sarah, 49
  William, 200
  William, Col., 193
**Hampton**, Rachard, 105
**Hanbury**, John, 191
**Hanest**, Hannah, 201
*Hanover*, 7
**Hanslap**, Henry, 3
  Joseph, 3
**Hanson**, Benjamin, 101
  Sarah, 101
*Haphazard*, 147
**Harbert**, Anne, 138
**Hardesty**, Mary, 222
*Hardshift*, 147, 149, 151
*Hardship*, 160
**Harman**, Abraham, 191
**Harnet**, ___, 53
*Harnisham*, 201
**Harper**, Mary, 199, 203
**Harris**, Anna, 18
  Cordelia, 45, 47, 53
  George, 12, 18, 45, 47
  John, 15
  Margaret, 196
  Mary, 18
  Moses, 15
  Nathan, 45
  Orrellana, 45, 47
  Rachel, 47
  Samuel, 190, 196
  Sarah, 9, 15
  Thomas, 45, 47

William, 85
Harrison, Ann, 122
  Richard, 187
  Samuel, 78
  Sarah, 151
Hart, Sophia, 113
Harvey, Frances, 183
  Isabella, 20
  John, 12
Harwood and Letchworth, 92
Harwood, Mary, 34
  Richard, 34, 35
  Richard, Jr., 34, 177
Hatchet, The, 64, 71, 73, 74, 183
Hatton, William, 130
Hawkins, Elizabeth, 56, 136
  H., 134
  Henry Holland, 66, 136
  Henry, 137
  Martha, 137
Hayes, John, 157
  Edward, 193
  Hugh, 165
  William, 120
Hayward, Thomas, 176
Hazard, 152
Head, ____, 66
  Ann, 66
  Kendall, 66
  William, 66
Hearts Delight, 136
Heighe, Betty, 79
Helleber's Spring, 20, 21
Hellelewy, 158
Hempstone, Charity, 7
Henderson, Jacob, 127
Hendrickson, William, 22
  William, Sr., 21
Henson, Samuel, 8
Henstone, Mary, 8

Hepburn, ____, 6
  John, 7
  Patrick, 99
Herbert, William, 166
Hewit, Henry, 42
Hickory Plains, 14, 15
Hiders, Christopher, 159
Higdon, Benedict Leonard, 139
  Benjamin, 138, 139
  Charles, 138
  Clare, 139
  Ignatius, 139
  John, 138
  Martha, 139
  Menesenca, 138
  Susannah, 139
  Thomas, 138, 152
  William, 138, 139, 152
  William, Sr., 138
Higgins, James, Rev., 47
Higginson, Elizabeth, 109
Hildson, Richard, 68
Hill's Choys, 30
Hill, ____, 159
  Abel, 116
  Ann, 160
  Clement, 135, 136
  Clement, Jr., 136, 160
  Edward, 157
  Eleanor, 135
  Henry, 62, 159, 160, 205
  Henry, Jr., 205
  Margaret, 191
  Sarah Galloway, 205
  William, 183
Hillaley, 157
Hillary, Eleanor Sprigg, 170
  Mary, 177
  Thomas, 100, 168, 170, 171, 179

**Hilliard**, Ann, 209, 210
**Hilliday**, John, 213
*Hilton's Purchase*, 198
**Hilton**, James, 4
  John, 4
**Hines**, William Bois, 50
**Hinkle**, Barsheba, 22
  Charlotte, 22
  Elizabeth, 21
  George, 21, 22
  John Jacob, 22
  Margaret, 22
  Sarah, 22
**Hinman**, \_\_\_\_, 109
  Margaret, 108
*His Lordship's Favor*, 137
*His Lordship's Manor*, 111
**Hitchins**, Priscilla, 85
**Hobbs**, Basil N., 49
  J. T., 10
  Janet, 46
  Kitty, 46
  Nicholas, 48
  Philemon Dorsey, 46
  Rachel, 22, 46
  Samuel, 46
  Sarah, 48
  Warner, 46
  William, 46
  William, Jr., 46, 51
**Hodges**, Charles Ramsey, 27
  Mary, 27
  Sarah, 28
  Thomas Ramsey, 17
**Hodgkins**, Theodore, 201
**Hoen**, Rebecca, 38
*Holland's Choice*, 44
**Holland**, Col., 190
  Francis, 185, 189, 196
  Francis, Jr., 190
  Margaret, 185, 189
  Richard, 9
  Thomas, 9
  William, 185, 189
  William, Col., 189
**Holloway**, John, Dr., 165
  Priscilla, 164, 165
**Hollyday**, Anne, 137 138
  John, 114
  Leonard, 73, 83, 95
  Leonard, Col., 135
  Thomas, 64, 66, 71, 138
**Hollyway**, L., 138
**Holmes**, John H., 10
**Homewood**, Anne, 36
**Honeyman**, Gale, 1
**Hood**, Hannah, 53
  John, Jr., 53
**Hooker**, Thomas, 42
**Hoover**, Henry, Jr., 20
*Hope, The*, 31, 135
*Hopewell*, 215
*Hopkins' Search*, 28
**Hopkins**, Ann, 196, 198
  Elizabeth, 18, 197, 198, 204
  Ephraim Gover, 197
  Gerard, 18, 25, 111, 121, 204
  Henrietta, 18
  Jane, 121
  Johanna, 18
  Joseph, 196, 198, 204
  Mary, 18, 196, 198, 199
  Philip, 197
  Samuel, 197
  Thomas, 158
  William, 196
**Hoskins**, Bennett, 140, 154
  Mary Ann, 154
**Houldsworth**, Robert, 64
*Howard's Patapsco Range*, 25

*Howard's Range*, 24
**Howard**, Elizabeth, 37
  Henry, 45
  Honour, 55
  Joseph, 56
  Philip, 105
  Rachel, 56
**Howe**, Tho., 71
**Howell**, William, 143
*Hugh's Labour*, 30, 31
**Hughes**, William, 13
**Hughs**, Thomas, 186, 188
**Hundley**, John D., 49
*Hunt's Chance*, 75, 76, 77
**Hunter**, William, 133
*Hunting Lott*, 8, 9, 10
**Husband**, Joseph, 18
  Lydia, 18
  Susanna, 18
**Hussey**, Stephen, 10
**Hutchings**, William, 171
**Hutton**, Charles, 148
**Hyatt**, Charles, 32
**Hynes**, William Rose, 50

**Idle**, Ester, 100
**Ijams**, Ann/e, 33, 37, 38, 40
  Ariana, 34
  Artridge, 36
  Cassandra, 35
  Charity, 33, 36, 39
  Elizabeth, 33, 34, 36, 37, 38
  Ellen, 37
  George Washington, 37
  George, 34, 40
  Henrietta, 36
  Isaac Plummer, 37
  Isaac, 38, 39
  Jacob, 34

  John, 33, 34, 35, 36, 37, 38, 40, 47, 108
  Lewis, 37
  Margaret, 35, 38
  Mary, 33, 34, 35, 36, 37, 38
  Nancy, 37
  Plummer, 33, 34, 38, 39, 108
  Plummer, 110
  Rachel, 36
  Rebecca, 36, 37, 38
  Richard, 33, 34, 35, 36
  Ruth, 34, 38, 39
  Sarah, 35, 36
  Susanna, 34, 36
  Thomas Musgrove, 36
  Thomas Plummer, 37
  Thomas, 33, 35, 36, 37, 38
  William Fletcher, 37
  William, 2, 34, 35, 36, 37, 38, 40
  William, Jr., 33
  William, Sr., 33
*Indian Creek with Addition*, 66
*Indian Field*, 136
*Indian Town Land*, 39
**Ingledue**, Hannah, 15
*Inlargement*, 149
*Invasion, The*, 44
**Ireland**, Joseph, 72
**Isaac**, Richard, 32
*Island Neck*, 64

**Jackson**, Joseph, 26
  Mary, 3
  William, 2, 32
*Jacob's Branch*, 35
**Jacob**, John, 39
  Morda., 127
*Jamaica*, 137
**James II**, 43

Jameson, Elizabeth, 156
  Sarah, 159
  Thomas, 132, 133
  Thomas, Jr., 161
Janney, Amos, 14
  Ann/a, 11, 12
  Israel, 11
  Jacob II, 15
  Mahlon, 14
Jarboe, John, 130
  Mary, 129, 130, 148, 149, 152, 156, 159, 161
Jarrett, Abraham, 198
Jean, Wm., 57
Jee, John, 138
Jenkins, Edward, 153
  Elizabeth, 150
  Henrietta, 153
  Mary, 153
  Thomas, 150, 153
Jennings, Ann, 87
  Samuel Kennedy, 53
  Thomas, 87
*Jerico*, 39
*Jerusalem*, 81
Johns, Abraham, 11, 85
  Benjamin, 192
  Cassandra, 195
  Elizabeth, 85, 191
  Kinsey, 19, 85, 85
  Margaret, 83, 84, 87
  Mary E., 15
  Mary, 13, 85, 192
  Richard, 42, 85, 92, 93, 187, 190, 199
  Stephen Stuart, Maj., 84, 87
Johnson, ____, 144
  Anna, 53
  Benjamin, 85, 86
  Edward, 77

  Edward, Dr., 77
  Gov., 84, 87
  Jane, 166
  Janney, 86
  Mary, 144
  Peter, 220
  Phoebe, 101
  Thomas W., Dr., 46
  Thomas, 87
  Thomas, Jr., 161
  William, 118, 174
Johnston, Mary, 6, 7
  Thomas, 6, 7
Jones, ____, 176
  Albert, 45
  Edward, 219
  Elizabeth, 35
  Henry, 19
  Hugh, 71, 81
  Isaac, 37
  Jacob, 19
  James, 160
  Joseph, 17, 27
  Lewis, Jr., 221
  Pierce, 122
  Rebecca, 5, 37
  Richard, 190
  Ruth, 8, 218
  Samuel, 19
  Sarah, 212
  William, Capt., 165
*Joseph and Mary, The*, 93, 95, 97
Joslin, Margaret Nuttall, 163
  Thomas, 163
Jowles, Henry Peregrine, 172
Joy, Peter, 183

Keely, John, 215
  Mary, 215
Keene, John Henry, 54

Richard, 103
*Kellering*, 102, 168
Kelly, Jane, 58
Kendall, Anna, 116
Kennedy, Janet, 46
  Philip, 46
Kent, Ann Wheeler, 109
*Kenton's Purchase*, 189, 190
*Kequotan's Choice*, 214
Kerrick, Hugh, 134
Key, ____, 156
  Elizabeth, 188
  Francis Scott, 83
  John, 43
  Philip, 157, 158
  Susannah, 157
Kidd, Margaret, 121
  William, 121
King, Charles, 171, 176
  Elizabeth, 171
  Francis, 103
  Joseph, 153
  Susannah, 176
Kingsbury, James, 77, 106
Kirk, George, 4
Kirschner, Elizabeth, 51
*Knighton's Purchase*, 185, 186, 189, 198

Ladd, Nancy, 27
*Ladsford's Gift*, 71
Lafayette, Gen., 81
Lamar, Elizabeth, 112
  James, 28
Lambert, Ann, 98
  Elizabeth, 214
Lambeth, ____, 213
Lambrest, Balderfott, 56
Lancaster, ____, 156
  Corry, 152

Elizabeth, 152
John, 140, 152, 154, 158
Joseph, Capt., 139
Mary, 158
*Land of Promise*, 11
*Land's Land*, 69
Lane, Samuel, 210
Lang, John, Rev., 120
Langton, Ann, 13
Lanham, Alexander, 222
  Catherine, 222
  Verlinda, 222
  William, 222
*Lanterman*, 131, 152
Larkin, William, 115
Lathan, Catherine, 222
Lawrence, Ann, 41, 61
  Ann West, 50, 51, 91
  Anna Lavinia, 51
  Benjamin (2), 60
  Benjamin, 41, 42, 43, 44, 45, 47,
    48, 49, 50, 55, 56, 59, 60, 61,
    104, 222
  Benjamin, Jr., 41
  Betsy, 44, 45
  Caleb Dorsey, 54
  Caroline Dorsey, 54
  Charles Augustus, 50
  Elhannan, 48
  Elias Dorsey, 48
  Elizabeth, 42, 43, 47, 50, 55, 56,
    58, 61
  Emma West, 51
  Hammond Dorsey, 54
  John Dorsey, 44, 50, 90
  John Peter, 50
  John Stephen, 50
  John, 43, 44, 45, 51, 52, 53, 54
  Josephine Elizabeth, 50
  Julianna Mahala, 50

Larkin, 54
Leucey, 56
Levin, 43, 44, 45, 47, 50, 52, 54, 55
Levin, Jr., 54
Lucy, 41, 42, 59, 60, 61, 222
Margaret, 43, 55
Margaretta, 50, 52
Martha E., 50
Martha, 51, 52, 91
Mary Elizabeth, 50, 52
Mary, 41, 48, 49, 60
Nehemiah, 41, 60
Otho William, 55
Peggy, 44, 45
Polly, 47
Rachel, 43, 44, 44, 45, 47, 50, 52, 55
Rebecca, 47, 49, 54, 55
Ruth, 44, 52
Samuel, 47, 48
Sarah Dorsey, 54
Sarah Margaret, 50
Sarah, 53, 54, 54, 55
Sophia, 43, 44
Stephen Decatur, 50
Susanna/h, 45, 47, 49, 50, 51, 52, 91
Thomas, 41, 42, 60
Upton Sheredine, 50, 51
Urith O., 48
Urith, 48, 49, 50
**Lawson**, Alexander, 80, 193
   J., 69
**Lazenby**, Robert, 180
**Lazsher**, \_\_\_\_, 23
   Asa, 23
   Elizabeth, 23
   Jefferey, 23
   Sally, 23

*Leaf's Forrest*, 44
**Leatherwood**, John, 105
   Samuel, 105
**Leconby**, Thomas, 133
**Lee**, Abraham, 18
   Cassandra, 193
   Corbin, 193
   Elizabeth, 190, 192, 193
   James, 192, 193
   James, Jr., 192
   Josiah, 194
   Margaret, 192, 193
   Mary, 193
   Parker Hall, 193
   Priscilla, 193
   Rachel, 194
   Richard, 193
   Samuel, 193
   Stephen, 25
**Leeke**, Henry, 35
**Leigh**, Sopha, 154
*Leonard's Neck*, 60
**Leonard**, Mary, 36
*Letchworth's Chance*, 85, 92, 93
*Letchworth's Cypress*, 92
*Letchworth's Hills*, 92
*Letchworth*, 92, 97
**Letchworth**, \_\_\_\_, 93, 96
   Ann/e, 67, 93, 95, 96
   Elizabeth, 71, 92, 94, 95, 96
   Joseph, 64, 71, 87, 92, 93, 94, 95, 96
   Mary, 64, 93, 95
   Thomas, 68, 70, 71, 92, 93, 94, 95, 96, 97
   widow, 92
**Letton**, Elizabeth, 163
*Level Addition*, 2
**Leverton**, Ephram, 131
**Levett**, John, 103, 104

Robert, 103, 104
Elizabeth, 103, 104
**Lewes**, Rev. Mr., 158
**Lewin**, Ann, 106, 118, 221
  Christiana, 118
  Elizabeth, 118
  Francis, 106, 118
  Henrietta, 118
  Lewis, 117, 118, 119, 120
  Lewis, Jr., 117, 118
  Margret, 118
  Mary, 117, 118
  Richard, 76, 106, 117, 118, 119, 221
  Samuel, 118
  Sarah, 106, 117, 118
*Lincey*, 159
**Lindle**, see Linle
*Lingan's Purchase*, 77
**Lingan**, George, 72
  Thomas, 76
*Linganore Hills*, 50
**Linle**, Sarah, 128, 129, 131, 142, 146, 147
*Little Bristol*, 122
**Littler**, Rachel, 16
**Livers**, Arnold, jr., 158
  Mr., 158
**Livingood**, Daniel, 36
**Lloyd**, Henrietta Maria, 132
  Maria, 90
**Lockwood**, Robert, 210
*Locust Grove*, 137
**Longman**, Daniel, 211
**Lord Baltimore**, 172, 173, 174
**Lord**, Elizabeth, 139
**Lowe**, Abraham, 75
  Dorothy, 136
  Henry, Col., 147
**Lucas**, Ann Smith, 215

  Basil, 60
  Dorothy, 169
  Thomas, Jr., 169
  Thomas, Sr., 169
**Ludwigg**, Wm., 107
**Luhn**, Edgar Ray, Maj., 218
**Lumar**, John, 18
**Lux**, William, 58
*Lyford*, 3, 4, 24
**Lyles**, Barbara, 89
  Eleanor, 88, 181
  Hillary, 178, 179
  James, 178
  Margery, 9, 28
  Martha, 89
  Priscilla Bowie, 178
  Priscilla, 89, 178
  Robert, 72, 178, 221
  Thomas, 182
  William, 89
  Zachariah, 9, 178
**Lyons**, Aurelia, 82
**Lytle**, Hannah, 16
  Richard Humphreys, 16

**Maccubin**, Deborah, 46
  Elizabeth, 88
  Zachariah, 212
**Mackall**, Ann, 67, 68, 71, 96
  Barbara, 80
  James, 67, 71, 73
  Jno., 64
  John G., 83
  John, 71
  Mary, 71, 75, 79
  Susannah, 71
**MacLughlin**, Peter, 27
**Maddox**, Notley, 84, 87
**Madison**, Pres. James, 82

Magruder, Alexander, 69, 94, 95, 96
  Elizabeth, 94
  Enoch, 178
  George Frazier, 178, 179
  Nath., 95
  Samuel, Sr., 168
*Maiden's Dowery*, 99
*Maiden's Fancy*, 39
*Maidstone*, 118
*Major's Lott*, 32
Malone, Lucy, 60
Mankin, James, 57
Manly, Elizabeth, 37
*Manor of Collington*, 102
Mansell, \_\_\_\_, 57
  Ann West
  Cordelia, 51
  Elizabeth Lawrence, 51
  Estella, 51
  John L., 51
  Louisa, 51
  Martha West, 51
  Mary Lawrence, 51
  Susan D., 51
  Thomas, 51
  Susanna, 56
Mariarte, also see Meriate
  Ann, 100
  Arden, 100, 101
  Daniel, 100, 104
  Daniel, Capt., 43
  Edward, 42, 98, 99, 101
  Elinor, 99, 100
  Elizabeth, 103
  Honor, 42
  John, 101, 102
  Margaret, 100, 101, 102, 168
  Ninian, 100
  Rachel, 42, 102, 104

  Thomas, 100
  William, 104
Mariott, Joshua, 36
Marquis, John, 79
Marriott, Joseph, 36
  Rachel, 36
  Sarah, 36
Marshall, Thomas, 221
*Marsham's Rest*, 135, 137
Marsham, George, 72
  Katherine, 159
  Richard, 135, 136, 137, 150
  Sarah, 135
*Marshes Seat*, 216
Martin, Agnes, 216, 217
  George, Capt., 215
  Thomas, Jr., 126
Mathews, Ann, 142, 145
  Ignatius, 142, 143
  Mary, 129, 130, 142, 143, 147
  Sarah, 142, 143
  Thomas, 130, 142, 143
  Thomas, Jr., 143
  Victoria, 132
  William, 149
Matly, John Paptis, 141
  Thomas, 141
Mattingly, John Baptist, 141
Maynadier, Daniel, 122
Maynard, Ann, 119
  Elizabeth, 120
  Samuel, 119, 120
  Sarah, 120
  William, 120
McCally, Zach., 181
McClane, James, 24
McCray, see McRae, 222
McCrea, see McRae, 222
McElderry, Patrick, 182
McGill, John, 28

McMachan, Alex., 58
McPherson, William, Jr., 161
McRae, Alexander, 222
   Duncan F., 222
   Farquire, 222
   Susanna, 222
   Susannah Maria, 222
McWilliams, Thomas, 158
Means, Mary, 20
Mears, 82
*Meekine Hill*, 118
Mendinhall, James, 12
Meriarte, also see Mariarte
   Daniel, 98, 99
   Edward, 98, 99
   Eliza, 99
   Elizabeth, 98
   Honor, 98, 99
   Margaret, 98, 99
   Rachel, 98, 99, 101
   Sarah, 101
*Merryvale*, 48
Mewthis, Margret, 160
Michaell, Mr., 173
Middleton, Ann, 150
   Eleanor, 151
   Elizabeth, 218
   John, 156, 159, 218, 219, 221
   Mary, 158
   Rachel, 4, 5, 218
   Sarah, 5, 8, 116, 218
   Thomas, 5, 8, 9, 218
   Thomas, Jr., 218
   Thomas, Sr., 8
Milford, John, 159
*Mill Place, The*, 48
*Miller's Folly*, 81, 86
Miller, Nehemiah, 25
   William, Jr., 74
Millhouse, Jane, 10

Mills, John, 96, 97
   Joseph, 11
   Richard, 73
   Robert, 97
   William, 97, 158
Mollison, \_\_\_\_, 78
Monk, Mary, 64
Monroe, Elizabeth, 112
Montgomery, Mary, 38
Moon, John, 23
Moore, Hannah, 90
   James, 105
   James, Jr., 105
   John, 193
   Mary, 9
   Moridcay, 56
   Richard, 9, 90
   Samuel Preston, 90
   Stephen West, 90
   William, 64
*Morefield*, 125
*Morefields Adventure*, 124
Morgan, Cassandra, 193, 194
   Elizabeth, 193, 194
   Sarah, 193, 194
   William, 193, 194
Moriarty, Donald P. II, 98
Morris, Elizabeth, 102
   Martin, 201
Morsell, Mary, 10
   Rachel, 10
   William, 10
Mott, Ann, 98
*Mouls Success*, 193
*Mount Pleasant*, 92, 97, 135, 136, 137
Mudd, Ann, 143
   Barbara, 142, 143
   Bennett, 145
   Elizabeth, 144, 145

Ellinder, 145
Ezekiah, 145
Francis, 144
George, 143, 145
Henrietta, 144, 145
Henry, 142, 143, 144, 145
Ignatius, 144
Jane, 143, 145
John, 131
Joseph, 144
Juliana, 143
Luke, 144
Mary, 144
Monica, 145
Richard, 141, 144
Sarah, 142, 143, 144
Thomas (2), 142
Thomas, 141, 142, 143, 144, 145, 146
**Muffett**, James, 71
**Mullikin**, Belt, 181
Elizabeth, 203
Mary, 181
Phoebe, 49
Samuel, 124
Sophia, 181
**Mumford**, Joseph, 212
**Murdock**, Elinor, 177
George, 180
George, Rev., 170
Rev., 178
William, 137
**Murphe**, Francis, 111
**Murray**, Dr., 135
**Musgrove**, Eleanor, 36
**Mussetter**, Christopher, 38
**Myer**, Jacob, 58

**Nailor**, George, 92
**Neale**, \_\_\_\_, 156
Ann/e, 132, 155, 158
Anthony, 158
Bennett, 158
Charles, 137
Clare, 156, 158
Eleanor, 155
Elizabeth, 139, 140, 152
Henry, 157, 158
James, 139, 140
James, Capt., 132
Jane, 132, 133, 139, 140
Mary Ann, 139, 140, 154
Mary, 157
Mary, Jr., 158
Raphael, 131, 134, 140, 148, 154
Raphael, Jr., 134
Richard, 154
Sarah, 137
William, 147, 154, 155
**Neemes**, D., 120
**Nell**, Thomas, 218
**Nelson**, Katherine Murdoch, 55
Roger, Gen., 55
*Newfoundland*, 127
*Newington*, 74
**Newman**, Harry Wright, 34, 162
**Newton**, Benjamin, 153
Sarah, 220
**Nicholas**, Elizabeth, 59
**Nicholson**, \_\_\_\_, 58
John, Jr., 33
Lucy, 57
**Nicols**, Mary, 35
**Noones**, D., 119
**Norman**, Priscilla, 112
**Norris**, \_\_\_\_, 39
Sarah, 39, 40
Thomas, 208
*Northampton*, 102, 168

Norwood, John, 42
  Rachel, 43
  Thomas, 42, 104
Nugent, Edmond, 143
*Nuthall,* 166
Nuthall, Ann, 176
  Araminta, 176, 177
  Arthur, 167
  Barbara, 169
  Brent, 169, 170, 171, 172, 173, 174, 175, 176, 177
  Charles, 171, 177
  Elias, 166, 167, 168, 183, 214
  Elinor, 166, 167, 169, 170, 177
  Elizabeth King, 176
  Elizabeth, 166, 170, 171, 175, 176, 179, 183
  James (2), 183
  James, 74, 163, 166, 167, 170, 182, 183
  John (2), 166, 170
  John (3), 170
  John, 163, 165, 167, 169, 171, 174, 175
  John, Jr., 172
  John, Sr., 169, 173
  Margaret Brent, 171, 176
  Margaret, 74, 176
  Mary Brent, 171, 177
  Mary, 170, 180, 183
  Nicholas, 167
  Oliver, 168
  Priscilla, 170, 178
Nuttall, Charles, 163
  Elijah, 163, 164
  Frances, 163
  James, 163
  John, 163, 164
  Lindsay, 164
  Martha, 163
  Mary, 163
  Nelson, 164
  Thomas, 163
*Nutthall,* 167

O'Bannon, Susan, 49
O'Neil, Bernard, 137
  Elizabeth, 137
  Mary, 137
Odell, Henry, 100
  James, 180
  Martha, 179
  Sarah, 127
  Thomas, 100
Oden, Benjamin, 90
Offutt, Sarah, 45
Ohrendorff, Mary Magdalena, 51
Oliver, John, 31
*Orchard,* 79
Orme, Elizabeth, 219
  John, 219
  Robert, 185
*Orphan's Gift,* 127
Ouchterlong, Agnes, 29
  John, 17, 18, 29
  Margaret, 29
  Mary, 17
  Priscilla, 4
Owen, Jos., 99
Owens, Ann, 112
  Benj., 19
  Isaac, 111, 112
  Thomas, 112
Owings, Anne, 53, 54
  Ariana, 53
  Beale, 47, 53
  Christopher, 55
  David, 53
  Elizabeth, 53
  Harriet Harris, 47

Harwood, 53
Isaac, 53
Jesse, 53
Joshua, 53
Levin Lawrence, 52
Levin, 53
Maria, 53
Mary, 47
Matilda, 53
Nathan Harris, 47
Rachel, 53
Richard, 47
Ruth, 53
Samuel, 47, 48, 52, 53, 55, 53
Susanna, 53
Thomas Beal, 53
Thomas Beale, Dr., 47
Thomas, 52, 53
Thomas, Dr., 53, 54
Urith, 47
William, 53

*Paca's Convenience*, 193
*Paca's Delight*, 193
*Paca's Enlargement*, 193
*Paca's Park*, 193
Paca, Aquilla, 192, 194
   James, 192
   John Stokes, 192
   John, 193
   John, Jr., 192
   Margaret, 193
Padison, John, 125
Pancoast, John, 16
Parker, Gabriel, 64, 66
Parlitt, William, 200
Parnham, Francis, 155
   John, 148
Parret, Thomas, 214
   William, 214

Parrott, Christian, 38
   Gabriel, 210
   Richard, 114
Patterson, Jeremiah, 15
   Rachel, 15
Pattison, James John, 83
*Peace*, 46
Pearce, John, Jr, 168
   William, 89
Pearson, John, 186
Peart, John, 212
Peerce, Edward, Capt., 167
Penn, John, 24
   William, 106, 116
Pennington, Henry, 56
Penson, William, 168
Perregory, Elizabeth, 23
   Henry, 23
Pervail, Gidian, 197
Phelps, John J., 34
Phillips, Jonathan, 164
Pickering, James, 213
   Mary, 213
Pierpoint, Ann, 56, 57
   Charles, 57
   Francis, 57
   Henry, 57
   John, 57
   Joseph, 57
   Margaret, 57
   Rachel, 57
   Samuel, 57
Pigman, Nathaniel, 39
Pile, Ann, 148
   Bennett, 148
   Eleanor, 155
   Elizabeth, 102, 148
   John, 133
   Joseph, 131, 132, 148
   Joseph, Capt., 143, 148

Joseph, Jr., 218
Mary, 132, 148
Richard, 31
Richard, Dr., 102
*Pillage Resurveyed*, 46
**Pinckney**, Chris., 65
**Pindell**, Gassaway, 201
  Sarah, 201
  Thomas, 178
*Piney Hedge*, 100
*Pinner*, 159
**Piper**, Nancy, 27
*Pleasant Meadow*, 8, 11
**Plomer**, Henry, 1
  John, 1
**Plowden**, ____, 156, 158
  Edmund, 169, 172
  Edward, 159
  George, 172
  Henrietta, 158, 162
**Plumer**, Richard, 1
*Plummer's Delight*, 13, 24
*Plummer's Delight, Resurvey to*, 13
*Plummer's Hunting Lott*, 24
*Plummer's Pasture*, 25
*Plummer's Purchase*, 6, 7, 19
**Plummer**, ____, 25
  Aaron, 11, 12
  Abiezar, 3, 4, 17, 26, 27, 28, 29
  Abner M., 10
  Abraham, 8, 9, 14, 15, 23, 24, 26
  Achsah, 21
  Alice, 24
  Amelia, 5
  Amey, 22
  Ann Thomas, 18
  Ann/e, 5, 6, 10, 11, 13, 14, 15, 17, 25, 28, 29
  Anna, 7, 8, 10, 11, 12, 15

  Artridge, 26
  Asa, 12
  Ascah, 19
  Barrach, 27
  Benjamin, 5, 28
  Bezor, 18
  Cager, 18
  Caroline, 20
  Cassandra, 8, 14
  Catharine, 20
  Charity, 7, 27
  Charles H., 28
  Charles, 7, 27
  Christina, 23
  Cineh, 40
  Daniel, 25, 26
  Deborah, 12, 13
  Dinah, 40
  Donesphlar, 7
  Dorcas, 4, 6, 7, 19, 24
  Dorilla, 13
  Drusilla, 6, 7, 8
  Ebenezer, 116
  Eleanor Walker, 10
  Eli, 12, 40
  Elijah, 27
  Elinor, 40
  Elisha, 13, 27
  Elizabeth, 2, 3, 4, 8, 10, 11, 13, 15, 19, 20, 22, 23, 24, 25, 26, 27, 33
  Ellen, 10, 11
  Emily N., 12
  Esther, 29
  Evan, 13
  Ezra, 11, 12
  George, 3, 4, 5, 17, 18, 19, 23, 24
  Gerard, 18
  Greenbury Griffith, 10

## Index

Gulielma, 26
Hannah, 24, 40
Harriet, 25
Hester, 108
Isaac, 10, 12, 26
Israel E., 10
Israel, 13
James, 1, 3, 4, 5, 8, 13, 17, 18, 19, 25, 26
Jane, 6
Jeminia, 17
Jeremiah, 6, 7, 8
Jerome, 1, 3, 4, 5, 18, 19, 23, 107
Jesse Baker, 10
Jesse, 10, 11, 12
John, 1, 3, 4, 7, 15, 17, 18, 19, 20, 21, 22, 25, 27, 28, 40
John, Jr., 18
Jonathan, 13
Joseph Pemberton, 18
Joseph West, 11t, 12
Joseph, 5, 8, 9, 11, 12, 22, 27, 28, 29, 109
Joshua, 5, 23, 24
Kezia, 19, 21
Levi, 27
*Lot*, 12
Lydia Griffith, 10
Mahala, 12
Margaret, 2, 24, 29
Maria, 13
Marian, 11
Martha, 6
Mary Ann, 27
Mary P., 10
Mary, 2, 4, 6, 8, 11, 15, 18, 19, 26, 32, 206, 207
Micajah, 3, 4, 19, 24, 107, 110
Miriam, 11
Mordecai, 28, 29, 108
Moses, 11, 12
Nancy, 23
Nelly, 7
Patsy, 7
Phebe, 40
Philemon, 3, 4, 18, 19, 20, 21, 22, 24, 40
Philemon, Sr., 21
Philip, 10
Phoebe, 3, 4, 6, 18, 29
Priscilla, 3, 4, 6, 15, 17, 18, 25, 26, 29
Rachel, 5, 6, 8, 11, 13, 15, 20, 21, 26
Rebecca, 11, 14, 23, 26
Richard, 10, 26
Robert, 15, 25, 26
Ruth, 4, 6, 8, 9, 10, 11
Sallie, 10
Samuel W., 13
Samuel, 1, 3, 4, 5, 8, 9, 11, 12, 14, 15, 18, 19, 26, 218
Samuel, Jr., 12
Sarah, 8, 9, 11, 12, 13, 14, 15, 16, 17, 19, 20, 21, 23, 26, 27, 28, 29, 109
Sophia, 20
Susanna/h, 2, 4, 6, 8, 9, 12, 16, 20, 25, 26, 32
Tacy, 12
Thomas (1), 2, 3
Thomas (2), 2, 4, 8, 17, 18, 19, 24, 26, 29
Thomas (3), 4
Thomas (4), 5
Thomas Griffith, 10
Thomas Morsell, 10
Thomas, 1, 3, 4, 6, 9, 12 18, 21, 25, 27, 32, 33, 40
Thomas, Sr., 9

Ursula, 8, 9, 15
widow, 17
William B., 10
William W., 11
William, 4, 5, 6, 7, 8, 10, 13, 22, 25, 27
Yate (2), 25
Yate, 15, 18, 19, 24, 26, 27
Zephaniah, 6, 7, 8
**Popel**, Margaret, 77
*Poplar Spring Garden*, 44, 45, 54
*Poplar Thicket*, 30
*Popular Spring Meadows Garden*, 54
*Port Vernon Plantation*, 215
**Porter**, Hannah, 57
Philip, 58
*Portland Manor*, 110, 111
*Pottenger's Discovery*, 110
**Pottenger**, Jemina, 110
John, 114
Robert, 114
Samuel, 110
Susanna, 113
**Poultney**, Anthony, 16
Elizabeth, 16
James, 17
Jesse, 17
John, 10, 16
Mary, 16
Rachel, 17
Samuel, 16
Sarah, 16
Thomas, 16
William, 17
**Powell**, Anne, 122, 124
Daniel, 122
Howell, 126
Mary, 100
**Prather**, Aaron, 179, 180

Eleanor, 179
Elizabeth, 179, 180
Isaac, 180
Jeremiah, 179, 180
Jeremiah, Jr., 179
John Smith, 179, 180
Jonathan, 168
Josiah, 179, 180
Martha, 168, 179, 180
Rachel, 179, 180
Thomas, 168, 179
Zachariah, 179, 180
**Pratt**, Elinor, 177
John, 177
**Presby**, George, 193
*Preston's Neck*, 61
**Preston**, Elizabeth Talbott, 222
James, 41, 61
John, 107
Margaret, 24, 61, 107
Rebecca, 41, 42, 61
Richard, 61
William, 107
**Price**, Philip, 51
**Prockter**, Betty, 133
**Proctors**, Elizabeth, 134
**Pryce**, Robert, 193
**Pue**, Anne, 90
**Pumphries**, \_\_\_\_, 36
*Purchase*, 70
**Purnell**, Ann, 39
Elizabeth, 213
John, 117
Mary, 117
Richard, Jr., 213
Samuell, 114
Sarah, 117
**Pusey**, Elizabeth, 192
Mary, 18
**Pye**, Walter, 160

Queen, Edward, 160
  Marshall, 134
  Marsham, 134, 149

Ralston, Mary, 10
Ramsay, John, 205
Randall, Sarah, 60
  Urith, 47, 52, 55
Ransom, George
*Rapatta*, 189, 190, 198
Raper, Richard, 157
*Rattle Snake Point*, 124
Rawlence, Paul, 95
Rawlings, ___, 34
  Elizabeth, 35
Ray/e, William, Sr., 211
  Thomas, 7
Reed, John, 157
  Mary, 126
  Thomas, 155
  William, 69
Redgrave, Elizabeth, 195
Rencher, William, 176
*Repulta*, 199
*Reserve, The*, 63, 64, 70, 73, 74, 75, 80, 81, 83
*Resurrection Manor*, 167, 169
Rhoades, Nicholas, 7
*Rich Hills*, 8, 9
*Rich Lands*, 151
*Rich Level*, 2
*Rich Meadows*, 48
Richards, Sarah, 27
Richardson, Daniel, 61, 191
  Elizabeth, 61, 191
  Hannah, 191
  John, 178
  Joseph, 9, 61, 100, 106
  Joseph, Capt., 205
  Nathan, 190, 191

  Richard, 57
  Sapphira, 61
  Sarah, 100, 191
  Sophia Elizabeth, 61
  William, 42, 58, 61, 191
Ricketts, Thomas, 32
Rider, Robert, 63
Ridgely, Ann, 45
  Elizabeth, 46
  Katherine, 45
  Rachel, 56
  Westall, 207
  William, 46
Rigbie, Elizabeth, 55, 56, 58
  James, 56
  John, 55, 56, 58
  Nathan, 106
Riggs, Amelia, 46
  Delilah, 23
  Samuel, 46
*Riley's Discovery*, 32
*Riley's Folly*, 30, 31, 32
*Riley's Gift*, 30, 31
*Riley's Horse Pasture*, 31
*Rileys Lott*, 31
*Riley's Range*, 30, 31, 32
Riley, Elizabeth, 31
  Hugh, 2, 29, 30, 31, 32
  Hugh, Jr, 30
  Lydia, 30
  Margaret, 30
  Mary, 31, 32
  Rachel, 31
Roach, Ann, 177
Roberts, Andrew, 121
  Ann Grace, 59
  Ann, 121
  Elizabeth, 189, 198
  Henry, 106, 121
  Mary, 115

Samuel, 218
Sarah, 121
William, 59
**Robertson**, Daniel, 68
George, 39
Mary, 200
Samuel, 117, 118, 200
Sarah, 120
**Robins**, Henry, 121
Ruth, 106
**Robinson**, Elsie, 37
Richard, 41
**Rodery**, Sarah, 32
**Rogers**, Ann, 77
Benjamin, 76, 77, 79
Eleanor, 79
William, 79
**Rollson**, Nicholas, 42
**Roper**, Catherine Graves, 102, 167
Richard, 158
*Rose's Purchase*, 9, 32
**Rose**, Richard, 9
**Roseman**, Nathan, 131
**Ross**, Aquilla, 86
Thomas, 76
**Rothery**, Solomon, 32
**Roundall**, Samuel, 69
**Routhorn**, Joseph, 160
**Routhoume**, Joseph, 133
**Rowles**, William, 25
**Rumeny**, Nathaniel, 44
**Russell**, James, 78
Mary G., 11
**Ryan**, Charity, 37
Philip, 183
**Ryley**, see Riley

**Salsbury**, Elizabeth Ann, 145
**Sanders**, Ann, 119, 120

Edward, 119, 120
Elizabeth, 119, 120
Henry Childs, 119, 120
John, 106, 107, 119, 120, 130
John, Jr., 110
John, Sr., 110
Joshua, 141
Mary, 131, 148
Rebecca, 87
Sarah, 16, 106, 107, 119
Thomas, 12
**Sandsbury**, William, 200, 201
**Sanks**, George, 38
*Saplin Hall*, 1
*Sapling Range*, 46
*Saxon's Neck*, 124
*Scantley*, 106
*Scott's Lott*, 2, 32
**Scott**, Alice, 114
Charity, 114
Elizabeth, 113
Stephen, 16
**Scraggs**, Charles, 24
*Scrap*, 63, 74, 83
**Scrivener**, Elisha, 214
Elizabeth, 117, 213
Francis, 117, 118
George, 115, 116
John, 117, 213, 214
Mary, 114
Richard, 117, 213
Richard, Sr., 214
Sarah, 114
William, 117, 213, 214
*Seaman's Delight*, 2, 3
*Second Lott*, 32
*Second Thought*, 46
**Seever**, Mary M., 5
**Sellman**, ____, 57
Elizabeth, 56

Gassaway, 57
**Semmes**, Henrietta, 140
  Marmaduke, 140
  Susanna, 140
**Senier**, John, 41
**Ser__ett**, Edward, 99
**Sevell**, Abraham, 105
  Charles, 136
  Henry, 105
  Mary, 161
  Peter, 73
  Susanna, 161
**Shain**, Synthia, 113
*Sharp's Addition*, 124
**Sharp**, Ann, 106, 122, 124, 126
  Birckhead, 122, 124, 125, 126
  Catharine, 125
  Elisabeth, 125, 126
  Henry, 124, 125
  Katharine, 126
  Lydia, 125, 126
  Margaret, 125, 126
  Mary, 125, 126
  Nancy, 125, 126
  Peter, 122, 124, 125
  Peter, Jr., 124
  Richard, 125
  Samuel, 122
  Solomon, 124, 125
  William, 122, 124, 125, 126
  William, Dr., 122, 124
**Shaw**, John, 191
*Shaws*, 160
**Sheckell**, Samuel, 111
**Sheetz**, Joseph, 53
**Sheppard**, Mary Esther, 52
**Sherburn**, Baker Brooks, 159
  Clare, 131
  Nicholas, 159, 161
  Richard, 160, 161

  Richard, Dr., 159
**Sherbutt**, Ann, 214, 215
  Benjamin Batty, 214
  Elizabeth, 214
  John, 214
  Mary, 214, 215
  Sarah, 214
  Thomas, 214
**Sherwood**, John, 30
**Shileck**, John, 158
**Shipley** Louise, 54
**Shipley**, Peter, 44
  Robert, 56
  Sarah, 56
**Shircliff**, Tecla, 146
  William, 146
**Shirk**, Ida Morrison, 42
**Shoemaker**, Caroline, 18
**Short**, James, 155
**Shreve**, Catherine Lawrence, 52
  Catherine, 52
  Eliza Ann, 52
  Judge William, 52
  Levin Lawrence, 52
  Thomas Talliafeero, 52
  Upton Lawrence, 52
  William Martin, 52
**Shriner**, Peter, 50
  Sarah Maria, 50
**Sidwell**, Ann, 15
  Henry, 40
  Margaret, 40
*Silence*, 46
**Simmons**, Abraham, 215
  Cephas, 113
  Elizabeth, 114, 117, 120
  Enos, 114
  George, 116, 120
  Henry Childs, 113
  Isaac, 115, 116, 116, 120, 215

Jane, 42
Jonathon, 113, 114
Joseph, 114
Knighton, 120
Margaret, 120
Richard, 113
Robert, 113
Samuel, 113
Susannah, 113
Tyler, 114
William, 113
William, Jr., 118, 120
*Simpson's Supply*, 152, 154
**Simpson**, Comfort, 60
  Elizabeth, 145
  Ignatius, 144, 145
  Thomas, 201
**Sims**, Mary Brooke, 55
  Mary, 138
*Sinkin*, 154
**Sinks**, George II, 20
**Sister Juliana**, 51
**Skinbnor**, Mary, 107
*Skinner's Chance*, 72
*Skinner's Reserve*, 63
**Skinner**, Adderton, 63, 64, 66, 72, 73, 80, 81, 83, 85, 87
  Alexander, 70
  Amelia, 76, 83, 84
  Andrew, 121, 164
  Ann, 64, 65, 67, 68, 71, 72, 73, 75, 76, 79, 80, 82, 86, 87
  Arthur, 75, 77
  Benjamin, 67, 68, 70, 83, 84, 87
  Beulah L., 82
  Clarke, 63, 64, 71, 72, 73, 74, 87
  Clement, 81, 85, 86
  Dorcas, 80, 81, 85, 86
  Elisabeth, 75, 83
  Elisha, 79, 83, 84, 87

Elizabeth Greenfield, 84
Elizabeth, 70, 71, 74, 76, 77, 79, 83, 84, 87
Frederick H, 82
Frederick R., 69
Frederick, 80, 81, 82, 83, 84
Gabriel, 75, 77
Henrietta Maria, 69
Henry, 76, 77, 80, 81, 82, 83, 84, 85, 87
James H., 75
James, 74, 75, 76, 77, 80, 82
John S., 83
John Steuart, 82
John, 69, 74, 75, 76, 77, 78, 80, 84
Joseph, 74, 76, 77, 79, 80
Leonard, 74, 75, 77
Levin, 70
Mackall, 67, 68, 69, 71
Major, 80, 81, 84, 85
Margaret Johns, 83, 87
Margaret, 85, 86
Martha Erickson, 69
Martha, 74, 75, 87
Mary Ann, 85, 86
Mary, 63, 71, 74, 79, 81, 83, 84, 87, 93
Maryland, 70, 80, 81d, 83, 84, 85, 87
Nathan, 76
Nathaniel, 69, 70, 71, 75, 77
Nathaniel, Jr., 67
Orpha, 76, 79, 84, 87
Priscilla, 80, 84, 85, 86, 87
Rebecca, 81, 83
Richard, 81, 85, 86
Richard, Jr., 86

Robert, 63, 64, 67, 68, 70, 72,
  80, 81, 85, 86, 87, 92, 93, 94,
  96
Robert, Jr., 68, 69
Robert, Sr., 63
Ruth, 71
Samuel, 74, 75, 77
Sarah, 80, 81, 85, 86
Susanna, 76
Truman, 69, 83, 84, 85, 87
Truman, Col., 87
Walter, 83, 84
William, 63, 64, 71, 74, 75, 76,
  77, 80, 81, 84, 86, 87
William, Jr., 75
**Slack**, J. Marlene, 222
**Slater**, Ellis, 83
**Slye**, Ann/e, 156, 161
  Elizabeth, 141, 157
  George, 157, 158, 162
  Gerard, 156, 157, 161
  Gerard, Capt., 156
  Henrietta Maria, 156, 157, 158
  Jane, 156, 157
  Mary, 131, 157, 158
  Susannah, 156
*Smith's Addition*, 189, 198
*Smith's Farm*, 69
**Smith**, Alice, 62, 117
  Ann, 66
  Basil, 150, 160
  Cassandra, 108
  Charles, 157
  Clement, 29, 213
  Daniel, 108, 109, 117
  Dorothy, 157
  Elizabeth, 2, 3, 4, 8, 14, 17, 18,
    24, 26, 29, 117, 218, 219
  Esther, 28
  Fielder Bowie, 29, 109

Henrietta Maria, 69
Henrietta, 87
Hester, 28, 108, 109
James, 118
John Addison 78, 79
John, 3, 14, 43, 69, 80, 108, 160,
  168
Joseph, 221
Joseph, Sr., 105
Lucy Middleton, 29, 109
Lucy, 42
Lurana, 108, 109, 115
Lydia, 14
Margaret, 108, 109
Mary Hall, 69
Mordecai Finch, 109
Mordecai, 29, 108, 109
Nathan, 28, 107, 108, 115
Nathaniell, 107
Priscilla, 88, 89, 89
Rachel, 79
Rebecca, 79
Richard, 79, 88, 89
Sarah, 61, 62
Susannah, 145
Thomas, 43, 62
Walter, 68
Walter, Maj., 171
William, 97, 109, 136, 137, 218
William, Jr., 105
\_\_\_\_, 60, 91
*Smithfield*, 106, 110
**Smithson**, William, 193
**Smoot**, Charles, 152
  John, 153
*Sneaking Point*, 76, 77
**Snell**, George, 117
*Snowden's Manor Enlarged*, 206
**Snowden**, Elizabeth, 206, 207
  Mary, 207

Richard, 21, 206
Samuel, 208
Susan, 50
**Sollers**, Basil, 53
  John, 187
  Sarah, 11
  Thomas, 11, 53
**Soper**, Eleanor, 113
  Elizabeth, 181
**Spalding**, Benedick, 141
**Sparrow**, Elizabeth, 62
  Solomon, 42, 99
  Thomas, 62
**Speagle**, Jno. Cole, 188
*Spitefull*, 127
*Sprigg's Request*, 177, 180, 181
**Sprigg**, Ann, 168
  Catherine, 168
  Edward, 102, 103, 177
  Edward, Jr., 179
  Eleanor, 103, 168, 171
  Elias, 168
  Elizabeth, 103, 168
  John, 168, 177
  Joseph, 178
  Margaret, 103t, 171
  Martha, 168, 179
  Mary, 168
  Nathaniel, 168
  Osborn, 100, 102, 103
  Priscilla, 103
  Samuel, 168
  Sarah, 168
  Thomas (1), 102
  Thomas (2), 102
  Thomas (3), 102
  Thomas, 103, 167, 168, 169, 170
  Thomas, Jr., 170, 171
  Thomas, Sr., 168

*Spring Garden*, 117
*St. Catherine's*, 143
*St. Dorothy's*, 134
*St. Elizabeth's*, 166
*St. George's Rest*, 131
*St. George's*, 155
*St. Johns*, 160
*St. Leonard's*, 83
*St. Mary's Hill Freehold*, 167
**Stafford**, Honor, 99
**Stallings**, Jacob, 76
  Richard, 188
*Stanfords Field*, 149
**Stanley**, William, 2
**Stansby**, John, 210
**Starbuck**, Elisha, 15
**Steele**, John, 118
**Stephens**, John, 186, 188, 189, 212
  Leowis, 212
  Rachel, 212
**Stevens**, Thomas, 125
  William, 164
**Steward**, William, 137
**Stewart**, Susanna, 221
**Still**, Thomas, 4
**Stimpson**, Thos., 56
*Sting, The*, 196
**Stirling**, Thomas, 67
*Stoakley*, 79
**Stockett**, Elizabeth, 2, 3, 32, 33
  Henry, 2
  Lewis, 37, 205
  Oliver, 168
  Thomas, 2, 168
  Thomas, Jr., 4
*Stoke*, 69
**Stone**, Eliza, 109
  James, 77, 91
  Mary, 220
  Robert, 220

Salathial, 37
William, 165
William, Gov., 220
*Stones Rest*, 159
Stonestreet, Sarah, 155
*Stoney Plaines*, 32
*Stoney Ridge*, 193
Storer, Ann, 63, 65
  Arthur, 63, 64, 65
  Edward, 65
  Katharine, 63, 65
Strahl, Elizabeth, 15
*Strawberry Patch*, 48
*Strife*, 28
Stuart, Alexander, 105
  Ann, 81
Stulls, Nicholas, 159
Sturney, Catherine, 81
  William, 81
Sudler, Samuel, 118
Sulivan, Darby, 73
Summy, Frederick, Sr., 20
Sunderland, Benjamin, 112
  Eleanor, 109
  Thomas, 37
*Swanson's Lot*, 3, 26, 27, 28, 32, 33
Swanston, Dr., 33
  Francis, 2, 32
  Susanna/h, 3, 32
*Swearengen's Pasture*, 30
Swearingen, David, 126
  Laurana, 30
  Margaret, 30
  Mary, 30
  Samuel, 126
  Thomas, 30, 31
  Van, 30
Syllvain, Philip, 157
Symons, Abraham, 104

Tailor, Thomas, Col., 42
*Talbott's Resolution*, 43, 56, 58
Talbott, Anna, 13, 16
  Antionette, 52
  Daniel, 186
  Edward, 42, 61
  Elisha, 16
  Elizabeth, 16, 41, 55, 59, 60, 61
  Jesse, 16
  John, 13, 15, 61, 81
  John, Jr., 13
  Joseph III, 15
  Joseph, 13, 16, 81
  Mary, 16
  Rachel, 15, 16
  Richard, 41, 43, 52, 61, 186
  Richard, Jr., 61
  Ruth, 13
  Samuel, 13, 16
  Sarah, 16
  Susannah, 13
  Thomas, 81
  Upton L., 52
*Taney's Delight*, 74, 84, 86
*Taney's Right*, 74, 84, 86
Taney, Eliza, 94
  John, 67, 68, 92, 96
  Michael, 68, 92
Taneyhill, Andrew, 67, 68
  Ann Mackall, 68
  Ann, 108
  Cassandra, 109, 115
  Eleanor, 109
  Elizabeth, 68
  Hannah, 109
  John, 68, 109, 115
  John, Jr., 109
  Leonard, 109
  Lurana, 108
  Mordecai, 109

Philip, 109
Phoebe, 114
Thomas, 109
William, 68, 109
**Tarcey**, Thos., 94
**Tate**, John, 97
**Taylor**, Elizabeth, 139
Grace, 10, 26
Joseph, 36
Mary, 11
Susannah, 36
**Tayman**, Sarah, 101
**Tench**, Thomas, 104, 217
**Tettershall**, Mary, 130
**Thomas**, Elizabeth, 211
Hezekiah, 219, 220
Jacob, 10
John, 220
Richard, 207
Samuel, 207
Tristram, 125
*Thompson's Rest*, 130
**Thompson**, \_\_\_\_, 52
Ann, 154
Anna Maria, 153
Baltis, 153
Elizabeth, 153
Henrietta, 152, 153, 154
James, 132
Jane, 153
Jean, 212
John Baptist, 153, 154
John, 147
Joseph, 154
Mary Jane, 132
Mary, 132
Mildred, 146
Raphael, 153, 154, 162
Richard Walbert, 153, 154
Richard, 153, 155

William, 132
*Thomson Hopyard*, 110
*Thomson Pasture*, 110
**Thornbury**, Catherine, 212, 213, 214
Eliz, 214
Lois, 214
Richard, 187, 196
William, 213, 214
**Thornton**, Posths., 80
**Thorold**, George, Rev., 134
*Three Sisters*, 170, 171
**Tidings**, Eliza, 205
Richard, 99
**Tilly**, Joseph, 59
**Todd**, Francis, 56
**Tomson**, Henrietta, 153
**Tottershell**, Philllip, 71
**Tottle**, Mary, 112
*Tower Hill*, 138
**Towgood**, Josias, 170
Mary, 117
Meriton, 170
*Town Land*, 167
*Townhill*, 35
**Trabue**, Judge James, 86
**Trew**, Richard, 129
*Triller*, 85
**Troth**, \_\_\_\_, 122
Ann, 124
Elizabeth, 122
Henry, 122, 124
William, 122, 124
William, Jr., 122
**Trott**, Elizabeth, 107
James, 120
Thomas, 107
**Troutman**, Mary, 114
*Truman's Choice, Remainder of*, 127

*Truman's Reserve*, 63
**Truman**, Ann, 66, 87
  Edward, 94, 96
  Elizabeth, 65, 66, 67, 94, 96
  James, 66, 67
  James, Dr., 63, 65
  Martha, 65, 66, 67, 83
  Mary, 67
  Nathaniel, 65, 67
  Thomas, 65, 67, 87
**Tucker**, John, 77
  Lydia, 12
  Mary, 12
  Robert, 12
  Saborne, 186
  William, 188
**Tull**, Mary, 34
*Tune*, 201
*Turner's Pasture*, 201
*Turner's Place*, 201
**Turner**, Elizabeth, 19
  John, 5, 9, 19
  John, Sr., 8, 17
  Mary, 148
  Monica, 133, 138
  Sarah, 19
  Sol., 9
  William, 187
*Twekesbury*, 17
**Twisden**, Levina, 174
*Twiver*, 69
*Two Sisters* (ship), 205
**Tydings**, Elizabeth, 59
**Tyler**, Elizabeth, 110
  Grafton, 28
  Mary, 17
  Robert, 17
  Robert, Col., 84
  Samuel, 28

*Upper Getting*, 9

**VanCleave**, Gideon, Dr., 194
  Mary, 194
**VanSwearingen**, Mary, 166
  Sarah, 156, 161
**Veach**, Daniel, 6, 7
  Verlinda, 22
**Vernon**, Ann, 211, 212, 215, 217
  Christopher, 211, 212, 215, 216, 218
  Elizabeth, 212
  Ephraim, 211, 215, 216, 217
  John, 215, 217
  Lois, 211, 212, 215
  Lucy, 211, 215
  Sophia, 215
  Thomas, 211, 215, 216
  William, 211, 212, 213, 214, 215, 217
**Virgin**, John, 220

**Wade**, \_\_\_\_, 168
  Elizabeth, 168
  Robert, 168, 171
**Waitt**, Thomas, 4
**Wake**, Ann Barnett, 52
**Walker**, \_\_\_\_, 137
  Charles, 97
  Eleanor, 9, 16
  Rebecca, 37
  Sarah, 10
  William, 9
**Walley**, Mary, 161
**Wallis**, Benj., 95, 96
**War**, Peter, 51
*Warburton Square*, 104
**Warburton**, Cassandra, 143
**Ward**, Ann, 13
  Benjamin, 118

Edward, 188
Eleanor, 117, 118
Elizabeth, 14, 118, 186, 188
James, 32
John, 186, 187, 188, 196
Robert, 14, 188
Sam, Jr., 111
Sarah, 14
Susannah, 32
William, 26
Yate, 26
*Ware Park*, 32
**Warfield**, Absolom, 117
Alexander, 117
Anne, 55
Azel, 117
Benjamin, 46
Catherine, 46
Charlotte, 55
Davidge, 117
Elizabeth, 117
Joseph, 55
Rezin, 55
Sarah, 46
Vachel, 46
**Waring**, Ann/e, 135, 136, 137, 138
Basie, 137
Basil, 66, 135, 136, 137
Basil, Capt., 181
Eleanor, 136, 138
Elizabeth, 137
Francis, 137
Henrietta Maria, 137
Henrietta, 136, 137
Henry, 136, 137
James, Haddock, 136
John, 84, 136, 137
Marsham, 135, 136, 137, 138
Marsham, Jr., 137

Martha, 181
Mary, 138
Richard Marsham, 135, 136
Richard Marsham, Jr., 136
Sarah, 135, 136, 137
Thomas, 181
**Warner**, James, 105
Barton, 152
Elizabeth, 152, 153
Marsham, 132
Thomas, 155
*Wartinton*, 77
**Washington**, Gen., 84
*Water Mill*, 74
*Water's Purchase*, 39
**Waters**, Ann, 39, 40
Anna Marie, 10
Arnold, 39, 40
Artridge, 15, 25
Basil, 181
Charity, 39, 40
David, 54
Eliza, 211
Elizabeth, 39
Ezekial, 24
Jacob Holland, 40
Jane, 181
John III, 6
John, 35, 37, 39, 190, 211
Margaret, 9, 12
Mary, 37, 38, 39
Mordecai, 40
Nathan, 54
Rachel, 37
Samuel, 12, 25, 39
Samuel, Jr., 26
Sarah, 12, 39
Stephen, 181
Susannah, 39, 40
Thomas, 39, 40

William, 39, 40
Wathen, ____, 144
  John, 131
  Sarah, 145
  Susannah, 150
Watkins, Anne, 34
  Elisabeth, 34
  Gassaway, 34, 35
  Gassaway, Jr., 35
  James, 26
  Jane, 35
  John Gassaway, 34, 35
  John, 34, 35, 42
  Margaret, 35
  Mary, 35
  Nicholas, 35
  Susannah, 36
  Thomas Gassaway, 35
Watson, Andrew, 129
  William, 92
Watton, Ann, 136
Wayman, Daniel, Sr., 20
  Leonard, 5
Webb, Ann/a, 11, 58
  Elizabeth, 11, 127
  George, 11
  Sarah, 124
  Thomas, 127
  William, 193
Webber, Elizabeth, 213
Webster, Hannah, 190, 195
  Isaac, 190, 191
  John, 40, 191
  Margaret, 190, 191
*Wee Bit*, 157
Weems, David, 119, 214
  John, 28
  Marianna Ewell, 116
  Susanna, 214
*Welch Poole*, 108

Welch, see Welsh
Wells, ____, 17
  Frances, 17, 29, 32
  Leah, 23
  Mary, 2, 121
  Nathan, 18
  Ricahrd, 61
  Samuel, 76
  Susanna, 28
  Thomas, 121
Welsh, Ann, 112
  Benjamin, 38
  Jamina, 38
  John, 121
  Richard, 33, 113
  Robert, 112
  Thomasin, 121
  William, 193
Wess, Elizabeth, 127
*West Puddington*, 56
West, Ann, 88, 90
  Christian Hannah, 90, 91
  Eleanor, 88, 89
  Elizabeth, 88, 89, 91
  Harriet, 90
  John Henry, 88, 90
  John Stephen, 90, 91
  John, 88, 91
  Joseph, 90
  Martha, 50, 88, 89, 90
  Mary Magdalene, 88, 90
  Mary, 10, 88, 89, 90, 91
  Priscilla, 88, 89
  Rachel Sophia, 90
  Rebecca Ann, 88, 90
  Richard Williams, 90
  Richard, 40
  Robert, 88, 89
  Stephen (2), 90
  Stephen, 50, 58, 88, 89, 91

William Henry, 90, 91
Weston, 30
Wharton, Jesse, 137
  Jesse, Dr., 220
Wheeler, Robert, 181
  William, 42
Whitaker, Alexander, 220
  Robert, 69, 94, 96
White Hall, 55
White Plain, 28
White's Adventure, 219
White, Benjamin, 209, 210, 218, 219, 220
  Eleanor, 219, 220
  Elizabeth, 210, 218, 219
  Guy, 209, 218
  Guy, II, 5
  Hester, 219, 220
  James (2), 210
  James, 209, 210, 211
  James, Jr. (3), 211
  Jane, 219, 220
  John, 209, 219, 220
  Lettice, 209
  Margaret, 209, 210
  Mary Ann, 209
  Mary, 219
  Nathan Smith, 219, 220
  Rachel, 209
  Rebecca, 209
  Sarah, 209, 219
  Susanna, 210
  William, 209, 219
  Wm., 99
Whiten, James, 17
Whittington, Francis, 118
  Thomas, 118
Whittle's Rest, 86
Wickham's Good Will, 17
Wickham, 110

Widdow's Purchse, 32
Widow's Discovery, 153
Wight, John, Capt., 102
  Margery, 102
Wilfred, Neale, 158
Wilkinson, Betty, 80
  Elizabeth, 79, 80
  James, Gen., 80
  Joseph, 79, 80
  Joseph, Gen., 80
  Joseph, Jr., 79
Willett, Edward, 168
  Mary, 111
William's Purchase, 74
Williams, Anne, 34
  Baruch, 177, 178
  Baruch, Jr., 177
  Benjamin, 103
  Christian, 90
  Eleanor, 182
  Elisha, 182
  Elizabeth, 180, 182
  Hannah, 90
  Hilleary, 178
  John, 40
  Joseph, 38, 103, 108
  Joseph, Sr., 18, 29
  Lilben, 13
  Lucy, 177
  Margaret, 103
  Mary, 39, 40, 99, 177, 178
  Phoebe, 4
  Rachel, 181, 182
  Richard, 33, 37, 40
  Richard, Capt., 90
  Richard, Jr., 33
  Ruth, 103
  Stockett, 39, 40
  Theodore, 204
  Thomas, 157

Thomas, Col., 182
Williamson, Capt. John, 53
  Rebecca, 53
  widow, 49
Wills, George, 18
  Walter, 29
Wilson, Ann, 222
  Benjamin Kidd, 192
  Benjamin, 198
  Benkid, 121, 190, 192, 198
  Cassandra, 190, 194, 195
  Edward, Sr., 4, 5
  Elizabeth, 195, 198
  Faith, 211
  Gover, 194
  Henry, 121, 190, 192, 194, 198
  Henry, Sr., 195
  James, Capt., 70
  John (1), 121
  John (2), 121
  John (3), 121
  John, 106, 120, 121, 169
  John, Jr., 217
  John, Sr., 217
  Joseph, 121, 222
  Josiah, 104
  Josiah, Jr., 103
  Lingan, 104
  M. J., 54
  Nancy, 54
  Priscilla, 190, 194, 195
  Rachel, 106, 194
  Rebecca, 222
  Ruth, 121
  Samuel, 193, 194, 196
  Sarah, 4
  William, 106, 107, 121, 183, 194, 222
  William, Jr., 194
Wimmonds, William, Jr., 119

Winchester, Amanda, 50
  Benjamin, 49
  Lavina L., 49
  Louisa, 50
  Mary, 49
  Olivia, 50
  Richard, 49
  William Chambers, 50
Winkelman, Agnes, 1, 60
Wiseman, Jane, 163
Woellas, James, 11
*Wolleston Manor*, 160
Wood, Joel, 16
  John, 74
  Margaret J. Skinner, 84, 87
  Margaret, 12, 114
  Mary Stuart, 87
  Nathan, 12
  Peter, 83, 87
  Robert, 89, 185, 186, 188, 189, 200
Woodten, Turner, 103
Woodward, Mary, 138
*Woollestan Mannor*, 140
Worthington, Elizabeth, 53
  John, 196
  Sarah Chew, 194
Wright, Elisabeth, 16
  F. Edward, 94
  Hannah, 14
  Henry, 103
  Rebecca, 143
Wyley, George, 76
Wythe, Richard, 163
Wyvill, Marmaduke, 120

Yardley, Mary, 14
Yate, George, 2, 105
  Joseph, 2
  Priscilla, 24

**Yoakley**, Stephen, 168
**Yoe**, John, 74
    W. H., 87
**Young**, Ann, 126
    Arthur, 67

Other Heritage Books by Elise Greenup Jourdan:

*The Greenup Family*

*Abstracts of Charles County, Maryland Court and Land Records:*
*Volume 1: 1658-1666*
*Volume 2: 1665-1695*
*Volume 3: 1694-1722*

*Colonial Records of Southern Maryland:*
*Trinity Parish & Court Records, Charles County; Christ Church*
*Parish & Marriage Records, Calvert County; St. Andrew's*
*& All Faith's Parishes, St. Mary's County*

*Colonial Settlers of Prince George's County, Maryland*

*Early Families of Southern Maryland:*
*Volume 1 (Revised) and Volumes 2-10*

*Settlers of Colonial Calvert County, Maryland*

*Settlers of Colonial St. Mary's County, Maryland*

*The Land Records of Prince George's County, Maryland:*
*1702-1709*
*1710-1717*
*1717-1726*
*1733-1739*
*1739-1743*

with Francis W. McIntosh

*1840 to 1850 Federal Census: Tazewell County, Virginia*

*1860 Federal Census: Tazewell County, Virginia*

*1870 Federal Census: Tazewell County, Virginia*

www.ingramcontent.com/pod-product-compliance
Lightning Source LLC
Chambersburg PA
CBHW061954180426
43198CB00036B/887